Kintyre to Ardnamurchan

Published by
Imray, Laurie, Norie & Wilson Ltd
Wych House St Ives Cambridgeshire PE27 5BT England
☏ +44 (0)1480 462114
Email ilnw@imray.com
www.imray.com
2018

© Clyde Cruising Club Publications Ltd 2018
First edition 2014
Second edition 2018

ISBN 978 184623 902 1

Clyde Cruising Club Publications Ltd has asserted its right under the Copyright, Designs and Patents Act 1988 to be identified as the author of this work.

British Library Cataloguing in Publication Data.
A catalogue record for this title is available from the British Library.

CAUTION

Whilst the Publishers and Author have used reasonable endeavours to ensure the accuracy of the contents of these Sailing Directions they contain selected information and thus are not definitive and do not include all known information for each and every location described, nor for all conditions of weather and tide. They are written for yachts of moderate draft and should not be used by larger craft. They should be used only as an aid to navigation in conjunction with official charts, pilots, hydrographic data and all other information, published or unpublished, available to the navigator. Skippers should not place reliance on these Sailing Directions in preference to exercising their own judgement.

To the extent permitted by law, the Publishers and Author do not accept liability for any loss and/or damage howsoever caused that may arise from reliance on these Sailing Directions nor for any error, omission or failure to update the information that they contain.

The UK Hydrographic Office (UKHO) and its licensors make no warranties or representations, express or implied, with respect to this product. The UKHO and its licensors have not verified the information within this product or quality assured it.

PLANS

The plans in these Sailing Directions are not to be used for navigation.
They are designed to support the text and should at all times be used with navigational charts.

This product has been derived in part from material obtained from the UK Hydrographic Office with the permission of the UK Hydrographic Office, Her Majesty's Stationery Office, Licence No. GB AA - 005 - Imray
© British Crown Copyright, Kintyre to Ardnamurchan 2018
All rights reserved.

The copyright in a number of plans reproduced in this publication is owned by Bob Bradfield and Antares Charts, who have kindly given permission for their reproduction in this publication.

The last input of technical information was January 2018.

CORRECTIONAL SUPPLEMENTS

These Sailing Directions may be amended at intervals by the issue of correctional supplements. These are published on the internet at the web sites www.clyde.org and www.imray.com and may be downloaded free of charge. Printed copies are also available on request from the publishers at the above address.

The Publishers and Author will at all times be grateful to receive information which tends to the improvement of the work.

Printed in Croatia by Zrinski

CCC Sailing Directions and Anchorages

Kintyre to Ardnamurchan

Incorporating The Yachtsman's Pilots by Martin Lawrence

Edited by **Edward Mason**

Imray Laurie Norie & Wilson Ltd

50'

N

Loch Eil *p.135*

Loch Sunart *p.146*

**8. Sound of Mull
and Loch Sunart**
p.136

Loch
Linnhe
p.128

**7. Loch Etive and
Loch Linnhe**
p.114

40'

Ardmore
Point

10. Coll and Tiree
p.172

Coll
p.173

Tobermory
p.143

Caliach
Pt

Lynn of Morvern

Lismore

30'

Tiree
p.178

Treshnish
Isles
p.159

Ulva

Salen
p.140

p.138

*Passage of
Tiree*

Loch
na Keal

MULL

**9. West Coast
of Mull** *p.154*

Loch
Spelve

Firth
of
Lorn

6. Firth of Lorn
p.96

**5. Loch Crinan to the
Firth of Lorn** *p.70*

Loch Melfort *p.89*

20'

Skerryvore

Iona
p.186

Ross of Mull

Garvellachs
p.98

56°N

Loch
Craignish
p.74

11. Ross of Mull *p.180*

10'

Colonsay
p.52

Crinan
p.72

*Crinan
Canal*

Oronsay
p.51

JURA

Ardrishaig

Loch
Tarbert
p.47

Loch
Sween
p.64

Lower
Loch
Fyne

**3. West coasts of Islay
and Jura; Colonsay**
p.42

*Sound
of Jura
p.61*

56°N

50'

Rhinns of Islay

ISLAY

*Sound
of Islay
p.40*

**4. Sound of
Jura** *p.54*

Isle
of
Bute

*West Loch
Tarbert
p.26*

40'

Gigha
p.22

*Firth
of
Clyde*

ARRAN

Port
Ellen *p.30*

Kintyre

**2. Southeast Islay and
Sound of Islay**
p.28

*Kilbrannan
Sound*

0   10   20   30

Nautical Miles

Campbeltown *p.18*

20'

Rathlin I

Mull of
Kintyre

**Republic
of Ireland**

Sanda

**1. Mull of Kintyre to
West Loch Tarbert**
p.16

*North
Channel*

10'   7°W   50' Portrush   30'   20'   10'   6°   50'   40'   30'   20'   10'   5°

Contents

Preface

'This narrow strait' (the Sailing Directions said),
'Is full of rocks, and difficult to enter;
Whirlpools are common here at every tide;
There are uncharted reefs on every side
And currents (twenty knots) along the centre.'
'Come,' said the Skipper, 'we will go in there.'
(We went in there.)

'There is no sand' (the Sailing Directions said),
'The anchorage is thoroughly unsafe.
There is no shelter from the frequent squalls,
Save on the west, among the overfalls.
Boats should go on to Loch MacInchmaquaif.'
'Come,' said the Skipper, 'we will anchor here.'
(We anchored here.)

From *The Log of the Blue Dragon (1903)*
C.C. Lynam

An incidental benefit resulting from the merging of the CCC Sailing Directions with those of Martin Lawrence is that I now feel free to repeat the above lines (entitled *Nimium ne Crede Experto,* which translates roughly as: 'Don't put too much trust in the experts') that were previously quoted by Martin in the

The canal basin at Crinan, the starting point for many west coast cruises

Edward Mason

preface to his first book, *Crinan to Canna*. As they were originally published in 1903 it is reassuring to know that they cannot have been referring to the Sailing Directions of the CCC - the Club was not founded until 1909 - but nonetheless, even with regard to our current books, I must admit that a relentless recital of potential hazards can create an air of impending doom that is at odds with what is intended to be a leisure pursuit.

It is hard to see how it could be otherwise: experienced skippers with well-found and strongly-crewed boats might well sail happily through overfalls and anchor in dubious places but the novice with a trusting family aboard will weigh every word - and rightly so. Inevitably, sailors of all abilities use these directions and each individual skipper will need to assess how the information given within them might affect their own vessel, taking into account the capabilities of her crew.

Having said that, it is also important to bear in mind the advice that is included in the *Caution* on the first page of all our books: 'Skippers should not place reliance on these Sailing Directions in preference to exercising their own judgement'; advice with which the skipper of the *Blue Dragon* would no doubt have heartily concurred. His cavalier disregard for the Sailing Directions may well have been a gross exaggeration, dreamt up by an awestruck crew member, but there was surely more than a grain of truth in it.

Lynam was in fact a highly experienced yachtsman who had sailed on the Scottish west coast, winter and summer, for many years and more than once had ventured into places where no yacht had been before. It must also have helped that the *Blue Dragon* was a stoutly built, 25-foot, centreboard yawl and she was all too familiar with taking the ground, both intentionally and unintentionally.

Acknowledgements

This is the last of the Clyde Cruising Club's four books of west coast Sailing Directions to be merged with Martin Lawrence's Yachtsman's Pilots; in this instance the books in question were the latter part of *Clyde to Colonsay* and *The Isle of Mull*.

Edward Mason

'Capella of Lorne' anchored in Bagh Gleann Righ Mor, Loch Tarbert, Jura: a loch as remote and dramatic as any on the west coast

The whole project has taken four years and throughout the course of it I have been always acutely aware of Martin's vast knowledge of the west coast and his skill in communicating it to the reader. As this is a Club publication it has been necessary to leave out some of his more personal observations and reflections but I hope that his enthusiasm and love of the area still shows through. The Club, myself and future editors, will always be grateful to him for making his text and photographs so freely available and I trust that the combined volumes will offer the best possible pilotage advice to yachtsmen on the west coast of Scotland.

Sadly, I have to pay a final tribute to Arthur Houston, my predecessor, mentor and dear friend. Arthur died not long after returning his meticulously marked-up proof of this book, precisely on the day that he had promised; punctilious to the end. He was a long-standing member of the CCC whose experience of sailing the west coast went back over sixty five years and there were few places of which he had no knowledge. It was always a great comfort to know that my drafts were to be subjected to his thorough checking and correction and I cannot thank him enough. He will be sorely missed.

A relative newcomer to the scene is Bob Bradfield who started surveying and charting Scottish anchorages at about the same time as the first CCC–Imray publication, *Firth of Clyde*, was in preparation. Although that book was not able to benefit from any of his work, Bob's rate of progress was so prodigious that by the time *Kintyre to Ardnamurchan* was underway there were well over two hundred anchorages in his *Antares Charts* portfolio. Bob has been most generous in allowing us to use information from his charts and many plans in this present book have been based on his accurate surveys.

Lastly, Jimmy Dinsmore has once more subjected the final proofs to his painstaking scrutiny and successfully eliminated many simple and, when pointed out, obvious errors. Any that remain are mine.

During the production of the four volumes it has been a pleasure to work with the professionals in the Imray publishing team: Elinor Cole has very capably looked after the general editing and production; Debbie Wilson has, over the series, re-drawn more than four hundred plans to an extremely high standard and Liz Cook has prepared the comprehensive index to each book. I thank them all and especially Willie Wilson, who has given encouragement and strategic advice throughout, forming a relationship which I hope will endure for many years to come.

Edward Mason, Editor
CCC Sailing Directions, September 2014

Preface to the second edition

The principal developments that have occured since the first edition was published in 2014 are the establishment of further serviced pontoons at Gigha, Sound of Ulva and the long awaited transit marina in Oban Bay.

The latter has coincided with a significant increase in ferry traffic in Oban and accordingly the Code of Conduct for the safety of navigation in the bay has been extensively revised. This will affect every yacht that enters Oban Bay and it should be carefully studied before doing so (see pp.106-110). Buoyage in Kerrera Sound has also been changed and it is planned to introduce summer season-only buoys in the northern entrance to Oban Bay.

The Club also hopes that 2018 will see the eventual replacement, by the NLB, of the increasingly inconspicuous beacon, erected by the CCC many years ago, on the Cleit Rock in Cuan Sound.

Edward Mason, Editor
CCC Sailing Directions, January 2018

Introduction

The Scottish west coast, between the Mull of Kintyre and Ardnamurchan Point offers some of the best and most varied sailing that can be found anywhere in Europe. From the exposed passage around the Mull of Kintyre, through the turbulent tidal sounds north of Crinan to the rock-strewn entrances to Loch Teacuis, it provides challenges that will test even the most experienced yachtsman. Yet, within the same easy two-day sail from all its main harbours and marinas, there is an abundant choice of welcoming islands, sheltered lochs, tranquil anchorages and secure moorings to attract those who prefer to take it a little more gently.

Most of the passages to reach these destinations are within sounds or lochs or along a shore entailing only short hops across open sea, so that navigation is, in the main, a matter of pilotage by eye and satisfying yourself that what you see corresponds to the chart. Only when the visibility clamps down is it necessary to resort to navigation as such, which these days invariably involves consulting the chart plotter, or even your smartphone, before laying off a course.

That said, we make no apologies for the fact that throughout this book and its companion volumes, we continue to include full details for pilotage using traditional clearing lines, transits, bearings and daymarks. Not only can GPS signals be lost, batteries fail or the charted information be inadequate (see p.5) but there is considerable satisfaction to be derived from using the same methods that sailors have used in these waters for centuries. This has the additional benefit that, when entering a harbour or anchorage, there is much to be said for looking around rather than concentrating on a screen which, however technically advanced, may not show converging vessels or the odd creel marker buoy.

At night most of the main passages are fairly well lit, at least for a passage under power or with a fair wind, but they are not up to the standard of Scandinavian countries as there is not enough traffic to justify more lights. A few anchorages or passages are very well lit for local commercial users but for the most part, at least during June and July, there is little need to sail at night unless you are making a longer passage.

Entering Cumhann Beag, Loch Tarbert, Jura (p.47), and looking out for the leading marks; a place where a moment's inattention could land you in trouble

Edward Mason

However, despite all the talk of sheltered lochs and tranquil anchorages, the Argyll coast is no place for anyone who is unable to deal with adverse conditions, which may arise unexpectedly. The proximity of the shoreline, of such interest and delight in fine weather, can rapidly become a hazard in the event of gear or machinery failure and a prudent skipper will have a contingency plan in mind when the going gets rough. Fortunately, because of the nature of the coastline, shelter is usually not far away and in the majority of cases it is safe to enter in heavy onshore weather, unlike many estuaries and harbours found on more open coasts around the British Isles. Ironically, in a few lochs this shelter can create problems of its own in the form of squalls generated in the lee of the higher hills, but at least the sea state will be less.

These Directions set out to provide, clearly and concisely, as much information as may be useful to small-boat visitors to these waters. The upper limit of size for which they cater is a draught of 2 metres, and they include information specifically applicable to shoal-draught boats, centreboarders, trailer-sailers, twin-keel boats, multihulls and motor cruisers. In many anchorages there are parts which are only accessible to shoal-draught boats, particularly those which can dry out fairly upright. However, while the smallest boats, even cruising dinghies, may be at home in much of the area described in this pilot, they must be soundly equipped and competently handled by experienced crews.

The small number of navigational marks (and the large number of unmarked rocks) together with the strong tides in several passages, will require some adjustment on the part of the navigator. To set against these is the relative absence of commercial shipping. Ferries, fish farm service vessels, small coasters and, very occasionally, cruise ships are those most likely to be encountered. However visibility is usually good – except in rain, and fog is fairly rare.

Charts

These Directions contain many plans but they are not intended as a substitute for Admiralty charts. Although many of the plans in the book are of a larger scale than the charts and include more detail, they cover only small areas and it is essential to have a comprehensive set of charts at both small and large scales. A complete list of current charts is given in the Appendix. For passage-making, Imray's charts C64 and C65, at a scale of around 1:150,000, give better coverage than any current Admiralty charts and are more convenient to use. Admiralty Leisure Folio 5611 covers the whole of the area with which this book deals and the Imray Chart Pack 2800 covers from Crinan to Ardnamurchan at 1:50,000 scale.

When plotting a position it is important to be aware that the conversion of Admiralty charts to WGS84 datum was only completed for the west coast of Scotland in August 2016. Therefore even fairly recent charts may be referred to the horizontal datum OSGB36, on which a position given by geographical co-ordinates may differ by as much as 100 metres from the position on current charts.

The increasing use of chart plotters has greatly reduced the practice of plotting on paper charts and, accordingly, there is less need to be aware of the discrepancies discussed above. However, the limitations of the charts used as the basis of the plotter display must be recognised and allowed for. This is particularly the case on the west coast of Scotland where much inshore pilotage is conducted in relatively deep water but in close proximity to sunken rocks.

This is acknowledged by the UKHO which over the past few years has added the following cautionary note to many of their charts:

'Mariners are warned that positions obtained from Global Navigation Satellite Systems such as GPS, may be more accurate than the charted detail, due to the age and quality of some of the source information. Mariners are therefore advised to exercise particular caution when navigating close to the shore or in the vicinity of dangers.'

The ability to enlarge the area of interest on a plotter display to a size much bigger than the original chart can easily lead to a false sense of security and must be guarded against. Even the latest editions of UKHO charts using information from recent surveys are unlikely to incorporate more accurate detail in the many intricate anchorages into which a yacht may sometimes enter. If traditional bearings, transits and leading lines are available they should be used in preference to blind reliance on a plotter.

In an attempt to overcome some of the above problems a group of enthusiasts has recently been conducting surveys in many west coast anchorages and publishing the results, under the name of *Antares Charts*. These comprise a series of very large scale electronic charts, intended for use in conjunction with a GPS derived position. Using information gathered by sophisticated sounding and sidescanning equipment linked to marine surveying software the resulting charts can be run with suitable plotting software on PCs or Macs, certain Garmin handheld plotters, iPads and other tablets and even mobile phones.

To date, around 240 locations have been surveyed and many of these are in the area covered by this book. A full list of these is given in the Appendix and further details can be found on the Antares Charts website: *www.antarescharts.co.uk*

Alastair Cameron

'Dreamcatcher' at Gigha, in a bay off the spit joining Gigha to Eilean Garbh; a good place to anchor in easterlies (pp.23-24)

Maps

Ordnance Survey maps at 1:50,000 are well worth having on board to make up for the lack of topographical detail on current charts. In places where the charts are at a small scale the Ordnance Survey maps actually provide useful navigational detail. In some cases the OS Explorer series of maps at 1:25,000 supply essential detail where there is no Admiralty chart at an adequate scale.

Note that OS maps use a different grid of coordinates which do not even align with those of an Admiralty chart. Some GPS receivers can display OS coordinates.

Tides

In general terms the flood runs north and west increasing in strength in the northern part of the Sound of Jura, with rates of up to eight knots at springs among the islands, until the Firth of Lorn is reached where the direction of the flood turns northeast.

Tidal streams are strong wherever the movement of a large body of water is constricted by narrows and there are often overfalls at the seaward end of narrow passages, particularly with wind against tide.

Overfalls also occur off many headlands, especially those to the west of Islay and Mull and, of course, the Mull of Kintyre. This is covered in detail in Chapter 1.

There are also usually overfalls wherever two tidal streams meet such as, for example, the ebb streams from the Sound of Mull and from Loch Linnhe. These eddies and overfalls are too common to be mentioned individually.

In the Dorus Mor, close north of Crinan, the streams turn up to 2½ hours before HW and LW Oban, but in the Sound of Mull they turn about an hour after HW and LW Oban. This means that at least nine hours of fair tide can be carried going north although of course at the expense of the return passage.

The spring range throughout the northern part of the area is up to four metres but south of Fladda it reduces to about two metres and at the southern end of the Sound of Jura it is less than a metre and at neaps can be almost negligible. Most of the rise and fall in the Sound of Jura occurs during the first half of each period, as regular tidal curves do not apply, and strong streams can be expected within minutes of the change of direction.

Weather

On the west coast of Scotland the weather is very variable at any time, being influenced by the passage of depressions from the Atlantic, and rapid changes can frequently be experienced; an effect which is even more noticeable in the more open waters west of Islay and Mull. The prevailing wind is between south and west, with a higher proportion of northerly and easterly winds in May and June, when an anticyclone is more likely to become established to the north of Scotland.

Visibility is usually good and fog is rare though heavy rain or drizzle can reduce visibility markedly, though generally only for a short time. The *Admiralty Pilot* says that 'visibility of less than ½ mile may reach 3 days per month in midsummer' and visibility of less than 2 miles 'does not average more than 3 days per month during the worst summer weather at Stornoway and Tiree'.

Gales occur on average on less than half a day per month south of Skye during April-September and one day per month in the far northwest during May-August.

Rainfall is greatly affected by the proximity to high ground, and annual figures vary from less than 1000mm in the outermost islands to between 2300 and 3000mm at the heads of those lochs that penetrate furthest into the mountains.

Weather forecasts

The majority of yachtsmen rely on the Maritime Safety Information (MSI) forecasts broadcast by the Maritime and Coastguard Agency (MCA). The area covered by this book is divided between two coastguard stations: Belfast and Stornoway.

Coastguard Broadcasts

• These are issued at three-hour intervals, that is eight times a day, and the coastguard complete most transmissions around the coast within one hour. Four broadcasts provide new forecasts and four are repeats.

• Two of the new forecasts include gale warnings, the shipping forecast and inshore waters forecast and outlook, as well as navigation warnings and the three-day fisherman's forecast when applicable (in winter time only).

• The other two new forecasts include inshore waters forecasts, a repeat of the previous 24-hour outlook and any gale warnings or strong wind warnings. Mariners thus have new inshore waters forecasts every six hours.

• The repeats are for the benefit of mariners who missed the new forecast made three hours previously and consist of the inshore waters forecasts and gale warnings and any new strong wind warnings.

• The full broadcasts are based on 0710 and 1910 start times so as to catch navigators at the beginning of the sailing day or night passage. All broadcasts are in local time to avoid confusion between UTC and BST.

• Forecasts for UK inshore waters are issued by the Met Office four times a day at 0500, 1100, 1700 and 2300 local time and cover the next 24 hours. Outlooks for the following 24 hours are only issued at 0500 and 1700.

• Warnings for all forecasts are transmitted on VHF Ch 16, indicating the forecast on VHF Ch 62, 63, 64 and 10. Aerials are combined for the warnings to avoid apparent repetition.

• Warnings are brief: 'All stations – this is Stornoway Coastguard – for a weather information broadcast listen channel 83', but made slowly. The forecast broadcasts are made clearly and at dictation speed.

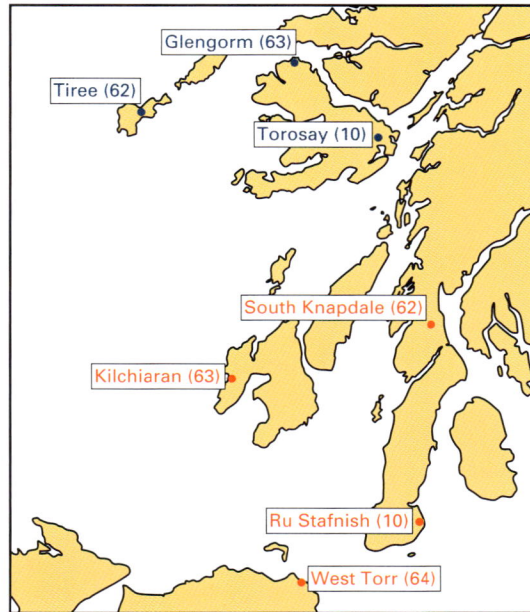

Aerial sites used by Belfast (shown in red) and Stornoway Coastguard (shown in black) for broadcasting Maritime Safety Information (MSI) throughout the area covered by this book. VHF channels shown in brackets.

Coastguard forecast areas

Belfast Coastguard covers the area from the Mull of Galloway to the north of Jura. From here Stornoway Coastguard covers the mainland coast and islands norhwards to Cape Wrath. The above diagram shows the location of transmitting stations that can be received throughout the area covered by this book, together with the channels on which they transmit.

The forecasts broadcast by Belfast Coastguard are made every three hours at: 0210, 0510, 0810, 1110, 1410, 1710, 2010 and 2310. Those by Stornoway Coastguard are made at: 0110, 0410, 0710, 1010, 1310, 1610, 1910 and 2210. The times given are not precise as forecasts may be delayed or omitted during casualty working. **All times are Local Time.**

BBC Radio Forecasts

Shipping Forecast
BBC Radio 4 198 kHz (1500m). Sea areas Malin and Hebrides. Broadcast at: 0048, 0520, 1201 and 1754.

Inshore Waters Forecast
BBC Radio 4 198 kHz (1500m) and VHF frequencies. Sea areas The Minch and Ardnamurchan Point to Cape Wrath. Broadcast at: 0053 and 0525.

Landward forecasts
BBC Radio Scotland 810 kHz (370m) and VHF frequencies.

Navtex

Navtex reception on the west coast of Scotland and in the Outer Hebrides has now been much improved by the establishment of a transmitter at Malin Head. This broadcasts Inshore Waters forecasts for sea areas The Minch and Ardnamurchan to Cape Wrath on 490kHz (A) at the following (UTC) times: 0000, 0400, 0800, 1200, 1600 and 2000.

The anchorage off the slate pier, Easdale

Anchorages, moorings and berthing

Heading north from the Mull of Kintyre there are no secure anchorages for twenty miles or so but once Islay or Gigha are reached the number of options rapidly increases. By no means all of the anchorages are suitable for all conditions but, with careful reading of the forecast and these Directions, it should always be possible to find a safe and comfortable refuge should bad weather be encountered.

As with the rest of the Scottish west coast, if it is to be properly explored it is essential for the yacht to be well equipped with ground tackle and the crew thoroughly familiar with anchor handling. Though visitors' moorings and pontoons are becoming more plentiful and it is now possible to cruise throughout the area without anchoring once, this will mean missing the opportunity to visit some of the finest anchorages in Europe. Although the anchorages close to the centres of sailing activity between Crinan and Tobermory tend to be well-used at the height of the season there are still many unfrequented places to be found, especially in fair weather.

The holding ground varies widely, and although sand and mud of varying consistency are the most common, weed is frequently found, and occasionally rock. If strong winds are expected it is worth taking special care to ensure that the anchor is well set.

These Sailing Directions aim to provide details of less familiar anchorages as well as the more popular ones, although they make no claim to be comprehensive and, under suitable conditions, independently minded yachtsmen will find, with the help of charts, sketch plans and experience, anchorages other than those described in this book.

Choosing an anchorage

Many places are only suitable for a short daytime visit in settled conditions and the inclusion of an anchorage in these Directions is no indication that it is suitable for all conditions. It is the skipper's responsibility to decide whether to use an anchorage at all, and for how long, in light of conditions (both current and predicted) and all the information available. Even the most apparently sheltered place will sometimes have the crew standing anchor watches throughout the night. Nor is the mere presence of pontoons or moorings a guarantee of adequate protection from wind, sea or swell in all weathers and at all times. Many can be badly exposed in some directions.

The description 'occasional anchorage' is intended to convey that the place described is only suitable for use under certain conditions; perhaps for a brief visit ashore during daylight, or in winds from certain directions to await a change of wind or tide. In ideal conditions it might be possible for it to be used overnight.

The description 'temporary anchorage' is used to describe an anchorage which must be used with caution even in good conditions and which would rarely ever be suitable for leaving a boat unattended or anchoring overnight.

Conversely, the absence of the description 'occasional' or 'temporary' should not be taken as a recommendation that an anchorage may be used in any weather.

Some anchorages, and particularly piers and boat harbours, are only suitable for shoal-draught boats, and this should be obvious from the description; the inclusion of an anchorage does not imply that it is suitable for all yachts.

Within some anchorages there are often several suitable places to lie depending on weather conditions and the type of boat. It is not always practicable to describe them all, or to mark each one on the plans.

Steep high ground to windward is unlikely to provide good shelter; in fresh winds there may be turbulent gusts on its lee side, or the wind may be deflected to blow from a completely different direction. Conversely, trees to windward will absorb a lot of wind and provide good shelter.

Rivers, burns and streams generally carry down debris, often leaving a shallow or drying bank of stones, sand or silt, over which the unwary may swing, invariably in the middle of the night.

Fish farms

Fish farming is a major industry throughout the west coast and their cages, ropes, feeding pipes and buoys can be found almost anywhere with suitable mooring depths in sheltered waters. They are usually outside the most popular places and their ever-increasing scale often means that they are located in areas that are not suitable for anchoring a yacht. However, some of the smaller ones can obstruct what appears to be a suitable anchorage and the temptation to anchor too close to them must be resisted.

There are two main forms: cages for 'fin fish' (usually salmon), and rows of buoys from which ropes are suspended, on which shellfish are 'grown'. These buoys may have ropes between them on, or close to, the surface. Fish cages may be moved around within a bay or their designated area and the symbols on charts or the plans in this book should be taken as an indication that a fish farm may be present, rather than its precise location.

The boundary of an area licensed for fish farming is sometimes marked by buoys, usually yellow and sometimes lit. These are often a long way from the cages, and there may or may not be moorings or other obstructions within the area marked out by the buoys. Anchor well clear of all fish farming equipment and, if in doubt, use a tripping line.

Moorings

Many bays and inlets offering conditions suitable for anchoring often appear to be taken up by moorings for fishing boats and other small local craft although, with care, space may well be found to anchor. Vacant moorings should not be used without first checking their ownership, availability and suitability. Do not pick up a buoy unless you are sure that it is a mooring buoy and not marking creels for storing live prawns – or another yacht's anchor buoy!

The allocation of licences for moorings is the responsibility of the Crown Estates and new applications are rarely approved unless they have satisfied themselves that some anchoring space for visiting yachts is set aside. This is done through consultation with RYA Scotland and the West Highlands Anchorage and Mooring Association (WHAM). The latter would be interested to learn from cruising yachtsmen of any apparently unauthorised obstruction or over-proliferation of moorings and can be contacted through their website *www.whamassoc.org.uk*

Visitors' moorings

Visitors' moorings are provided by local hotels free of charge to yachts whose crews patronise their establishments, as well as by local harbour and mooring associations and the occasional boatyard or charter operator. They are arranged (as they have to be) to suit the largest boats likely to use them. As a boat on a mooring behaves differently from a boat at anchor the effect of this is often to reduce rather than increase the number of visiting boats that can use an anchorage. There is no guarantee that a mooring is suitable for any boat intending to use it.

These moorings generally have large blue or yellow buoys marked 'visitors 15 tons'. The majority of these moorings are now provided with a pick up buoy and strop, which makes mooring easier than when a rope had to be fed through a ring on the top of the buoy. Even so, the strop should be examined for wear and if in doubt an additional line should be attached to the buoy as described below.

In the case of having to moor to a buoy which has only a ring, all yachts should carry a good length of nylon anchorplait made up with a hard eye at one end through which a snap shackle, or similar, can be used to connect it to the ring. Failing this it will be necessary to attach the rope to the ring using a Fisherman's bend which will stop chafe but will be hard to undo and may even have to be cut in the morning. In both cases plastic tubing should be used to prevent chafe at the bow roller. It is best practice to have at least two lines between the boat and the mooring. A simple slip rope should be used only as a temporary arrangement whilst the main line is being attached or released. The practice of

The visitors' moorings at Craighouse, Jura, where the alternative of anchoring is problematical because of the poor holding

rafting up together on these moorings is not now encouraged.

When visitors' moorings were first established, about forty years ago, they were owned by the Highlands and Islands Development Board (HIDB) and no charges were levied. This is no longer the case and virtually all moorings are now owned and operated by local interests. In larger harbours, such as Tobermory, dues may be collected by boat every evening but in the majority of places it is the responsibility of those who use a mooring to go ashore and seek out either the harbourmaster, a local hotel or shop, boatyard, sailing club or honesty box and pay their dues. If mooring buoys are to be maintained it is vital that those using them make every effort to ensure that they pay their way. If there is no obvious place where payment can be made it is highly likely that the moorings will not have been maintained and they will be dangerous to use.

There are at least two dozen locations where visitors' moorings are provided and they are listed in the quick reference table in the Appendix on p.200.

Marinas and yacht centres

There are nine marinas in the area between Loch Crinan and Loch Linnhe, ranging from major boatyards offering all facilities and services for yachts up to 40 tonnes to smaller yards with limited services but nonetheless providing a good place to base a yacht for a season at a more modest cost. At all these establishments a berth or mooring will usually be found for a visiting yacht; the charges vary widely and cost-conscious skippers will do well to enquire first.

Details of all the above are listed in the table in the Appendix (p.200) and further information can be found in the publication *Welcome Anchorages* which is published annually and available free from marinas and marine companies all over Scotland, or on the internet at *www.welcomeanchoragesscotland.com*

Pontoons

In addition to the above marinas there is now an ever-growing number of harbours and anchorages where berthing or dinghy landing is possible at a pontoon. At the latest count there were ten such places, some of which, as at Tobermory, offer up to fifty serviced finger berths together with facilities for taking on diesel. Others may provide only two or three berths for short-stay visits. Again, details are given in the Appendix and *Welcome Anchorages*.

Quays, piers, jetties, slips, linkspans

These, and related structures, need some definition and description. The categories overlap somewhat and a structure identified on the chart may have fallen into disuse, or been replaced by one of a different type, or have a description well above its status. The definitions used in this book are as follows, and give some indication of what you might expect to find.

A quay, wharf or pier is used by fishing boats and occasional coasters, and usually has at least 2 metres of water at its head at chart datum. It is often constructed of piles or open framing, or stone or concrete with vertical timber fendering, alongside which it is difficult for a small yacht to lie without a robust fender board. A pier projects from the shore, but a quay or wharf is either part of a harbour or parallel to the shore.

Ferry terminals, such as those at Colonsay, Craignure and Port Askaig have a linkspan for a bow-loading car ferry. The inner end is hinged and the outer end, supported between concrete towers, is raised or lowered to match the height of the ramp on the ferry, according to the state of the tide. The linkspan is usually at one end of a quay alongside which the ferry lies.

A jetty is smaller and, for yachts, more user-friendly but often dries alongside. Newer jetties are constructed of more or less smooth concrete, older ones of stone, often with a very uneven surface; a few are of timber.

A slip, or slipway, runs down at an angle into the water, although its outer end may be above water at low tide and it may be used by a ferry to an inshore island. There is sometimes sufficient depth for a yacht to go alongside a slip for a brief visit ashore for stores.

With the enormous growth in inshore fishing and fish-farming, many of these structures are in regular use by fishermen whose livelihood depends on being able to land their produce quickly, and yachts should take care not to obstruct them.

The stone pier at Ardbeg, Islay, is rough but has deep water alongside and a small tidal range

Martin Lawrence

Equipment

This should be as robust and reliable as for a yacht going a similar distance offshore anywhere in the English Channel or the North Sea.

Anchors

A boat needs at least two anchors, of the sizes recommended by anchor manufacturers or independent reference books, rather than those supplied as standard by boat manufacturers which are often on the light side.

Chain rather than rope will prevent a yacht roving around in gusts and at least 60 metres of chain is recommended. If you do use rope it will help to have a weight ('angel', 'chum') which can be let down to the seabed on a traveller.

In view of the variety of conditions two different types of anchor should be carried. The choice is very much a matter of individual preference but about half the yachts moored in marinas still carry a CQR pattern anchor. However, the adoption of 'second generation' anchors such as the Delta, Spade and Rocna seems to be gathering momentum and they certainly get good reports from those who have used them in Scottish waters. Some have the ability to penetrate certain types of weed, an attribute which was formerly thought to be restricted to the traditional Fisherman anchor.

Chartering

The area covered by this book is the centre of the yacht charter business in Scotland and in any popular anchorage a fair proportion of yachts will be bareboat or skippered charter boats. Most are based in the Oban to Crinan area and all the major marinas have one or more charter firms operating out of them.

Details of the various charter firms and much more information is given in the excellent 75-page full colour brochure published by Sail Scotland which is freely available direct from them or many marinas. It can also be read and downloaded from *www.sailscotland.co.uk*

Conservation

The editor is grateful to Dr. Sarah Cunningham of Scottish Natural Heritage, in conjunction with Dr. Graham Russell of RYA Scotland, for supplying much of the following information.

Under the Marine (Scotland) Act 2010 the Scottish Government and Scottish Natural Heritage have agreed to identify a network of protected marine areas (MPAs) around our coasts to safeguard important species and their habitats. Marine Scotland have provisionally identified 17 possible MPAs in Scottish inshore waters, of which there are 10 sites on the west coast, covering a range of marine life including burrowed mud, flameshell beds, maerl beds, common skate, black guillemot, and the largest aggregation of the rare fan mussel in UK waters, as well as areas of marine geological

Scottish Natural Heritage

Basking sharks can frequently be seen, later in the summer, especially to the west of Mull

interest. A public consultation was completed in late 2013 and the outcome and final designation of the new MPAs is awaited in due course. There are also three other MPA search areas still being considered on the west coast, for species such as basking shark and minke whale. Six Marine Special Areas of Conservation (mSACs) have already been designated under the European Habitats Directive within the area covered by this volume. None of these should be considered a threat to recreational sailing. Rather the opposite: they help protect the essential character of these important sailing waters.

There is no intention to restrict access to mSACs or MPAs where activities are not having negative effects on the habitats and species of a site, which is normally the case; indeed, that would be counterproductive as the aim is to make everyone aware of the special features of the sites so that they can be appreciated. However, if you are lucky enough to see whales, dolphins, porpoise, seals or basking sharks whilst in these waters, please adhere to the Scottish Marine Wildlife Watching Code (*www.marinecode.org*), to minimise any disturbance to these animals.

In a couple of existing SACs some types of fishing are prohibited because of their potential to damage the sea life on the bottom, e.g. the fragile serpulid worm reefs in Loch Creran, where anchoring is also restricted to certain areas to protect the reefs. It is possible that there may be a few places where restrictions on anchoring are introduced in the MPAs when they are designated but RYA Scotland has been working closely with Scottish Natural Heritage and Marine Scotland to ensure that these are kept to a minimum. Many of the protected substrates are ones which recreational sailors do their best to avoid due to poor holding. Permitted anchorages in Loch Creran have been identified and the restrictions have been detailed on the relevant entry on p.122. If any other no-anchoring zones are identified they will be published in the annual amendments to these Directions at *www.clyde.org* and incorporated into future editions.

Services and supplies

Compared with the areas covered by our other west coast volumes, the *Outer Hebrides* and *Ardnamurchan to Cape Wrath*, provisioning and fuelling rarely poses any problems, except when cruising to the west of Mull, and even then nothing is more than a day's sail away.

The quick reference table on p.200 in the Appendix gives an overview of what can be expected and where it will be found, but it must be treated with a degree of caution as changes can take place rapidly from season to season, especially with regard to small shops and restaurants.

Diesel

Between Crinan and Tobermory diesel by hose is readily obtainable at a good number of dedicated yacht pontoons. Outside this area it is less easy and marine diesel may only be available from local fishing boat suppliers or a garage which could involve some telephoning or a longish walk.

Water supplies

As with diesel, replenishing water alongside by hose presents few problems in the more populated areas. Elsewhere, most piers usually have a tap of some sort and a yacht with built-in tanks should have a portable container or two, together with a straight-sided funnel, with which to fill the tank. A 20-metre hose of the flat variety on a reel, with a universal coupling to fit on any sort of tap, is also well worth carrying.

Bottled gas

Where Calor Gas is referred to, Camping Gaz is often also available, especially in marinas, and caravan sites, though this cannot always be assumed to be the case in remote outlets.

Provisions

These are obtainable at almost all the places mentioned in the table in the Appendix and the majority have well stocked local stores or even supermarkets.

At the entrance to the Sound of Mull off Duart Point, avoiding a Calmac ferry is a frequent occurrence

Repairs

Nowhere within the area is more than a day's sail from a yacht yard which will be able to offer almost all the facilites and skills that could be needed and these are listed in the Appendix.

Eating ashore

The possibilities for eating and drinking ashore are still improving and the choice is wide. Hotels, restaurants and pubs are mentioned in the text, although not usually by name and without specific recommendations as management and standards may change rapidly. Several provide moorings for patrons.

Communications

Mobile phones

2G coverage throughout the sea area from Kintyre to Ardnamurchan is generally good though there are a few small patches of limited reception. However, many anchorages are surrounded by high ground so any important calls or internet connections should be made before making the approach.

The above comments relate to the Vodafone and EE networks which are generally acknowledged to provide the best coverage of Scottish west coast waters.

VHF radiotelephones

VHF reception is generally good in open water but, as with mobile phones, close proximity to high ground may interfere with the signal.

The map on p.7 shows the names and channels of the stations used for VHF transmissions and it may help users to tune into the best channel for reception of the Coastguard weather forecasts.

Travel

There are regular bus services from Glasgow to Campbeltown (Mull of Kintyre), Ardrishaig (for Crinan, Ardfern and Craobh), Oban and Fort William. Rail services run from Glasgow and Edinburgh to Oban and Fort William. Scheduled air services operate from Glasgow to Tiree and Islay.

Caledonian MacBrayne run ferry services from Oban to Craignure (Mull), Colonsay, Coll and Tiree. Also from Tayinloan (Kintyre) to Gigha and West Loch Tarbert (Kintyre) to Port Ellen and Port Askaig (Islay). They also run smaller ferries from Tobermory to Kilchoan (Ardnamurchan), Fionnphort (Ross of Mull) to Iona and Loch Aline to Fishnish (Mull).

Journeys by public transport, both within and to Scotland, should be planned in advance and this is easily done by using the website *www.travelinescotland.com* who also produce an iPhone/iPad app. This resource will give the timings and also the names and contact information for all the operators.

Donald MacDonald

Charles Warlow

Access rights

In Scotland, since the Land Reform (Scotland) Act 2003 came into force, everyone has the statutory right of access to all land for recreational purposes, excluding hunting, shooting or fishing. These rights must be exercised responsibly and do not apply to houses and gardens, farmyards, growing crops and other commercial uses which are defined more fully in the Access Code published by SNH and available from tourist offices and the website *www.outdooraccess-scotland.com*

Access rights apply equally to islands, despite the efforts of some owners to declare them private and forbid landing. However the privacy of houses and any other buildings on an island must be respected.

Emergencies

Serious and immediate emergencies (including medical emergencies) are usually best referred to the coastguard.

Coastguard

Following the reorganisation of coastguard services the area covered by these Directions is divided between two stations: Stornoway coastguard station being responsible for the area north of Jura and Belfast coastguard covering the remainder southwards from there.

Both stations are 24 hour Maritime Rescue Subcentres and maintain a continuous listening watch on VHF Ch16, and operate a safety service on Ch 67. Stornoway can be contacted by telephone on ☎01851 702013 and MMSI 002320024 and Belfast on ☎02891 463933 and MMSI 002320021.

Lifeboats

All-weather lifeboats are stationed at Campbeltown, Port Askaig (Islay), Oban and Tobermory.

Notes on sailing directions and plans

Arrangement

These Directions are written starting at the Mull of Kintyre. This is dealt with fully in the CCC volume *Firth of Clyde* but, as the timing of arrival at the Mull is crucial to passage planning in the waters to the west of it, directions for rounding the Mull itself are repeated in this book. Gigha, Islay and the west coast of Jura, including also Colonsay and Oronsay, follow next before heading northwards up the Sound of Jura. Chapter five then covers Crinan and the lochs north of it with the subsequent chapters continuing north through the Firth of Lorn to Oban, Loch Linnhe, the Sound of Mull, Tobermory and Loch Sunart. The last three chapters deal with the west coast of Mull, Coll, Tiree and the Ross of Mull before returning eastwards to the Firth of Lorn.

Each chapter begins with general information relating to the whole: tides, shelter, marks, dangers and lights come first; then any passage directions, sometimes including certain anchorages where it is necessary to relate these to plans associated with the passages; then any branches from the main passage; and finally individual harbours and anchorages, usually in the same south to north sequence and all described as approached from seaward.

Although fully open to the south, David Balfour's Bay, Ross of Mull, is a delightful anchorage in settled weather

It should be noted that marks and dangers are listed in separate paragraphs only in the introductory sections, which usually cover large expanses of water across which yachts may be passage making in many different directions. In describing narrow lochs, sounds and the approach to anchorages and harbours, any dangers and marks are included under the heading *Directions* in the order that they will be encountered. This reduces repetition.

Bearings and distances

All bearings, both in text and on the plans, are from seaward and always refer to true north. All plans are orientated with true north at the top as the plan is read, except where stated.

Distances are given in nautical miles and cables (tenths of a nautical mile); distances of less than a cable are generally expressed in metres.

Depths and heights

These are given in metres to correspond with the current Admiralty charts. Depths are related to the current chart datum which is generally lower than that on older charts. This datum is the lowest level to which the surface of the sea is expected to fall owing to astronomical causes (LAT). If high barometric pressure and/or strong offshore winds coincide with a low spring tide the water may fall below this level, in which case there will be less depth than shown on the chart, or sketch plan.

Heights are now given as the clear height in metres above the highest astronomical tide (HAT) which is higher than the previously quoted MHWS used on older charts and previous editions of the Sailing Directions.

Tides

Heights of tides are represented by five figures; these are: Mean High Water Springs, Mean High Water Neaps, Mean Tide Level, Mean Low Water Neaps, Mean Low Water Springs. The word Mean is important because (for example) Low Water Springs in any particular fortnight may be substantially higher or lower than the mean.

If you have tide tables which give heights of tides at Oban you will be able to relate the height of tide on any particular day to the mean figures there (4·0 2·9 2·4 1·8 0·7 for Oban) and judge whether the rise and fall is greater or less than the mean.

The difference between times of tides at Oban and at Dover may vary by as much as 40 minutes, so that local tide tables will give more accurate results than those for Dover. In addition to Admiralty tide tables and commercial almanacs, pocket tide tables for Oban are supplied by local chandlers, boatyards and marinas.

References to tidal constants and timing of streams give the nearest Standard port first followed by the Dover equivalent in brackets. If times refer to neither a Standard port nor Dover they relate to local HW or LW.

Plans

Plans of anchorages and passages in these Directions are often at a larger scale than those on current charts, and the information in them is compiled from many sources. These include the Admiralty's original surveys, Ordnance Survey, aerial photographs, observations and surveys by other yachtsmen and, latterly,

One of the pleasures of cruising Islay is being able to anchor off and visit a distillery. Ardbeg also has a good restaurant

Edward Mason

Google Earth. Some of them are based directly on British Admiralty charts, with the permission of the Hydrographer of the Navy.

Generally the conventions used on Admiralty charts have been followed so that these Directions may be used in conjunction with them. Symbols used on plans are illustrated on this page and also on the front cover flap.

All plans are drawn with north at the top (except where noted) and all depths are in metres. None of the plans is to a recognised scale and the drawn scale should be used to estimate distances. Only information relevant to craft up to 2 metres draught, for which these Directions are primarily written, is given and they are intended as an illustrated guide to the text and should not be used for navigation.

Background information

In previous editions of the Sailing Directions a note regarding items of special or historic interest was often included but this has now been omitted as a result of the publication in 2010 of the Club's Companion to the Sailing Directions, *Cruising Scotland*. This fully illustrated, hardback book, updated in 2015, sets out to provide the cruising yachtsman with much of the supplementary information that would ideally be included within the Sailing Directions but has often been omitted due to shortage of space. Page references to *Cruising Scotland* are given throughout.

Place names

In some cases the popular name for a place, or its spelling, differs from that on Admiralty charts. The latter is usually given, and both where appropriate. The spelling of many names appears to vary greatly – see the Gaelic Glossary in the Appendix – and throughout these Directions and on the plans we have endeavoured to use that shown on the relevant Admiralty chart.

Changes, corrections, and supplements

Despite appearances, things do change on the west coast. Buoys, lights, piers, pontoons and many shoreside facilities slowly evolve. Readers are asked to bear this in mind and to make sure that they have the latest amendments issued at intervals on the CCC and Imray websites, and also to report any discrepancies, or even uncertainties, which may be further investigated by other readers.

This is greatly appreciated not only by the Club and publishers, but also by the Hydrographic Office to whom any relevant information is forwarded.

Principal chart symbols

Symbol	Description
	HW mark
	LW indicating mud, sand or shingle
	Shoreline rocks
	Isolated rocks
	2 metre line
	Towns, buildings
5	5 metre line
10	Other contours
✳	Drying rock
⌗	Rock awash at chart datum
+	Rock with less than 2 metres at chart datum
	Fuel
	Water
	Fish farm
V **⚓**	Visitors' berth/mooring
	Harbourmaster
☆	White light
☆	Red light
☆	Green light
☆	Sectored light where sectors not shown
☆	Major light on small scale plans
	Harbour with yacht berths
	Yacht harbour/marina
⚓	Anchorage
	Slip
	Chimney
▶	Yacht/sailing club

Abbreviations

1₅ or *(1₅)*	On a reef or beside a drying rock symbol indicates drying height above CD
1₅ or *(1₅)*	Within a 2m contour or beside a submerged rock symbol indicates least depth below CD
5 or (5)	On or beside a rock or islet indicates height above MHWS
M	Miles on land (1760 yards) Miles at sea (6080 feet)
m	Metres
c	Cable (1/10 nautical mile)
bn	Beacon

1. Mull of Kintyre to West Loch Tarbert

Admiralty Chart
2724, 2168, 2798
Admiralty Leisure Folio
5611.1B, 3
Imray Chart
C63, C64
Ordnance Survey
60, 61, 62, 68
Cruising Scotland
pp.61-62

Mull of Kintyre to the Sound of Jura

Once round the Mull of Kintyre, vessels heading north enter the wide, nameless, stretch of water between Kintyre and Islay leading to the Sound of Jura itself. Free from hazards, if Islay and Gigha are given a wide berth, much of it is open to the west and subject to the full Atlantic swell.

Tides

North-going stream begins +0400 Oban (−0130 Dover)
South-going stream begins −0225 Oban (+0430 Dover)

Generally the rates are up to 2 kn throughout the main body of water increasing to 5 kn close to the Mull of Kintyre itself and 4·5 kn towards the Mull of Oa.

Between Islay and Kintyre and through the Sound of Jura as far as Fladda the rise and fall of tides is related to a phenomenon known as an amphidrome which is a tidal pivot point where the range is nil. This occurs about halfway between Port Ellen and the Mull of Kintyre, but its exact location moves during the tidal cycle; there is less range of tide on the southeast coast of Islay at the time of spring tides because the amphidrome is nearer to Islay at that time. This (rather simplified) is the reason for the curious observation which used to appear in the Admiralty Tide Tables that 'it is neaps at Port Ellen when it is springs at Machrihanish'.

Shelter

Good shelter can be found at Port Ellen and Ardminish Bay, Gigha. If heading northwards and confronted by strong northerlies once round the Mull, Rathlin Island is worthy of consideration (see *Firth of Clyde* Sailing Directions p.99). If heading south or east and needing to wait for a favourable tide or conditions at the Mull, Macrihanish Bay (see below) is useful in offshore winds.

Anchorage

Machrihanish Bay, on the west side of the Mull of Kintyre at the south end of sand dunes 7½ miles north of Mull of Kintyre lighthouse, provides temporary anchorage to wait for more favourable conditions to round the Mull southward, but can be a trap if the wind comes onshore, or particularly if any swell comes into the bay. Skerrivore rocks extend 4 cables northwest from the southwest point of the bay and submerged rocks lie up to 2 cables off the south shore. Anchor off the mouth of a burn at the southeast side of the bay.

Lights

Mull of Kintyre Fl(2)20s91m24M
Rathlin West Fl.R.5s62m22M
Altacarry Head (Rathlin East) Fl(4)20s74m26M
Rue Pt. Fl(2)5s16m14M
Otter Rock S card. buoy Q(6)+L.Fl.15s
Eilean Chuirn (Ardmore Is.) Fl(3)18s26m8M
McArthur's Head Fl(2)WR.10s39m13/10M
Cath Sgeir W card. buoy Q(9)15s
Gamna Gigha Lt. Bn. Fl(2)6s7m5M
Na Cuiltean Fl.10s9m9M

Machrihanish Bay. Note that the Skerrivore Rocks are covered

Martin Lawrence

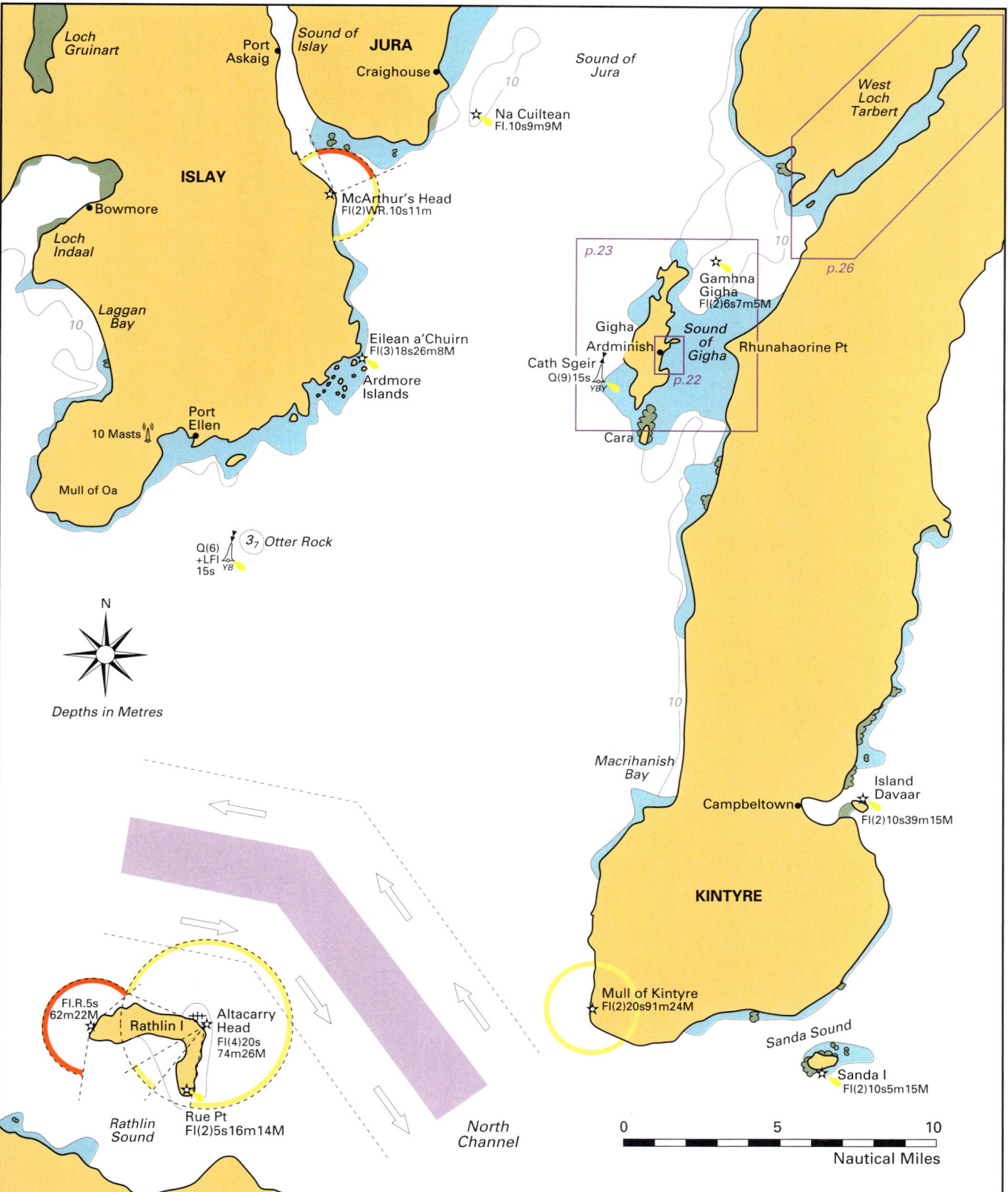

Loch Gruinart

Port Askaig

Sound of Islay

JURA

Craighouse

Sound of Jura

West Loch Tarbert

Na Cuiltean
Fl.10s9m9M

ISLAY

Bowmore

McArthur's Head
Fl(2)WR.10s11m

p.23

p.26

Gamhna Gigha
Fl(2)6s7m5M

Loch Indaal

Laggan Bay

10

Eilean a'Chuirn
Fl(3)18s26m8M

Gigha
Ardminish

Cath Sgeir
Q(9)15s
YBY

Sound of Gigha

Rhunahaorine Pt

p.22

Ardmore Islands

10 Masts

Port Ellen

Cara

Mull of Oa

Q(6)
+LFl
15s YB

3₇ Otter Rock

N

Depths in Metres

Macrihanish Bay

10

Island Davaar
Fl(2)10s39m15M

Campbeltown

Fl.R.5s
62m22M

Rathlin I

Altacarry Head
Fl(4)20s
74m26M

KINTYRE

Mull of Kintyre
Fl(2)20s91m24M

Rue Pt
Fl(2)5s16m14M

Rathlin Sound

North Channel

Sanda Sound

Sanda I
Fl(2)10s5m15M

0   5   10

Nautical Miles

MULL OF KINTYRE TO SOUND OF JURA

Admiralty Chart
2798
Admiralty Leisure Folio
5611.1B
Imray Chart
C63, C64
Ordnance Survey
68
Cruising Scotland
pp.61-62

Mull of Kintyre

A passage round the Mull of Kintyre requires great care and due regard must be paid to appropriate wind conditions and the times and nature of the strong tidal streams, overfalls and eddies which, in wind over tide conditions, can cause dangerous seas. Conditions can deteriorate rapidly and the timing of the passage, whether north or southbound, is most important. Small craft unless properly equipped and able to batten down all hatches should not attempt this passage in unsettled weather.

Tides

There are two distinct tidal streams off the Mull of Kintyre:

The offshore stream occurs south and west of Sanda Island and the Mull and attains at springs a rate of over 3 knots. During the last 2 hours of the west-going offshore stream a dangerous race forms off Sron Uamha (Deas Point). This race can be violent and dangerous to yachts in fresh to strong southerly winds.

The inshore stream passes in both directions through Sanda Sound and close to the south and west shores of the Mull and turns one hour earlier than the offshore stream. This stream achieves 5 knots in each direction just west of the Mull and in the Sound of Sanda. At times in the tidal cycle, and also where wind and swell conditions are adverse, the boundary between this inshore stream and the main offshore stream can be an additional cause of turbulent seas.

There are several races in Sanda Sound and its NE approaches. Races also extend west and SW of Sanda Island. None of these races should present problems in conditions suitable for rounding the Mull.

The extract from the *Admiralty Tidal Atlas* is of particular value in understanding the timing and direction of these streams and the timing of the inner stream is amplified below:

In Sanda Sound (mid-channel)
West-going stream begins:
–0230 HW Greenock (–0110 HW Dover)
East-going stream begins:
+0340 HW Greenock (+0500 HW Dover)
5 knots springs in either direction.

Close west of Mull of Kintyre
North-going stream begins:
–0250 HW Greenock (–0130 HW Dover)
South-going stream begins:
+0310 HW Greenock (+0430 HW Dover)
5 knots springs in either direction.

Passage planning

The importance of accurate timing cannot be overstated. West and northbound yachts, by using Campbeltown or Sanda as a point of departure, can reduce the approach distance to the tidal gate thereby ensuring that they round the Mull at the optimum time.

For south and eastbound yachts heading south from Gigha, the distance to the Mull is at least 23 miles and it is vital to make full use of the southgoing ebb down the west coast of Kintyre if a fair tide is to be carried all the way to Sanda.

Allowance should be made for sudden, unforecast changes of weather partly because they are more inclined to happen at a turning point such as the Mull and partly because the distance from shelter is greater than usual.

Directions

Northbound: from Campbeltown to Gigha (using the inner tidal stream)

In ideal conditions leave Campbeltown at about –0410 HW Greenock (–0310 Dover). Arriving at Sanda Sound around –0230 HW Greenock (–0110 HW Dover) gives at least 7 hours of favourable tide along the south Kintyre shore, round the Mull and north to Gigha or beyond. However, if wind against tide conditions or a westerly swell is expected off Sron Uamha (Deas Point) and at the Mull, delay departure from Campbeltown by 1 or 2 hours. Aiming to be at Sanda Sound at –0120 HW Greenock (HW Dover) allows time for these seas to subside but, if early, keeping close inshore, 1-2 cables off, should avoid the worst of the race off Deas Point.

A series of reefs at the north side of Sanda Sound are marked at each end by red can light buoys at the Arranman's Barrels and the Macosh Rock. An experimental seabed-moored tidal turbine lies NE of the Macosh Rock buoy and is marked by a Fl.Y.5s buoy.

Northbound: from Campbeltown to Islay (using main tidal stream south of Sanda Island)

If making for Islay and wishing to avoid the inner tidal stream with its races, overfalls, and potentially dangerous seas, leave Campbeltown at –0320 HW Greenock (–0200 HW Dover). Aim to arrive well south of Sanda Island at –0120 HW Greenock (HW Dover) and keep well east to avoid Paterson's Rock, marked by a R can light buoy, which should be given a wide berth. Keep at least 2 miles offshore from the Mull, or more, provided that your course coincides with the NW-going lane of the Traffic Separation zone.

Southbound: from Gigha to Campbeltown
Leaving Gigha between +0440 HW Greenock and +0505 HW Greenock (6 hours after and 6 hours before HW Dover) gives slack then increasingly favourable tides towards the Mull. This allows at least 5 hours of east-going tidal flow to pass through Sanda Sound, (note that the tide turns west-going in Sanda Sound at –0230 HW Greenock (–0110 HW Dover) and can reach 5 knots springs), or more than 6 hours of the east-going main tidal stream passing south of Sanda Island, when making for the Firth of Clyde.

Leaving Gigha earlier than +0440 HW Greenock (6 hours after HW Dover) results in increasing opposing tides. Reaching the lighthouse at the Mull earlier than +0440 HW Greenock (+0600 HW Dover) risks entering a dangerous race off Sron Uamha (Deas Point). This race exists for about 1hr 45 mins between +0310 HW Greenock and +0450 HW Greenock (+0430 HW Dover and +0610 HW Dover) when the east-going inner stream meets the west-going main stream. It is especially violent and dangerous in fresh to strong southerly winds.

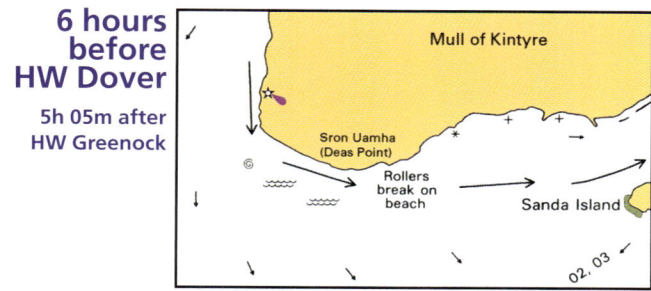

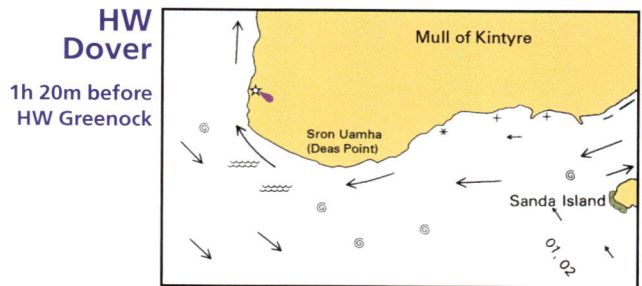

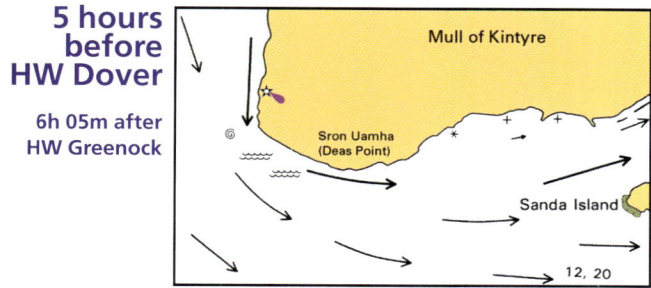

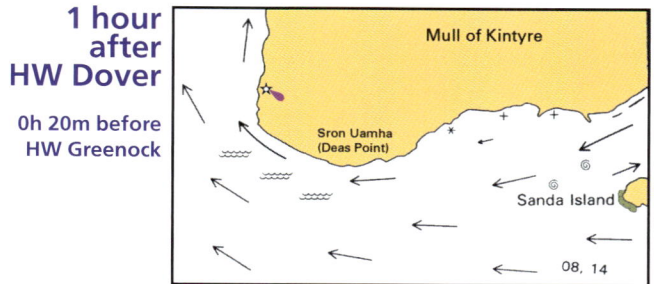

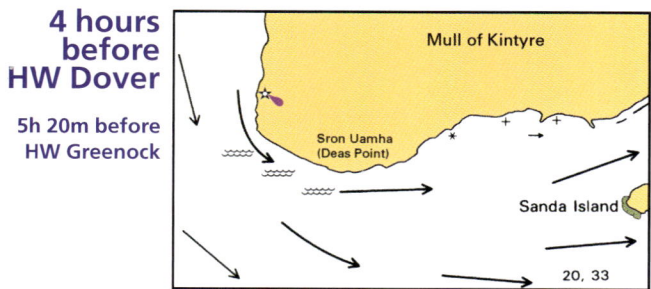

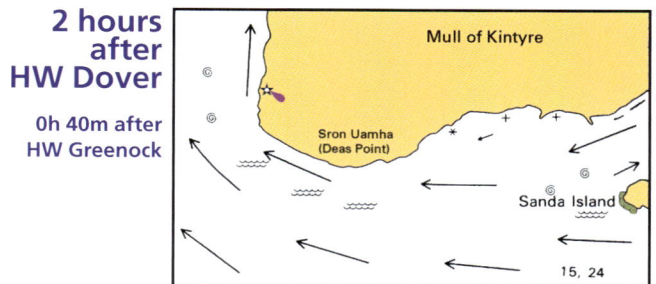

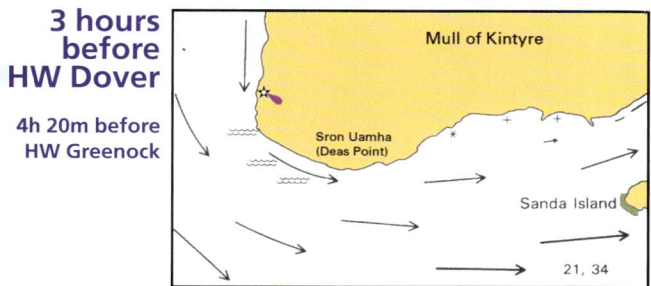

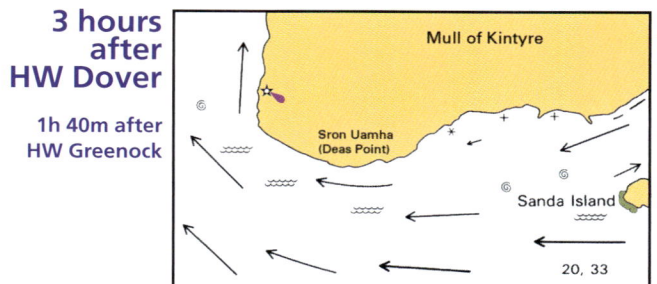

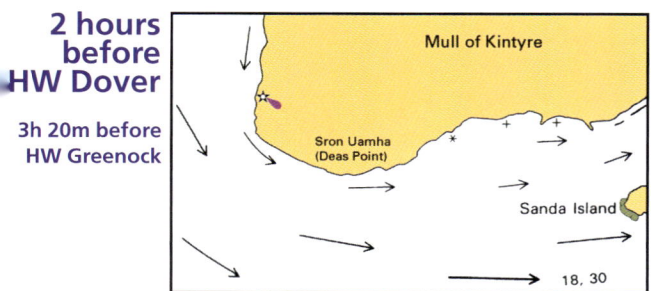

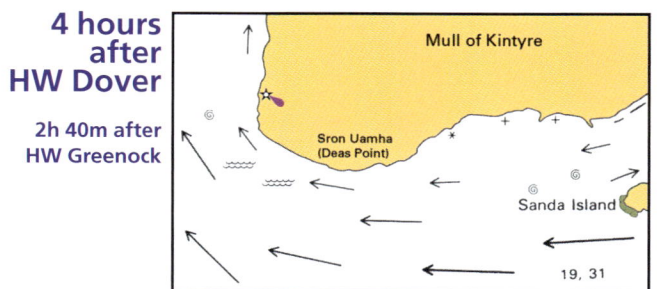

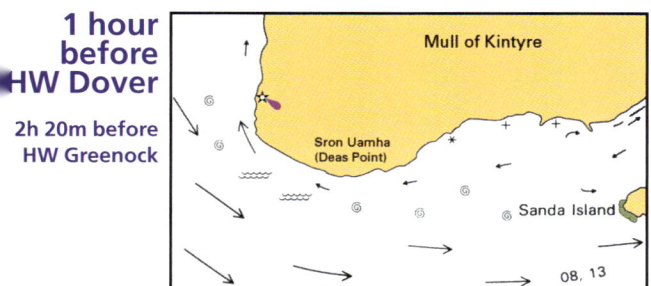

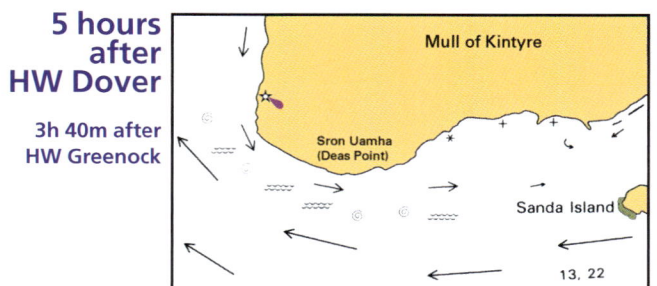

6 hours before HW Dover

5h 05m after HW Greenock

02, 03

5 hours before HW Dover

6h 05m after HW Greenock

12, 20

4 hours before HW Dover

5h 20m before HW Greenock

20, 33

3 hours before HW Dover

4h 20m before HW Greenock

21, 34

2 hours before HW Dover

3h 20m before HW Greenock

18, 30

1 hour before HW Dover

2h 20m before HW Greenock

08, 13

HW Dover

1h 20m before HW Greenock

01, 02

1 hour after HW Dover

0h 20m before HW Greenock

08, 14

2 hours after HW Dover

0h 40m after HW Greenock

15, 24

3 hours after HW Dover

1h 40m after HW Greenock

20, 33

4 hours after HW Dover

2h 40m after HW Greenock

19, 31

5 hours after HW Dover

3h 40m after HW Greenock

13, 22

Taken from the Admiralty Tidal Atlas for the Firth of Clyde and Approaches (NP 222) and reproduced with the permission of the UKHO

Rounding the Mull - further considerations

From the Clyde to the west side of Kintyre, if the wind is southwesterly, there is little point in using Sanda Sound. The tidal stream will be either against you or against the wind; no distance would be saved if tacking and motoring would be uncomfortable (to say the least). Despite this, local yachtsmen usually take the inshore passages at Sanda and the Mull, preferring to endure discomfort and save distance.

If using the outer route, pass at least ½ mile east of Paterson's Rock buoy and a mile south of Sanda, or 2 miles off if the wind is more than Force 3; plan to be south of Sanda about the time that the tide turns to the west.

When the Mull of Kintyre lighthouse comes into sight, the temptation to bear away too soon should be resisted; pass two miles off to avoid a south-going eddy inshore.

If the wind is northwesterly Sanda Sound can be used, but if it is any more than light, conditions will probably be unattractive when the west side of the Mull is opened up. Standing further offshore will take you into the Traffic Separation Scheme.

If making for Gigha or the Sound of Jura, moderate winds between northeast and south present little problem. In all wind directions except between south and west, aim to be at the east end of Sanda at −0230 HW Greenock (−0110 HW Dover).

If making for Islay aim to be clear of the Mull of Kintyre by +0430 HW Greenock (+0550 HW Dover), but if late keep well clear of the east-going stream inshore; an adverse tide in the deep water clear of the Mull is much weaker than near the shore.

The passage eastward can present fewer problems in that easterly winds do not blow from the open sea, but a following westerly wind can build up large and, at times, steep seas.

Distances

Distances between anchorages are more significant than is usual on the west coast of Scotland. The shortest distance between anchorages (other than Sanda) on a passage round the Mull from Campbeltown is about 44 miles.

Lamlash, Arran to Sanda Island	26 miles
Campbeltown to Sanda Island	11 miles
Sanda Island to Mull of Kintyre	9 miles
Sanda Island to Port Ellen, Islay	32 miles
Sanda Island to Gigha, Ardminish Bay	32 miles
Sanda Island to Ardmore Islands, Islay	33 miles
Sanda Island to Craighouse, Jura	41 miles
Sanda Island to Loch Crinan	59 miles
Sanda Island to Ardfern, Loch Craignish	64 miles

Traffic Separation zone

The eastern extremity of the Traffic Separation Scheme lies 2¼ miles southwest of Mull of Kintyre lighthouse, limiting the distance off the point at which yachts may round the point unless passing along the northwest-going lane of the scheme. Be aware that the tidal streams can carry a yacht rounding the Mull into this zone.

Tidal generators

Because of the significant tidal streams off the Mull the area is of interest to developers of renewable energy installations. At the time of writing (2017) only a single experimental unit is in place: the seabed moored turbine northeast of the Macosh Rock buoy (p.16). However, further developments are under consideration and when they are established amendments to these directions will be issued. In the meantime yachtsmen should be aware that new and unfamiliar buoys marking them may appear without notice.

Lights

At night the waters around the Mull of Kintyre are well provided with powerful lights, but in an area ENE of Sanda Sound three out of the four nearest lights are obscured.

For more than 5 miles northeast of Sanda, Sanda Island lighthouse, Island Davaar and Ailsa Craig lights are all obscured, leaving only Pladda visible, at least 13 miles away, and the two light buoys in Sanda Sound.

Mull of Kintyre Fl(2)20s91m24M
Sanda Island (Ship Light) Fl.10s50m15M
Arranman's Barrels buoy Fl(2)R.12s
Macosh Rock buoy Fl.R.6s
Tidal turbine marker buoy Fl.Y.5s
Paterson's Rock Fl(3)R.18s
Altacarry Head Fl(4)20s74m26M; the northeast point of Rathlin Island, 12 miles west of Mull of Kintyre
Rue Point Fl(2)5s16m14M; the SE point of Rathlin Island

The lighthouse on the Mull of Kintyre

Scottish Viewpoint

Susan Allan

The new pontoon and pier at Ardminish Bay, Gigha, with visitors' moorings beyond (p.22)

Ardminish Bay, Gigha, from the southeast (p.22)

Patrick Roach

Gigha

Admiralty Chart
2475, 2168
Admiralty Leisure Folio
5611.2
Imray Chart
C64
Ordnance Survey
62
Cruising Scotland
pp.69-70

On passage from the Mull of Kintyre to the Sound of Jura the most direct route is to the west of Gigha, but Gigha itself is such a convenient staging post that most boats choose to make the detour through the Sound of Gigha and stop at Ardminish. From here, if southbound, it is easier to time one's arrival at the Mull at the most suitable time (see p.18).

Gigha is a well-populated fertile island, renowned for its sub-tropical gardens. The main centre of population on the island is Ardminish which overlooks the principal anchorage

Sound of Gigha

The sound has the reputation of being difficult to navigate but aids to navigation have been improved and, in moderate weather and reasonable visibility, it will present little difficulty.

Tides

North-going stream begins +0430 Oban (–0100 Dover), South-going stream begins –0200 Oban (+0500 Dover).

Constant varies between approximately –0200 Oban (+0500 Dover) at springs and –0500 Oban (+0300 Dover) at neaps.

Height in metres

MHWS	MHWN	MTL	MLWN	MLWS
1·5	1·3	1·0	0·8	0·6

Directions

Approaching from the south keep at least a mile off the mainland shore to avoid Sgeir an Tru, a drying rock about 1¾ miles southeast of Cara. Identify Cara Island and from a position 3 cables east of Cara steer 013° between Gigalum and the W Cardinal pillar buoy marking Gigalum Rocks, with Eilean Liath in line with Ardminish Point. From a position 1½ cables east of Eilean Liath steer 026° leaving the G can buoy marking Sgeir Gigalum to starboard. Pass east of Sgeir Nuadh R can buoy and then west of Badh Rock, marked by a G can buoy. Gamhna Gigha (2) at the north end of the Sound, marked by a concrete tower and beacon, may be left on either hand but should be given a fair berth.

From the north pass east of An Dubh-sgeir (3), avoiding the submerged rocks extending 2 cables east of it. Identify Gamhna Gigha (see above) and then aim to pass close to the west of Badh Rock buoy; bring that buoy onto a bearing of 026° astern and steer to a position 1½ cables due east of Eilean Liath and continue to pass west of the Gigalum Rocks W cardinal buoy; when past that buoy alter course to 193° or thereby to bring Eilean Liath in line with Ardminish Point bearing 013°, until clear south of Cara Island.

Lights

Gigalum Rocks W card. buoy Q(9)15s
Sgeir Gigalum G con. buoy Fl.G.6s
Sgeir Nuadh R can buoy Fl.R.6s
Badh Rock G con. buoy Fl(2)G.12s
Gamhna Gigha Concrete twr. & Bn. Fl(2)62

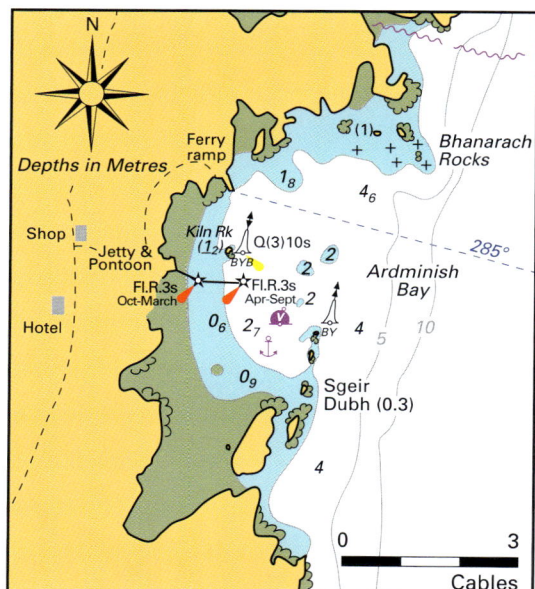

ARDMINISH BAY

Ardminish

Ardminish Bay (photos p.21) is well sheltered from the west but totally exposed to the east, when better shelter will be found in the anchorages off the northwest of the island (see p.24).

Directions

There are extensive reefs off both horns of the bay. Many of those on the south side are awash at LW and the outermost extremity is marked by a N cardinal buoy. On the north side of the bay the Bhanarach Rocks extend a cable southeast from the north point; they are unmarked and are a dangerous hazard.

Approaching from the north keep at least 2 cables off Ardminish Point on a course of not more than 205° with the Sgeir Nuadh buoy astern. To avoid the Bhanarach Rocks do not turn into the bay until the car ferry ramp on the north side of the bay bears 285°. From the south leave the N cardinal buoy no more than 1½ cables to port but note the 2m rock patches north of it. The only danger in the bay is Kiln Rock which dries 1·2m and is now marked by an E cardinal buoy.

Anchorage

There is a berthing pontoon having depths varying from 2·7 to 2·0m with 22 visitors' moorings east of it. Exposed to swell in southerly winds. Anchor in 3–5m south of the moorings or outside them. Bottom hard sand. Some shelter from the south and east will be found behind the reef at the south side of the bay.

Facilities

Shop, Post Office, telephone, hotel and restaurant. The former boathouse now has a bistro, toilets, showers and a launderette. Water at jetty. Calor Gas and auto diesel at shop. Golf course.

N

Depths in Metres

An Dubh Sgeir (3)

Gamhna Gigha (2.4)
Bn
Fl(2)6s

Port Mor

Eilean
Garbh

Rubh a'
Chairn Bhain

West Tarbert
Bay

East Tarbert
Bay

Fl(2)G.12s

Badh Rock

Outer Red
Rock

Inner Red
Rock

p.24

Sgeir
Blath-shuileach (1)

Sgeir
Cainnteach (1)

Fl.R.6s

Sgeir Nuadh

Druimyeon
Bay

Druimyeon
Reef

Sgeir Mhor (0.6)

Ardminish Point

Rhunahaorine Point
Bn
RW

GIGHA

Ferry
slip

Bhanarach Rocks

Ardminish

Ardminish Bay

Pier

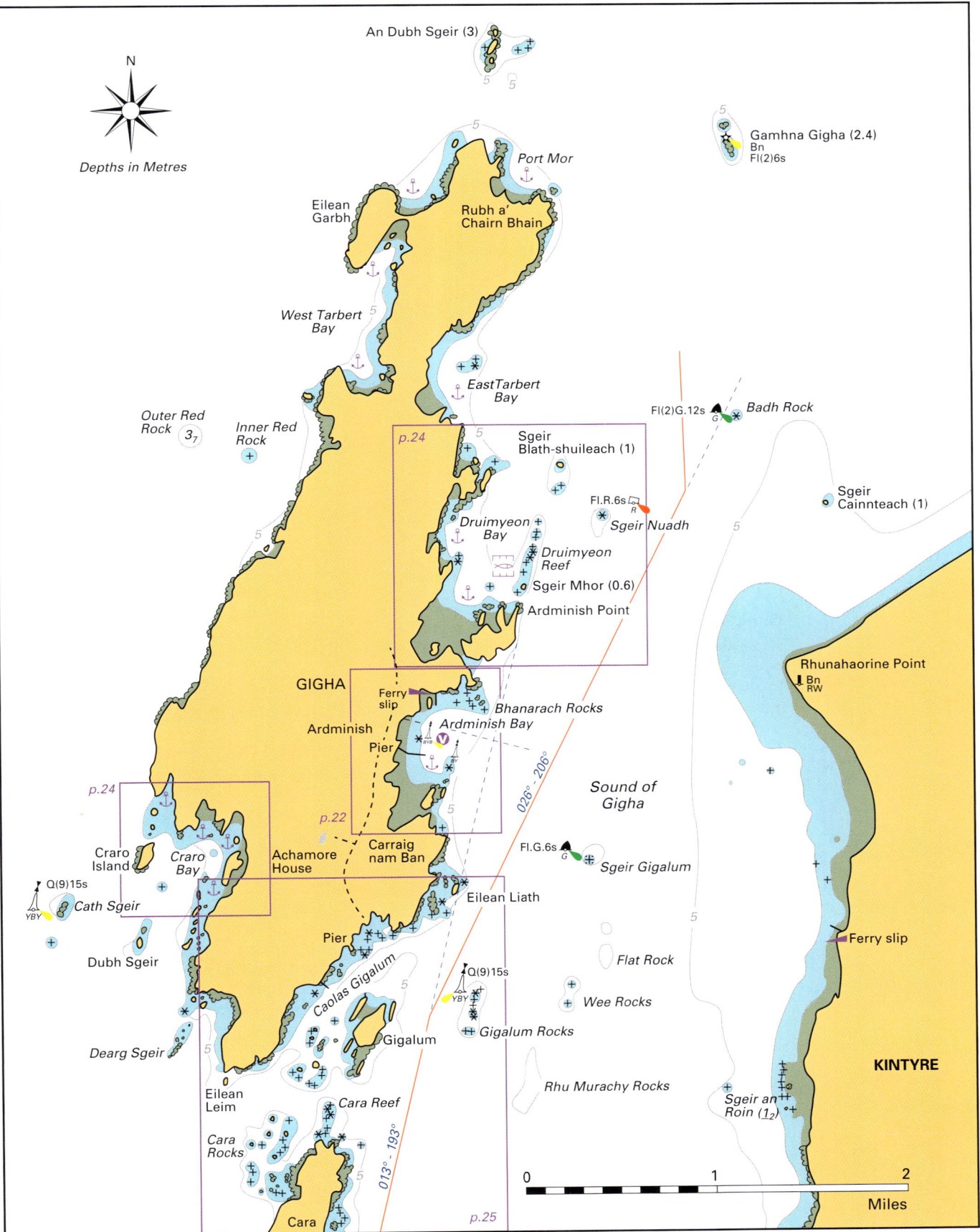

Sound of
Gigha

026° - 206°

p.24

p.22

Craro
Island

Craro
Bay

Achamore
House

Carraig
nam Ban

Fl.G.6s

Sgeir Gigalum

Cath Sgeir

Q(9)15s

YBY

Eilean Liath

Ferry slip

Dubh Sgeir

Pier

Caolas Gigalum

Flat Rock

Q(9)15s

YBY

Wee Rocks

Gigalum

Gigalum Rocks

Dearg Sgeir

Rhu Murachy Rocks

KINTYRE

Eilean
Leim

Cara Reef

Sgeir an
Roin (1₂)

Cara
Rocks

0   1   2

Miles

Cara

p.25

SOUND OF GIGHA

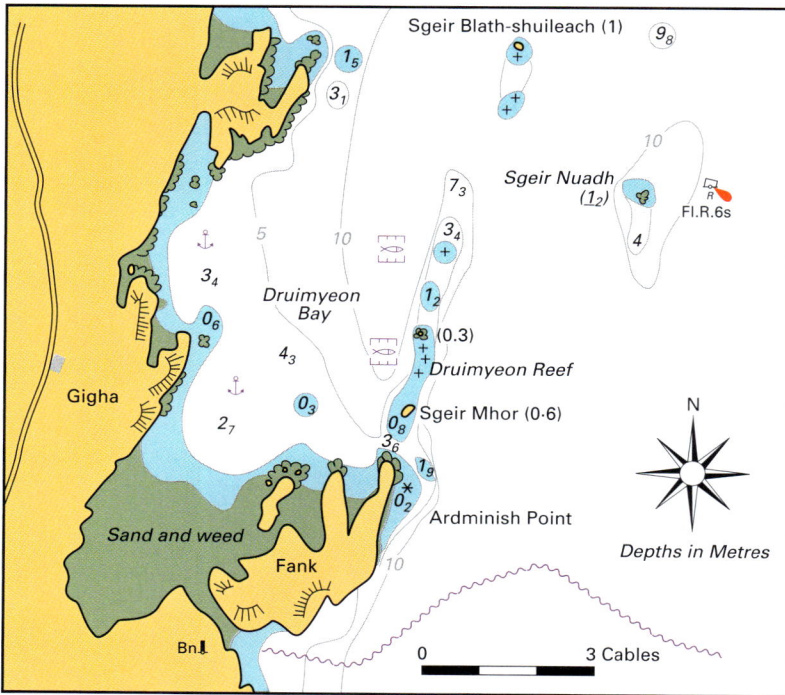

DRUIMYEON BAY

Depths in Metres

Druimyeon Bay

A more peaceful anchorage than Ardminish but not very convenient to find a way ashore. Fish cages are moored west of Druimyeon Reef.

Directions

From the north approach by the northwest side of Sgeir Bhlath-shuileach (Bhlar Rock). From the south pass between Ardminish Point and Sgeir Mhor (0·6 metres high) which lies ¼ cable from the point, but keep closer to Ardminish

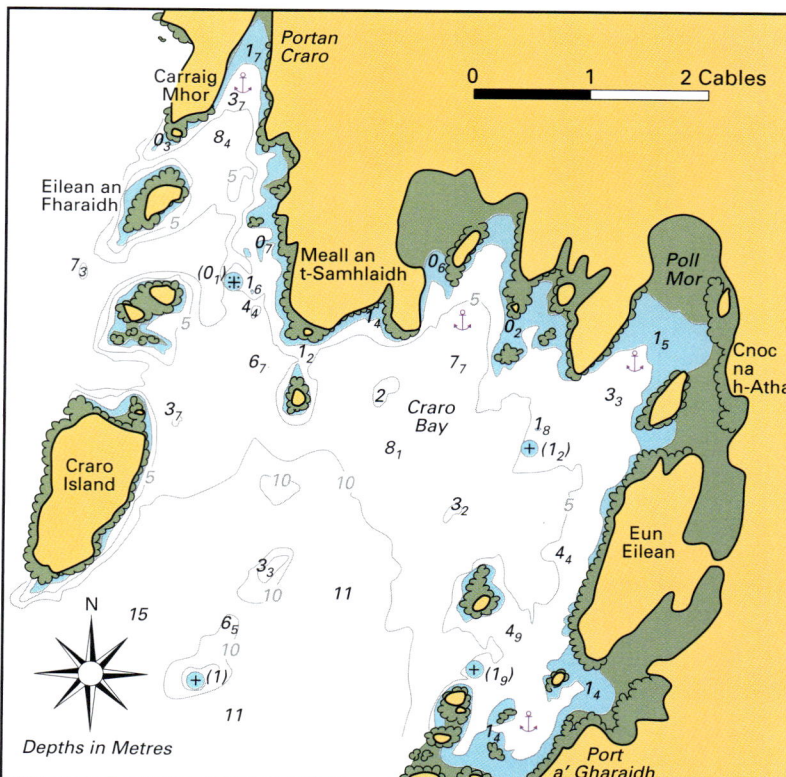

CRARO BAY

Depths in Metres

Point to avoid a rock spit extending south from Sgeir Mhor. A submerged rock with a depth of only 0·3m lies a cable offshore nearly 2 cables northwest of Ardminish Point, and drying rocks lie ½ cable northeast of Rubha Breac.

Anchorage

Anchor well offshore where shown. Bottom sand and weed. Good anchorage also close to the west shore, north of Rubha Breac.

Caolas Gigalum

This sound between Gigha and Gigalum, although strewn with rocks, is relatively straightforward to navigate in fair weather. The channel lies between the Gigha shore and the outer rocks west of Gigalum which are above HW, although less than a metre high. Take care to keep outside a line joining the outer end of the pier on Gigha and where the coast is steep-to east of En. Leum.

Anchorage

Anchor northeast or southeast of the pier, no closer to Gigha than the end of the pier. In easterly winds some shelter may be found north of the 3-metre-high rock near the west side of Gigha, but look out for a submerged rock between the 3-metre rock and the ferry mooring.

The pier is constructed of concrete piles which are not convenient to lie alongside. There is no regular steamer service, but a boat should not be left unattended at the pier. Temporary berths on the north side and by the low-level landing platform on the southwest side, both appear to have depths of about 1·2m.

Occasional anchorages

East Tarbert Bay is a wide bay immediately north of Druimyeon Bay. Anchor off the south side, avoiding Tarbert Rocks and shellfish floats in the middle of the bay.

Port Mor at the north end of Gigha is another possibility, as is the small inlet northwest of it.

West Tarbert Bay (p.23 and chart 2475) Anchor in 3-8m, sand and shingle, south of the spit joining Eilean Garbh to Gigha, or in the southeast corner of West Tarbert Bay.

Alternatively, the bay north of the shingle spit joining Eilean Garbh to Gigha gives better shelter in southerlies; anchor up to a cable off the west shore.

The three anchorages above can be subject to swell but are good alternatives in easterlies. Approaching them from the south, note the Inner Red Rock, with less than 2m over it, lying 3 cables offshore.

Craro Bay lies on the southwest side of Gigha, east of the Cath Sgeir W cardinal buoy. Although part of it is labelled *Not sounded* on the Admiralty chart, it has been surveyed by *Antares Charts*, revealing four pleasant occasional anchorages that, in settled weather, would make an interesting excursion if using their chart and GPS or, with great care, the adjacent plan.

Martin Lawrence

The two anchorages at Port Mor (lower left) and those inside Eilean Garbh (upper centre left)

0   5 Cables

Eilean Liath (4)

27

Gigha

026° - 206°

9₁

Caution
In Caolas Gigalum depths may
occasionally be less than charted

7

5₂

28

6₁

8₅

YBY
Q(9)15s
(1₂)

1₈

Pier

Caolas Gigalum

3₇

Perch

Gigalum Rocks

5

2₄

10

013° - 193°

10

3₁

Gigalum

5

2₇

4

(3)

5

7₆

(1)

8₈

En Leum

(1)   (1)

2₇

Cara Reef

2₃

(1)

10

5₂

N

16

Cara Rocks   (2)

(1)

5

(0₈)   (2)

Depths in Metres

5

6₁

10

(3)

House

8₂

16

Cara

5₈

6₇

17

.41

6₄   Cara Flat

7₉

CAOLAS GIGALUM

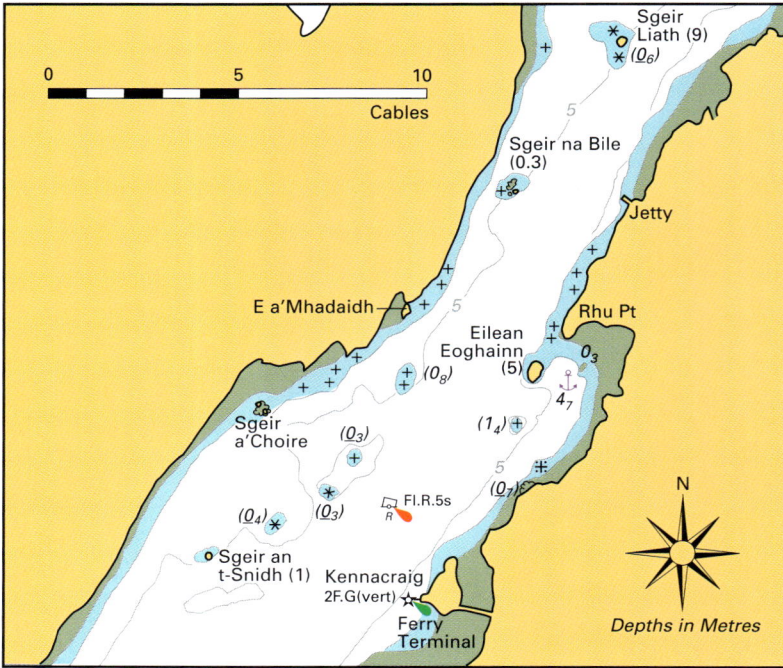

WEST LOCH TARBERT (CENTRAL SECTION)

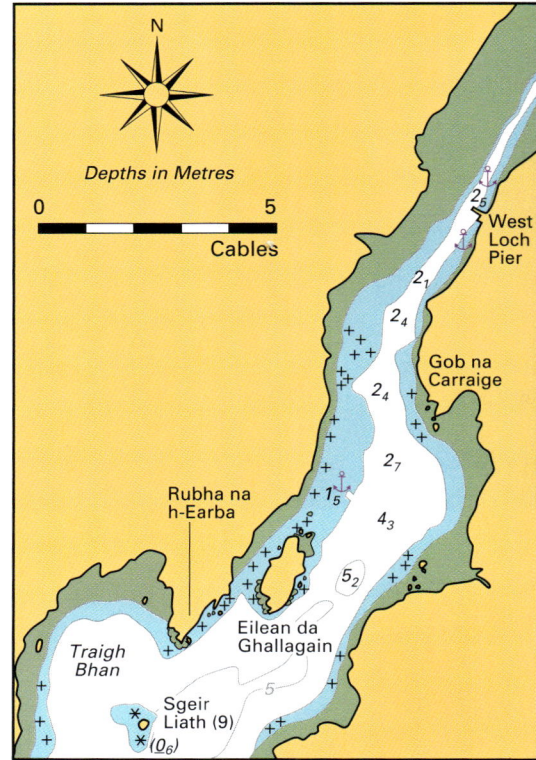

Sgeir Liath (9)
(0.6)

Sgeir na Bile
(0.3)

Jetty

E a'Mhadaidh

Rhu Pt

Eilean
Eoghainn
(5)
(0.8)

0.3

4.7

Sgeir
a'Choire

(0.3)

(1.4)

(0.4)

(0.3)

Fl.R.5s

Sgeir an
t-Snidh (1)

Kennacraig
2.F.G(vert)

Ferry
Terminal

(0.7)

Depths in Metres

Cables
0   5   10

WEST LOCH TARBERT (HEAD)

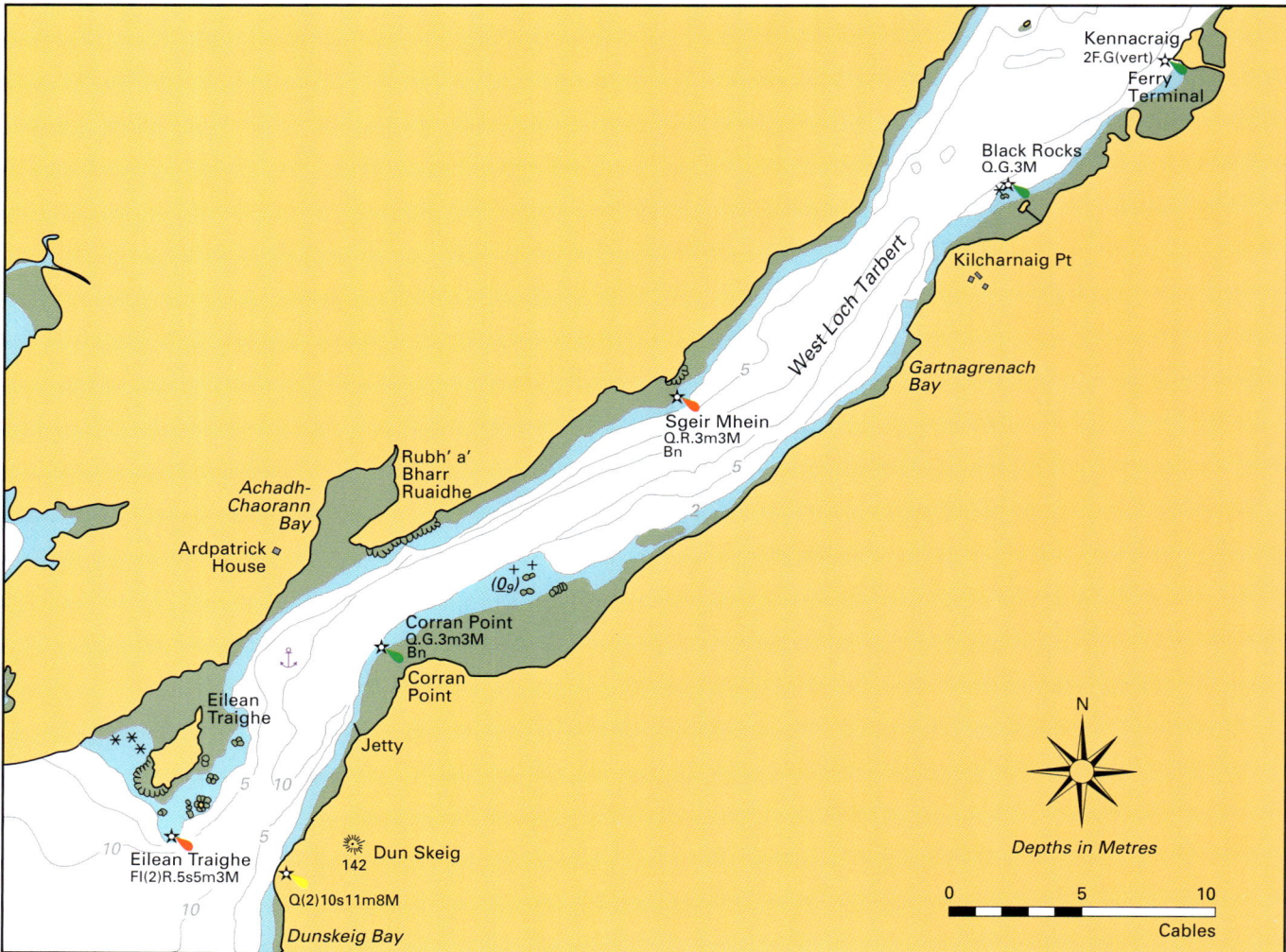

N

Depths in Metres

Cables
0   5

West
Loch
Pier

2.5

2.1

2.4

Gob na
Carraige

2.4

Rubha na
h-Earba

2.7

1.5

4.3

Eilean da
Ghallagain

5.2

Traigh
Bhan

0

Sgeir
Liath (9)
(0.6)

5

WEST LOCH TARBERT (OUTER - NOTE SMALLER SCALE)

Kennacraig
2.F.G(vert)
Ferry
Terminal

Black Rocks
Q.G.3M

Kilcharnaig Pt

Gartnagrenach
Bay

West Loch Tarbert

5

Sgeir Mhein
Q.R.3m3M
Bn

5

Rubh' a'
Bharr
Ruaidhe

(0.9)

Achadh-
Chaorann
Bay

2

Ardpatrick
House

Corran Point
Q.G.3m3M
Bn

Corran
Point

Eilean
Traighe

Jetty

5   10

5

Eilean Traighe
Fl(2)R.5s5m3M

Dun Skeig
142

10

Q(2)10s11m8M

Dunskeig Bay

N

Depths in Metres

Cables
0   5   10

West Loch Tarbert

A rather narrow, pleasantly wooded, loch with many hazards on either side but well marked as far as the ferry terminal for Islay, which is halfway up the loch; a pier at the head is extensively used by fishing boats. As the ferry runs from Kennacraig, 4 miles from the entrance to the loch, it may be preferable to proceed beyond the terminal to avoid the wash from the ferries, before anchoring.

Tides

In-going stream begins about +0430 Oban (–0100 Dover). Out-going stream begins about –0200 Oban (+0500 Dover).

Constant is approximately –0200 Oban (+0500 Dover) at springs, –0500 Oban (+0300 Dover) at neaps.

Height in metres

MHWS	MHWN	MTL	MLWN	MLWS
1·5	1·3	1·0	0·8	0·6

Directions

The entrance is identified by a conspicuous conical hill, Dun Skeig, 142 metres, on the south side of the entrance. Approaching from north a light beacon (a steel column) must be identified 2 cables south of Eilean Traighe, a low island on the north side of the entrance.

Pass south of the Eilean Traighe beacon and well north of Corran Point beacon, a mile further northeast, 1½ cables off the south shore.

For the next mile, keeping these two beacons in line astern will clear submerged and drying rocks 4 cables off the south shore. Note that close to Corran Point beacon this line leads close to the edge of a drying bank.

Two further beacons at approximately 1½ mile intervals are passed, the first to port and the second to starboard. Kennacraig ferry terminal is ½ mile further on the southeast shore, with a red light buoy ¼ mile northwest of it marking submerged and drying rocks which extend ½ mile from the northwest shore over a length of a mile.

Beyond Kennacraig the loch narrows and there are unmarked dangers, mostly on the north side. There are no beacons or buoys beyond Kennacraig. West Loch Pier, ¼ mile from the head of the loch, is owned by Tarbert Fishermen's Association and is well used, particularly at weekends. The head of the loch dries for about ⅓ mile.

Anchorage

Northeast of Eilean Traighe, sand and weed. Subject to severe wash from ferries and fishing boats, as in all bays south of Kennacraig.

South of Rhu Point, and southeast of Eilean Eoghainn (5). Enter by passing close to Eilean Eoghainn to avoid the 1·4m rock and the awash rock shown on the plan to the south of it.

Head of loch Anchor north or south of the pier, closer to the southeast shore and use a tripping line. Yachts should not be left unattended alongside the pier. Water at the pier, all facilities, including diesel, sailmaker and chandlery at Tarbert, 1½ miles by road.

Alternatively, anchor a cable northeast of Eilean da Ghallagain.

Loch Stornoway, 2 miles north of the entrance to West Loch Tarbert, is open to the southwest and subject to swell but provides an occasional anchorage in settled weather or winds from north to east. Drying rocks extend a cable northwest of Sgeir Choigreach (2), the outer islet on the south side of the entrance, but Montgomerie Rocks on the north side may extend further south than shown and it is recommended to keep closer to the islets. Anchor in the centre of the bay, off the beach in 3m, sand. Clear out if any sea is coming in.

Admiralty Chart
2476, 2168
Admiralty Leisure Folio
5611.28, B, C & D
Imray Chart
C64
Ordnance Survey
62
Cruising Scotland
p.70

The head of West Loch Tarbert. Tarbert, Loch Fyne, is visible beyond the head of the loch

Martin Lawrence

2. Southeast Islay and Sound of Islay

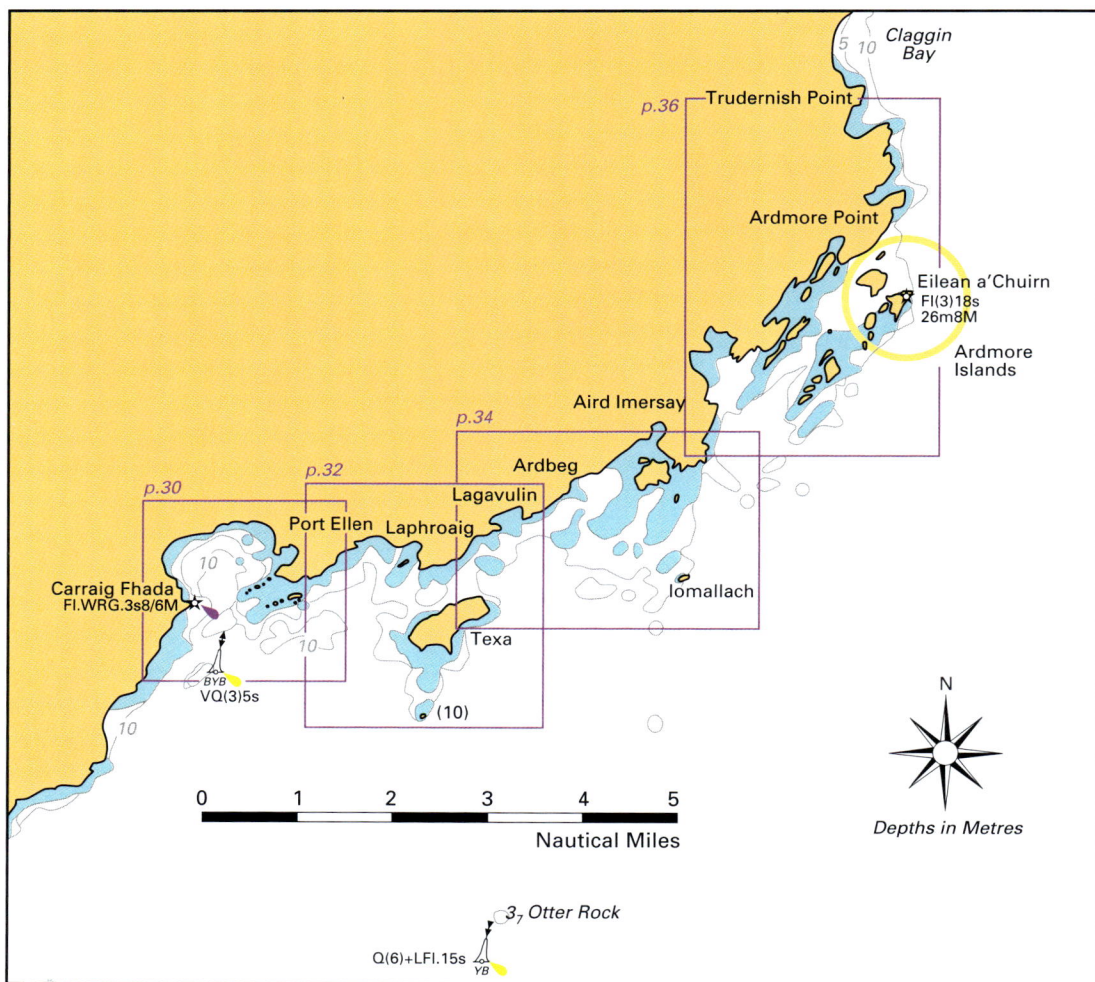

SOUTHEAST ISLAY

Map labels:
- Claggin Bay
- 5 10
- p.36
- Trudernish Point
- Ardmore Point
- Eilean a'Chuirn Fl(3)18s 26m8M
- Ardmore Islands
- Aird Imersay
- p.34
- Ardbeg
- p.32
- Lagavulin
- p.30
- Port Ellen
- Laphroaig
- Carraig Fhada Fl.WRG.3s8/6M
- BYB VQ(3)5s
- 10
- Iomallach
- Texa
- (10)
- N
- Depths in Metres
- 0 1 2 3 4 5 Nautical Miles
- 3₇ Otter Rock
- Q(6)+LFl.15s YB

Southeast coast of Islay

Admiralty Chart
2168
Admiralty Leisure Folio
5611.5
Imray Chart
C64
Ordnance Survey
60
Cruising Scotland
pp.65, 68-69

The southeast of Islay is rich in history – and distilleries. Dunyvaig Castle at the entrance to Lagavulin Bay was the headquarters of the Lords of the Isles after the Norsemen were defeated at the Battle of Largs in 1263, and the finest carved medieval stone cross in Scotland is at Kildalton Chapel, near Port Mor and Glas Uig, north of Ardmore.

The inner passages between Ardmore and Port Ellen have been used by local fishermen and traders for centuries, but have only been brought to the notice of yachtsmen comparatively recently by Michael Gilkes.

The Ardmore Isles and the passage inshore of them are designated as a Special Area of Conservation (see p.11)

There is no published chart of the area at a larger scale than 2168 (1:75,000), but Ordnance Survey Explorer map (scale 1:25,000) No.352 Islay South provides useful detail of this part of the coast. However, much of this section of the Islay coast has been recently surveyed by *Antares Charts* and the use of these will enable more of the coast to be explored than can be described in these *Directions*, not to mention the possibility of taking one or two short cuts.

Tides

There are strong tidal streams nearby, in particular at the Oa and the Rhinns of Islay, at the Mull of Kintyre, and in the Sound of Islay.

At Otter Rock the streams run east and west. The west-going stream begins about +0530 Oban (HW Dover) and the east-going stream begins about −0110 Oban (+0610 Dover).

Off Texa Island, tidal streams split, one stream running towards Ardmore, the other towards Rubha nan Leacan at the southeast point of the Oa beginning at about +0530 Oban (HW Dover), and running from those points towards Texa beginning about −0030 Oban (−0600 Dover).

Dangers and marks

Dangers and marks related to an extended coastal passage are described below in sequence from The Oa to Ardmore. Those related to individual anchorages and inshore passages are described in the relevant section.

The Oa, the south point of Islay, which rises to 200 metres, has a tall stone monument at Mull of Oa, its southwest point.

Otter Rock, with a least depth of 3·7 metres, 3 miles south of Texa, is marked by a south cardinal light buoy.

Texa Island is 2 miles east of Port Ellen. Tarr Sgeir, a detached rock 10 metres high, lies 6 cables south of Texa and there are other rocks between Tarr Sgeir and Texa.

Iomallach, 2·5 metres high, 1¾ miles ENE of the northeast end of Texa and a mile south of Aird Imersay lies at the extremity of an area of rocks south and southwest of Aird Imersay. A detached shoal patch of rock lies southwest of Iomallach and Ruadh Mor, 4 cables southwest of Iomallach has a depth of only 2·1 metres.

Edward Mason

The visitors' pontoons at Port Ellen (p.31)

Ardmore Point is the most easterly point of Islay. Eilean a'Chuirn, nearly a mile south of Ardmore and 5 miles northeast of Texa, is the most easterly of the Ardmore Islands. Eilean a'Chuirn light beacon is an inconspicuous tower.

The Ardmore Islands run northeast from Ceann nan Sgeirean, 1 mile northeast of Aird Imersay, for 1½ miles, and drying rocks lie up to 3 cables southeast of Ceann nan Sgeirean.

Port Ellen from seaward (pp.30-31)

Martin Lawrence

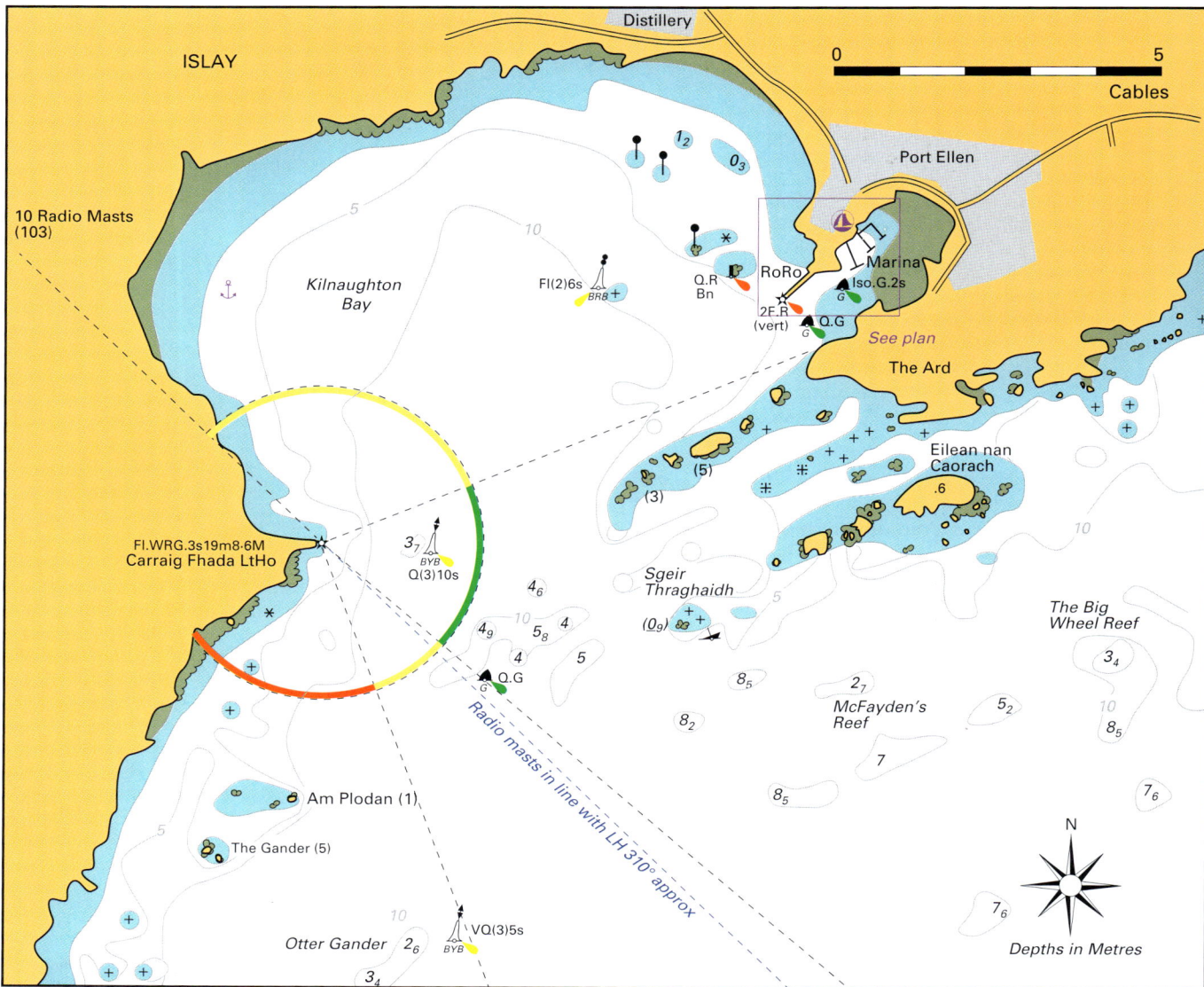

PORT ELLEN

Port Ellen

Admiralty Chart
2476, 2168
Admiralty Leisure Folio
5611.27B
Imray Chart
C64
Ordnance Survey
60
Cruising Scotland
p.68

This is the main ferry terminal and harbour on Islay. Pontoon berthing facilities have made it a popular alternative to Gigha as an arrival and departure point for Northern Ireland or the Mull of Kintyre.

Tides

Constant –0050 Oban (+0610 Dover) at springs, and –0530 Oban (+0130 Dover) at neaps. These times are very approximate because of the unusual tidal curves in this region. Digital sources will prove more accurate.

Height in metres

MHWS	MHWN	MTL	MLWN	MLWS
0·9	0·8	0·6	0·5	0·3

Directions

The Otter Rock (LD 3·7) S cardinal buoy lies 4½ miles southeast of the entrance to Port Ellen and is a good landfall mark if coming from the Mull of Kintyre.

Approaching from the east pass south of Tarr Sgeir (10), 6 cables south of Texa and head towards Carraig Fhada lighthouse. When this is

in line with the prominent radio masts on the hill above, bearing 310°, it will lead to a G conical buoy which should be left to starboard.

From the southwest, identify the E cardinal buoy marking the Otter Gander and steer to leave this to port before following the transit given above leading to the outer G buoy. From this buoy steer north until on a line between the lighthouse and the pierhead (the inner

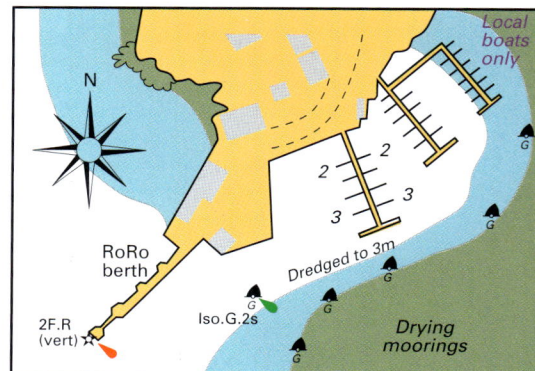

PORT ELLEN MARINA

Martin Lawrence

Port Ellen approach from the southeast

E cardinal buoy marks a shoal with 3·7m over it and yachts can pass either side of it). Turn to starboard to steer approximately 60° and approach the pierhead on that bearing.

Hold close to the southeast side of the pier before entering the dredged channel to the marina, which is marked by a starboard hand buoy (Iso.G.2s) and several small green starboard hand buoys. Shallow areas lie very close south of these buoys, and east of the two green buoys which mark the anchors for the ground chains of the pontoons.

Lights

Otter Rock S cardinal buoy Q (6) + L Fl.15s
Otter Gander E Cardinal buoy VQ(3)5s
Carraig Fhada LtHo Fl.WRG 3s 19m 8-6M
Outer buoy G conical buoy QG
Inner buoy E Cardinal buoy Q(3)10s
Beacon 1 cable west of pier Q.R.
Buoy south of pierhead G conical buoy Q.G.
Inner harbour channel G conical buoy Iso.G.2s

Anchorage and berthing

A small, self-service, marina with 36 visitors' berths has been positioned in a dredged area lying northeast of the pier. The depth is approximately 3m at the two outer ranges of pontoons. These are for visitors and yachts up to 15m can be accommodated. The inner range is reserved for local boats and is much shallower. Dues are collected by volunteer supervisors.

Kilnaughton Bay on the west, north of Carraig Fhada, affords shelter in westerlies and some protection from southerly swell.

Older, uncorrected, charts may show an anchor symbol southwest of the pier but on no account should yachts anchor in this position, or anywhere in the approach to the pier, as this could restrict ferry movements. The visitors' moorings off the distillery have now been removed.

Supplies

Marina berths serviced with water and electricity. Toilets, showers and washing machine are a short walk from the marina and diesel is available in cans at the filling station 500m away. Shops, Post Office, telephone, hotels and restaurant, Calor Gas. Car hire and distillery visits.

Port Ellen from the south; the finger pontoons have been removed for dredging and the photograph was taken before the northern pontoon was added

Martin Lawrence

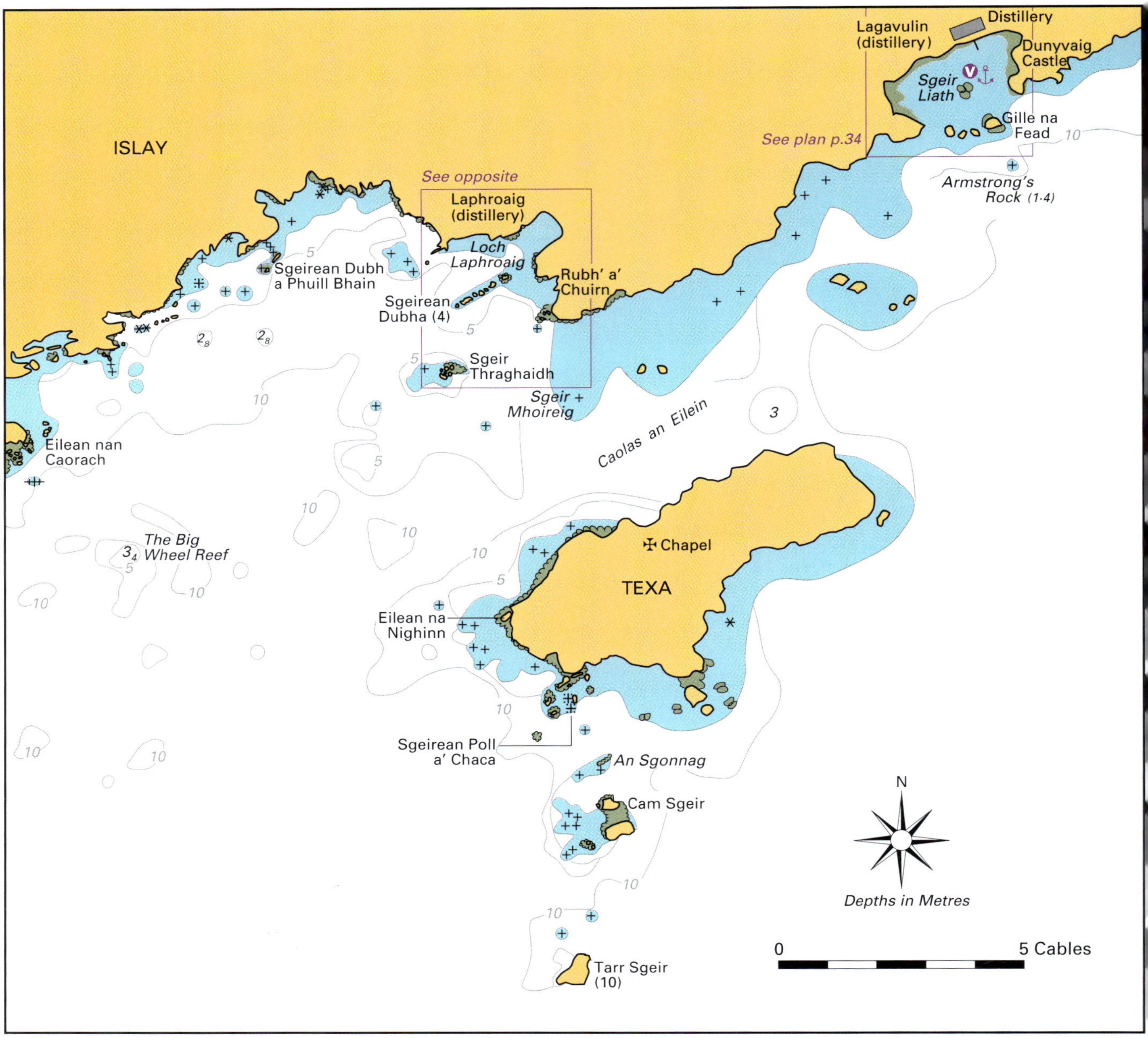

Labels on chart (clockwise/as shown):
Lagavulin (distillery)
Distillery
Dunyvaig Castle
Sgeir Liath
Gille na Fead 10
See plan p.34
Armstrong's Rock (1·4)
ISLAY
See opposite
Laphroaig (distillery)
Loch Laphroaig
Sgeirean Dubh a Phuill Bhain
Rubh' a' Chuirn
Sgeirean Dubha (4)
5
5
2₈   2₈
Sgeir Thraghaidh
Sgeir Mhoireig
Caolas an Eilein
3
Eilean nan Caorach
The Big Wheel Reef
3₄
5
10   10
10
10   10
10
10
10
Chapel
TEXA
Eilean na Nighinn
Sgeirean Poll a' Chaca
10
An Sgonnag
Cam Sgeir
N
10
Depths in Metres
0   5 Cables
10
Tarr Sgeir (10)

CAOLAS AN EILEIN

Port Ellen to Loch an t-Sailean

If heading east it is usual to leave Port Ellen by re-tracing the course described for entry and steering to pass south of Tarr Sgeir and thence northwards to the Sounds of Islay or Jura. However, if planning to visit any of the distilleries on this stretch of coast, some distance will be saved by passing through Caolas an Eilein, between Texa and Islay.

Chart 2476, which shows Port Ellen and the west end of Texa to a scale of 1:15,000, is useful for the first part of this passage, especially if aiming to visit Laphroaig.

Directions

Leave Port Ellen on the track described for entry (p.30) until a cable southeast of the outer G conical buoy. Then steer due east towards Texa for a mile until past The Big Wheel Reef

(LD 3·4), leaving Sgeir Thraghaidh (drying 0·9) and Macfayden's Reef (LD 2·7) to port. From here a course of 070° will lead to Caolas an Eilein between Texa and Islay. Take care not to be carried off this course by the tide as some of the above rocks, and several near Texa, are within a cable of it.

Caolas an Eilein is 4 cables wide but rocks above and below water lie on the Islay side so keep about a cable off the Texa shore. Note also that a submerged rock with less than 2m lies 1½ cables due west of Texa and about 1½ cables south of the above course. At the east end of Caolas an Eilein continue ENE until Lagavulin bears due north, then head northeast towards Loch an t-Sailean or pick up the entrance bearing of 333° if heading for Lagavulin. There is a temporary anchorage off the stone jetty on Texa.

Admiralty Chart
2476, 2168
Admiralty Leisure Folio
5611.27B, 5
Imray Chart
C64
Ordnance Survey
60
Cruising Scotland
pp.68-69

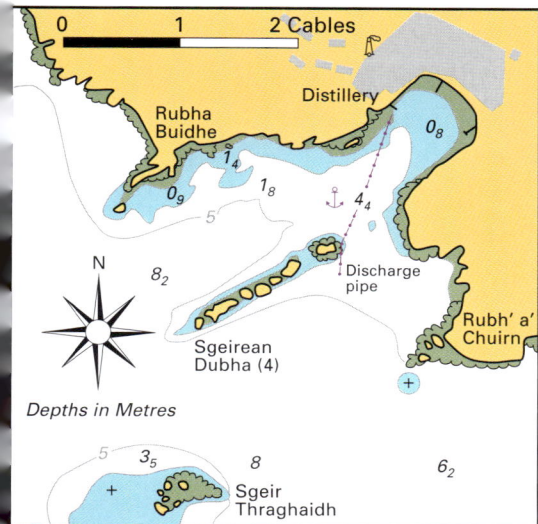

0   1   2 Cables

Distillery

Rubha
Buidhe

1_4

0_8

0_9 1_8

4_4

5

N

8_2

Discharge
pipe

Rubh' a'
Chuirn

Sgeirean
Dubha (4)

Depths in Metres

5   3_5 8 6_2

Sgeir
Thraghaidh

LOCH LAPHROAIG

Loch Laphroaig

Loch Laphroaig is less sheltered than Lagavulin Bay, which is just over a mile further north, but the entrance is deeper and less constricted. The white painted distillery buildings are conspicuous in the approach from the southwest. Entry from the east should not be attempted without Chart 2476 and only then with great care because of several unmarked sunken rocks.

Directions

On the passage between Port Ellen and Caolas an Eilein the distillery will be clearly seen about 1½ miles to the northeast. Follow the course described opposite but when the middle point of Eilean nan Caorach bears due north alter course to port on to 055°, heading for the right hand building on which the name 'LAPHROAIG' is painted.

After about half a mile, identify the small group of above-water rocks, Sgeir Thraghaidh (not to be confused with the drying rock of the same name off Port Ellen and recently passed to port) and note that submerged rocks extend up to 1½ cables southwest of it.

Continue on 055° and enter Loch Laphroaig leaving the string of islets, Sgeirean Dubha (4), about 30m to starboard. Anchor in 4·5m when the innermost islet (6) bears due south, noting and avoiding the discharge pipe shown on the plan. There is much kelp in the loch but clear patches exist near, and to the east of, the anchor symbol.

Loch Laphroaig and the distillery from the southwest. Sgeir Thraghaidh to the lower right

Martin Lawrence

Lagavulin Bay from the southeast. The red chimney of the distillery can be seen in front of the large building on the left

Martin Lawrence

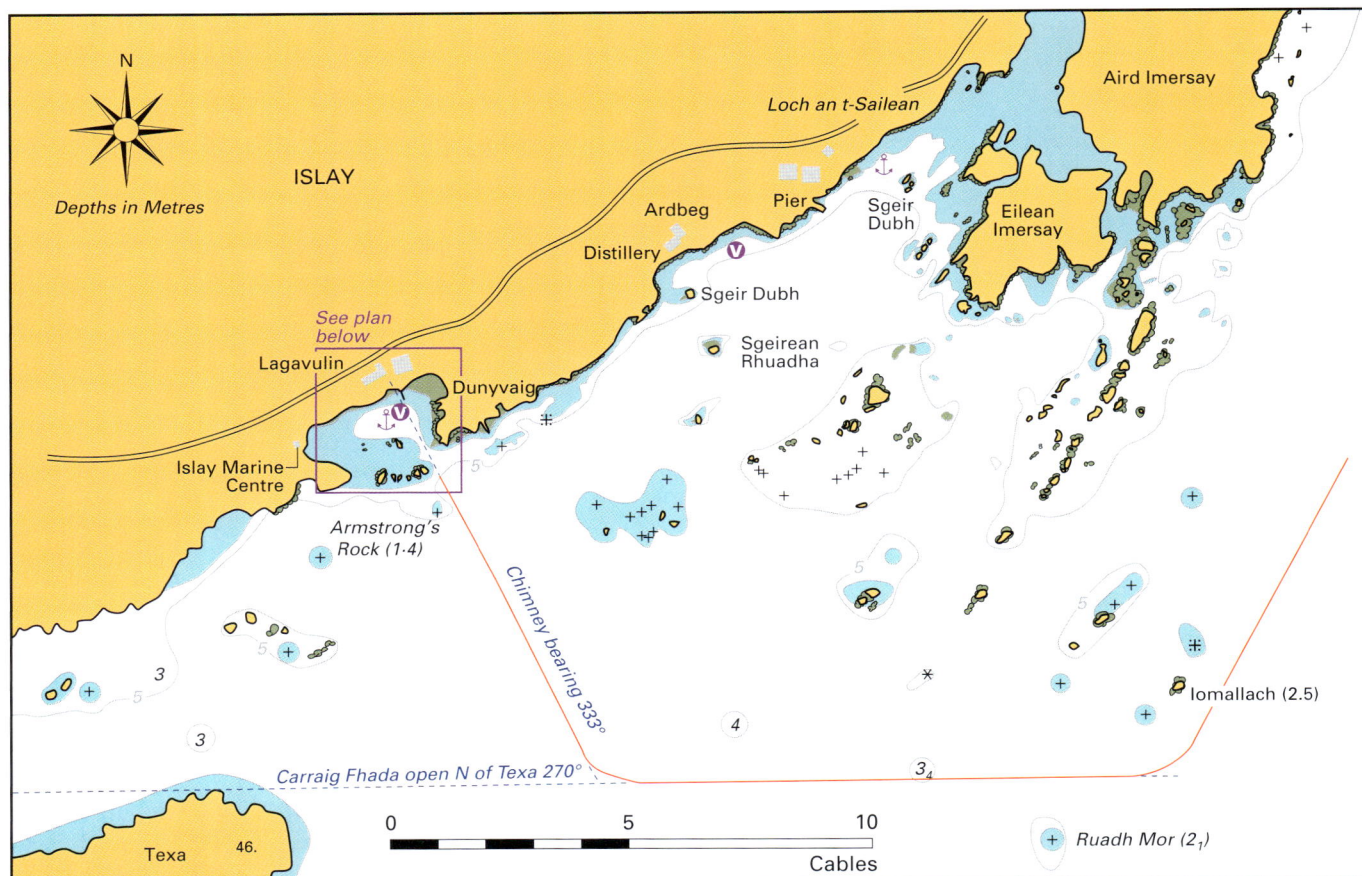

LAGAVULIN & ARDBEG

Lagavulin Bay

Admiralty Chart
2168
Admiralty Leisure Folio
5611.5
Imray Chart
C64
Ordnance Survey
60
Cruising Scotland
pp.68-69

From the southeast two distilleries will be seen, Lagavulin, and Ardbeg which is ¼ mile further northeast, both of which have their names conspicuously painted on the wall.

Lagavulin Bay is small and shallow and the entrance, marked by substantial port and starboard beacons, is shallower still, having only 2·1m in it plus a number of boulders with even less and much kelp. However, with care, yachts of moderate draught should have no difficulty in feeling their way slowly in.

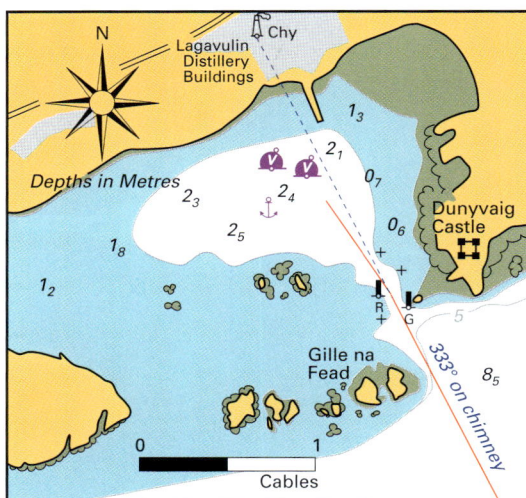

LAGAVULIN BAY

Tides

As Port Ellen:

Constant −0530 Oban (+0130 Dover) at springs, and −0050 Oban (+0610 Dover) at neaps.

Height in metres

MHWS	MHWN	MTL	MLWN	MLWS
0·9	0·8	0·6	0·5	0·3

Directions

From the east or northeast, identify Texa Island and Iomallach (2·5 m high). Pass a cable south of Iomallach to avoid an unmarked rock (2m) southwest of it. From a point close to Iomallach, steer with the north point of Texa Island in line with Carraig Fhada lighthouse at Port Ellen. This course takes you over a rock with a depth of 3·4 metres. Identify the distillery and when the conspicuous red chimney bears 333°, alter course to starboard and steer that course towards the entrance, noting and avoiding Armstrong's Rock (1·4m) close to port.

From the southwest pass south of Tarr Sgeir (10) and keep at least two cables off the east end of Texa. Steer northeast until picking up the bearing of 333° on the red chimney before approaching the entrance on that bearing.

From the southeast avoid Ruadh Mor (LD 2·1), 3½ cables southwest of Iomallach, by keeping towards Texa before picking up and following the 333° bearing above.

Approaching the entrance identify the prominent red and green beacons and leave the above water rock due south of them about 20m to port. Aim to cross a line between the two beacons at its midpoint, at an angle of less than 45°. Then pass 10-12 metres from the red inner (west) beacon to avoid boulders on the starboard side. When this beacon is abeam alter slightly to port to steer with the distillery pier 10° on the starboard bow. Do not stray to starboard of this line as the northeast part of the bay is very shoal.

Anchorage

Anchor in 3m, mud, in the middle of the pool just south of the visitors' moorings. Subject to swell. Two visitors' moorings are provided by Islay Marine Centre (pay at chandlery). Shoal patches have been reported in the approach to the visitors moorings.

Facilities

The distillery is open to visitors on weekdays. Showers and toilets at Islay Marine Centre, on the southwest side of the bay, which also provides chandlery, slipping, storage, grp and engine repairs, diesel and water (cans). Land at dinghy pontoon.

Loch an t-Sailean (Ardbeg)

The route into Loch an t-Sailean passes yet a further distillery, Ardbeg, where three visitors' moorings are located off the buildings (see photo p.14). Better shelter can be found near the head of the loch.

Directions

Approach as for Lagavulin and then, noting the unmarked and underwater rocks east of Dunyvaig Castle, follow a course north-eastwards between 1 and 1½ cables from the shore which clears them. Leave the islet, Sgeir

Sara Mason

Dubh, lying a cable off Ardbeg Distillery to port and Sgeirean Rhuadha, a small group of three above-water rocks to starboard. Thereafter the way is clear past the Ardbeg distillery to the islet, another Sgeir Dubh, at the head of the loch.

Using the *Antares* chart it is possible, in calm conditions, to pass through the skerries to the south of Eilean Imersay and reduce the distance between Ardbeg and the Ardmore Islands, but no visual pilotage directions for this passage can be given.

Anchorage

Anchor northwest of Sgeir Dubh in 3m. The bottom is sand with some rock and weed but good holding can be found and it is well sheltered by the numerous skerries which break up any swell. It is possible to lie alongside the stone pier (see photo p.10) beyond the distillery but the stonework is rough.

Facilities

The Ardbeg distillery has a visitor centre with a restaurant and provides three visitors' moorings.

Looking northwest into Lagavulin Bay from a position slightly east of the leading line

Loch an t-Sailean at Ardbeg; Sgeir na Maodail lies at the lower right with Sgeiran Ruadha above. Sgeir Dubh and the shallow spit are immediately below the distillery

Martin Lawrence

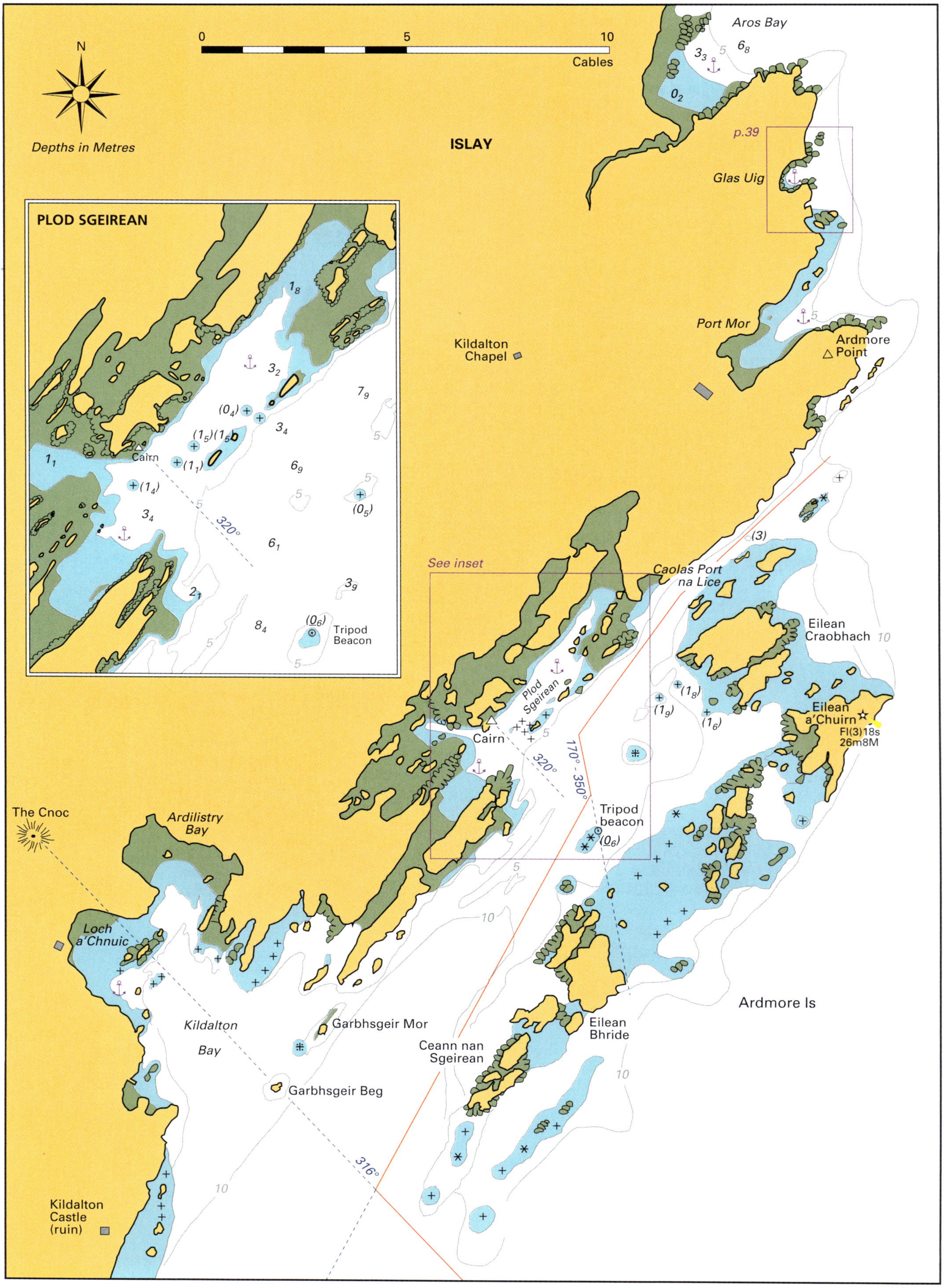

N

Depths in Metres

0   5   10
Cables

ISLAY

Aros Bay

3_3 6_8

0_2

p.39

Glas Uig

Port Mor

Ardmore
△ Point

Kildalton
Chapel

PLOD SGEIREAN

1_8

3_2

(0_4)

7_9

$(1_5)(1_5)$ 3_4

△ Cairn

(1_1)

1_1

(1_4)

6_9

5

3_4

5 5

(0_5)

6_1

3_9

2_1

8_4

(0_6) ⊙ Tripod
Beacon

5

5

See inset

Caolas Port
na Lice

(3)

Eilean
Craobhach 10

Plod
Sgeirean

(1_8)

(1_9)

Eilean
a'Chuirn ☆
Fl(3)18s
26m8M

△ Cairn

(1_6)

5

$320°$

$170° - 350°$

Tripod
beacon

(0_6)

The Cnoc

Ardilistry
Bay

Loch
a'Chnuic

Kildalton
Bay

Garbhsgeir Mor

Ceann nan
Sgeirean

Eilean
Bhride

Ardmore Is

10

10

Garbhsgeir Beg

$316°$

10

Kildalton
Castle
(ruin)

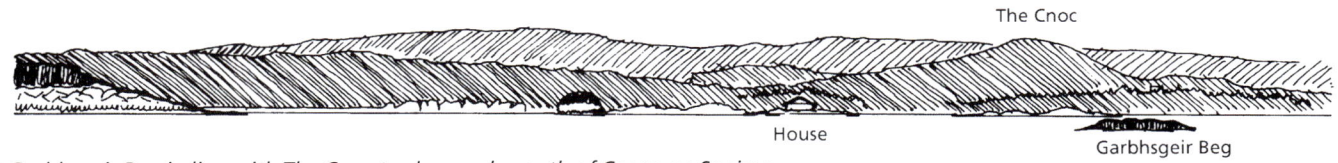

Garbhsgeir Beg in line with The Cnoc to clear rocks south of Ceann na Sgeiran

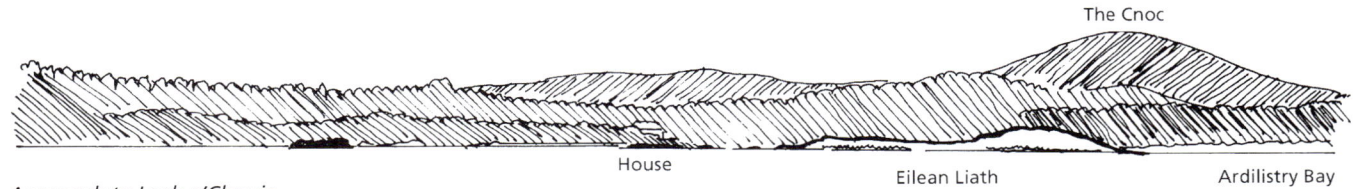

Approach to Loch a'Chnuic

Ardmore Islands

These offlying islands lie about a mile south of Ardmore Point, the eastern extremity of Islay, and give protection to several good anchorages. The passage inshore of them requires care as some of the features are not easy to distinguish and it should only be attempted for the first time in clear, quiet weather. It is also easier to make it from the north to the south.

Tides

As Port Ellen:

Constant –0530 Oban (+0130 Dover) at springs, and –0050 Oban (+0610 Dover) at neaps.

Height in metres

MHWS	MHWN	MTL	MLWN	MLWS
0·9	0·8	0·6	0·5	0·3

Directions

From the northeast keep ½ cable from the southeast side of Ardmore Point to pass inside the line of rocks north of Eilean Craobhach, 3 cables south of Ardmore Point and *not* the islets close south of the point. Keep in the middle of the canal-like channel, passing over or near to the 3m patch, then hold to the northwest side of the pool as it opens out as there are several rocks with less than 2m over them southwest of Eilean Craobhach.

When the tripod beacon north of Eilean Bhride is in line with the east point of Eilean Bhride bearing about 170°, steer towards the beacon on that line to avoid a rock awash in the centre of the pool. When about a cable from the beacon alter course to pass west of Ceann nan Sgeirean. To avoid drying rocks south of Ceann nan Sgeirean do not alter course southward until Garbhsgeir Beg is in transit with The Cnoc and do not pass north of Garbhsgeir Beg.

From the south or southwest pass east of Iomallach, and head NNE to pass northwest of the Ardmore Islands. From the southeast bring the detached islet Garbhsgeir Beg in line with the conical hill The Cnoc, bearing 316° to pass close southwest of drying rocks south of Ceann nan Sgeirean.

When Ceann nan Sgeirean is aft of the beam steer to pass northwest of the tripod beacon.

There is no clear mark to avoid the rock awash in the middle of the bay north of the beacon, but its west side should be cleared by keeping the tripod beacon astern in line with the east point of Eilean Bhride, bearing about 170°.

Steer on this line to within a cable of the skerries at Plod Sgeirean and then turn NNE to head for the narrow channel leading out of the pool to the north.

Anchorages

Kildalton Bay (Loch a'Chnuic) Approach from the southeast keeping Garbhsgeir Beg under The Cnoc on a course of 316°. Pass south of Garbhsgeir Beg and maintain this course until two detached above-water rocks lying off the southwest shore are identified.

Pass no more than 50m northeast of the second, more northerly, above-water rock, to avoid a rock with 2·1m over it lying ½ cable northeast of it. When midway between the above water rock and a group of islets and rocks to the north, come round to port and anchor in 2-3m, hard sand, off the southwest shore. The anchorage is subject to swell and if the wind goes to the south or east it is prudent to clear out as considerable swell gets up.

Plod Sgeirean This area is very remote and inaccessible and teeming with wildlife; the anchorage is within a sheltered pool ringed by skerries and islets. Enter between the islet which forms the south point of the bay and the first skerry to the northeast, keeping rather nearer to the northeast skerry as a drying reef extends off the southwest point. A white painted cairn has been built on the islet opposite the entrance which, when bearing 320°, indicates the line of approach.

To anchor at the north end keep heading towards the white cairn and turn to starboard when closer to the islet ahead than to the skerry northeast of the entrance, as submerged rocks lie west and northwest of the skerry.

If anchoring at the south end turn to port when the channel opens out and anchor as far south as depth allows.

Both anchorages have been found to be comfortable in southeast winds of F5.

Admiralty Chart
2168
Admiralty Leisure Folio
5611.5
Imray Chart
C64
Ordnance Survey
60
Cruising Scotland
p.69

Caolas Port na Lice, the narrow channel leading to Plod Sgeirean and the inshore passage west of the Ardmore Islands from the east (p.37)

Kildalton Bay and Loch a'Chnuich from the west showing, on the right, the two above-water rocks mentioned in the approach (p.37)

Anchorages north of Ardmore Point

Three open bays provide occasional anchorage north of Ardmore Point. These bays are all difficult to identify from seaward, but Ardmore Point has a triangulation point (a short tapering concrete pillar) near its summit and Port Mor has a large white house at its head.

Tides

As Port Ellen:

Constant –0530 Oban (+0130 Dover) at springs, and –0050 Oban (+0610 Dover) at neaps.

Height in metres

MHWS	MHWN	MTL	MLWN	MLWS
0·9	0·8	0·6	0·5	0·3

Anchorages

Port Mor is immediately northwest of Ardmore Point. The head of the bay shoals a long way. Hold to the southeast side as there is a line of rocks on the northwest side of the bay. The bottom is clean sand.

Martin Lawrence

Glas Uig is very difficult to distinguish and scarcely shows on chart 2168; it is about 3 cables north of Port Mor. Anchor on the north side of the bay to avoid the submerged reef off the quay on the south side.

Aros Bay is a clean open sandy bay ½ mile north of Ardmore Point; a pleasant place to spend a fine, windless day. Anchor in 3m in the centre of the bay.

Port Mor with the stone jetty on the right and the track leading to the road to Kildalton Chapel

Glas Uig showing the submerged reef off the old quay on the port side

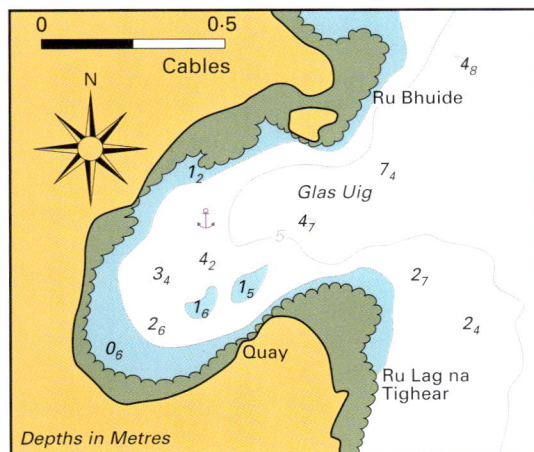
GLAS UIG

Martin Lawrence

Aros Bay with the Paps of Jura beyond

Martin Lawrence

Overfalls form at the north end of the sound on the flood with a northerly wind, and at the south end of the sound on the ebb, where it meets the ebb from the Sound of Jura. In wind over tide conditions these can be severe.

At Port Askaig
Constant −0030 Oban (+0500 Dover) at springs, and −0110 Oban (+0420 Dover) at neaps.

Height in metres

At Port Askaig

MHWS	MHWN	MTL	MLWN	MLWS
2·1	1·5	1·2	1·0	0·4

At Rubha a'Mhail

3·7	2·8	2·1	1·5	0·6

Note the difference in range in only 6 miles.

Directions

At the south entrance to the sound note the unmarked rock 3 cables southwest of Brosdale Island and give it a wide berth. Am Fraoch Eilean, 1½ miles west of Brosdale Island, has rocks drying 1½ cables south of it and a further mile northwest lie the Black Rocks, the principal danger in the sound. They are marked by a G con. buoy which from either direction is likely to appear nearer to the Islay shore than might be expected.

Pass south and west of this buoy and thereafter giving both shores a berth of a cable will clear all dangers until 3 miles north of Carraig an t-Sruith where Sgeir Traigh, a mass of grassy islets and rocks extends up to half a mile from the Jura shore. A clearing line of a conspicuous tower and the chimney on Caol Isla Distillery, north of Port Askaig, with Rubha Barr nan Gobag (cliffs 20-25m high on Jura) bearing 193° astern may be used.

If proceeding north to Loch Tarbert, Jura, continue to give the shore between Sgeir Traigh and the entrance to the loch a good berth as it is foul with off-lying rocks.

Anchorages

Port Askaig This village is on Islay, halfway up the sound, and is the port for the Kintyre and Jura ferries. There is no room to anchor but there is good shelter in the small inner harbour immediately south of the Jura ferry berth. This can be full of local boats but room should be found for a short stay, although rafting may be necessary. There is 2m depth in the outer part of the harbour.

Alternatively, if the wind is not in the north, there may be space in the small harbour north of the Calmac pier. *Facilities* Shop, PO, hotel, diesel and petrol, Calor Gas. Water hose on pier.

Whitefarland Bay A clean open bay on Jura opposite Caol Isla distillery, out of the main tidal stream. Anchor in 3m north of anchor-painted boulder. Holding poor in weed.

Bunnahabhainn (Bunnahaven) Bay This bay, 2½ miles north of Port Askaig is a convenient place to wait for a south-going tide. Anchor out of the main tide in 4m, ½ cable north of the pier.

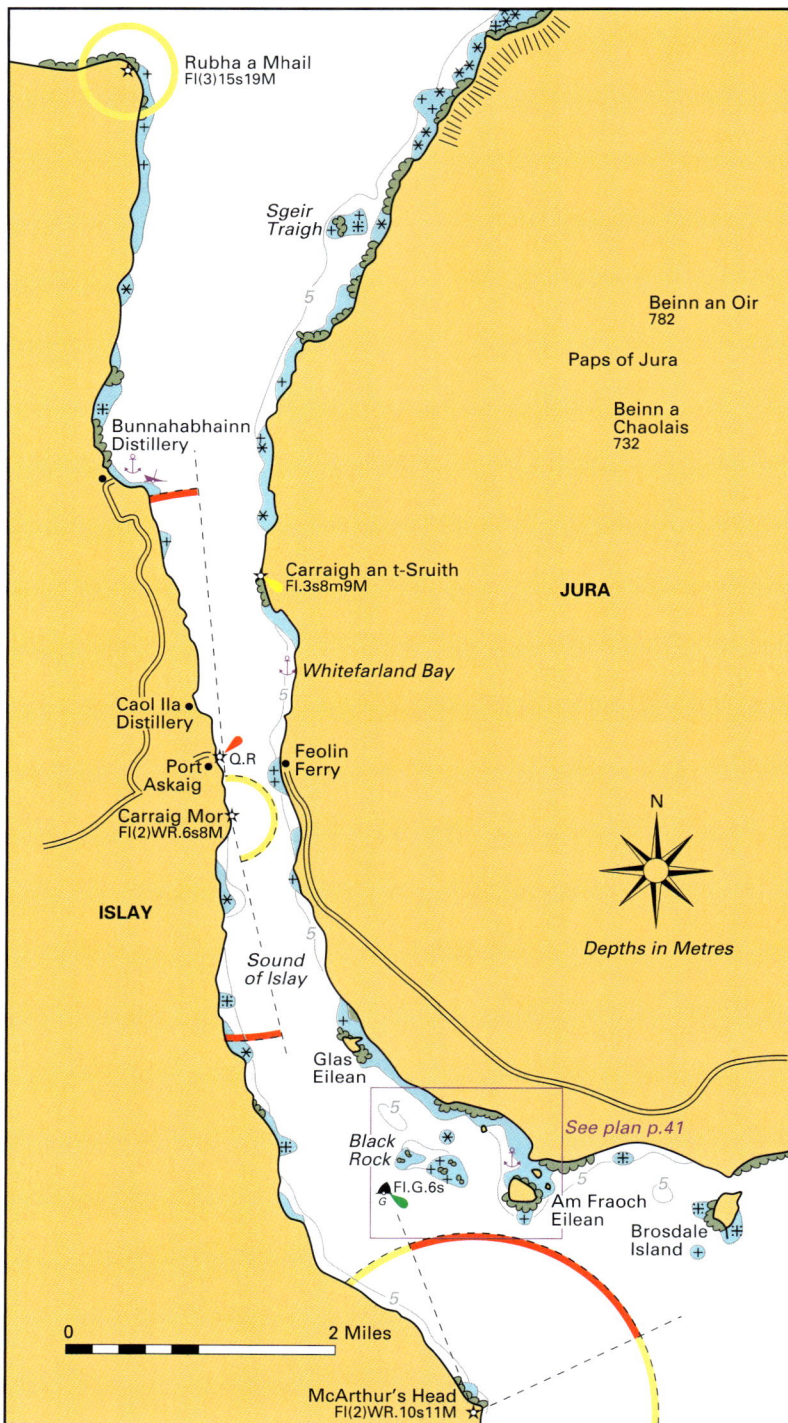

SOUND OF ISLAY

Admiralty Chart
2481, 2168
Admiralty Leisure Folio
5611.5, 7
Imray Chart
C64
Ordnance Survey
60
Cruising Scotland
pp.66, 76

Sound of Islay

The Sound of Islay separates Islay and Jura, and is eleven miles long. The navigation is straightforward, the Islay side being generally cleaner. The tide must be favourable as it runs at up to five knots in the narrows.

Tides

Tidal streams in the Sound of Islay run at up to 5 knots with eddies inshore.

The north-going stream begins about +0440 Oban (−0050 Dover), and the south-going stream begins about −0140 Oban (+0515 Dover).

Cottage

JURA

N

Depths in Metres

112°

5

Sgeir nan
Sian (2)

MacPhaill Rock
(0_6)

Black Rocks

(0_9)

Boathouse

Am Far Eilean

Quay To south fall of
Brosdale Island

Am Ploth

Fl.G.5s
G

Am Fraoch
Eilean

Ruin

Sound of Islay

003°

0   5

290°

5

Cables

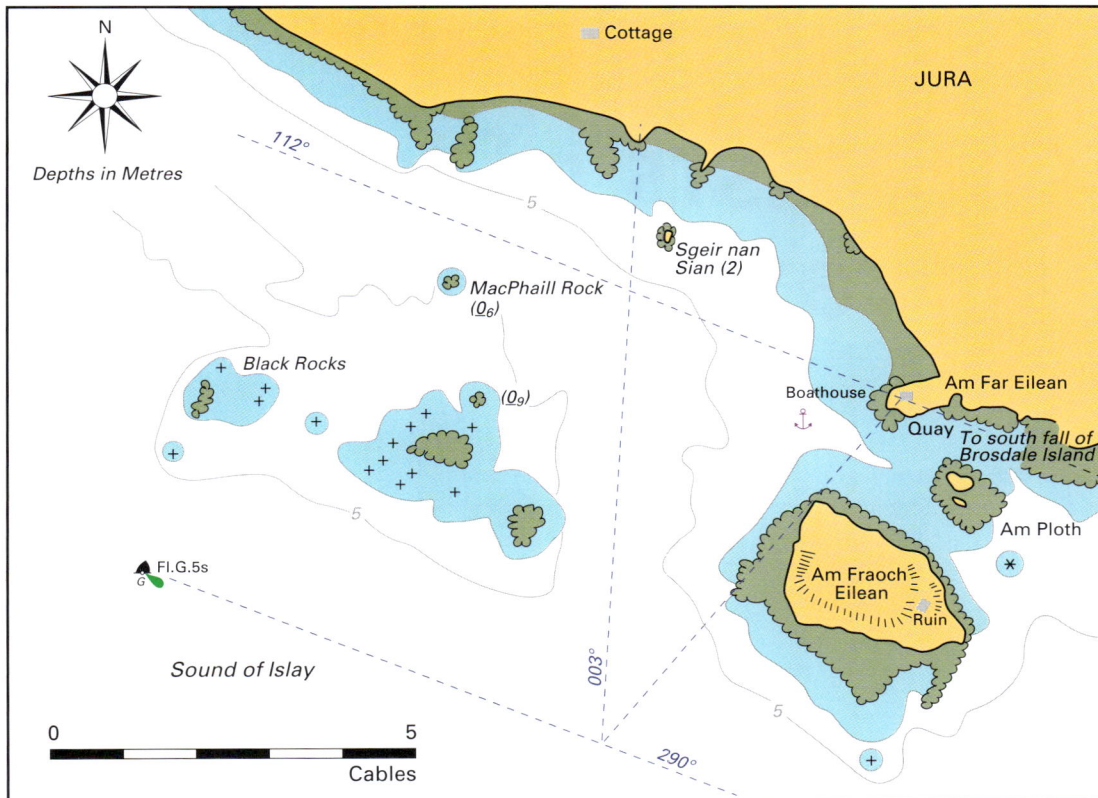

**AM FRAOCH ISLAND
PASSAGE**

Am Fraoch Island

This is a suitable place to wait for a favourable tide for a passage north through the sound. The passage north of MacPhaill Rock may also be used as an alternative to passing south of the Black Rocks to avoid a foul tide. Note the large areas of foul water around Am Fraoch Eilean and an unmarked rock 2 cables south of it.

Directions

From the southeast identify McArthur's Head lighthouse and the Black Rocks buoy. Approach the buoy on a course not less than 290° until McArthur's Head is abeam. When the boathouse behind Am Fraoch Eilean is seen, alter course to 003° and make for the rocky outcrop between Sgeir nan Sian and the cottage above the shore in line with McArthur's Head astern.

To continue passage north to avoid MacPhaill Rock and Sgeir nan Sian, keep the conspicuous boathouse at Am Far Eilean astern open of the south fall of Brosdale Island about 112°.

To make this passage from northwest to southeast, identify Am Far Eilean and Brosdale Island while passing Glas Eilean and reverse the directions given above.

Anchorage

Anchor off Am Far Eilean in 4m. Bottom sand and weed.

Lights

McArthur's Head lighthouse Fl(2)WR.10s39m13/10M
Black Rocks G con. buoy Q.G
Carraig Mor light beacon Fl(2)WR.6s7m8/6M
Carraig an t-Sruith light beacon Fl.3s8m9M
Rubha a'Mhail lighthouse Fl(3)15s45m19M

The Inner Harbour, Port Askaig, (see opposite)

Susan West, Geograph

3. West coasts of Islay and Jura; Colonsay

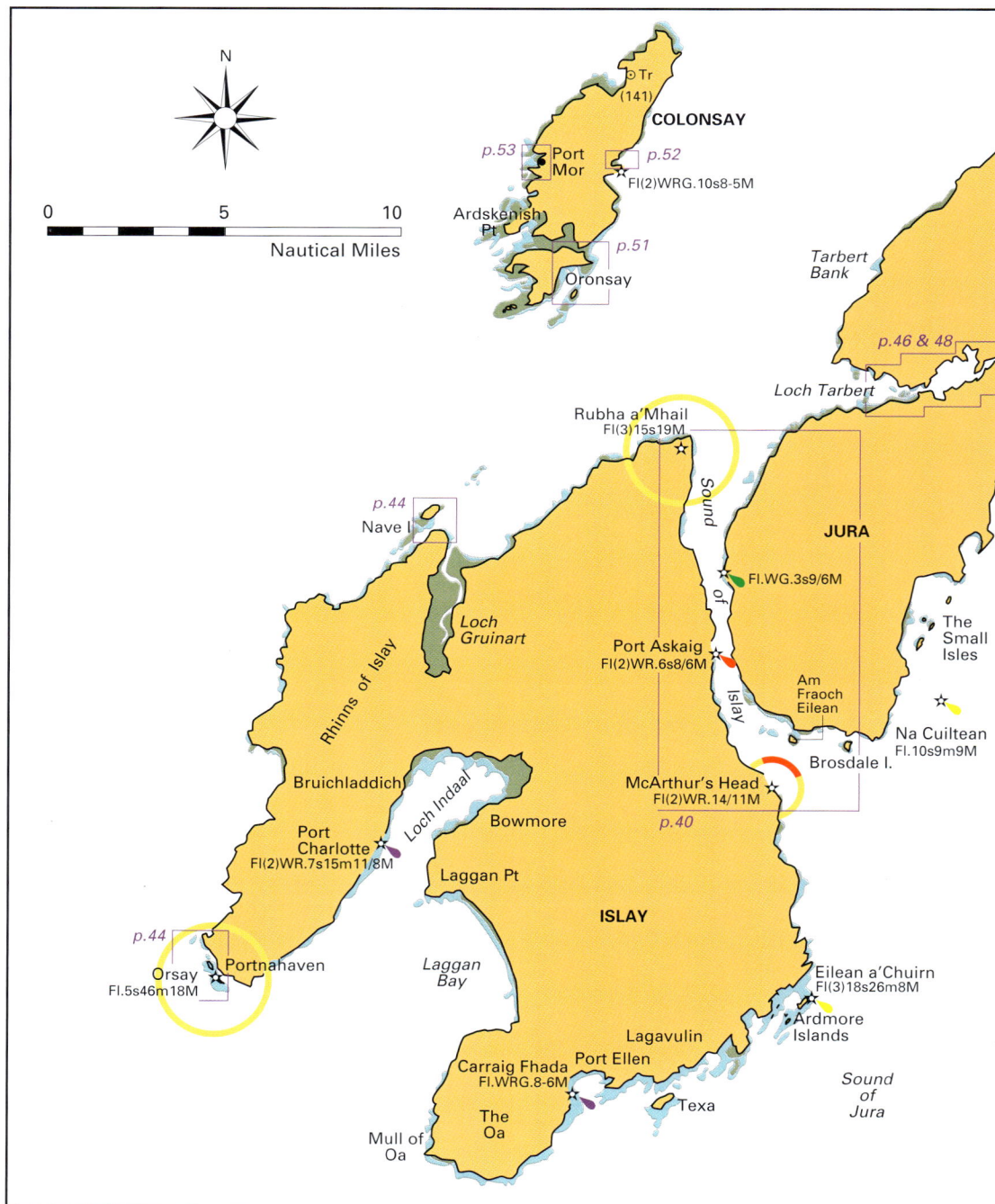

Map labels:

- Tr (141)
- COLONSAY
- p.53
- Port Mor
- p.52
- Fl(2)WRG.10s8-5M
- Ardskenish Pt
- p.51
- Oronsay
- Tarbert Bank
- p.46 & 48
- Loch Tarbert
- Rubha a'Mhail
- Fl(3)15s19M
- Sound of Islay
- p.44
- Nave I.
- JURA
- Fl.WG.3s9/6M
- Loch Gruinart
- The Small Isles
- Rhinns of Islay
- Port Askaig
- Fl(2)WR.6s8/6M
- Am Fraoch Eilean
- Na Cuiltean
- Fl.10s9m9M
- Brosdale I.
- Bruichladdich
- Loch Indaal
- McArthur's Head
- Fl(2)WR.14/11M
- p.40
- Bowmore
- Port Charlotte
- Fl(2)WR.7s15m11/8M
- Laggan Pt
- ISLAY
- p.44
- Orsay
- Fl.5s46m18M
- Portnahaven
- Laggan Bay
- Eilean a'Chuirn
- Fl(3)18s26m8M
- Ardmore Islands
- Lagavulin
- Port Ellen
- Carraig Fhada
- Fl.WRG.8-6M
- Texa
- Sound of Jura
- The Oa
- Mull of Oa

Scale: 0 — 5 — 10 Nautical Miles

N

WEST COASTS OF ISLAY AND JURA; COLONSAY

Passage to the west of Islay

Coming from the Mull of Kintyre and if bound for the west of Mull or the Outer Hebrides, yachts are faced with the choice of passing through the Sound of Islay or heading to the west of Islay. The majority opt for the Sound; not only is it the direct route but it gives the opportunity to visit many remote and attractive anchorages. For the few yachts choosing to take the outer passage the information below is given but reference to the Admiralty Pilot and charts, particularly with regard to tidal streams and overfalls, is also strongly recommended.

Tides

Off the Oa and the Rhinns the northwest-going stream begins about +0530 Oban (HW Dover) and the southeast-going stream begins about –0040 Oban (–0610 Dover). These streams reach a rate of 8 knots at springs off Orsay, Rhinns of Islay, and 5 knots off the Oa.

Overfalls form off the southeast side of the Oa during northwest-going streams and off its southwest side during southeast-going streams.

Some of the worst overfalls in the UK extend for up to 8M WSW of Orsay where there is an underwater cliff 50-75m high. This can be seen on the chart, where the overfalls are also shown. With any sea running at all the area must be avoided.

There are more overfalls in unsettled weather over West Bank, 4 miles northwest of Orsay, as well as over banks six miles further NNW.

Directions

Because of overfalls, both the Oa and the Rhinns of Islay should be passed at a distance of several miles (overfalls southwest of the Oa are worst with a southeast-going tide). As it is 36 miles from the Mull of Kintyre to the Rhinns of Islay only a motor yacht or fast sailing boat under very favourable conditions could pass these two points in a single tide, and it is normally best to take a foul tide in the open water between Kintyre and Islay, aiming to be at the Oa at slack water.

If conditions become unfavourable for a passage south of Islay, Port Ellen is the best place to find shelter, especially as it now offers secure berthing in the marina. Portnahaven, behind Orsay, provides good shelter but strong tides run across the entrance which can be difficult in deteriorating conditions.

Loch Indaal makes an interesting diversion in settled weather but it is shallow and totally exposed to the south and southwest and should not be considered as a safe place to seek refuge.

Continuing northwards from Portnahaven there is no shelter on the west or northwest coast of Islay, apart from an occasional anchorage inside Nave Island (18 miles), and in most instances passage making will be required to reach Colonsay (25 miles), Loch Tarbert, Jura (28 miles) or Iona (40 miles).

Lights

Rathlin West Fl.R.5s62m22M
Rhinns of Islay (Orsay Island) Fl.5s 46m18M
Rubh'an Duin (Loch Indaal) Fl(2)WR.7s15m11/8M
Rubha a Mhail (Ruvaal) Fl(3)15s19M
Dubh Artach Fl.(2)30s44m20M

Loch Indaal

Loch Indaal is a broad shallow loch whose interest is mainly in the several small towns and villages around it. Bowmore, the 'capital' of the island, has a distillery which provides guided tours. The Museum of Islay Life at Port Charlotte is worth visiting; there is a further distillery at Bruichladdich with a new one planned at Port Charlotte.

Tides

Constant –0040 Oban (–0610 Dover)

Height in metres

MHWS	MHWN	MTL	MLWN	MLWS
2·3	1·5	1·5	1·4	0·8

Directions

The loch is generally free from dangers and can be safely navigated using chart 2168 but note that off Laggan Point, the east point of the entrance, submerged rocks extend WSW for ½ mile, and rocks above water extend up to ¼ mile from the southeast shore.

Shellfish floats may be found ½ mile off the northwest shore and the head of the loch dries for ¼ mile and the shores all round the head are shoal with drying patches.

Bowmore

A small drying boat harbour is formed by a curved stone quay, but the 2-metre line is 2 cables offshore. A rock, and the end of a sewer outfall, 2 cables NNW of the quay are marked by a beacon.

A beacon 2½ cables southwest of the first beacon marks another rock. Anchor north of the north beacon. Although the harbour has been dredged, there is no depth for the average keelboat, and berths at the pontoons are fully occupied. Yachts, except those able to take the ground, should anchor off.

Supplies

Shops, Post Office, bank, telephone, hotels, restaurants; petrol and diesel at garage. Calor Gas at Bruichladdich. Indoor swimming pool and laundry at distillery. A whisky and music festival is held at the end of May / early June.

Occasional anchorages

Bruichladdich offers temporary anchorage off the recently extended pier which, having no wave screen, can give no protection to southerly swell but it could be used in very quiet weather. Shop, Calor gas and distillery.

Port Charlotte Temporary anchorage offshore. Museum.

Admiralty Chart
2168, 2169
Admiralty Leisure Folio
5611.5, 7
Imray Chart
C64
Ordnance Survey
60, 61
Cruising Scotland
p.65

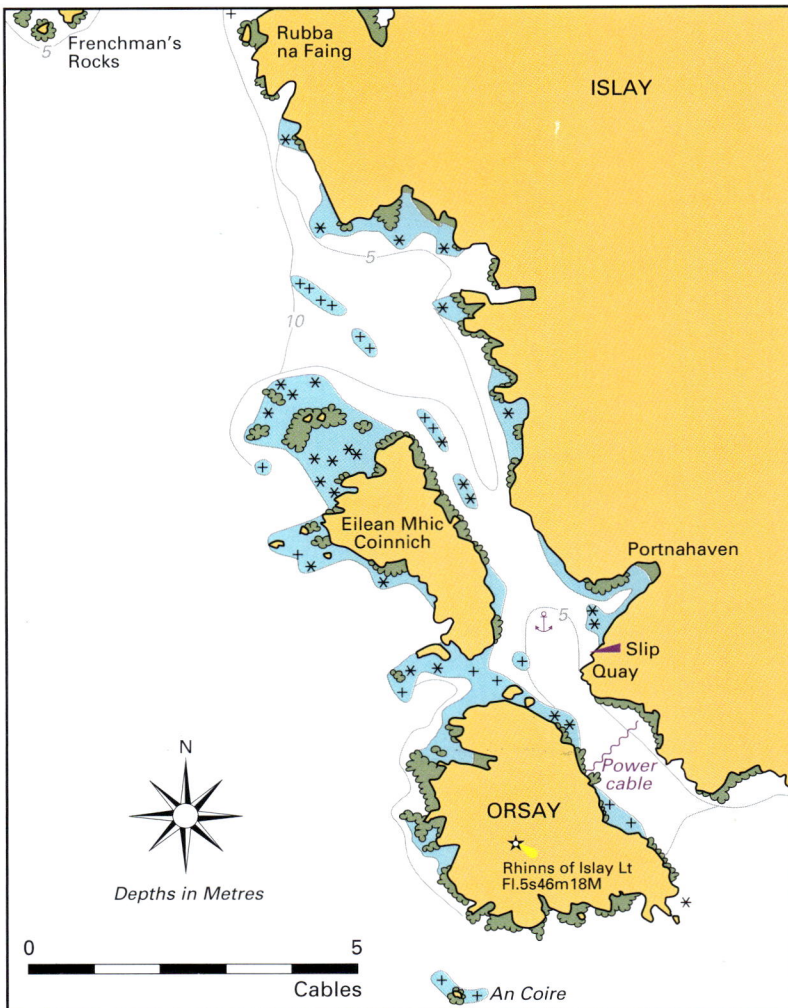

PORTNAHAVEN

From the southwest head for a white single-storey house by the shore on the northwest side of the entrance until about 25 metres from the shore. Weed on the reefs at the entrance is usually visible at any state of tide and a passage a few metres wide through the weed leads diagonally to the opposite shore, towards a house in the terrace ahead which has a rectangular extension on the roof.

Turn to head along the middle of the creek as soon as the reef to port is passed and drop anchor almost immediately. There are rings on either shore to which to take lines ashore. It may be possible to berth at the quay at the south side of the creek.

Supplies

Shops, Post Office, telephone, hotel. Portnahaven Boatyard ☎ 01496 860222 can repair wood and glassfibre, and can arrange for electrical and mechanical repairs. Slipway and alongside berth.

Nave Island

Nave Island lies north of Ardnave Point, at the NNW of Islay. Occasional anchorage can be made southeast of the middle of the island; drying rocks obstruct the south end of the channel.

Approach either from the northeast, or round the northeast end of Nave Island, keeping ¼ mile off to avoid a reef at the end of the island and to pass inshore of the Balach Rocks, which lie between 8 cables and 2 miles northeast of Nave Island.

Heading towards the Sound of Islay, Post Rocks lie 6 miles northeast of Nave Island and 1½ miles WNW of Rubha a'Mhail lighthouse. They are 7 cables offshore, dry up to 3·3 metres and rarely cover. A clearing mark for the Post Rocks is Beinn an Oir, the highest of the Paps of Jura, in line with Rubha a'Mhail lighthouse bearing 117°.

Portnahaven

The channel between Orsay and the Rhinns of Islay is well sheltered with a sandy bottom, but strong tides run across the south entrance. Entry should not be contemplated except in reasonably quiet conditions. Yachts using the anchorage can expect to lie to the tide.

Admiralty Chart
2168
Admiralty Leisure Folio
5611.5, 7
Imray Chart
C64
Ordnance Survey
60
Cruising Scotland
p.65

Tides

Constant –0055 Oban (+0605 Dover)

Height in metres

MHWS	MHWN	MTL	MLWN	MLWS
2·6	2·3	1·7	1·3	0·5

Directions

The north entrance is obstructed by submerged rocks and should not be attempted. Keep towards the Islay shore when approaching the south entrance unless it is certain that the tide is setting southeastwards, to avoid being carried onto An Coire, southwest of Orsay. Anchor northwest of the quay on the Islay shore, where the channel opens out.

Small, shoal draught, yachts can use a creek on the Islay shore northeast of the quay, but the approach is intricate and the creek is often full of small fishing boats. The following directions have been provided locally:

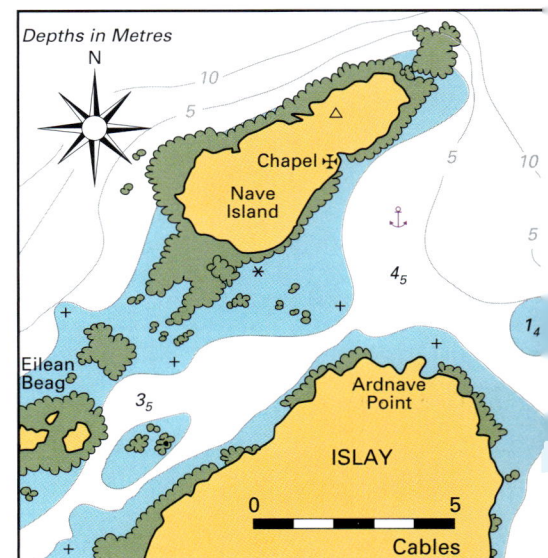

NAVE ISLAND

Orsay from the southwest with the ebb racing round An Coire

Nave Island from the east; the anchorage is just off the picture to the right

The magnificent raised beach southwest of Cumhann Mor, Loch Tarbert, Jura (p.47)

N

Depths in Metres

1 Mile

0.5

0

See p.48

Cumhann Beag

Cruib Lodge

10 23 5

0.6 (0.9)

0.6

1.7

Sgeirean Druim an Loch)0.3)

(0.9)

1.8

Eilean Ard

Loch Tarbert (Inner)

2.1

(0.6)

7

2.4

42

Cairidh Mhor

See inset above

Rubh' a Choire

Raised beach

Cumhann Mor

JURA

Rubha Liath

Sgeirean Bhudragain

Boghachan Baite (1.2 - 2.4)

(0.7)

Bagh Gleann Righ Beag

Aird Reamhar

Glenbatrick Bay

A

107°

Loch Tarbert (Outer)

Sgeir Agleann (5)

Rubhachan Eoghainn

Glenbatrick

Bagh Gleann Righ Mor

An Sailean

Eileanan Gleann Righ

Rubh' an t-Sailean

1.9 Bo Mor

4.7

(1.1)

1.3

2.1 8 (0.6)

2.1

2.1

2.7 7.6

10 5

42

13 7

23

7 4

6.7

Cairidh Mhor

090°

(4)

Rubh' a Choire

Cumhann Mor

19

107° W

13 0.4

10

060° 10

5

0.6

(2.1)

C

0.9

245° 2.7

4.3

7.3

B

Rubha Liath

8.2 5

Sgeirean Bhudragain

5.5

Rubh' a' Bhaillein

(0.7)

Boghachan Baite (1.2 - 2.4)

0.6

A

7.9

7.6

5 Cables

5

0

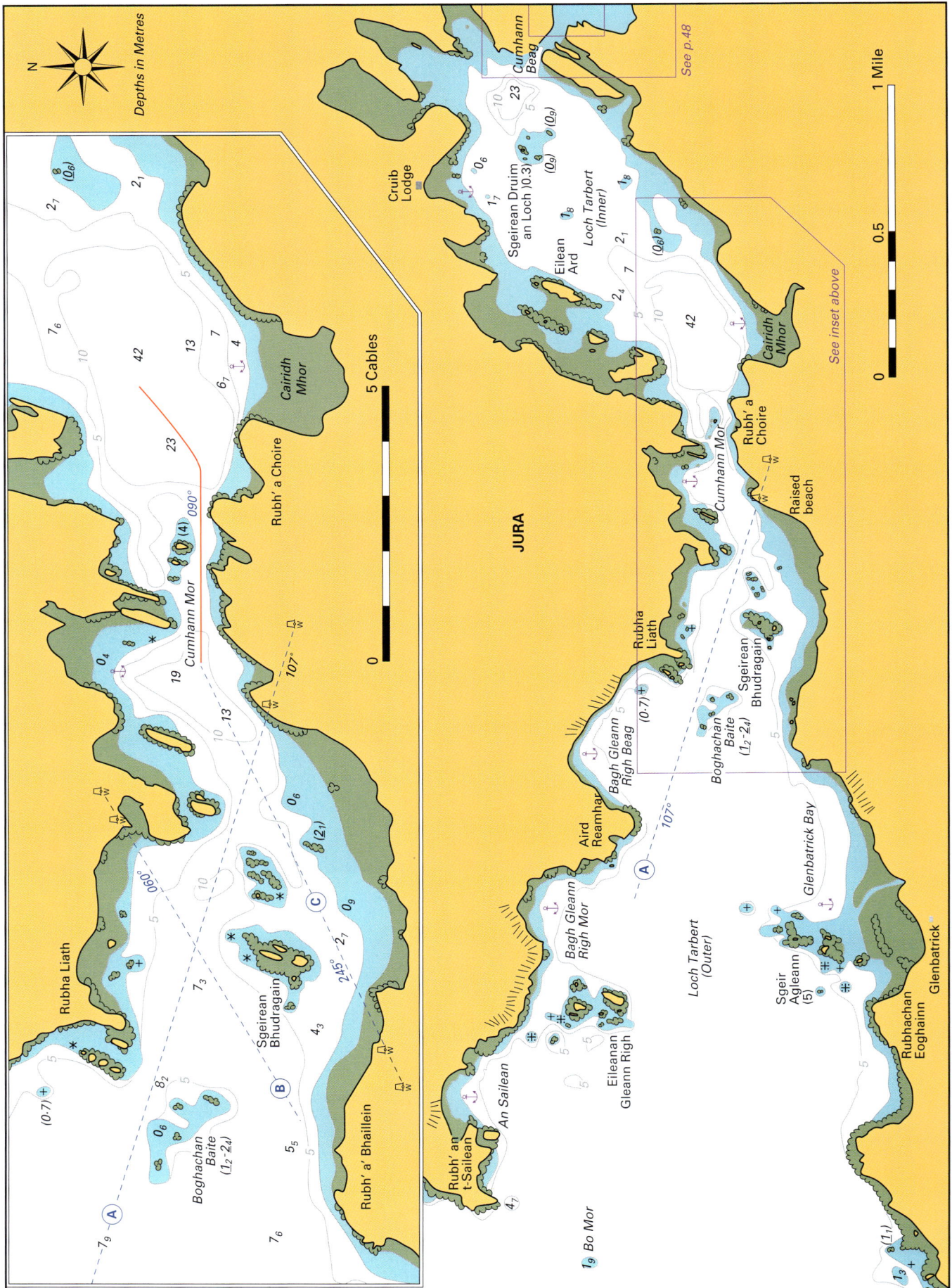

OUTER & INNER LOCH TARBERT, JURA WITH CUMHANN MOR INSET

Loch Tarbert, Jura

The wildest and most remote loch south of Ardnamurchan, Loch Tarbert comprises an Outer Loch where the open anchorages are quite exposed and an Inner Loch which offers much better shelter. Between these, the narrows of Cumhann Mor are not difficult to navigate although there are rocky patches in the approach. The narrow passage from the Inner Loch through Cumhann Beag to the Top Pool is a more serious undertaking which requires suitable conditions and careful navigation.

Leading lines

The key to navigation in Loch Tarbert is to be found in the leading lines, in the approaches to Cumhann Mor and in the innermost passage from Cumhann Beag to the Top Pool. They were established in 1960 by the late 'Blondie' Hasler for use by shallow draught Tarbert Estate vessels. There are now three groups of three lines, which have been designated for navigational clarity. Those leading into Cumhann Mor are designated A, B and C; the first three in Cumhann Beag are D1, D2 and D3; the final three approaching the Top Pool are E1, E2 and E3. (A previous line of approx. 151° to Glenbatrick no longer exists.) The first three lines, A, B and C, which were resurveyed and sounded in 2006, should be followed closely.

Marks

Each leading line is marked by a pair of pillars, which are all squat concrete obelisks 1·1–5m high. Most are plain white but two pairs in Cumhann Beag are black and white banded (six equal bands of each colour).

Tides

Constant at Scalasaig −0012 Oban (+0542 Dover).

Height in metres

MHWS	MHWN	MTL	MLWN	MLWS
3·9	2·7	2·2	1·6	0·5

Streams are generally imperceptible in both the Outer and Inner lochs except at the narrows. Through Cumhann Mor the ingoing stream begins about —0605 Oban (—0050 Dover) and the outgoing about —0010 Oban (—0540 Dover) and runs at about 2 kn. However in Cumhann Beag streams can reach 8kn

Outer Loch

From the north, enter 1 to 2 cables off Rubh' an t-Sailean, giving Bo Mor a good clearance. If approaching from the south keep 2½ cables north of Sgeir Agleann to avoid extensive reefs and an isolated submerged rock. Passage along the north shore is easier.

Anchorage

Anchor in any of three open bays on the north shore: An Sailean, Bagh Gleann Righ Mor (photo p.3) and Bagh Gleann Righ Beag. In Glenbatrick Bay (see above), east of Sgeir Agleann, there is good holding and shelter on the west side of the bay where the shore dries out for 2 cables. Beware of violent squalls coming down the glen in strong southerly winds.

Banded pillars on line D3, Cumhann Beag (see plan p.48)

Plain pillars on line E3, Eilean an Easbuig (see plan p.48)

Cumhann Mor

The approaches to Cumhann Mor are encumbered by two rocky patches, Boghachan Baite which dry about 1·8m, and the more extensive Sgeirean Bhudragain with 3m islets and drying rocks. From south of Aird Reamhar, Line A (107°) provides a deep clear route to the north of both patches. Alternatively Line B (060°) passes between them from a southwest approach, to join Line A. From line A turn ENE onto Line C (marks astern 245°). Then steer 090° through the narrows, between the south shore and the 4m islet.

Anchorage

Immediately before the narrows of Cumhann Mor in a bay off the north shore. Avoid drying rocks off the east side. Good shelter, with good holding in mud.

Inner Loch

Sheltered waters extend over a mile northeast from Cumhann Mor. To avoid the few drying or shoal patches it is easier to approach Cumhann Beag by passing north of Sgeirean Druim an Loch (conspicuous white rocks, see plan).

Anchorage

The usual anchorages are (i) Cairidh Mhor, on the south shore, about 3 cables east of Cumhann Mor, and (ii) off the north shore of the loch, SSW of Cruib Lodge. Both are shoal and dry out some distance. The Inner Loch is reported generally to have good holding in mud. Avoiding the deep holes near each of the narrows, and the few shoal patches, much of this loch could be suitable for anchorage.

Admiralty Chart
2481, 2169
Admiralty Leisure Folio
5611.27C
Imray Chart
C64
Ordnance Survey
61
Cruising Scotland
p.75

N

Depths in Metres

200

100

Metres

INSET B

107°

229°

046°

E3

E2

E1

Eilean a' Bhuic

Eilean an Easbuig

Eilean na Craoibhe-caorainn

Halfway Anchorage

Top Pool

Landing stage

The Hole

22

Moorings

3 Cables

Metres

Tracks
The red lines indicate suggested deviations from the leading lines

Depths
On this page the 1m contour is shown using a dark blue tint.
The 2m contour is tinted pale blue

See inset B

E2

E1

E3

See inset A

D3

D1

D2

Cumhann Beag

Inner Loch Tarbert

INSET A
Same scale as Inset B

054°

120°

148°

2.4

D1

D3

D2

BW

W

W

BW

BW

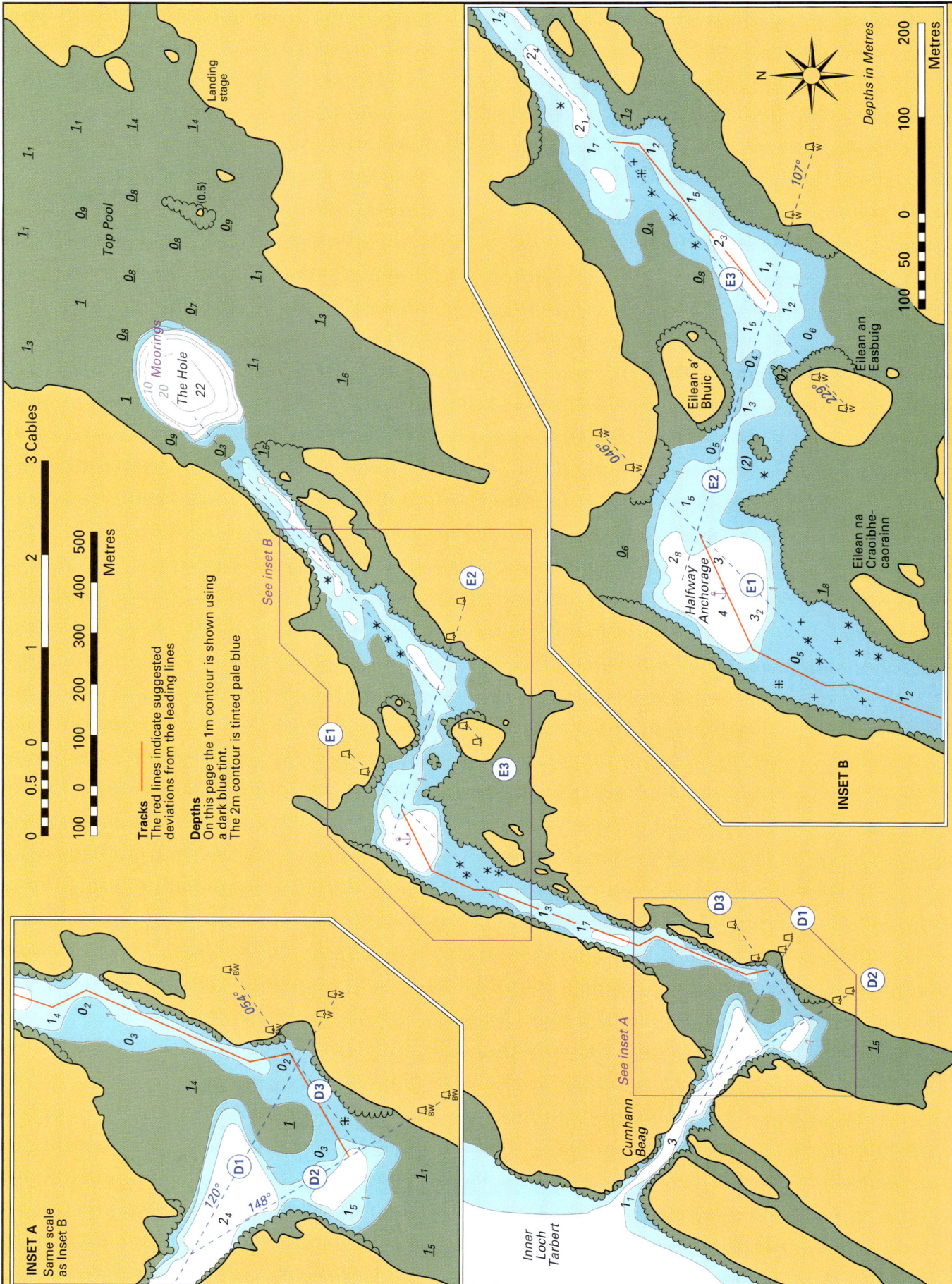

CUMHANN BEAG, LOCH TARBERT, JURA

Cumhann Beag from the west on line D1

Cumhann Beag on line D1 with beacons on D2 coming in to line

Cumhann Beag

The plan opposite has been based on the first survey, made in July 2006 by Randal Coe and Jon Hallam. Minimum depths over the boulders and rocks in this shallow channel may not have been found and further dangers may exist. Keep a keen eye on the sounder and a lookout on the bow.

Cumhann Beag to the Top Pool is the third section of Loch Tarbert, Jura. In this passage there are two groups of leading lines, D1–D3, and E1–E3. In general it is helpful to follow these leading lines.

The limiting depth for the passage is at the final sill, which dries about 0·3m. Similarly there are other shoals which just dry on lines E1 and E3, probably also over boulder banks, which could be avoided with small deviations off-line. The red tracks on the plan indicate where such deviations are suggested.

Tidal streams

Yachtsmen must be warned that there are spring rates of more than 8 knots throughout the channel. The passage from Cumhann Beag to the Top Pool must be taken towards the top of the flood tide and the return also needs to be negotiated around HW. This will usually provide adequate depth for 2m draught and manageable tidal streams. Avoid spring tides. Dangerous seas are reported in the approach, with strong onshore winds.

Directions

Cumhann Beag is to the northeast of Inner Loch Tarbert. The canal-like entrance is fairly narrow with craggy cliffs to port. Take centre passage and on the far shore is the first pair of pillars (line D1, approx. 120°). After 2 cables of 'canal' a further two pillars appear to starboard (D2 banded, 148°). These should be kept in line while passing close by the small headland to starboard. This line avoids an extensive drying spit to port. Past the spit, a third pair of pillars are seen to the northeast (D3 banded, 054°). Turn towards these a little before they come in line and then continue until quite close inshore (photograph p.47) before turning north up the fairway. Keep close to the east shore for just over 1 cable before making a dog-leg to centre passage.

Steer parallel to the west shore and maintain this heading. As Line E1 (046°) is crossed, approach and follow the west shore over a boulder bank (see plan inset B). Then veer away through the Halfway Anchorage until the next line (E2, 107°) can be seen to starboard. Follow this line until the last pair of pillars (E3, 229° astern) are seen in the gulley on Eilean an Easbuig (photograph p.47). When in line, use these up to the Top Pool but initially veering off line to avoid the boulder bank off the east end of Eilean a' Bhuic. Approach the sill before The Hole with caution as there may not be enough water at neap tides for a deep keel.

Anchorage

This is a problem in the Top Pool as there is only The Hole, 22m deep with very steep sides, which does not dry. The northeast part of The Hole is taken up with present (and no doubt many past) moorings laid for local boats. A doubtful anchorage could perhaps be found on the southwest side of The Hole, but with swinging to tide there could be a risk of drying out. In fact it is not recommended to anchor anywhere in the Top Pool unless the craft, say a bilge keeler, can safely take the ground. After visiting the pool at HW, a return to the Halfway Anchorage (see plan opposite) is a much safer option. There is plenty of swinging room in 4m and splendid views down the passage to the Paps of Jura.

See plan below

NORTHWEST JURA ANCHORAGES

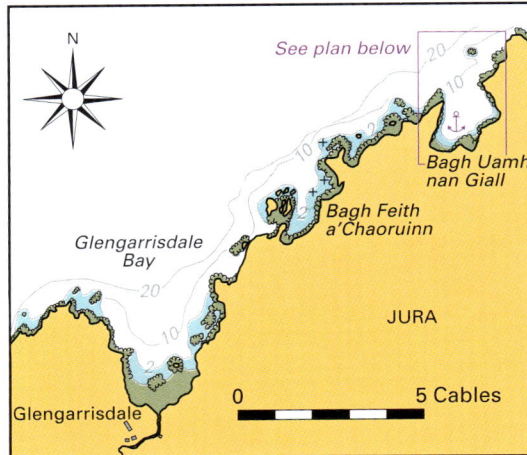

Bagh Uamh nan Giall

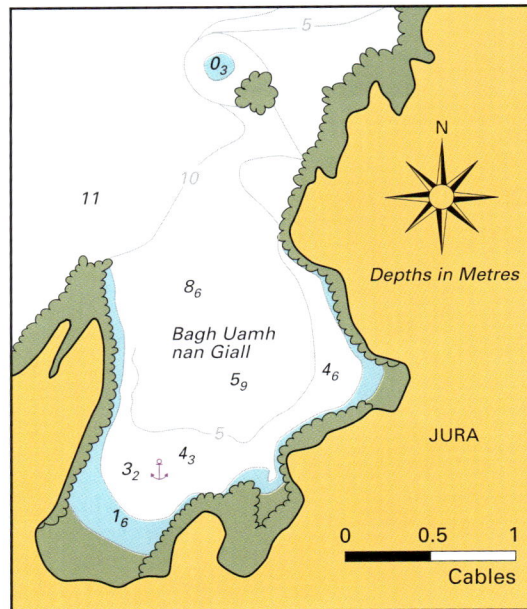

Bagh Feith a'Chaoruinn

Glengarrisdale Bay

JURA

Glengarrisdale

0   5 Cables

BAGH UAMH NA GIALL

0₃

11

8₆

Bagh Uamh nan Giall

5₉   4₆

Depths in Metres

N

JURA

3₂   4₃

1₆

0   0.5   1

Cables

Caolas Mor, Oronsay; the anchorage off the boathouse with Eilean Ghaoideamal and, beyond, the Paps of Jura

Northwest coast of Jura

Several bays provide occasional anchorage in settled weather if there is no swell; charts 2343 and 2326 are recommended.

Bagh Feith a'Chaorainn, ½ mile northeast of Glengarrisdale Bay, has been recommended as a useful place while waiting for the tide but it is quite restricted and at springs the seaward rocks might let a bit too much sea in. A submerged rock lies ½ cable off the east shore.

Bagh Uamh na Giall, lies ½ mile further northeast and is probably the better of the two, giving good overnight anchorage in settled weather from the east. A drying rock lies 1 cable from the shore north of the entrance.

Colonsay and Oronsay

Two relatively low-lying islands linked by a drying causeway. The east coast of both islands is clean if not approached nearer than 2 cables, but the south and southwest coasts should be given a very wide berth of at least 3 miles to avoid dangerous rocks extending up to 2 miles offshore. There are no all-weather anchorages on either island and all the anchorages can be troubled by swell.

From the northeast there is little to distinguish any part of the island, but from the north end of the Sound of Islay, Beinn Oronsay (91 metres) shows up as a wedge-shaped hill with a sheer cliff on its south side. Closer to Colonsay a monument on the skyline between Scalasaig and Loch Staosnaig is the best mark.

Tides
At Scalasaig
Constant −0012 Oban (+0542 Dover)

Height in metres

MHWS	MHWN	MTL	MLWN	MLWS
3·9	2·7	2·2	1·6	0·5

Edward Mason

Caolas Mor, Oronsay

Oronsay, the southerly of the two islands, provides several occasional anchorages in the sound between Oronsay and the islands southeast of it. Oronsay Priory, about a mile from the anchorages, is well worth a visit.

Directions

Approaching from the Sound of Islay pass ¼ mile north of Eilean Ghaoideamal; coming from northeast steer towards Eilean Ghaoideamal until the boathouse bears 270° and then steer to keep it on that bearing.

Anchorages

Off the boathouse (see photo opposite), take care to avoid Leac nan Geadh which covers and keep well offshore to avoid the 1·5m and 1·7m rocks shown on the plan below but not on the Admiralty chart.

North of Leac nan Geadh gives the best shelter. Approach on the south side of the bight to avoid drying rocks to the north and the 1·2m rock which is a cable northeast of Leac nan Geadh.

West of Eilean Treadhrach is sometimes preferred, and in southwesterly winds a better berth may be found on the north side of Eilean Treadhrach but note that a reef extends almost 2 cables northeast of Eilean Treadhrach and there are isolated rocks in the bay (see plan).

Admiralty Chart
2169, 2343
Admiralty Leisure Folio
5611.4, 6
Imray Chart
C64, 65
Ordnance Survey
61
Cruising Scotland
pp.76-77

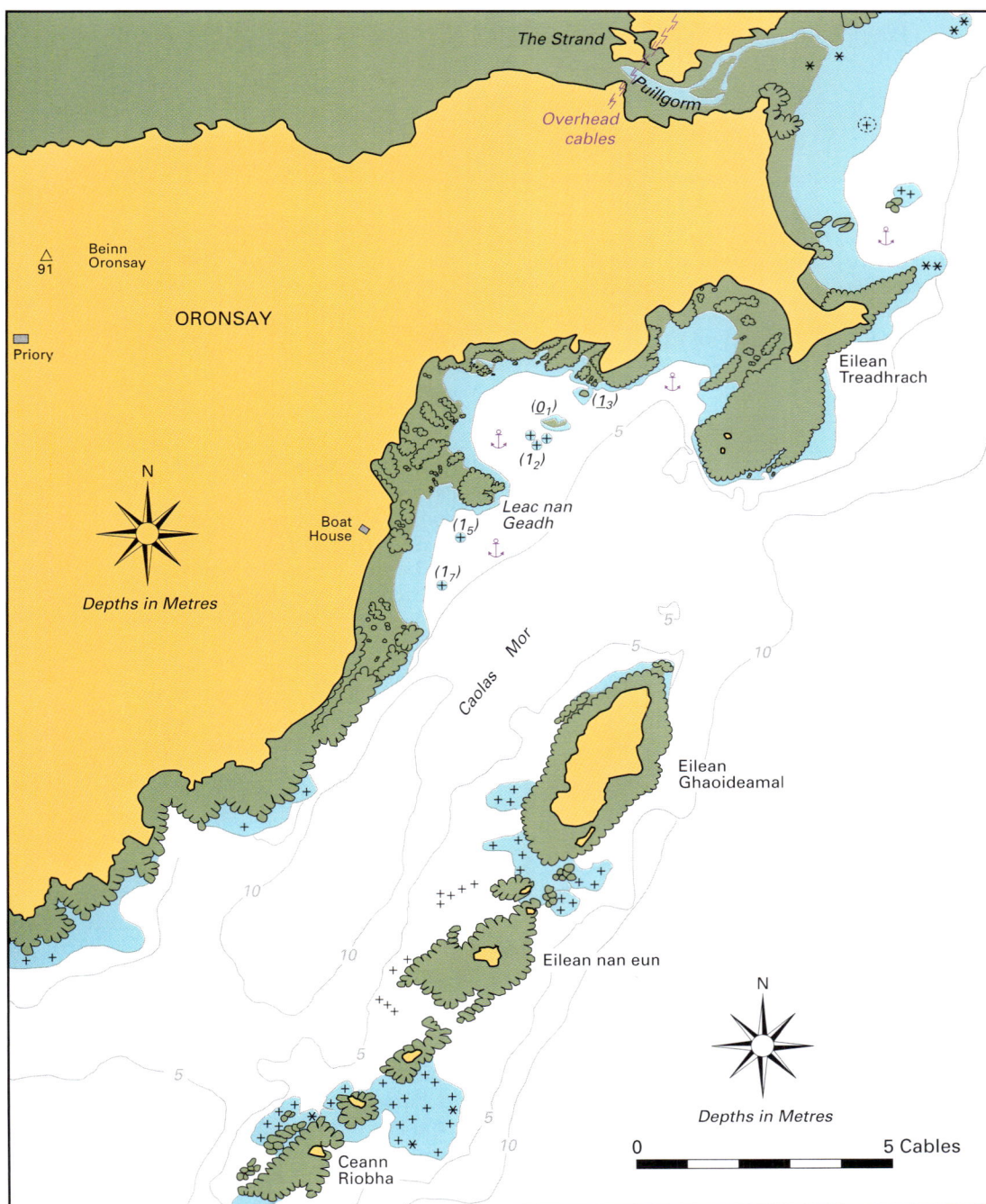

CAOLAS MOR, ORONSAY

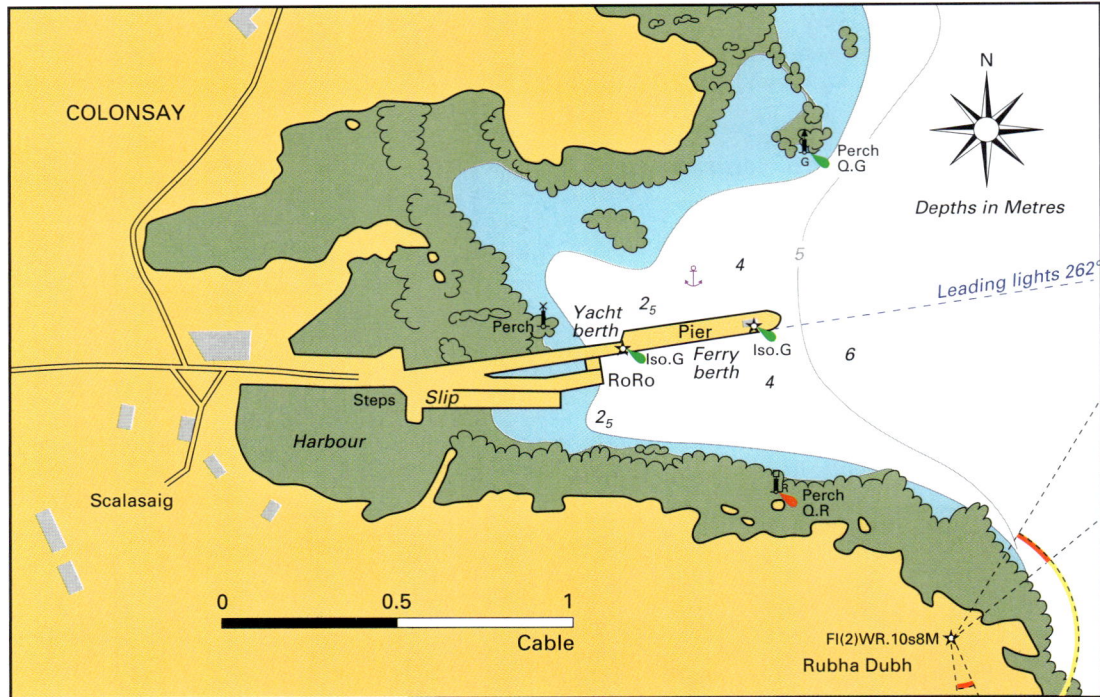

**SCALASAIG,
COLONSAY**

Admiralty Chart
2169, 2474
Admiralty Leisure Folio
5611.4
Imray Chart
C64, 65
Ordnance Survey
61
Cruising Scotland
pp.76-77

Scalasaig

Situated on the east coast of Colonsay north of Loch Staosnaig, this is the only village in the area and may be identified easily by the lighthouse, pier and a monument south of the village.

Tides

At Scalasaig
Constant –0012 Oban (+0542 Dover)

Height in metres

MHWS	MHWN	MTL	MLWN	MLWS
3·9	2·7	2·2	1·6	0·5

Directions

Even in westerly winds a swell usually works into Scalasaig and there is very little swinging room. On approaching from southward there is little sign of the village until it bears 270°, and the first mark to be seen is the monument on the skyline. A linkspan for a car ferry has been built on the south side of the pier.

Scalasaig, Colonsay

Patrick Roach

Anchorage and berthing

There is no room for yachts to anchor clear of the ferry terminal on the south side of the pier, and the bottom has been dredged down to bare rock. Yachts able to take the ground can dry out in the harbour.

North side of the pier The presence of reefs and a multitude of small fishing pot marker buoys makes anchoring there restricted. Bottom sand and rocks. Subject to swell.

Part of the north side of the pier screen near its root has been covered with timber boarding for visiting yachts to lie alongside. Depth at the yacht berth is 2·5m but a reef extending from the shore limits the space available. The extent of the reef is marked by an unlit perch.

Supplies

Water at CalMac building, phone box, toilets and rubbish skip at pier. Restaurant, hotel, shop and Post Office. Calor Gas, petrol and diesel in cans. Piermaster ☏ 01951 200320.

Loch Staosnaig

This bay is ½ mile south of Scalasaig and can be identified by the monument on the north side. An electricity cable runs close to the north side of Eileann Staosnaig on the transit of two large yellow diamonds on poles.

Because of the presence of the electricity cable the preferred anchorage is in the southern half of the bay but note submerged and drying rocks off both shores. Do not approach within a cable of the north shore. Good holding in sand but subject to swell, although there is more space than at Scalasaig.

Occasional anchorages on Colonsay

Bagh Lon A small, clean, sandy bay ¾ mile south of Loch Staosnaig. Anchor in the centre of the bay in 2·5m, sand. A drying reef extends a cable northeast of the south point of the bay.

Balnahard Bay A sandy bay, immediately north of Rubh a Geadha at the northeast tip of Colonsay, offers occasional anchorage in 6-10m sand and shingle. Keep towards Rubh a Geadha to avoid the rocky spit on the north side.

Kiloran Bay This wide sandy bay on the northwest coast of Colonsay provides excellent shelter in easterly weather although it can be subject to swell. Access is straightforward using chart 2169.

Port Mor is a small bay on the west side of Colonsay, 5 miles from the north end. It gives good shelter from the east but is very exposed to the south through west to northwest and subject to heavy southerly swell. It is best approached from the north because of the extensive reefs off the southwest coast of Colonsay.

From a point a mile west of the north end of Colonsay head southwest; this line will clear all offlying rocks. Do not approach the shore closer than 4 cables when making for the entrance until the line of the road passing the graveyard is completely open to avoid Bogha na Tuadh (drying 2·4m) and the rocks south of it. Then approach on the line of the road.

Passages past Colonsay to Mull and Tiree

The passage from the Sound of Islay past the east side of Colonsay is straightforward. In good visibility from a point 1 mile northeast of Colonsay steer 330° towards the highest point of the Ross of Mull, Beinn a Chaol-achadh, and the nearest point on the shore there, Rubh' Ardalanish, a distance of about 8 miles. Directions for the passage between the Torran Rocks and Mull are given on pp.190-191.

In the passages from the Sound of Islay and

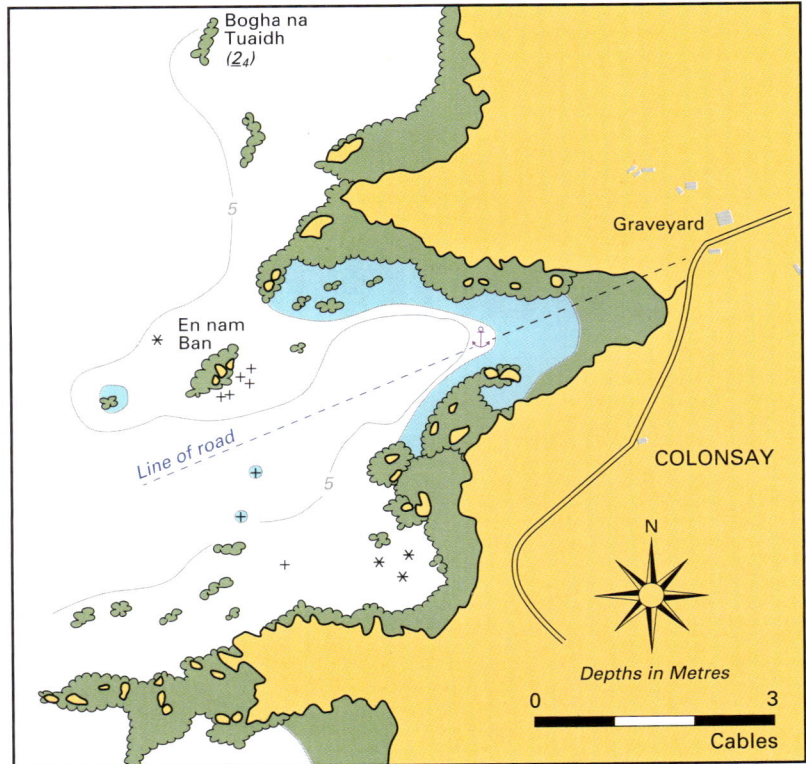
PORT MOR COLONSAY

south of Colonsay two specific hazards are the Post Rocks 1½ miles west of Rubha a'Mhail lighthouse and Bogha Chubaidth, awash 1½ miles southwest of Oronsay. Rubha a'Mhail lighthouse in line with Beinn an Oir, the highest, and from this direction the central hill of the Paps of Jura, bearing 117° leads well north of the Post Rocks, and the lighthouse in line with Beinn Shiantaidh, the more northerly of the Paps bearing 112° leads well south of Bogha Chubaidth.

Once clear west of Oronsay steer 315° to pass northeast of Dubh Artach lighthouse which is distinguished by a broad red band painted round it. Tiree is low-lying but has two hills in its western part, Ben Hynish and Ben Hough, which in clear weather will be the first part of Tiree to be seen.

Loch Staosnaig, Colonsay

Martin Lawrence

4. Sound of Jura

Admiralty Chart
2396, 2397
Admiralty Leisure Folio
5611.6
Imray Chart
C64, 65
Ordnance Survey
61, 55
Cruising Scotland
pp.70-75

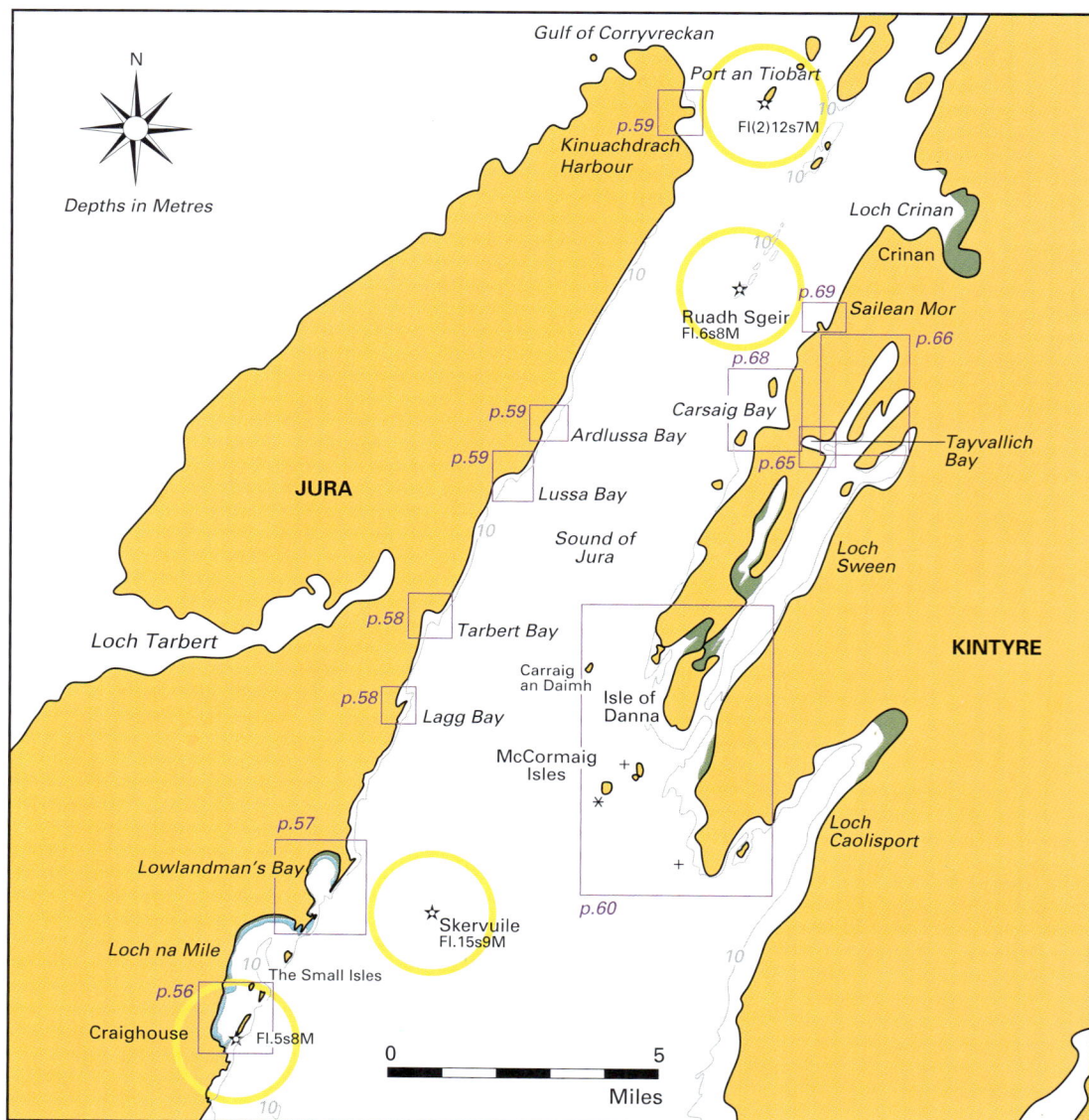

Gulf of Corryvreckan

N

Depths in Metres

Port an Tiobart
p.59
Fl(2)12s7M
Kinuachdrach
Harbour

Loch Crinan

Crinan

p.69
Ruadh Sgeir
Fl.6s8M

Sailean Mor
p.66

p.68

p.59
Ardlussa Bay

Carsaig Bay

Tayvallich
Bay

p.59
Lussa Bay

p.65

JURA

Sound of
Jura

Loch
Sween

Loch Tarbert

p.58
Tarbert Bay

KINTYRE

Carraig
an Daimh

Isle of
Danna

p.58
Lagg Bay

McCormaig
Isles

Loch
Caolisport

p.57
Lowlandman's Bay

Skervuile
Fl.15s9M

p.60

Loch na Mile

The Small Isles

p.56

Craighouse   Fl.5s8M

0   5

Miles

The Sound of Jura is, in the main fairway at least, a relatively hazard-free stretch of water and those hazards that do exist are well marked. Tidal streams are significant and can raise awkward seas with wind against tide in conjunction with the uneven bottom. The seas are at their worst when the wind is southerly, blowing from the open sea against an ebb tide, but eddies on the flood can be just as troublesome.

In this chapter the harbours and anchorages are described from south to north, starting with the Jura shore at Craighouse, continuing north as far as Kinuachdrach Harbour, then over to Kintyre from Loch Caolisport to just south of Crinan.

Tides

Throughout the sound most of the rise and fall occurs within the first three hours of each period. The height of tide is greatly affected by wind and barometric pressure; a southwesterly wind and/or low pressure raising the level by up to a metre, and a northeasterly wind and/or high pressure reducing it by a similar amount.

Throughout the greater part of the sound the north-going stream begins about +0545 Oban (+0015 Dover) and the south-going stream begins about –0015 Oban (–0545 Dover). The stream turns earlier on the east side, particularly at the entrance to Loch Sween. The rate at the south end of the sound is about 2 knots, and around Skervuile about 3–3½ knots.

Near Ruadh Sgeir at the north end of the sound the north-going stream begins about +0425 Oban (–0105 Dover) and the south-going stream begins about –0155 Oban (+0500 Dover), the rate in each direction being up to 4 knots.

Marks

Paps of Jura, a group of three conspicuous hills near the south end of Jura, provide a useful reference point unless they are obscured by cloud.

Na Cuiltean, a rock east of the south end of Jura, with a small white light beacon.

Skervuile, a larger light beacon in the middle of the sound.

MacCormaig Isles, off the entrance of Loch Sween.

Carraig an Daimh, an isolated rock 11 metres high 1¾ miles north of MacCormaig Isles.

Ruadh Sgeir at the north end of the sound is 13 metres high with a small light beacon.

Directions

There is little to add to the description already given except to emphasise the need to work the tides. If attempting a passage against the tide, some use may be made of eddies in the lee of any projection from the shore, but this will need very careful chartwork, especially on the mainland side. The most useful eddy is off Carsaig Bay.

Submerged reefs extend 4 cables NNE of Ruadh Sgeir at the north end of the sound, and there are strong eddies and overfalls north of that islet on the flood. The flood tide sets NNW across the reefs and must be allowed for if passing east of Ruadh Sgeir or south of Reisa an t-Sruith.

Lights

McArthur's Head LH Fl(2)WR.10s39m13/10M
Na Cuiltean light bn. Fl.10s9m9M
Eilean nan Gabhar (Goat Island) Fl.5s7m8M
Craighouse perch Fl.R.6s
Nine-foot Rock buoy Q(3)10s
Skervuile light beacon Fl.15s22m9M
Ruadh Sgeir light beacon Fl.6s13m8M
Reisa an t-Sruith Fl(2)12s12m7M

Loch na Mile, Jura with Craighouse, left centre, and the Paps of Jura

Patrick Roach

Admiralty Chart
2396
Admiralty Leisure Folio
5611.6, 28E
Imray Chart
C64
Ordnance Survey
61
Cruising Scotland
pp.74, 75

Anchorages on Jura

There are over half a dozen anchorages on the Jura side of the sound, some more obvious than others and, being often in the lee of Jura, they might be expected to offer good shelter. However, several of them are badly affected by cabbage kelp, with resulting poor holding, and the majority are subject to swell. With care, patches of better holding on sand can be found in some of them and in moderate conditions any swell, usually varying with the tide, is generally acceptable.

Craighouse Bay (Loch na Mile)

Craighouse, (see photo p.55) the largest settlement on Jura, lies in the southwest corner of an extensive bay sheltered by a row of islands, whose south end is 2½ miles from the southeast point of Jura. In spite of the apparent shelter there is often some swell, usually of a tidal origin, and the holding is poor, with much thick kelp, making the provision of visitors' moorings more than welcome. It is well lit and can be entered at night.

Tides

Tidal streams run strongly across the entrance.
Constant –0130 Oban (+0400 Dover) at springs, and –0430 Oban (+0100 Dover) at neaps.

Height in metres

MHWS	MHWN	MTL	MLWN	MLWS
1·2	0·9	0·7	0·4	0·3

Directions

From the north, Goat Rock (drying 0·3) is dangerous but it has recently been marked by an E cardinal buoy which should be left well to starboard when approaching from the north before opening up the entrance.

From the south, Na Cuiltean light beacon helps to identify the entrance and the distillery and houses are seen once the entrance is opened.

Loch na Mile is bordered by three islands on its east side and any of the passages between them can be taken, with care and using the

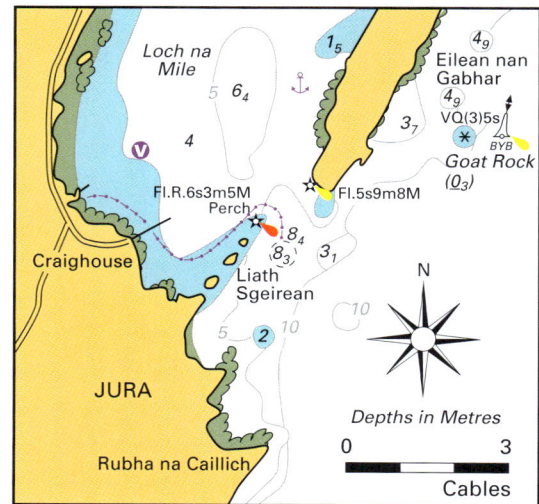

Drumnatuadh Bay, Lowlandman's Bay, gives good protection from most directions

Martin Lawrence

CRAIGHOUSE

chart. The main entrance is at the south end of the bay, between the south point of Goat Island (Eilean nan Gabhar) and a drying reef extending north from the south point of the bay. A small metal light beacon stands at the south end of Goat Island and a lit beacon stands about 20 metres south of the end of the reef (not at the end of the reef) on the south side of the entrance.

Anchorage and mooring

There are 16 visitors' moorings which, in view of the holding, are well worth the £10 a night charge, payable at the honesty box near the pontoon. Suitable depths for anchoring can be found outside the moorings or east of the pier but in the latter case beware of the outfall pipe shown on the plan. A dinghy landing pontoon has been installed off the old stone jetty; use the inner end to allow room for the Tayvallich ferry RIBs. There is good depth alongside the pier but it is of concrete frame construction so that it is difficult to keep fenders in place, although the range of tide is small.

Goat Island In easterly winds there is slightly better shelter west of Goat Island, as close to the island as the depth allows.

Loch na Mile (north) Anchoring is possible well off shore west of Rubha Bhride but do not be tempted to anchor in the bay east of Rubha Bhride where, contrary to older editions of chart 2396, the 2m depth contour should run northwest from a rock (drying 0·6) directly to Rubha Bhride. There are rocks inside this line (see plan opposite).

Supplies

Well-stocked community shop, water at pier, diesel, petrol, Calor Gas, Post Office, phone, hotel. Public toilets, showers at hotel.

Lights

Na Cuiltean light bn. Fl.10s9m9M
Eilean nan Gabhar (Goat Island) Fl.5s9m8M
Craighouse perch Fl.R.6s
Goat Rock buoy VQ(3)5s

Lowlandman's Bay

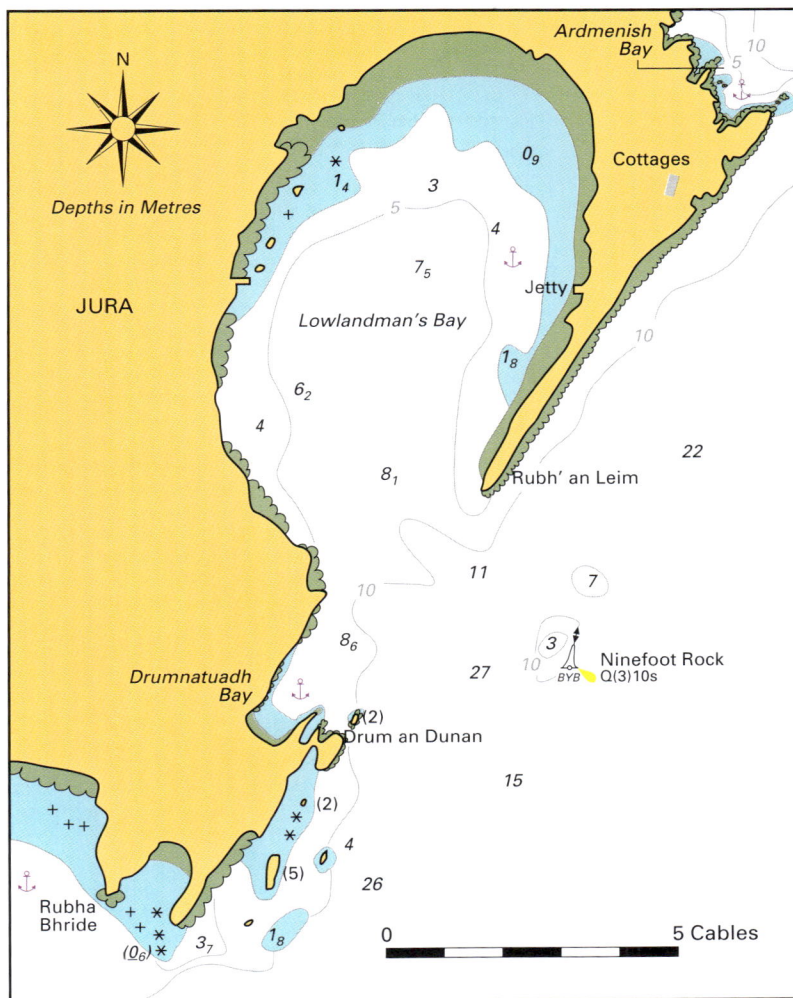

This bay lies just north of Loch na Mile. The former lighthouse-keepers' houses on the rocky ridge which shelters the east side of the bay are conspicuous, and Ninefoot Rock east cardinal light buoy (Q(3)10s) lies east of the entrance.

Anchorage

Lowlandman's Bay Much of the bay is shallow and the best anchorage is near the east side, off a stone jetty, southwest of the houses. Otherwise anchor wherever the best shelter can be found from wind and swell, but note that the bay shoals at the head for a considerable distance. Holding is poor in thick kelp.

Drumnatuadh Bay (Drum an Dunan) lies on the south side of the entrance to Lowlandman's Bay (photograph opposite) and is one of the better small anchorages on the Jura shore, having less weed than most. A large clear patch of sand gives good holding in 3m. Anchor just inside the east point of the bay which is well sheltered except from the east and northeast. It can be subject to tidal swell.

Ardmenish Bay offers a temporary anchorage for those who may want to explore the iron-age fort on the rocky point which encloses it on the southeast side. Anchor in 4–5m, west of the 0·9m islet off the point.

LOWLANDMAN'S BAY

A perfect evening in Lowlandman's Bay, below the Paps of Jura

Martin Lawrence

Admiralty Chart
2396, 2397
Admiralty Leisure Folio
5611.6,
Imray Chart
C64 C65
Ordnance Survey
61, 55
Cruising Scotland
p.75

Other anchorages on the east coast of Jura

There are several small bays north of Lowlandman's Bay before reaching the north end of Jura. All may be used with caution and in quiet weather. They are subject to the same conditions as Loch na Mile having cabbage kelp, swell, and small range of tide. The exception is Lussa Bay where there is a good area of sand.

As stated previously, none of them provide shelter in poor conditions but all are well worth considering as occasional overnight anchorages or convenient places for a lunch stop and an interesting run ashore. They are named on charts 2396 and 2397 and can be approached using these charts or the adjacent plans. Several more occasional anchorages on the east coast of Jura have been surveyed by *Antares Charts* and are available in their portfolio.

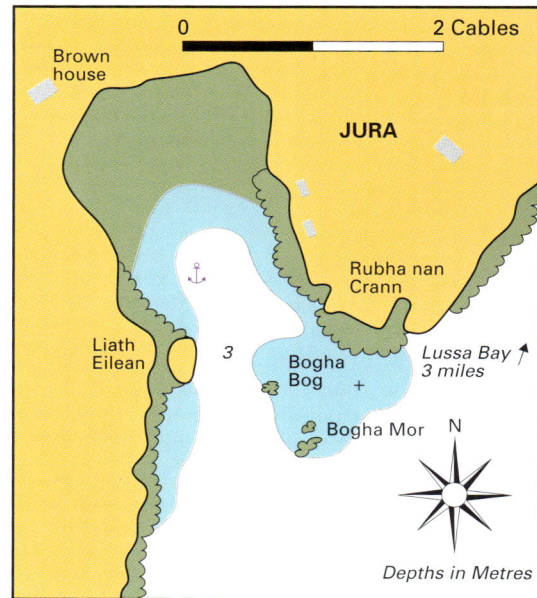

TARBERT BAY

LAGG BAY

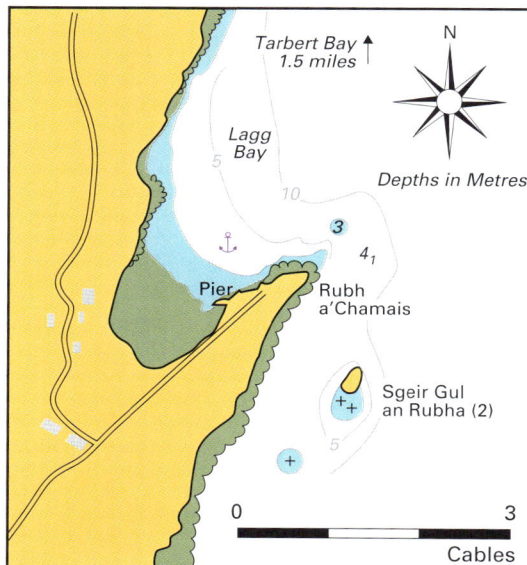

Lagg Bay; drying rocks extend north of the point

Lagg Bay, 4 miles north of Skervuile, was the original landing place for the mail ferry crossing to Jura. A power cable shown on older charts in this bay was disused many years ago.

Drying rocks extend ¼ cable NNE of the east point of the entrance. Phone box beside the road at west side of the bay.

Tarbert Bay, 1½ miles north of Lagg Bay, is identified by a dip in the skyline, as it is only ¾ mile from the head of Loch Tarbert on the west side of Jura (p.47).

The bay is shallow and almost entirely filled with dense broad-leafed seaweed, but a patch of clear sand north of Liath Eilean has a depth of about 2½ metres. Enter the bay from the south passing close to Liath Eilean, keeping a brown house closed behind, it until the island is abeam; from north and east pass at least 2 cables south of Rubha nan Crann before turning into the bay.

Martin Lawrence

Edward Mason

Lussa Bay, 3 miles NNE of Tarbert Bay, is straightforward, but give the east point of the entrance a berth of half a cable. Anchor where indicated; patches of sand can be found.

Ardlussa Bay, 1½ miles NNE of Lussa, provides little shelter except for a shoal-draught boat.

Port an Tiobart and Kinuachdrach Harbour lie north and south respectively of the Aird of Kinuachdrach, which is due west of the Dorus Mor. They provide alternative anchorages out of the tide which at this point in the sound can reach 4 knots.

Tarbert Bay; the small patch of sand can be seen below the anchored yacht

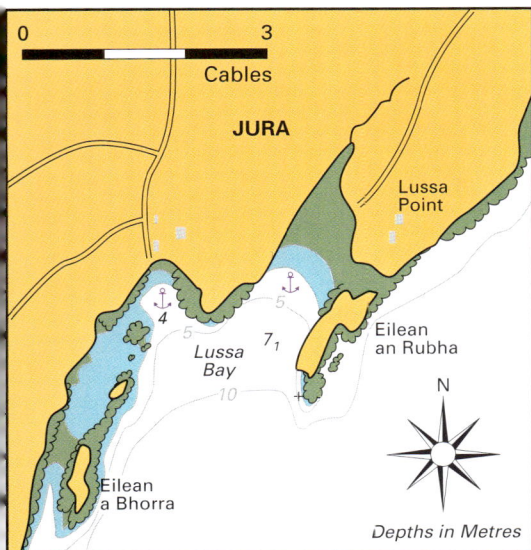

LUSSA BAY

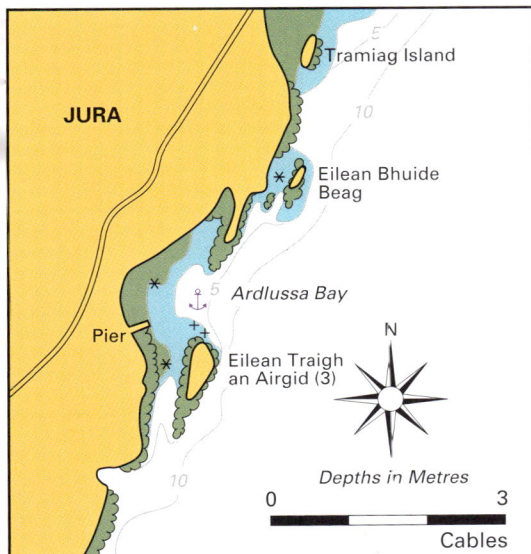

ARDLUSSA BAY

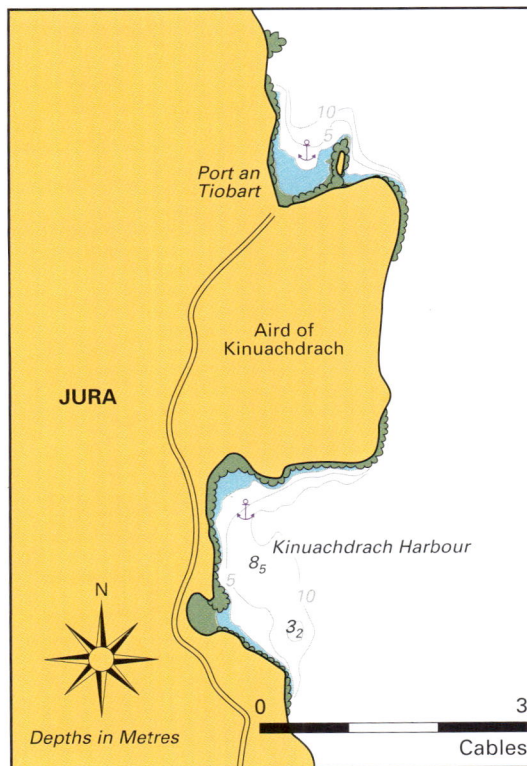

PORT AN TIOBART & KINUACHDRACH HARBOUR

N

Depths in Metres

Rubha Riabhag

Keills Chapel
Jetty

Loch Sween

018°

Loch Keills (Loch na Cille)

Rubha na Cille

Carraig an Daimh (12)

Dubh Sgeir (2)

Island of Danna

Castle Sween (ru)

Moorings

En Ghamhna touching Point of Knap leads W of Keills Rock 155°

3_4

Point of Knap in line with Corr En clears Corr Rocks

+ (1)
Keills Rock

+ (1)
Danna Rock

Lochfoot Rocks (1)

3_7

N point En Mor in line with N point Corr En

3_4

Corr Rocks
(1_8) +

Eilean Ghamhna

MacCormaig Isles

Corr Eilean

Eilean nan Leac

3_7

p.62

Eilean Mor

(0_6) *
Flat Rock

Kilmory Chapel

Dubh Sgeir (4)

Kilmory Bay

Muileann Eiteag Bagh

+ (0·9)
+ (1)
Eilean Traighe

Sound of Jura

Liath Eilein (15)

Caution

Tidal Streams

Tidal streams run strongly in this area and care must be taken to watch clearance bearings and transits

N going stream begins +0450 Oban (-0040 Dover)
S going stream begins -0110 Oban (+0545 Dover)

Rates and times vary at Springs and Neaps

Ruadh na Brogg +

Point of Knap

Loch Caolisport

Bow of Knap

Q(9)15s
YBY

Back Bow

(2_7)

0   5   10

Cables

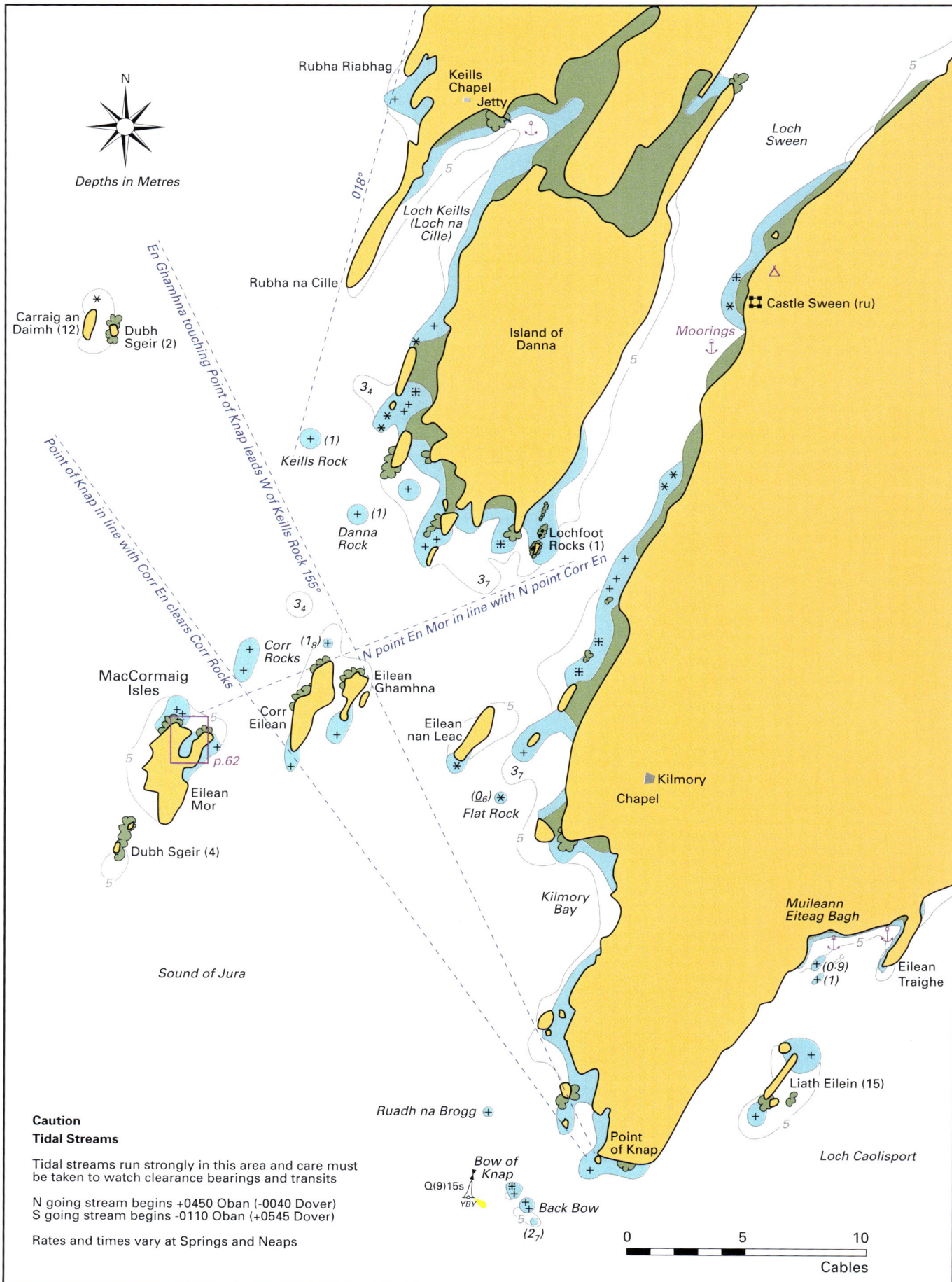

APPROACHES TO LOCH SWEEN

Sound of Jura - east side

Most of the dangers in the Sound of Jura are concentrated in the area around the MacCormaig Islands and affect the approach to Loch Caolisport and Loch Keills (Loch na Cille) as well as Loch Sween. On a direct passage through the sound they are easily avoided by keeping west of Eilean Mor and Carraig an Daimh.

Tides

Craighouse
Constant –0130 Oban (+0400 Dover) at springs, and –0430 Oban (+0100 Dover) at neaps.

Height in metres

MHWS	MHWN	MTL	MLWN	LWS
1·2	0·9	0·7	0·4	0·3

Tides run strongly and irregularly among the MacCormaig Isles and it is essential to watch clearing marks continuously.
The north-going stream begins about +0450 Oban (–0040 Dover) and the south-going stream begins about –0110 Oban (+0545 Dover).
Spring rates off the Point of Knap are 1½ knots. Among the islands and off Rubha na Cille, 2 miles north of the MacCormaig Isles, they are around 3 knots, with eddies and overfalls throughout the area.

Dangers

Clearing marks for avoiding some of these dangers are fairly distant and not easy to identify, but the adjacent plan and illustrations (p.62) should help. In poor visibility it may be necessary to resort to GPS and a chartplotter but bear in mind the strong currents and watch the cross-track error The principal dangers are as follows, from south to north:

Bow of Knap and Ruadh na Brogg, submerged and drying rocks ½ mile west and WSW of the Point of Knap on the north side of the entrance to Loch Caolisport. Bow of Knap is marked by a W cardinal light buoy, Q(9)15s.

Corr Rocks, 2½ cables west of the north end of Corr Eilean nearly uncover and weed shows at LW neaps. They are dangerous, especially if approaching Eilean Mor from the north or from Loch Sween. In the latter case they are best avoided by keeping close to the west side of Corr Eilean, which is clean.

Danna Rock and Keills Rock both have a least depth of 1·0m. Rubha Riabhag open of Rubha na Cille bearing 018° (see above) leads close west of Keills Rock. The north end of Eilean Ghamhna touching the Point of Knap bearing 155° leads west of these rocks, but take care not to mistake Keppoch Point, 5 miles further south, for the Point of Knap.

Loch Caolisport

An attractive loch with few hazards but being totally open to the southwest it offers little shelter from the prevailing winds, although in winds from north to east good anchorage can be found in some of the bays on the northwest side of the loch. There are no sheltered anchorages on the southeast side except in offshore winds.

Directions

From the south the approach presents no problems but from the north a decision must be taken whether to pass inside or outside Bow of Knap and Ruadh na Brogg, which lies 3 cables north of it. The former is now marked by a W cardinal buoy, Q(9)15s, but the rocks extend almost 3 cables east of the buoy. If taking the inside passage hold close to Eilean Glas and the islet south of it and give the Point of Knap a berth of about 1½ cables.

Anchorage

Muileann Eiteag Bagh A bay on the north shore of the loch about 1½ miles northeast of the entrance. Pass east and north of Liath Eilean and anchor off the beach, clear of rocks to the west, in 6-10m or between Eilean Traighe and the mainland. Bottom sand and shingle.

Chapel Bay, west of Eilean na h-Uamhaidh on the north shore near the head of the loch, gives good shelter in winds from northwest to east. Keep clear of off-lying rocks extending almost 1 cable southwest of the island and anchor in 4-6m, sand.

Approach to Loch Sween

The tidal streams around the MacCormaig Isles are irregular, and there are strong eddies making steering by compass course difficult. Great care should be taken to identify the islands correctly.

Directions

Entering from the south leave Eilean nan Leac to starboard, and Corr Eilean and Eilean Gamhna to port. From the north, identify the Carraig an Daimh islets and Eilean Mor, the most westerly island of the MacCormaig Isles group, which may be identified by the conspicuous stone cross on the summit and a small stone chapel.

To avoid Keills Rock and Danna Rock steer 155° from a position east of Carraig an Daimh, keeping the Point of Knap in line with the north end of Eilean Ghamhna until almost midway between Eilean Ghamhna and Danna Island (p.62).

Then steer 100° to avoid the Lochfoot Rocks (Sgeir Bun an Locha) which sometimes cover and may be difficult to see against the shore, until Castle Sween and the caravan site bears 030° before entering the loch. A useful clearance bearing for avoiding the Lochfoot Rocks is the north point of Eilean Mor in transit with the north point of Corr Eilean.

Loch Keills (Loch na Cille)

This is the open sandy loch immediately east of Rubha na Cille. The loch is free of dangers. Anchor as far up as depth permits near the jetty on the west side. The anchorage is subject to swell as it is quite exposed southward, but the swell is usually limited by the tide running past the entrance. If visiting Keills Chapel it is possible to use the jetty to land.

Admiralty Chart
2396, 2397
Admiralty Leisure Folio
5611.6,
Imray Chart
C64
Ordnance Survey
62, 55
Cruising Scotland
pp.70-72

Loch Sween approach - clearing marks for Danna and Keills Rocks from north

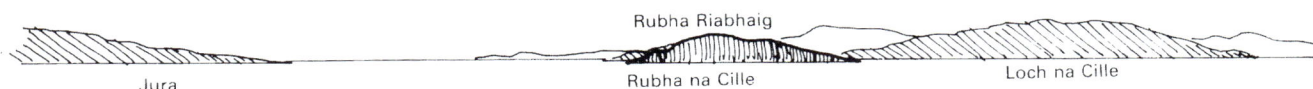

Loch Sween approach - clearing marks for Danna and Keills Rocks from south

Admiralty Chart
2396, 2397
Admiralty Leisure Folio
5611.6,
Imray Chart
C64
Ordnance Survey
62
Cruising Scotland
p.72

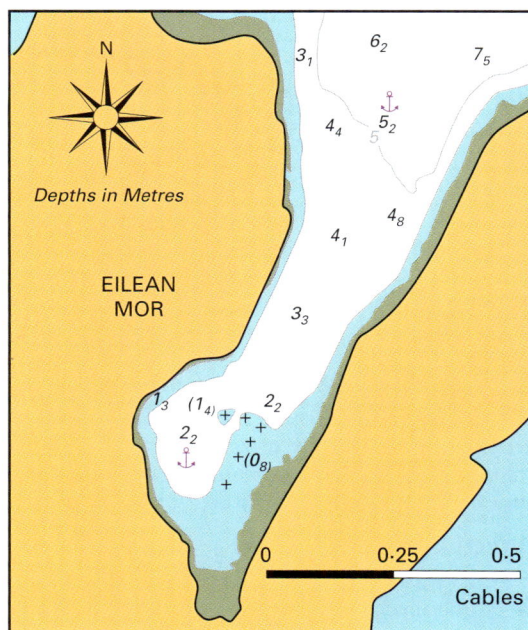

EILEAN MOR

Eilean Mor (MacCormaig Isles)

The most southwesterly of the MacCormaig Isles, identified by the ruined chapel about the middle of the island and a cross on a hill top near the south end.

Eilean Mor anchorage

Eilean Mor is a popular anchorage, particularly for day visits. The anchorage is a tiny inlet at the north end of the island with an uneven stony bottom and several individual rocks with depths of less than 2 metres.

The westernmost rock is said to have been dynamited but it still lurks at a depth of 1·4m and the others remain, as shown by the recent *Antares* survey on which the adjacent plan is based. Debris from the explosion litters the bottom and can cause trouble with anchors.

Directions

For dangers and clearing marks in the approach see p.61 and the plan on p.60. Corr Rocks, 3 cables NNE of the entrance are most dangerous if approaching from the north or from Loch Sween. The ebb tide divides to run past both sides of the island, and particular care needs to be taken to avoid being set off course

From the north take care to avoid the Corr Rocks lying west of Corr Eilean and aim towards the east side of the entrance to the anchorage to avoid the two rocks which lie ½ cable north of Eilean Mor. The anchorage is small with a very narrow entrance; take the centre of the channel and, when the pool opens out, veer to starboard to avoid the 1·4m rock. Shoal draught boats may be able to continue along the centre of the pool on the old leading line, a white painted cairn just above the shore in transit 194° with the post on the summit of the island, but must take care to avoid the 0·8m rock which lies to the east of this line.

Anchorage

Anchor on the west side of the pool in not much over 2m, using the mooring rings ashore to prevent swinging in the very restricted space. The holding is poor in kelp with many stones and if the anchorage is crowded, as it often is, it is preferable to anchor further out beyond the 5 metre contour where a sandy bottom has been reported. In the pool there is good shelter from all but northerly winds.

Looking over the Eilean Mor anchorage with Corr Eilean beyond and the mouth of Loch Sween in the distance

Tayvallich from the east with Carsaig Bay and the Sound of Jura over the isthmus

Admiralty Chart
2397
Admiralty Leisure Folio
5611.6
Imray Chart
C64
Ordnance Survey
62, 55
Cruising Scotland
p.72

Loch Sween

A picturesque loch, particularly in its upper parts, with several narrow arms running deep among wooded hills.

Tides

There are no strong tidal streams. There is effectively a 'stand' of tide for three hours at high water from −0330 to −0030 Oban, and +0230 to +0530 Oban at low water.

No official figures are available for the rise of tide in Loch Sween; the nearest are for Craighouse: constant −0130 Oban (+0400 Dover) at springs, −0430 Oban (+0100 Dover) at neaps.

Height in metres

MHWS	MHWN	MTL	MLWN	MLWS
1·2	0·9	0·7	0·4	0·3

Directions

The outer approaches to the loch are described on pp.60-61 and for the inner arms of the loch the dangers are described separately under the sub-headings on the subsequent pages.

Approaching from the north part of the Sound of Jura, identify the Lochfoot Rocks (Sgeir Bun an Locha) before turning into the loch. The north end of Corr Eilean in line with the north end of Eilean Mor astern bearing 247° leads southeast of Lochfoot Rocks.

To approach from south, by the east side of Eilean nan Leac, keep close to Eilean nan Leac with Castle Sween in sight open of the island bearing 028° to avoid Flat Rock, drying 0·6

Tayvallich Bay from the west; short stay pontoon slightly left of centre

metres 2 cables southeast of the island; the passage west of Eilean nan Leac is straightforward.

After entering the loch, pass west of the moorings at Castle Sween; there is shoal water inshore both north and south of the moorings. About 3 miles up the loch, identify Sgeirean a'Mhainn (Coffee Rock) and pass it on either side. At high water this rock is not easy to see (although there may be a pole on it), and it is best to keep well to the west side of the loch, so as to avoid Sgeir nan Ron (drying 1·2m) which lies a cable from the east shore, and 4 cables east of Sgeirean a'Mhainn.

Beyond this the main fairway of the loch is straightforward. 4½ miles NNE of Castle Sween the loch divides into three parallel branches, with Loch a'Bhealaich (Tayvallich) half a mile to the west.

Anchorage

Taynish Island provides an occasional anchorage for small boats, with limited swinging room north of this island on the northwest shore of the loch.

Castle Sween An extensive caravan site is situated both south and north of the castle. There is temporary anchorage in the south bay outside the numerous small craft moorings but north of the Castle a shoal extends 1 cable offshore. Shop, launderette and restaurant.

Martin Lawrence

Tayvallich

One of the most perfectly sheltered anchorages on the West Coast, but with several rocks both submerged and above water within. Most of the water deep enough for anchoring is occupied by moorings, but the harbour committee tries to keep two areas clear for visiting yachts to anchor, west and southeast of the central reef. The shores are shoal except on the east side.

Directions

Approach through Loch a'Bealaich avoiding submerged rocks which extend from the north side. The Oib Rocks, which extend furthest south, almost half way across the loch, are marked by a buoy with a S cardinal topmark which must be left to starboard and Quarry Rock is marked by a perch (see plan p.66).

Enter Tayvallich Bay by the more southerly of the two gaps in the outer reef (see diagram below) as the other is foul; turn to port and pass through the moorings leaving Sgeir Dubha (the rocky islet in the middle of the bay) to starboard. A shoal extends a considerable distance south of Sgeir Dubha, and is marked by a small south cardinal buoy which must be left on its south side.

Alternatively, it is possible to pass north of Sgeir Dubha, keeping a small south cardinal buoy (or beacon) marking a submerged rock on the north side of the passage to starboard. However, be aware that there is a rock in this passage with only 1·7m over it and to be sure of clearing this rock hold close to the north side of Sgeir Dubha (see plan).

Anchorage, berthing and mooring

The whole bay is more or less taken up by private moorings and these should not be used without permission. The Tayvallich Bay Association has made provision for visitors by installing three visitors' moorings and leaving space for anchoring. The locations of the moorings and anchoring zones are shown approximately on the plan above.

A wooden pier at the northwest side of the bay is used by fishing boats and visiting yachts should use the short-stay pontoon. This is attached to the pier adjacent to the shop/coffee shop and can be seen in the photograph. This

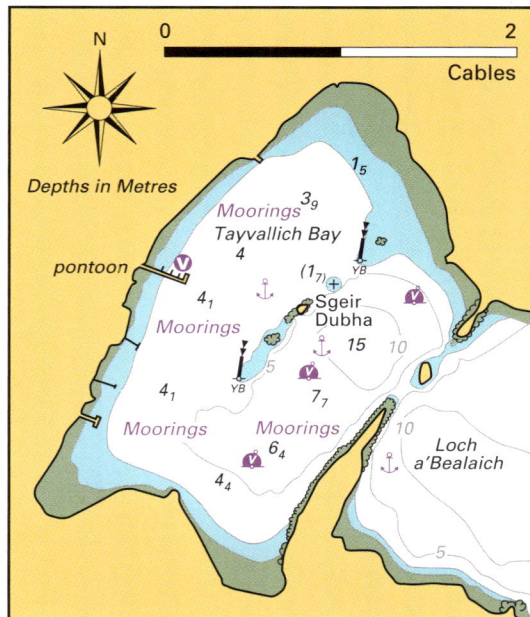

TAYVALLICH BAY

pontoon is owned and managed by the Tayvallich Bay Association and has been extended with two finger berths. The use of the pontoon is subject to the following rules: Maximum stay one hour, no boats to be left unattended, dinghies to be taken to the concrete pier, not left alongside the pontoon. Water is available at the pontoon and there is a collecting box for donations at the head of the pier.

An alternative anchorage is outside the bay to the south of the entrance, but much of the bottom consists of boulders and the holding may not be good in strong winds. It is reported that the bottom nearest to the promontory is slightly better.

Services and supplies

Showers and toilets are available at the shop during opening hours. Coffee shop/grocer/Post Office towards the south end of the village. Water tap at the pontoon. Phone box beside Post Office. Refuse disposal skip beside Post Office. Calor Gas at caravan site at north side of the bay. Tayvallich Inn restaurant ☎ 01546 870282. No fuel.

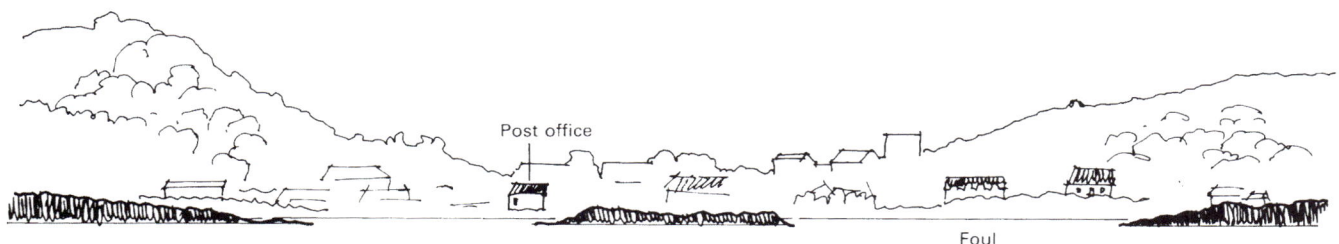

Tayvallich approach

N

Depths in Metres

Caol
Scotnish

8_6
(6)
(1)

7

Arinafad
Rock (0_2)

3

4

Caol
Scotnish

4

0_6

0_8
5_2

Stone jetty
Boat House

4

2_1

Scotnish
Farm

3
(0_2)

5_6

Scotnish Reef
Old pier
(0_2) 2
(0_7)
Scotnish
Rock

2_7

Fairy
Isles

2_6

Sgeir Bhuide

5

Sailean
Mhor

6

Tayvallich

5

Quarry Rock
4_3
Oib Rocks
(0_6)

Loch a'Bealaich

Loch Sween

Sron
Bheith

0   3

Cables

CAOL SCOTNISH AND THE FAIRY ISLES

Martin Lawrence

The anchorage in the Fairy Isles, Loch Sween: probably one of the most sheltered on the west coast

Caol Scotnish

A narrow inlet two miles long and in places only ¼ cable wide with sheer rocky sides; the upper parts are used for fish farming.

Directions

Enter between Oib Rocks, which extend 1½ cables into Loch a'Bealaich from the eastern point of the entrance, and Quarry Rock which extends almost a cable on the western side. The more dangerous Oib Rocks are marked at their extremity by a spherical buoy with a S cardinal topmark and there is a perch on the Quarry Rock.

The main hazards are Scotnish Reef and Scotnish Rock, 3 cables from the entrance and a cable south of the narrowest part. Leave Scotnish Rock, which occasionally covers, very close to starboard, about 10m, on a course which is about halfway between Scotnish Rock and Scotnish Reef (occasionally dries). This passage should never be attempted if Scotnish Rock is covered.

Half a mile beyond a stone jetty on the west side of the narrows, where the kyle opens up, Arinafad Rock (dries 0·2m) just west of mid-channel, is usually marked by a small buoy with a topmark of two balls, but it might be confused with other buoys at the fish farm, particularly if its topmark is missing. Above this point access to the head of the loch is straightforward if the chart is followed.

Anchorage

Anchor in the narrows south of Scotnish Rock. The bottom is thick weed, the holding is only fair and the tide runs at up to 1½ kn. Alternatively anchor in soft mud in the upper loch but beware foul ground where there may be old fish farm tackle.

Fairy Isles

This is a very snug little anchorage in an inlet on the west side of Sailean Mhor, the main arm of the head of the Loch Sween.

Directions

From Sailean Mhor enter through the deep passage northeast of Sgeir Bhuide, the first small island on the west side of the loch, keeping midway between it and the promontory to the northeast until well into the pool to avoid a sunken rock (LD 1·0) lying 40m northeast of Sgeir Bhuide.

Anchorage

Anchor in the middle of the pool northwest of Sgeir Buidhe in 4m. Bottom soft mud. Well sheltered.

The north part of the inlet is shown on the chart as being blocked by the submerged barrier of an abandoned fish farm but it is now reported that this is no longer a hazard. Access to the pool beyond is not recommended without the use of the *Antares* chart which shows a passage with a least depth of 2·3m leading into it.

Occasional anchorages

Achanamara at the eastern arm of the head of Loch Sween, is mostly shoal and occupied by boats on permanent moorings, though space to anchor could be found.

Port Lunna, the inlet north of Eilean Loain, has been cleared of fish farming installations and this provides another place to anchor though soundings are deep until near the head.

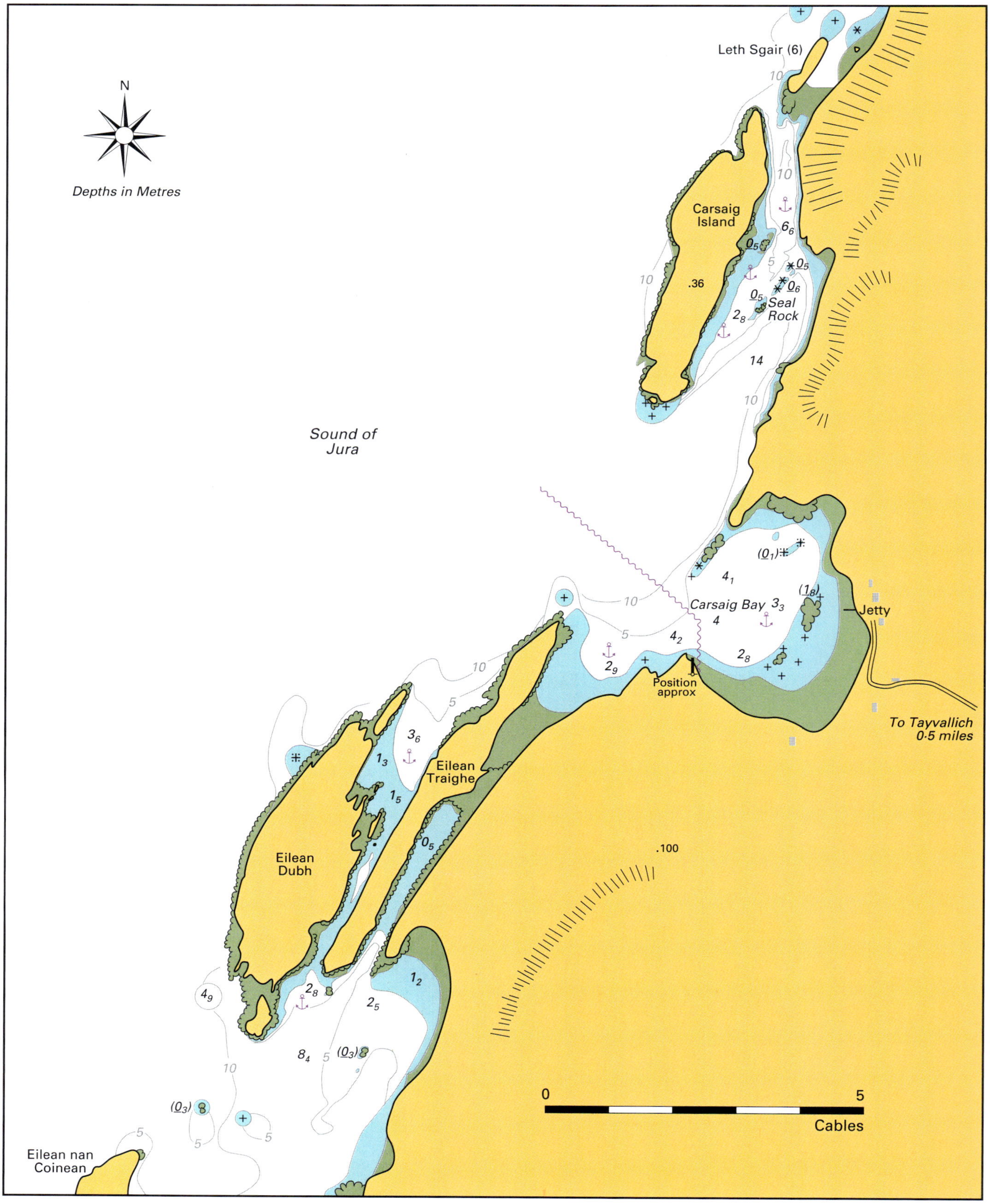

N

Depths in Metres

Leth Sgair (6)

10

10

Carsaig
Island

0.5

6.6

10

0.5

0.5

0.6

.36

0.5

Seal
Rock

2.8

14

10

10

*Sound of
Jura*

(0.1)

4.1

Carsaig Bay 3.3

(1.8)

Jetty

4

10

4.2

5

2.8

2.9

10

Position
approx

*To Tayvallich
0.5 miles*

5

3.6

Eilean
Traighe

1.3

1.5

Eilean
Dubh

0.5

.100

1.2

2.8

2.5

4.9

8.4 5 (0.3)

10

(0.3)

5

Eilean nan
Coinean

5

5

0   5

Cables

CARSAIG BAY ANCHORAGES

Carsaig Bay

This is the only bay between Loch Sween and Crinan with any number of houses and it can also be recognised by the drop in the skyline.

The entrance to the bay is partly blocked by a reef which extends more than halfway across it from the north point in a SSW direction. Rocks in the bay, both submerged and drying, lie up to 2 cables from the shore, and the parts of the bay which are clear of rocks are full of weed. A power cable crossing to Jura runs out in a northerly direction from a beacon on the south shore. For tidal streams see p.55.

Anchorage

There may be temporary anchorage off the jetty, but care must be taken to avoid the many covering rocks. More sheltered anchorage may be had inside the islands at the north and south headlands but if approaching these note the uncharted rocks off the south point of Carsaig Island and the north point of Eilean Traighe.

Carsaig Bay (South) Anchor either just inside Eilean Dubh, just abeam a dip in the island or inside Eilean Traighe, keeping well off Eilean Traighe Point and not going too far in. The latter anchorage is obstructed by moorings. The bottom in both anchorages is sand with good holding, if weed patches are avoided.

Carsaig Bay (North) This is inside Carsaig Island. Approach from the south giving a good berth to the island to avoid rocks off the southern tip. Anchor close to the island but be aware of Seal Rock and those north of it.

North end of Carsaig Island Except in northerly winds, the best shelter is east of the north part of Carsaig Island. Approach from the northwest keeping close to Carsaig Island and well clear of Leth Sgeir, which has drying reefs off its southwest end.

A narrow passage, 3-4 metres deep, connects this anchorage to the south anchorage. Keep close to the mainland shore to avoid the drying rocks that extend more than ¾ of the way across the channel. The tide runs fast here at times.

Occasional anchorages

Eilean Dubh (south) This is in the conspicuous bay a mile south of Carsaig Bay. There are several sunken rocks in the main part of the bay but by holding close to the islet off the south end of Eilean Dubh (see plan opposite) access can be gained to the northern part of the bay where anchorage can be found in 6-8m, mud; a useful alternative to the southern anchorages in Carsaig Bay in northerlies.

Sailean Mor A small bay affording occasional anchorage, lying mid-way between Carsaig and Ardnoe Point, west of Crinan, which can be difficult to identify. Dounie, a large grey house to the north is partially hidden by trees but can be seen from the south. Anchor west of the centre of the bay in 4m. The space for anchoring is limited as the head of the bay shoals a long way out before shelving quite abruptly. Exposed to the north, and subject to heavy northerly swell.

Admiralty Chart
2397
Admiralty Leisure Folio
5611.6
Imray Chart
C64
Ordnance Survey
55
Cruising Scotland
p.72

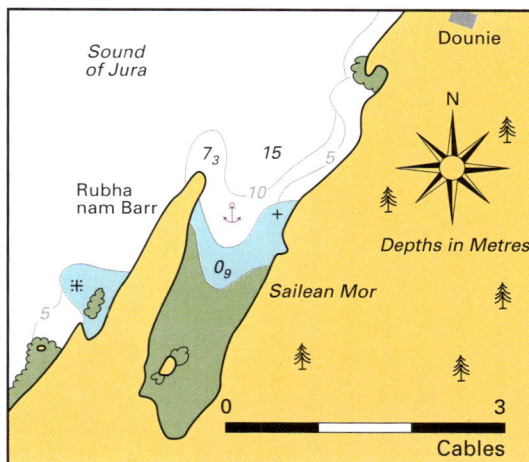

SAILEAN MOR

Valerie Talacko

The anchorage inside the north end of Carsaig Island

5. Loch Crinan to the Firth of Lorn

Admiralty Chart
2326
Admiralty Leisure Folio
5611.12, 14, 16, 27A
Imray Chart
C65, 2800.2
Ordnance Survey
55
Cruising Scotland
p.78

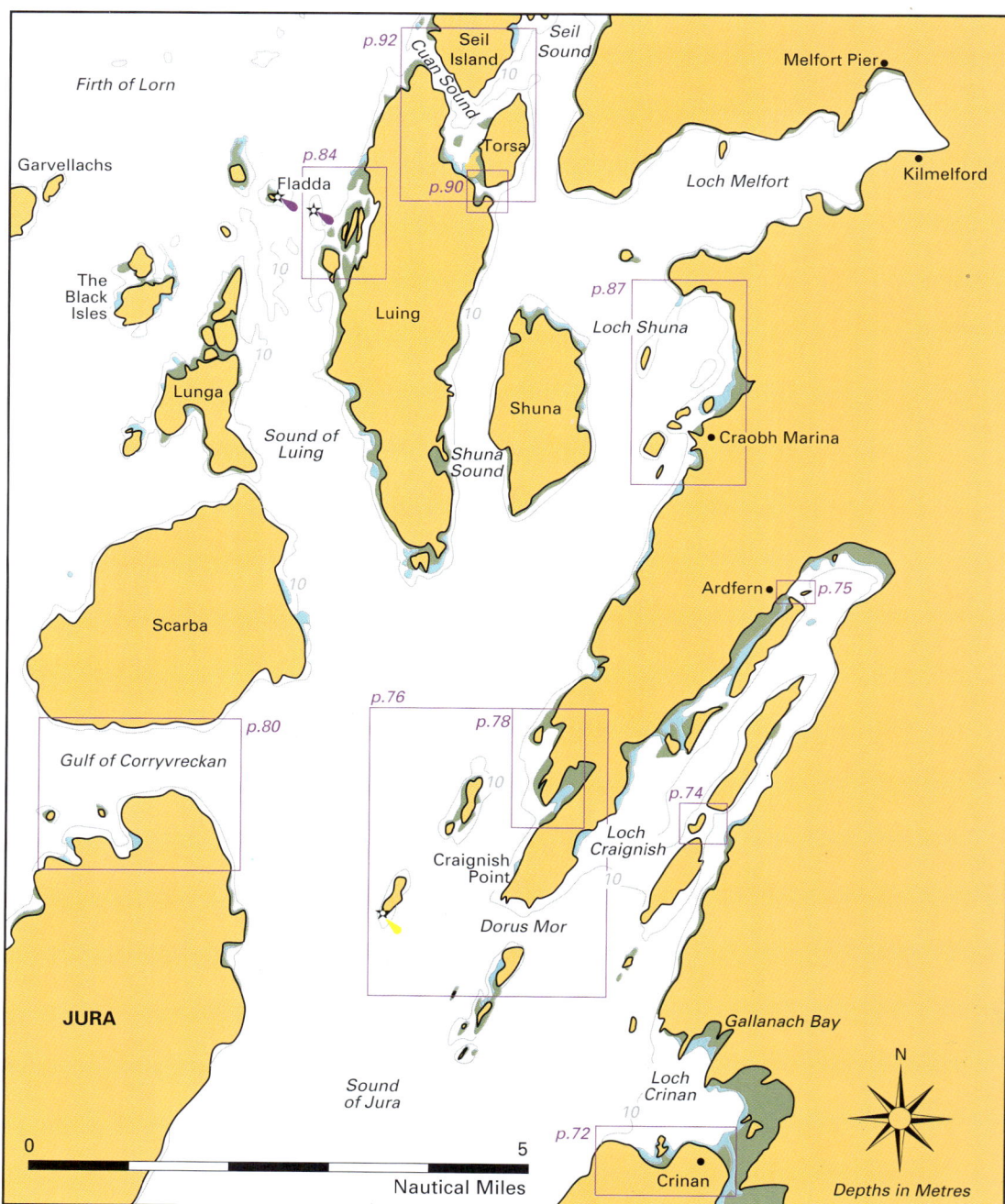

Firth of Lorn

p.92

Cuan Sound

Seil Island

Seil Sound

Melfort Pier

p.84

Torsa

Garvellachs

p.90

Fladda

Loch Melfort

Kilmelford

The Black Isles

Luing

p.87

Loch Shuna

Lunga

Shuna

Craobh Marina

Sound of Luing

Shuna Sound

Ardfern

p.75

Scarba

p.76

p.78

p.80

Gulf of Corryvreckan

p.74

Craignish Point

Loch Craignish

JURA

Dorus Mor

Gallanach Bay

Sound of Jura

Loch Crinan

p.72

Crinan

N

0   5

Nautical Miles

Depths in Metres

LOCH CRINAN TO THE FIRTH OF LORN

John Anderson

Crinan to the Firth of Lorn

Most yachts visiting the west coast will pass through these waters, unless they go to the west of Jura, and Admiralty chart 2326, at a scale of 1:25,000, is essential. There are probably more islands and passages in the area covered by this chart than in any equivalent area off the British mainland. Tidal streams in passages covered by chart 2326 are as strong as most around Britain; there are few artificial marks, and plenty of hidden dangers. However most of the passages are completely sheltered from the open sea and the hazards are easily avoided with care.

Several yacht centres of varying degrees of sophistication have grown up in this area in the last twenty five years and hundreds of yachts are now berthed in these waters. Inshore of a line between Ardnoe, the south point of Loch Crinan, and the south end of Luing the land is relatively pastoral, but the islands west of this line are bleak and rugged and almost uninhabited. The character of the tidal streams differs on either side of the same line; to the east the tides present few problems, but to the west they need close attention.

This chapter begins with Lochs Crinan and Craignish, probably the starting point for the majority of yachts, continues with the passages through the Dorus Mor, Corryvreckan and the Sound of Luing followed by the lochs and sounds to the east of Luing and ends with Cuan and Clachan Sounds which join Lochs Shuna and Melfort to the Firth of Lorn.

Tides

The tidal range inside Jura and the islands northward is little more than two metres at springs but to the west of Jura it is more than three, so that the whole volume of water in the Sound of Jura has to pour out through a few narrow channels on the flood and back again on the ebb; each of these channels has tidal streams at springs of six to eight knots. It is therefore essential to work the tides unless you have a really hefty engine. Full details of these significant tidal streams are given in the subsequent sections.

Looking northwest from above Crinan, across the Craignish Peninsula and up the Sound of Luing towards the Firth of Lorn and Mull

Martin Lawrence

The head of Loch Crinan with the River Add in the foreground

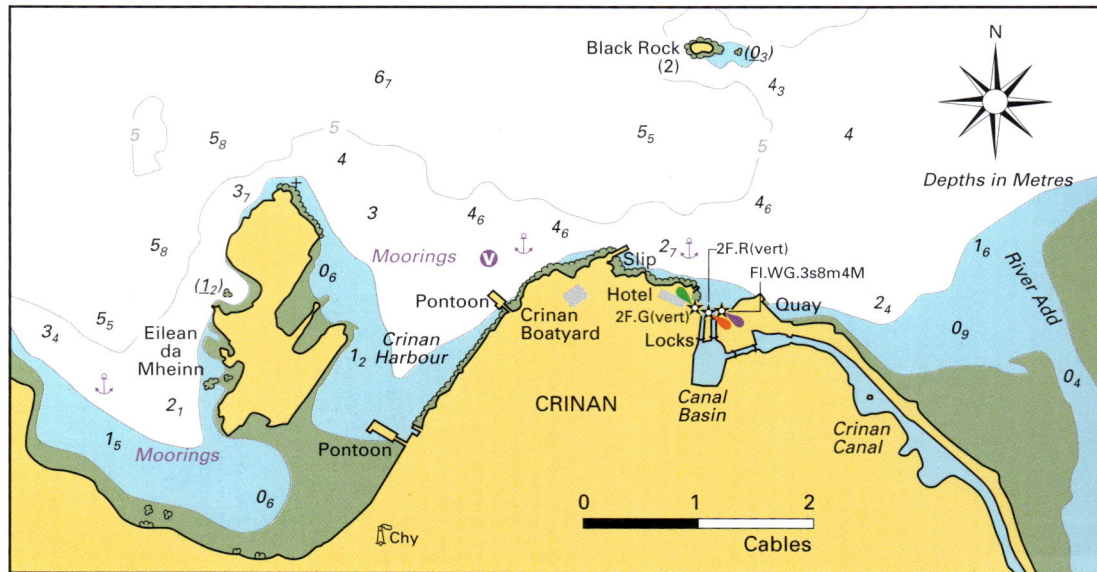

CRINAN HARBOUR
AND THE CANAL

Loch Crinan

Admiralty Chart
2326
Admiralty Leisure Folio
5611.12,
Imray Chart
C65, 2800.2
Ordnance Survey
55
Cruising Scotland
p.78

Loch Crinan is sheltered from the open sea, but because it is shallow quite a steep chop can build up and NW and SE winds can blow stronger in Loch Crinan than in surrounding waters. Leaving Crinan in a fresh northwesterly, do not be deterred from carrying on north as the wind will likely be less strong and more westerly towards the Firth of Lorn.

The moorings and anchorages are exposed to the north and northwest but otherwise reasonably sheltered. Total shelter can be found in the canal basin.

Tides

Constant −0100 Oban (+0600 Dover).

Height in metres

MHWS	MHWN	MTL	MLWN	MLWS
2·4	1·7	1·4	1·1	0·3

Tidal streams east of the 10-metre contour are slight.

Directions

Coming from the south, give Ardnoe Point a berth of ½ cable and from the Dorus Mor make for the Crinan Hotel, a conspicuous white building.

From Loch Craignish either pass southwest of Eilean nan Coinean (Rabbit Island), or east of it, keeping at least a cable off Scodaig, the point of the mainland here, to avoid submerged rocks southwest of the point. A rock half a cable east of Rabbit Island normally stands above water but may be covered by a very high tide. Within the loch the only danger is Sgeir Dubh (Black Rock), north of the canal entrance, with a drying reef extending 1 cable eastwards.

Anchorages

Off the hotel Anchor keeping clear of the approach both to the canal lock and to the quay, poor holding in weed reported. Yachts may berth temporarily at the quay but permission should be obtained from the head lock-keeper.

Crinan Harbour This is full of private moorings but Crinan Boatyard operate about 10 visitors' moorings on the outer trots. Contact Crinan Boatyard VHF Ch 16/12. The boatyard also own a small pontoon where water and diesel may be taken on. Space for anchoring has been left to the northeast of the visitors' moorings and north of the private moorings in the western bay.

Canal Basin Excellent shelter can be found in the basin (see *Crinan Canal* opposite). If the the basin is full, berth in the canal itself above the first lock.

Gallanach Bay opposite Crinan provides a good alternative anchorage to Crinan in northerly winds. Anchor southwest of the islets in 3-4m, sand and weed.

River Add is only suitable for shoal-draught boats, and is then only accessible in quiet weather, although well sheltered once inside (photo p.71). A bar with a least depth of 0·1m lies between drying sandbanks at the river mouth, and the position of the channel at the bar may be marked by two small buoys. It has recently been surveyed by *Antares Charts*.

To enter the river keep Black Rock astern in line with the 10-metre islet at the south end of Garbh Reisa (off Craignish Point) bearing 304°; this should lead to the north side of the channel at the bar. When you have almost run out of water turn to head for the tangent of the west side of the river bank and feel your way in. A pool with a depth of two metres lies off the old ferry slip on the west side.

Services and supplies

Fully equipped boatyard, chandlery and chart agent (Crinan Boatyard). Diesel and water from their pontoon. Launderette and showers at boatyard. Water by hose in canal basin and above lock 14. Calor Gas at chandlery. Skip for refuse in public car park. Diver available locally.

Limited range of provisions at chandlery and at coffee shop; hotel with bar and restaurant, coffee shop beside canal basin. Infrequent bus service to Lochgilphead.

Lights

Light Beacon (east of sea lock) Fl.WG.3s8m4G
Sea lock entrance 2FR(vert) & 2FG(vert)

Communications

Phone box beside canal basin. Post Office at Bellanoch.
Crinan Boatyard VHF Ch 12, 16, Sea Lock VHF Ch 74
WiFi at some moorings
Crinan Boatyard ☎ 01546 830232
Crinan Hotel ☎ 01546 830235
Lock-keeper ☎ 01546 830211
Canal Office (Ardrishaig) ☎ 01546 603210
Yot Spot (Ardrishaig) ☎ 01546 602777
Taxi (Ardrishaig) ☎ 07850 645671

Crinan Canal

Full details will be found in the *CCC Sailing Directions for the Firth of Clyde*, p.78 and a *Skipper's Guide* issued free to users by the Crinan lock-keeper also explains everything very clearly.

Sea lock

The sea lock is normally left open, day and night, and vessels can usually go straight in, unless it is filling or emptying or they are directed to stand off. There is often quite a strong current out of the sea lock from the run-off from the canal, so it is best to get the bow line ashore first; however, if the lock-keeper is standing by to take your lines he may prefer to take the stern line, in which case keep some way on to stem the current and avoid being swung across the lock. Ladders are provided in case there is no one available to take your lines.

Hours of opening

The canal is open seven days a week from May to September, Monday to Saturday during spring and autumn and Monday to Friday during the winter until Christmas. It is frequently closed for repairs during January and February.

In the summer season, times for all locks (including sea locks) are as follows: First locking 0830 - Last locking 1700 with a lunch break from 1200–1230.

In peak season (mid June to mid-August) last locking times for the Crinan sea lock are extended to 1900 on Thursdays through to Sundays. If in doubt exact dates and times should be checked with the Canal Office or try calling Ch 74 during working hours.

Size of vessels

Length overall 26·8m (88ft), beam 6·1m (20ft), draught 2·9m (9ft), maximum air draught under cables 29·2m (95ft).

Canal transit assistance

Vessels requiring assistance with operating locks can obtain this from Yot Spot who can provide it for a charge of £60 per boat, or £42 per boat if more than one are grouped together.

The sea lock and canal basin at Crinan

Charles Warlow

Admiralty Chart
2326
Admiralty Leisure Folio
5611.12,
Imray Chart
Ç65, 2800.2
Ordnance Survey
55
Cruising Scotland
p.82

Loch Craignish

An easily entered, picturesque loch which is divided by a chain of islands running down its east side. The eastern channel is narrower than the main loch but navigable for its full length. The loch contains several good anchorages and the Yacht Centre at Ardfern offers comprehensive facilities.

The two main islands on the east side are Eilean Macaskin and Eilean Righ, and others on the west side are Eilean Dubh and Eilean Mhic Chrion which give shelter to a large lagoon.

Tides

Constant –0100 Oban (+0600 Dover).

Height in metres

MHWS	MHWN	MTL	MLWN	MLWS
2·4	1·7	1·4	1·1	0·3

The height of tide is very much affected by wind and barometric pressure, and a strong southwesterly may raise the tide one metre higher than predicted in tide tables, and a strong northeasterly depress it, although to a lesser extent. Tidal streams throughout the loch are generally no more than one knot.

Directions

The main fairway is almost entirely free from hazards, other than very close inshore, although if coming from Crinan, or tacking, note that a reef along with a group of small islets extends 6 cables SSW of Eilean Macaskin.

East side

A passage the full length of the loch is possible in the channel between the mainland to the east and the group of islands comprising Eilean Macaskin, Eilean nan Gabhar and Eilean Righ.

If entering between Eilean nan Coinean (Rabbit Island) and the mainland shore, Scodaig Point, which is foul to the south and west, should be given a berth of at least 1 cable.

The chart should be studied carefully because of the rocks which abound to the east of Eilean Macaskin, running parallel with the island's shore. The southwest rock is closer to mid-channel than its position on the chart would suggest and the rock shown as *Rep 1969* does exist. Accordingly in this area hold well towards the mainland shore.

There is a shoal bank off the upper east side of Eilean Righ, and a reef which runs out for fully a cable off the island's northeast corner. This ends in a rock which is almost in the mid-channel zone. The mainland shore should be kept aboard till well past this point. There is a passage close to the island, but it should only be attempted with local knowledge.

West side

Sgeir Dubh Mhic Lartai (Black Rock) 0·3m high, lies 1½ cables SSW of Eilean Dubh, with shoal banks extending half a cable to the north and south. Eilean Buidhe is connected to the shore by a drying reef. The passage between Eilean Buidhe and Eilean Dubh is shallow (LD 1·3) and narrow and should not be attempted without local knowledge.

East of the northeast end of Eilean Mhic Chrion, in the approach to Ardfern, Sgeir Dubh, 0·6 metre high, has shoal water southwest and northeast of it, the latter extending a good 1½ cables.

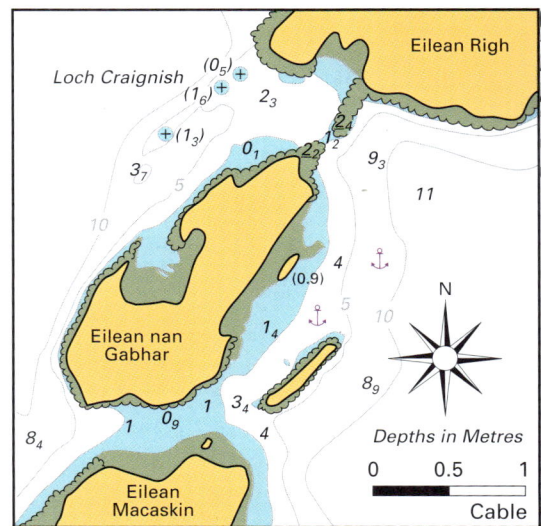

GOAT ISLAND

Anchorages

Goat Island (Eilean nan Gabhar) between Eilean Macaskin and Eilean Righ is a popular place to anchor. The anchorage lies to the east of Goat Island and should be approached from the eastern channel, although local boats do use, above half tide, the shallow passages north and south of Goat Island.

If attempting the northern passage, note the rock (LD 0·5) off the southwest point of Eilean Righ; use of the *Antares* chart is recommended. The passage south of Goat Island has a least depth of 0·9 metre and a bottom of clean sand.

Elsewhere the bottom is sand with some clay and gives good holding over a wide area.

East side of Eilean Righ Anchor in stiff mud and clay at the south end of the bay half way up the island, just north of the jetty and pontoon. Good holding and shelter. The north end is foul with seaweed.

In easterly winds shelter may be found in bays on the east side of the channel, if space can be found clear of the fish cages.

Bagh na Cille on the west side of the loch, about a mile northeast of Craignish Point is a suitable anchorage for quiet weather, but a drying reef lies towards the southwest side of the bay, and a submerged rock with less than 2m lies in the middle of the bay (plan p.76).

The Lagoon (Eilean Dubh) A long pool between Eilean Dubh and Eilean Mhic Chrion and the Craignish peninsula which contains many private moorings. Approach through the narrow channel between Eilean Dubh and Eilean Mhic Chrion.

In this channel, close inshore northeast of Eilean Dubh, there are two small islets with an awash rock east of them in the main channel, so keep well offshore before approaching the passage from the east. Pass midway between the more northerly islet and Eilean Mhic Chrion. An anchorage area for visiting yachts is marked out by lateral buoys between the entrance and the NW shore. There are also two red visitors' moorings; pay at an honesty box by the dinghy landing.

Ardfern Yacht Centre

Ardfern Yacht Centre lies north of Eilean Mhic Chrion. It is well sheltered except from strong northeast winds; many yachts are left on moorings here over the winter. There is almost no space for anchoring as most of the area is taken up with moorings. An apparently inviting space north of the moorings is occupied by a drying rock with a rock awash ¼ cable east of it; these rocks are ½ cable south of the smaller and more southerly of two tidal islets close to the mainland.

Directions

In the approach to the marina note the above-water rock, Sgeir Dubh (0·6), with shoals extending southwest and almost 1½ cables northeast of it. Enter between the pontoon breakwater at the south end of Eilean Inshaig, with a Fl.G.3s light on its south end and a Fl.R.3s buoy close to Eilean Mhic Chrion, which is steep-to. The passage north of Eilean Inshaig, which is east of the moorings, is also straightforward.

Visitors' berths are on the outer pontoons as shown on the plan, or as advised by marina staff. A berth can usually be found alongside.

Space for anchoring is limited but southeast of Inshaig is clear of moorings though a good anchor light is needed here. In easterlies anchor at the head of the loch in the northeast corner.

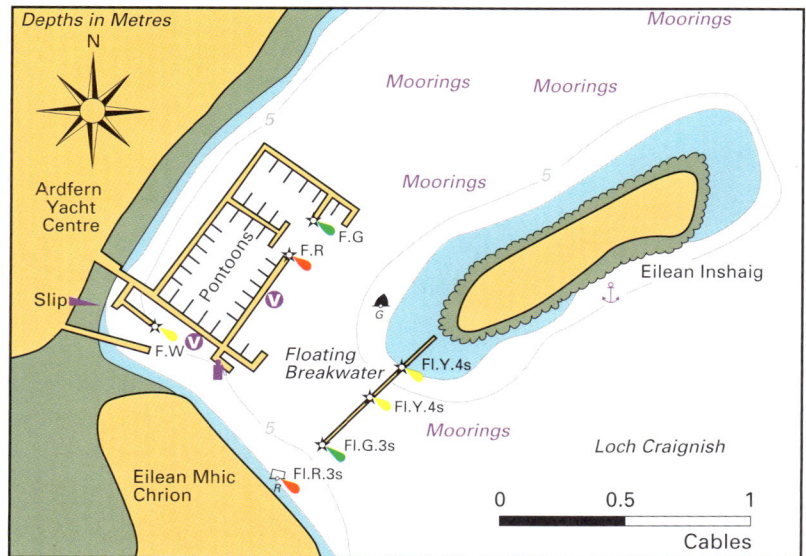

ARDFERN YACHT CENTRE

Services and supplies

Ardfern Yacht Centre provides moorings and pontoon berths, and has a 40-ton mobile hoist and laying up space ashore. Slip for trailer-sailers. All types of repairs. Diesel berth at south end of pontoons. Electricity and water at pontoons; chandlery and Calor Gas. Refuse disposal, showers, laundry. Hotel, restaurant and bar, ¼ mile to the south. Well-stocked shop halfway to the hotel. Infrequent bus to Oban and Lochgilphead.

Communications

Phone box at marina and beside hotel.
VHF at marina Ch 80 during working hours; Ch 16 should not be used.
WiFi at pontoons
Yacht Centre ☎ 01852 500247
Galley of Lorn Hotel ☎ 01852 500284

Loch Craignish from the east with the Craignish peninsula in the middle distance and a yacht anchored off Goat Island, lower right

Martin Lawrence

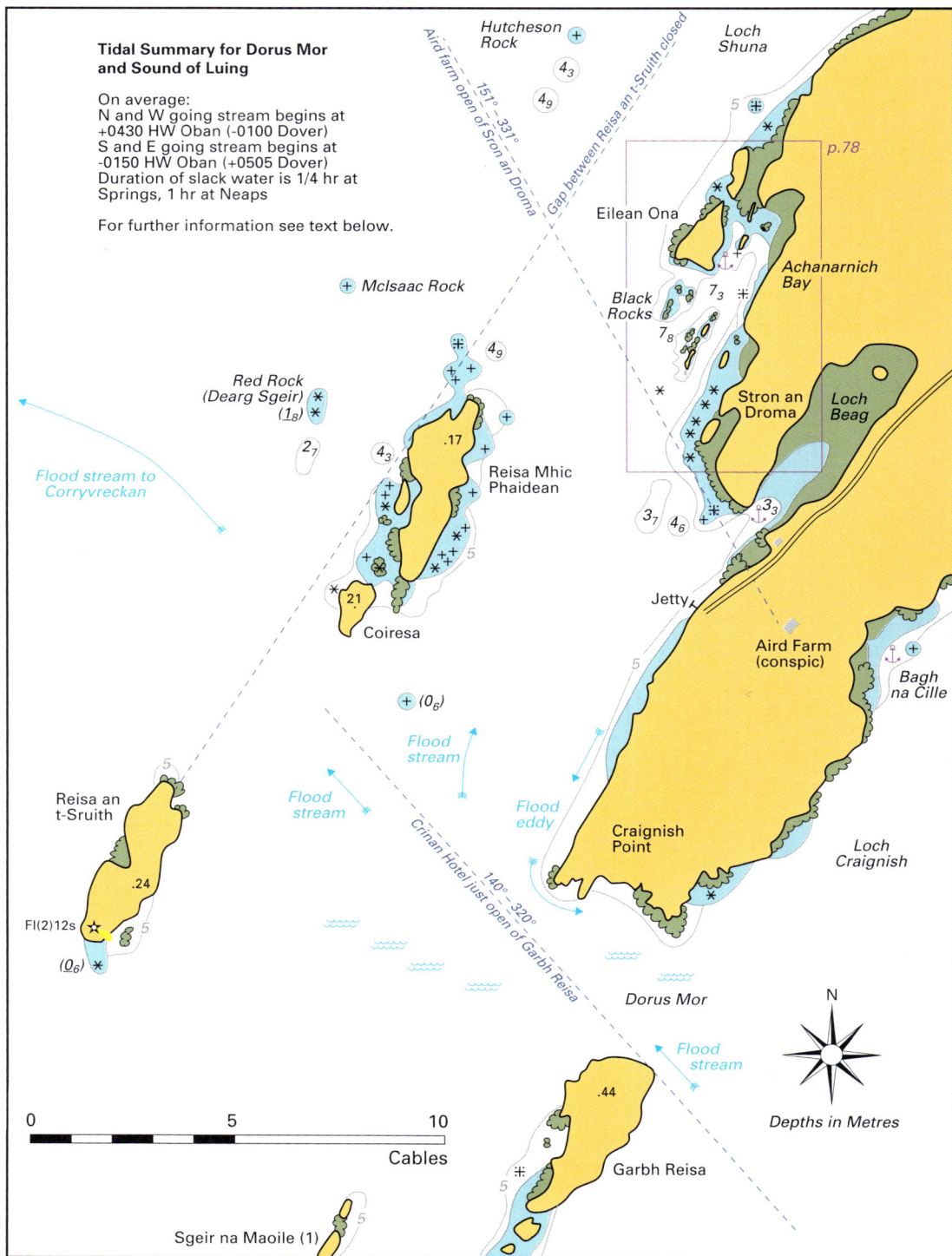

Tidal Summary for Dorus Mor and Sound of Luing

On average:
N and W going stream begins at +0430 HW Oban (-0100 Dover)
S and E going stream begins at -0150 HW Oban (+0505 Dover)
Duration of slack water is 1/4 hr at Springs, 1 hr at Neaps

For further information see text below.

DORUS MOR

Dorus Mor

Admiralty Chart 2326, 2343
Admiralty Leisure Folio 5611.12,
Imray Chart C66, 2800.2
Ordnance Survey 55
Cruising Scotland p.78

The Dorus Mor is a deep, unobstructed channel, 3 cables wide, between Craignish Point and the island of Garbh Reisa. It is noted, not only for the strength of its tidal streams, but also for their complex and fascinating nature. Small whirlpools, patches of deceptive calm, swirls and overfalls are all present in varying degrees, depending on the state of the tide. Full details of the tides are given opposite but a simple tip taken from the old CCC 'Blue Book' is:

'If proceeding north from Crinan through the Dorus Mor, the favourable flood tide will be carried for maximum time if time of departure from Crinan is 1 hour before the GMT of HW Dover. Therefore, when BST is in force, you should leave Crinan at the same hour BST as the GMT of HW Dover. But during or after heavy weather it is advisable to time departure so that the passage from Pladda to Sheep Is. is done as near slack water as possible.'

Martin Lawrence

Sron an Droma

Airds Farmhouse

Tides

Both flood and ebb reach 8kn Sp, 6kn Np, and attain their fastest rate within the first 2 hours of their run. The flood runs from east to west and the ebb from west to east.

The north or west-going stream begins +0430 Oban (–0100 Dover) at springs & +0515 Oban (–0015 Dover) at neaps.

The south or east-going stream begins –0145 Oban (+0515 Dover) at springs & –0100 Oban (+0600 Dover) at neaps.

These times can be advanced considerably by prolonged strong west winds. Turbulence and overfalls are increased, especially when wind opposes tide. The duration of slack water is ¼ hr at springs, 1 hr at neaps.

The flood flows north from the Sound of Jura and west through the Dorus Mor. One part of the main stream flows between Reisa an t-Sruith and Coiresa towards the Corryvreckan. The other part splits into two branches the first of which runs north between Craignish and Reisa Mhic Phaidean, off whose east side a race forms, and the second, when past Coiresa, breaks north towards the Sound of Luing and the remainder towards Corryvrechan. During the flood an eddy runs south down Craignish Point, turning east along the south shore. Turbulence is created where it meets the main west-going stream at the northeast corner of the Dorus Mor.

The flood stream flowing north past the west side of Garbh Reisa also creates a strong eddy which turns east along the north end of this island, but quickly loses strength, creating little disturbance where it meets the main stream. There can be overfalls between the eddies and the main stream and turbulence occurs over the whole area between the Dorus Mor, Reisa an t-Sruith and Coiresa.

The ebb flows east through the Dorus Mor, and is at its strongest on the south side, close to Garbh Reisa. There is a west-setting eddy along the Craignish shore. In its approach the ebb flows south from the Sound of Luing, and east from the Corryvreckan, meeting southeast of Rubha na Una (southeast Scarba) in a long series of tiny overfalls.

The ebb is exceptionally strong down the west side of Craignish, and off the northwest entrance to the Dorus Mor there are heavy overfalls when there is a strong southerly wind. These conditions also produce heavy, confused seas midway between the north ends of Reisa an t-Sruith and Garbh Reisa.

Dangers and clearing marks

Half a mile northwest of Craignish Point, towards Coiresa, lies a submerged rock with 0·6m of water over it. The Crinan Hotel kept just open north of Garreasar, bearing 140°, leads south of it.

A quarter of a mile west of Reisa Mhic Phaidean, Red Rock (Dearg Sgeir) dries 1·8 metres. McIsaac Rock, with less than two

metres over it, is 3½ cables northward of Red Rock. Both of these are cleared by keeping Ruadh Sgeir light beacon (to the south) touching or hidden behind the east side of Reisa an t-Sruith, bearing 191°.

To the east of Reisa Mhic Phaidean submerged and drying rocks on both sides of the channel are avoided by keeping near the middle of the channel. If tacking, a close eye must be kept on the chart or plotter.

Nearly a mile to the north of Reisa Mhic Phaidean lies Hutcheson Rock with less than two metres, over it. A line to pass southwest of the rock is to keep Aird farmhouse open of Sron an Droma at the west side of Loch Beag, bearing 151°. To pass east of Hutcheson Rock keep Reisa an t-Sruith touching Reisa Mhic Phaidean, bearing 211°.

Directions

Going north it is worth planning to be at the Dorus Mor as soon as, or slightly before, the tide turns northwards; another (lesser) tidal gate lies 20 miles further north, at Duart Point, but with reasonable speed through the water a fair tide can be carried to Tobermory. Note carefully the various clearing marks described above, and take care to avoid being carried towards Corryvreckan, especially under sail in light weather.

Going south the tide presents fewer problems except in strong southerly winds when there will be heavy overfalls in some areas between Craignish Point and Scarba. If facing an adverse tide at the Dorus Mor it is possible to take advantage of the eddy by keeping close to Craignish Point and into the bay beyond.

By night or if arriving after dark at the end of a passage, Reisa an t-Sruith and Ruadh Sgeir light beacons in line bearing 188° lead well clear to the west of Dearg Sgeir (Red Rock). You only have a few minutes to identify correctly the lights at Crinan on 140°and to turn to keep them in sight through the Dorus Mor.

Airds Farmhouse open west of Sron an Droma bearing 151° leads south of Hutcheson Rock

Admiralty Chart
2326, 2343
Admiralty Leisure Folio
5611.12
Imray Chart
C65, 2800.2
Ordnance Survey
55
Cruising Scotland
p.78

Achanarnich Bay

Achanarnich Bay is a pleasant anchorage, tucked behind Eilean Ona on the west side of the Craignish peninsula, 1½ miles north of Craignish Point. Both entrances require the utmost caution due to sunken rocks and strong cross-currents.

Directions

The SSW entrance can be difficult to identify, but a slow approach reveals the eastern channel between two lines of long, whalebacked rocks. Take care not to cut the corner when entering the channel between the whaleback rocks and beware the reef extending ½ cable northeast of the last whaleback rock to port. Therefore keep towards the mainland shore before turning towards Eilean Ona to avoid a rock (LD 0·5m) on the mainland side.

Coming from the west, cut across the tide and enter when the south shore of Eilean Ona is just open. From the north beware of a rocky shoal 40m off the island's southwest point. Hold 20m off the island's south shore before opening up the anchorage and turning to port.

Anchorage

A 2m patch lies just south of the long rock in the middle of the inner bay. Anchor where shown on plan in sand and weed between this rock and Eilean Ona, or off the lone boulder on the mainland shore, abreast the long rock. Exposed only to SSW.

Loch Beag 1 mile NNE of Craignish Point provides good anchorage within the entrance in 3-6m. The head dries out for 3½ cables, and a rock (LD 0·8) ¾ cable west of the northern point of the entrance must be watched. Exposed to southwest.

Looking over the Craignish peninsula from the northeast towards the Sound of Luing, Scarba and Corryvreckan

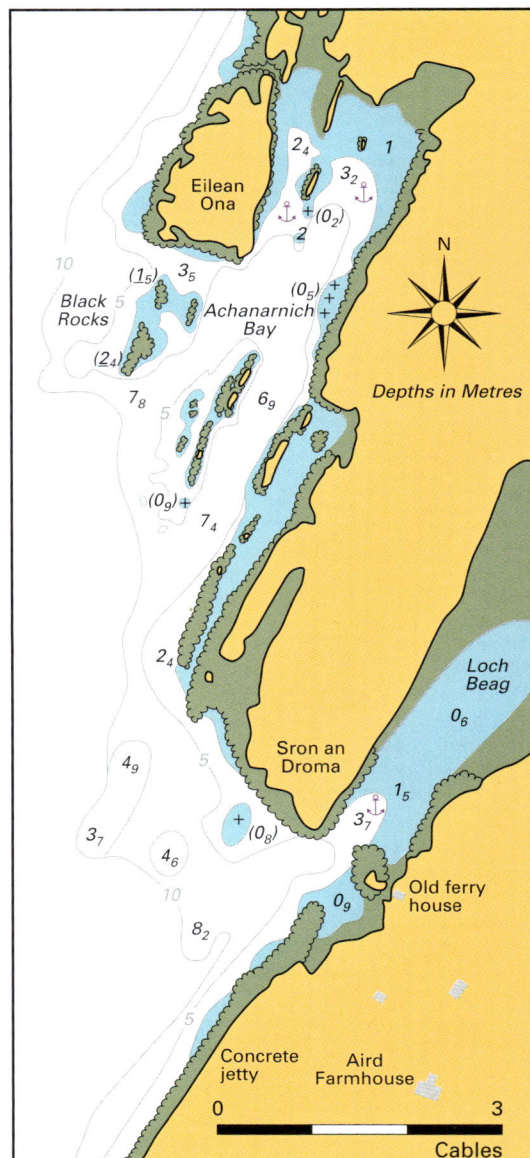

Eilean Ona

Black Rocks

Achanarnich Bay

Depths in Metres

N

Loch Beag

Sron an Droma

Old ferry house

Concrete jetty

Aird Farmhouse

0   Cables   3

ACHANARNICH BAY

John Anderson

A windy day in the Dorus Mor

Achanarnich Bay, on the west side of the Craignish peninsula, from the southwest

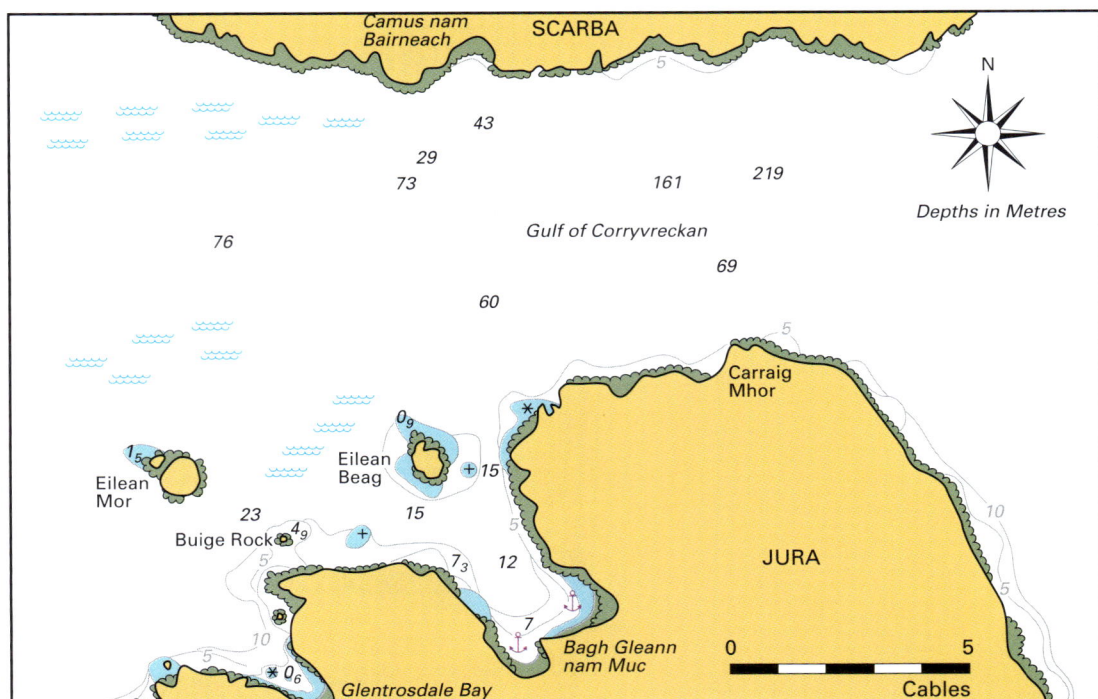

GULF OF CORRYVRECKAN

Gulf of Corryvreckan

Admiralty Chart
2343, 2326
Admiralty Leisure Folio
5611.14
Imray Chart
C65, 2800.2
Ordnance Survey
55
Cruising Scotland
pp.78-80

The Gulf of Corryvreckan, between Scarba and the north end of Jura is one of the most notorious stretches of water anywhere around the British Isles, although it is half a mile wide, with no hazards near the surface. With one significant exception it is more than 100 metres deep for the greater part of its width.

The hazardous nature of this passage is due to three factors: the strength of the current, the turbulence at the boundary of eddies on both sides (and overall whenever the tidal stream is opposed to the wind), and the presence of one rock which has a least depth over it of 29 metres, which is where the famous whirlpool is formed.

The warnings which invariably accompany descriptions of this stretch of water should be carefully heeded. Definite distinctions can be drawn between the flood and the ebb, whether these are springs or neaps, and the prevailing weather conditions. Bearing this in mind, these warnings may be tempered with caution and judicious timing. In calm weather at slack water the whole gulf becomes placid, and gives no hint of its ferocious nature under certain conditions of wind and tide. It is at its most dangerous when an Atlantic swell, having built up after several days of strong west winds, meets a flood tide. A passage at this time would be unthinkable.

Tides

The flood sets through from east to west, and the ebb from west to east. Both reach 8½ kn springs, 6½ kn neaps, in mid- channel, and these rates are attained within the first 2 hours of their run. South winds will raise the levels of tides and north winds will lower them but neither will alter their timing appreciably. This, however can be advanced considerably by prevailing strong west winds. On average the tide changes at the same times as the Dorus Mor and Sound of Luing.

The west-going stream begins: +0430 Oban (–0100 Dover) at springs & +0515 Oban (–0015 Dover) at neaps.

The east-going stream begins: –0145 Oban (+0515 Dover) at springs & –0100 Oban (+0600 Dover) at neaps.

The duration of slack water is ¼ hr at springs & 1 hr at neaps.

The flood surges over the deep, uneven bottom, and is impeded by a high shelf which stretches out from Scarba, ending abruptly at the 29m sounding, 3 cables southwest of Camas nam Bairneach. Above the comparatively shallow shelf the flood gains in velocity, but meets resistance in the water ahead where a backward-rearing overfall is formed which even in calm weather can be 4m high. A heavy westerly swell can double its height. The remaining dangerous overfalls extend 5 miles west up to and beyond the longitude of the Garvellachs.

In quiet weather the water remains smooth during the first 30 minutes of a flood. Turbulence at the shelf begins after 1 hour and lasts almost until the following slack water. It reaches its maximum in a little under 2 hours.

Beware of the flood in a sudden calm preceded by several days of strong west winds. On the last of the remaining swell an overfall can occur north of Carraig Mhor (northern extremity of Jura). Prolonged strong westerly winds can make an overfall, perhaps better described as a solid wall of water, stretch from here and also from the shelf, right across the Gulf.

The ebb: The rise to the shelf from the west end is more gradual than that from the east, and in consequence the overfalls are less severe. There can still be turbulence, dangerous when strong westerly winds have prevailed, off Camas nam Bairneach. In these conditions overfalls can extend from the shelf to the east end of the Gulf.

Directions

The ideal time for a passage is in calm weather at slack water, especially slack water neaps. Both the Jura and Scarba shores are very clean, and can be approached to within 10m if necessary. Eddies close to both shores are strong, but create no great turbulence. A passage should not be attempted with an unreliable engine, all hatches should be closed, and all crew would be well advised to have a lifeline attached if going forward.

However, with careful judgement of the conditions, passages are possible at other times:

From west to east: This poses fewer problems provided the gulf is not approached while the flood is still running and a course between mid-channel and not less than 3 cables off Eilean Mor is followed. If approaching on the ebb from the west of Jura beware of huge overfalls which develop over a shallow patch extending a cable off the northwest corner of Eilean Mor. The passage between Eilean Mor and the Buige Rock is more straightforward.

From east to west: Unless passing through at slack water this passage should only be made in quiet weather and only if you are confident that there is no swell. Keep within 1-2 cables of the Jura shore. With a powerful engine it may be preferable to make the passage against the first or last of the adverse ebb.

A passage with west wind and swell opposing a flood tide should never be attempted. In unsettled weather, or if there are any doubts whatsoever, the gulf should be given a wide berth.

Anchorages

Bagh Gleann nam Muc (The Bay of Pigs) is on the south side of the west entrance of Corryvreckan. The tidal stream provides shelter from any swell, except from northwest at slack water.

Owing to the strength and uncertain direction of the currents among the islands this anchorage should only be approached or left within half an hour of slack water at springs, or within an hour at neaps.

A submerged rock lies in mid-channel between Jura and Eilean Beag. The ground is foul between this rock and Eilean Beag. Keep 20m off Jura

Martin Lawrence

until past Eilean Beag; another submerged rock lies 1½ cables east of Buige Rock. The head of the bay is divided by a rocky promontory; the better anchorage is on its west side.

Bagh Gleann a' Mhaoil on the southeast of Scarba provides temporary anchorage out of the main tidal stream, in which to wait for a favourable tide through the gulf.

Corryvreckan, in a comparatively placid mood, seen from Scarba

Bagh Gleann nam Muc, the eastern anchorage

David Houston

Admiralty Chart
2326
Admiralty Leisure Folio
5611.14
Imray Chart
C65, 2800.2
Ordnance Survey
55
Cruising Scotland
p.81

Sound of Luing

The Sound of Luing, 5 miles long and 1 mile wide, is the direct route north from the Sound of Jura to the Firth of Lorn and it takes a large share of the tidal flow between these bodies of water. Towards the north it is not unlike the Dorus Mor, with its intriguing tidal races. It is clear throughout in mid-channel.

The normal passage north is between Fladda to the west and Dubh Sgeir to the east then heading either NNW to the west of Bono Rock buoy or north, passing to the east of Bogha Ghair buoy as described on p.97.

Tides

On average the tide changes at the same times as the Dorus Mor and Gulf of Corryvreckan.

The north-going stream begins: +0430 Oban (–0100 Dover) at springs & +0515 Oban (–0015 Dover) at neaps.

The south-going stream begins: –0145 Oban (+0515 Dover) at springs & –0100 Oban (+0600 Dover) at neaps.

The duration of slack water is ¼ hr at springs and 1 hr at neaps. Both flood and ebb are very strong, their rates increasing progressively from south to north. From 3kn springs at Ardluing, they reach a maximum of 7kn springs and 5kn neaps, between and among the islands around Fladda.

On the flood a tide race develops north of Rubha Fiola, continuing to the west of Ormsa and Belnahua. There is an eddy on both streams off the Luing shore at Rubha na Lic, to the north of it on the flood, and south of it on the ebb. The Lunga shore is better if going south with the last of the ebb, which continues to run here for approximately 1 hour after the flood begins in mid-channel.

Dangers

At the southeast entrance to the sound, the drying island of Rubh Ard Luing has numerous rocks lying up to a cable off it on all sides. The island should be given a berth of 1½ cables to clear these hazards. Ardluing S cardinal buoy marks the safe passage to the west.

By keeping 1½ cables off the Luing, Scarba and Lunga shores, various rocks and shoals can all be avoided. This safe distance also applies to the island of Eilean Mhic Chiarain and the smaller islands to the northeast. These are all but connected to each other, and in turn to Luing itself, by drying shoals with below and above-water rocks.

Camas a Mhor-Fhir, Lunga, on the west side of Grey Dogs which can just be seen on the extreme left

Donald MacDonald

Two cables northwest of Funaich Mhor is a rock with a possible depth of less than 1·8m over it. A rock with 1·8m over it also has to be watched almost halfway between Rubha Fiola and Fladda.

3 cables WNW of Fladda is the island of Belnahua, with a shoal bank extending 3 cables north, and ending in a rock which dries 0·3m.

Directions

The passage through the Sound of Luing is straightforward enough but eddies and overfalls make it necessary to keep a very close watch on the course at all times, especially under sail in light weather. It is easy to be carried off course and, although the hazards are quite easily avoided in good visibility, they are there and a constant check on position must be kept. In poor visibility very careful chartwork is needed or, if using GPS, a continuous watch on cross-track error should be maintained.

In anything like heavy weather with wind against tide the Dorus Mor and the passage between there and the south end of Luing would be actually dangerous to a small boat. The photograph on p.79 was taken from Craignish Point looking west towards Corryvreckan with a flood tide and a southerly wind about Force 7 (that is, the wind and tide were running the same way).

Anchorage

Poll nan Corran A bay on the east side of Lunga only exposed to the fetch across the sound – holding has been found to be poor, with thick weed. Enter north of the islet there and anchor off the beach. The islet shoals badly to the east where it must be given a berth of fully a cable.

Black Mill Bay on Luing, almost opposite Poll nan Corran, a bay which shoals out for ½ cable. Exposed to the west.

Fladda There is a temporary anchorage on the northeast side of the island, off the slip below the light beacon.

Camas a Mhor-Fhir Temporary anchorage on the west coast of Lunga, enclosed by the southwest headland of Lunga. Useful if waiting for slack water in the Little Corryvreckan. Exposed to southwest.

Cullipool and Poll Gorm see pp.84, 85.

Lights

Ruadh Sgeir Fl.6s13m8M
Reisa an t-Sruith Fl(2)12s12m7M
Ardluing S cardinal buoy Q(6)+LFl.15s
Fladda Fl(2)WRG.9s13m11–9M
169°-R-186°-W-337°-G-344°-W-356°-R-026°
Dubh Sgeir Fl.WRG.6s9m6/4M
000°-W-010°-R-025°-W-199°-G-000°
With these sectored lights a night passage of the Sound of Luing is fairly straightforward.

Martin Lawrence

Grey Dogs

Bealach a' Choin Ghlais on the charts, and sometimes known as the Grey Dogs or Little Corryvreckan, the passage between Lunga and the north end of Scarba is at times more hazardous than Corryvreckan itself. It is less than a cable wide at its narrowest point, with a group of islets and rocks above water in the eastern entrance. The tide runs like a mill race, reaching on flood and ebb 8½ kn springs, 6½ kn neaps, with slack water periods of 15 minutes and 1 hour respectively.

Tides

The flood tide runs westwards, beginning about +0430 Oban (–0100 Dover) at springs; +0515 Oban (–0015 Dover) at neaps.

The ebb runs eastwards, beginning about –0145 Oban (+0515 Dover) at springs; –0100 Oban (+0600 Dover) at neaps.

However, even locals say that it is difficult to forecast, to within an hour either side of the expected time, when it will turn.

The spring rate is about eight knots. Strong eddies, and standing waves in the fairway, arise, particularly at springs, and of course there is much less space to manoeuvre than in the Gulf.

Except at slack water the eddies make it very difficult to keep a boat under control, and the ebb is more dangerous in that it tends to set a boat onto the islets.

Directions

It should be attempted only in quiet weather at or near slack water, keeping 10-20m off the clean Scarba shore to avoid the islets in the middle. Due to the velocity of the tide, the narrowness of the channel, and the restriction caused by the islets in the middle, manoeuvrability is all but impossible, except at slack water. It should be treated at all times with the same caution as the Gulf of Corryvreckan. If necessary, wait on the east side just north of a jetty half a mile south of the north end of Scarba, or on the west side at Camas a' Mhor-Fhir, a deep inlet on the southwest side of Lunga.

Grey Dogs with standing waves at the height of a spring flood

Grey Dogs from Scarba. A prawn-fisherman going west with a flood (west-going) spring tide has hit the east-going eddy which runs at 6-8 knots

Martin Lawrence

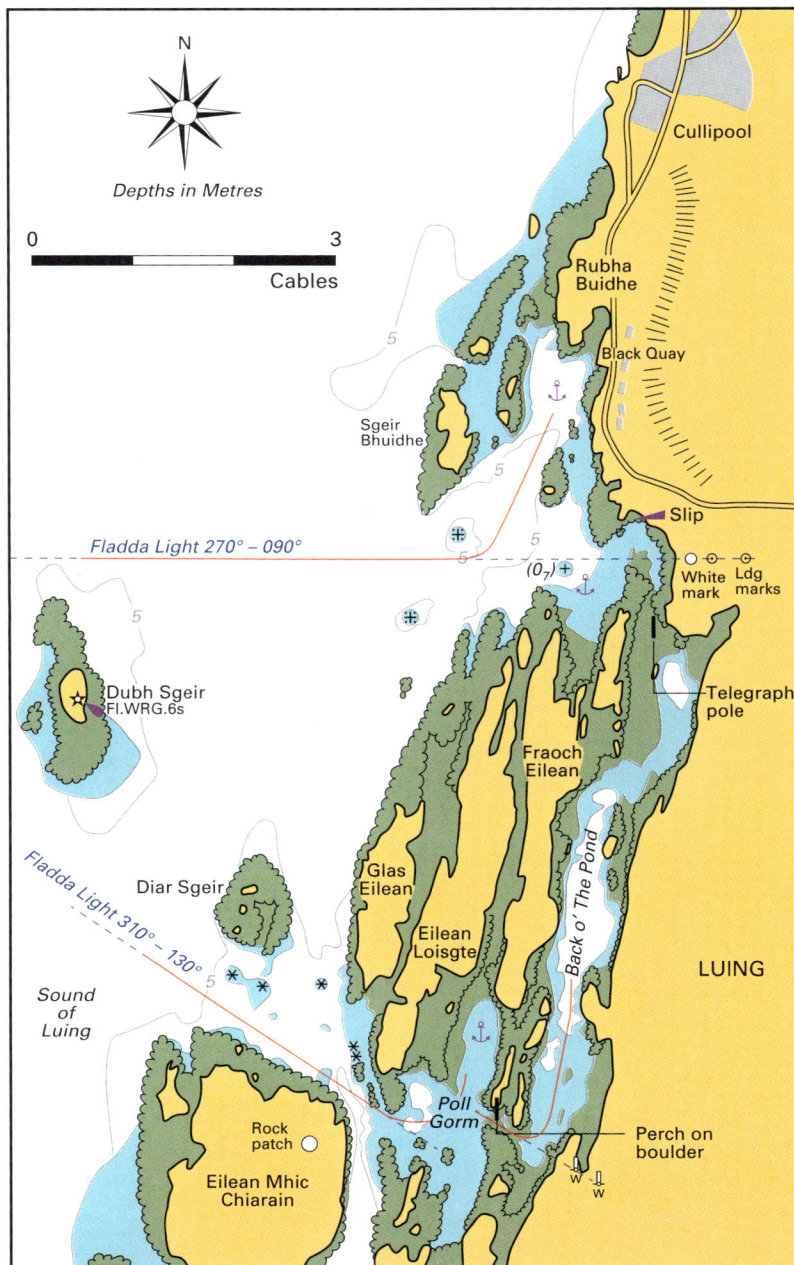

**CULLIPOOL, POLL GORM
& BACK O' THE POND**

Admiralty Chart
2326
Admiralty Leisure Folio
5611.14
Imray Chart
C65, 2800.2, 3
Ordnance Survey
55
Cruising Scotland
p.81

Cullipool

To the south of Cullipool, an old slate mining village on the northwest of Luing, the many islets and rocks enclose several occasional anchorages. The majority of these are best approached at slack HW and, even then, only by vessels drawing less than about 1·2m as they are within the labyrinth of shallow, and very narrow, channels leading to the Back o' the Pond, a well protected pool giving shelter to local lobster boats and their catch.

The area has been surveyed by *Antares Charts* and it is strongly recommended that their chart, being to the largest scale and the most up to date, is used in conjunction with these *Directions*.

Tides

Firth of Lorn (as Carsaig, Mull)
Constant −0010 Oban (−0540 Dover).

Height in metres

MHWS	MHWN	MTL	MLWN	MLWS
4·1	3·1	2·4	1·8	0·6

Directions

From the west approach with Fladda lighthouse bearing 270° astern, keeping the beacons (triangular topmarks) and white paint mark on the shore bearing 090°. Note the awash rock to the north and also the uncharted rock (LD 0·7) lying very close south of the leading line and almost due north of the northern tip of Fraoch Eilean.

Unless intending to anchor in the inlet to the northeast of Fraoch Eilean, there is no need to go as far east along the leading line as the 0·7 rock, as access to the Back o' the Pond through the northern entrance is not advisable without local knowledge. The channel leading to it is narrow and rocky and dries throughout, in places almost to 2m. Local fishing boats use it but only at HW.

Anchorages

Black Quay lies south of Rubha Buidhe. From the west hold onto the leading line described above until the passage west of Rubha Buidhe is clearly open, to avoid the rock awash a cable south of Sgeir Bhuidhe. Steer with Rubha Buidhe bearing about 011° to pass close west of the skerries south of the point and anchor between the quay and the skerries southwest of it in about four metres, black mud. The tide runs through the anchorage at about one knot. This anchorage is very congested with local moorings but to the south of it there are some visitors' moorings which are maintained by the community.

Fraoch Eilean Anchor in the mouth of an inlet between Fraoch Eilean and the islet northeast of it. Take care not to turn into the inlet until it is fully open so as to avoid the 0·7m rock mentioned above.

Poll Gorm Virtually whole of this inlet is within the 1m contour and it is mainly of interest to shoal draught boats. Approach on a course of 130° with Fladda bearing 310° astern taking care to compensate for any cross tide, although it is much better to wait for slack HW. Pass 25m off the north side of Eilean Mhic Chiarain and, as the coast trends south, a light coloured outcrop of rock appears on the slopes of Eilean Mhic Chiarain. When about 75m beyond this, head approximately east until about a cable east of Eilean Mhic Chiarain when Poll Gorm will be fully open to the north. Turn into the anchorage, keeping well clear of rocks on the west side, and anchor so as to leave clear access to the lobster pond to the north of the pool. Shelter is excellent but the tide runs strongly in the approaches.

Martin Lawrence

Back o' the Pond The pool known as Back o' the Pond lies east of Fraoch Eilean and should be approached from the south but, as with Poll Gorm, not by vessels drawing more than about 1·2m. The very narrow, drying, channel leading to it may be marked by a perch on a boulder at the south end of a low rocky spit at the entrance. Leading marks, two white posts, on the Luing shore may also be visible but they are not well maintained.

Follow the directions above for entry to Poll Gorm until either the perch or at least one of the leading marks can be picked up. Head for the leading marks on a course of 118° and aim to shave the perch very close to port and then follow the channel, which is visible between rocks, to the southeast. Once through the channel turn to port and proceed carefully towards the north. If neither the perch nor any of the leading marks can be seen it would be advisable to anchor in Poll Gorm and make an exploratory trip in the dinghy, but beware of a strong tidal set if it is not slack water.

Once in the anchorage, deeper water lies towards Cullipool and anchorage may best be found at the north end. The pool is very sheltered.

Poll Gorm, lower right, from the northeast. White arrow indicates the line of the channel through to the south end of the Back o' the Pond

H King

Cullipool from the north end of Luing at a low spring tide. Note all the drying rocks in the approach to Cullipool

Martin Lawrence

Clearing line for the Culbhaie Rocks coming from the south. Kilchoan Farm is the white building in the centre and Eilean Creagach is on the right

Admiralty Chart
2326
Admiralty Leisure Folio
5611.12, 16
Imray Chart
C65, 2800.2,
Ordnance Survey
55
Cruising Scotland
p.84

Loch Shuna and Shuna Sound

The area east of Luing is sheltered except from strong southerly winds, and the surrounding shores are rather more gentle in character than much of the rest of the coast. Craobh marina with a residential development stands on the east shore.

Tides

Loch Beag
Constant –0100 Oban (+0600 Dover).

Height in metres

MHWS	MHWN	MTL	MLWN	MLWS
2·4	1·7	1·4	1·1	0·3

Seil Sound
Constant -0025 Oban (-0555 Dover).

Height in metres

MHWS	MHWN	MTL	MLWN	MLWS
2·7	2·0	1·6	1·1	0·4

Tidal streams are generally negligible except in Shuna Sound where they reach one knot on the flood and two knots on the ebb.

Dangers and marks

At the south entrance to Loch Shuna, Culbhaie, a group of rocks ¼ mile off the east shore, dries 1·5 metres with other rocks within ½ cable of its west side. These are cleared to the west by keeping Kilchoan Farm, a conspicuous white house on the north side of Loch Melfort bearing 011°, open west of Eilean Creagach, which is about a mile south of Arduaine Point (see photo above). Heading south the east side of Reisa an t-Sruith bearing 208°, open of the west side of Reisa Mhic Phaidean, clears the west side of Culbhaie (see sketch below).

The passage between Shuna and the two main islands to the east is clean except for a rock awash ¾ cable due north of Sgeir Creagag (2) on the northeast side of Shuna. East of these islands careful attention to the chart is needed, although a direct passage from southward of Eilean Creagach to Craobh Marina or to Asknish Bay is straightforward. The dangers here are described opposite.

Shuna Sound is generally clean on the Shuna side, but there are rocks off the Luing shore both submerged and drying, notably off its south end and off a drying bay a mile north of the south end; keeping outside the 15-metre contour clears these.

A mile north of Shuna, Scoul Eilean has a rock awash one cable south of its south end and a submerged rock close southeast of the island. Degnish Point at the south of the entrance to Seil Sound has several drying and awash rocks up to ¾ cable off off its west and south sides.

Directions

From the south see Dorus Mor (pp.76–77). Note the clearing marks described above to avoid Culbhaie which dries 1·5 metres, ¼ mile from the east shore. Pass between Shuna and the islands to the east of it, or through Shuna Sound, to the west of Shuna.

From the west – unless coming through Cuan Sound – keep two cables off Ard Luing, or outside the 15-metre contour to avoid rocks inshore. To the north of Shuna and the Arduaine peninsula note the various hazards described above under the heading 'Dangers and marks'.

If waiting here for a fair tide in the Sound of Luing, there is a temporary anchorage off a bay ¼ mile north of Ard Luing – not the bay one mile north of the point, in the mouth of which there are many rocks.

Anchorages

In Shuna Sound

Bagh na h'Aird (Ard Bay) at the southeast corner of Luing. Temporary anchorage 1 cable off-shore.

Kilchattan Bay or Toberonochy. On Luing shore 1¾ miles north of the south end of the island. Anchor in the bay north of the village and well offshore as it is shoal all round. Anchor clear of the moorings, of which there are quite a few.

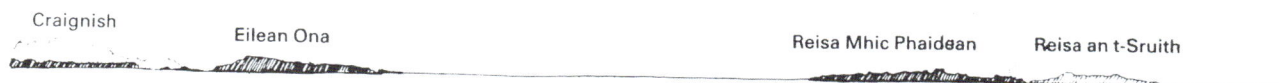

Craignish   Eilean Ona   Reisa Mhic Phaidean   Reisa an t-Sruith

Culbhaie clearing mark - Reisa an t-Sruith just open west of Eilean Mhic Phaidean leads west of Culbhaie 208°

North end of Shuna Island Anchor in a small bay just inside the point. Do not go beyond a stone quay to starboard, as there is less than 2m here. Beware of a rock ½ cable north off the eastern point. Holding ground is reported as firm mud provided weed is avoided.

In Loch Shuna

Poll na Gile This bay lies on the east side of Shuna Island and provides good anchorage south of the fish farm.

Bagh an Tigh-Stoir (East of Eilean Arsa) In depth 3m. Good shelter from northeast to southeast.

Asknish Bay Approach from the south, but take care to avoid the drying rocks three cables off the east shore.

A line of drying rocks, Eich Donna, extends three cables SSW from the Arduaine peninsula towards Eilean Creagach, and a drying reef extends more than half a cable NNE from the islet at the north end of Eilean Creagach with a clear passage 2½ cables wide between the reef and Eich Donna. Some local yachtsmen use a passage between the most northerly rock of Eich Donna, which dries 1·5 metres, and Arduaine, keeping about 20 metres from the shore.

Anchor as convenient, clear of moorings in sand and weed; or, if visiting the hotel, use one of the moorings provided for visitors. The best landing is in a crack in the rocky promontory south of the hotel.

An alternative anchorage north of Arduaine (see p.88) is preferable in southerly winds.

Loch Melfort Hotel has a restaurant and provides bar lunches and showers. ☎ 01852 200233.

Craobh Marina

The former anchorage known as Craobh Harbour (pronounced 'Croove') has been transformed by the construction of causeways between the shore and off-lying islands to provide a well-sheltered marina with full shoreside facilities.

Directions

From the west, leave the green conical buoy north of Eilean an Duin to starboard.

From the north beware of an extensive patch of drying and submerged rocks lying 2½ cables north of Eilean Buidhe with many drying rocks lying inshore and to the NNE of Eilean Buidhe.

Pass between the breakwaters and immediately inside the entrance, on the port hand, a line of red can buoys marks submerged rocks on the east side of the harbour.

In the bay on the west side of the harbour a drying reef projecting more than half the width of the bay from its north side is marked by a perch.

Lights

A sectored light beacon stands on the head of the east breakwater, Iso.WRG.5s.10m5-3M showing white from 162° to 183°.

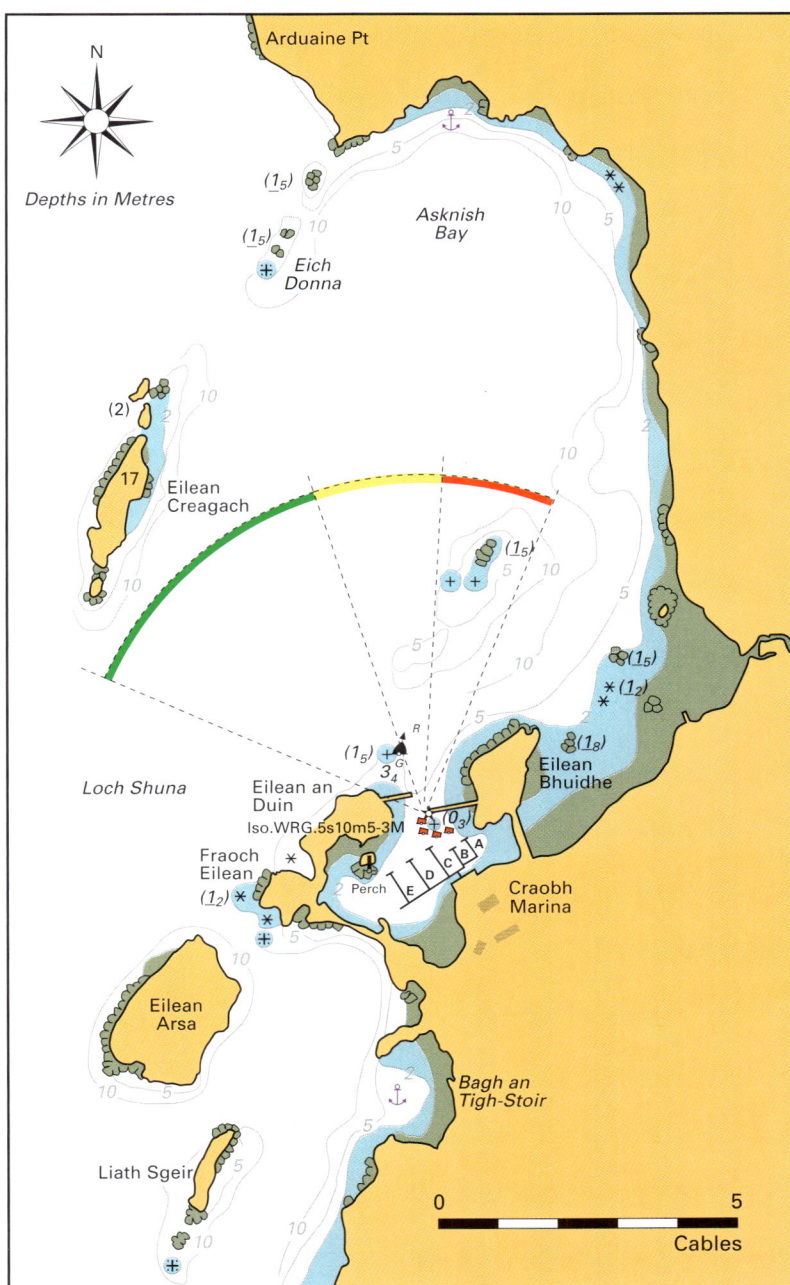

CRAOBH MARINA

Services and supplies

Pontoon berths, boatyard with slip and mobile hoist. Divers, refuse disposal, showers, launderette. Water, diesel, Calor Gas, chandlery. Hotel, pub/restaurant, shop (essentials only). Limited bus service to Oban.

Communications

Craobh Marina ☎ 01852 500222
VHF Ch 37 and 80 call sign *Craobh*.
Phone box.

Craobh Marina from the east

The moorings in Fearnach Bay, Loch Melfort, looking SSE across to Loch na Cille and Kilmelford Yacht Haven

Loch Melfort

Loch Melfort is the northeast branch of Loch Shuna and lies north of the Arduaine peninsula. It is another attractive, sheltered loch and, with a long-established boatyard at its head, it is home to many yachts.

Directions

Campbell Rock, in the middle of the loch, has 1·8 metres over it but for most boats this would rarely be a hazard. The south side of Eilean Gamhna touching the north point of Shuna 245° leads southeast of Campbell Rock.

On the north side of the loch, Eilean Coltair has a drying reef extending one cable from its south end and a drying rock one cable from its east side. A rock two metres high stands 3½ cables east of Eilean Coltair.

Other hazards in Loch Melfort lie within half a cable of the shore, or within bays and anchorages where they will be referred to separately.

Anchorages

North Asknish Bay, a bay ½ mile ENE of the west point of Arduaine (Asknish) Point. A rock, drying 1·6m, lies close inshore about 1½ cables east of the western point of the bay. Other rocks shown on Chart 2326 have been found not to exist. Anchor in 7m, east of the moorings and clear of the fish farm.

Kames Bay on the south side of the loch, nearly two miles from Arduaine Point, lies behind a promontory on which stand several bungalows facing west. On the south side of the bay a concrete pier stands at the end of a small promontory.

A reef, with intermittent heads just submerged, extends 1½ cables northwest of the pier. Some of the bay is occupied by fish cages. Much of the southwest bight of the bay dries but an area of deep water lies between the reef and the drying foreshore, although most of the best water is taken up by moorings. There is said to be space for a few visiting yachts to anchor at the south end of this bight.

Keep away from the pier (even with dinghies) as it is heavily used by the fish farm's workboats.

Kilmelford Yacht Haven

The head of the loch, Loch na Cille, dries off for two cables, and the inlet is full of moorings, some of which are available for visitors who should contact the Yacht Haven.

Directions

At the entrance to Loch na Cille a red perch with a red can topmark stands on the end of a reef on the north side, and a green perch with a green triangular topmark marks a rock awash on the south side of the inlet. This perch can be difficult to identify as it is often surrounded by moored yachts.

Services and supplies

The pier, on the south side, has a floating pontoon with diesel and water. Chandlery, Calor Gas, repairs to engine, hull and rigging. Moorings for hire; slipping, and winter storage ashore. Shop, Post Office, telephone, and hotel at Kilmelford, one mile.

Communications

Kilmelford Yacht Haven ☏ 01852 200248 VHF Ch 80
Cuilfail Hotel, Kilmelford ☏ 01852 200274

Fearnach Bay and Melfort Pier

Fearnach Bay is a wide bay on the north side of Loch Melfort, open to the south and southwest but usually comfortable in most summer weather. There is a small development of holiday houses around the pier and there are several visitors' moorings for hire.

In the approach to the bay a newly-charted rock with a LD of 1·7m lies more than ½ cable southwest of Rubh' Aird an Sturra. A drying rock lies ½ cable off the west side of Fearnach Bay and the northeast corner dries out for at least a cable.

Services and supplies

Short term berthing is available at a pontoon alongside the pier, depth 2m approximately. Alternatively berth at the pier itself in one metre. Yachts may dry out alongside the inner end of the pier for repairs (within the limitations of the tidal range); ask first at the office. Space is reserved for visiting yachts to anchor off the pier.

Water at the pier. Shower room, laundry and telephone. Moorings for hire (up to 17m outer trot, 6m inner trot, enquire at office).

Restaurant (The Shower of Herring) ½ mile east of the pier, shop, Post Office, telephone, and hotel at Kilmelford, 1½ miles.

Communications

Melfort Pier and Harbour ☏ 01852 200333
Shower of Herring restaurant ☏ 01852 200345

Melfort pier; the pontoon is on the far side of the pier and the small harbour, for dinghies only, is further to the right

Admiralty Chart
2326
Admiralty Leisure Folio
5611.16
Imray Chart
C65, 2800.3
Ordnance Survey
55
Cruising Scotland
p.84

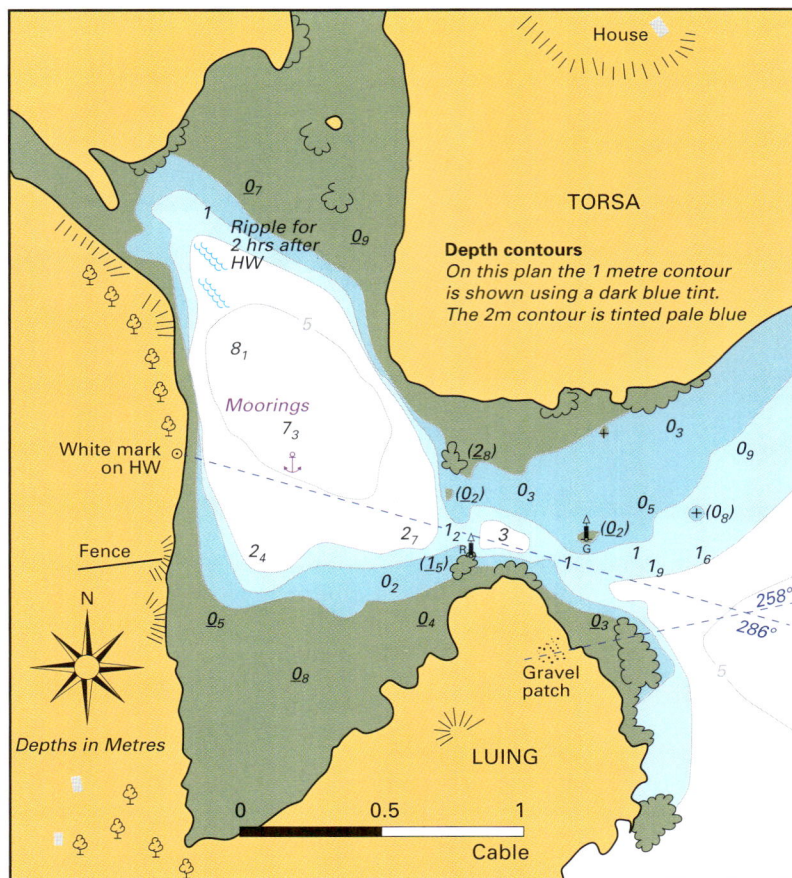

Tide

Constant -0020 Oban (-0550 Dover).

Height in metres

MHWS	MHWN	MTL	MLWN	MLWS
2·7	2·0	1·6	1·1	0·4

Directions

Consult the sketch plan carefully, noting the reef (dries 0·3m) east of the gravel patch and the extensive shoal area and rock ledge off Torsa, also the positions of the two perches; the outer G one marking the centre of a drying 0·2m reef and the inner R perch (established 2007) standing on the rock (dries 1·5m) on the south side of the entrance to the pool. Neither perch stands on the edge of the rock it is marking.

From the south, with Scoul Eilean astern, head towards the house on Torsa bearing 330° until the white painted mark on a rock face on the west side of the pool shows clearly between the two perches, bearing 286°, then turn in and head for the mark on this bearing. Keep not less than 20m south of the outer perch and aim to pass 15m north of the inner perch.

From the north do not head for the entrance channel until the gravel patch bears 258° to avoid the considerable shoal area off Torsa. Head for the shore south of the entrance, noting the reef, and follow the above directions when the white mark bears 286° as above.

When entering or leaving the anchorage the deepest water in the narrow passage between the inner perch and the rocks to the north of it will be found by keeping the outer perch in transit with the far south point of the Degnish peninsula (not Degnish Point itself as shown on chart 2326).

Anchorage

Anywhere north of a line between the entrance and a track at the south end of the bay. South of this the bay shoals. The north quarter of the bay may be affected by tide running from Cuan Sound. Holding is sometimes poor in weed.

ARDINAMIR

Ardinamir

Admiralty Chart 2326
Admiralty Leisure Folio 5611.16
Imray Chart C65, 2800.3
Ordnance Survey 55
Cruising Scotland p.84

A popular anchorage with a notorious narrow entrance, lying between the islands of Luing and Torsa, south of Cuan Sound. For many years now, the anxiety engendered by the difficult entrance has been relieved by the erection of two perches by the CCC. Even so, there is barely a 1m in the entrance, south of the outer perch, and only 1·2m depth north of the inner perch so access is not possible for many yachts at or near LW.

Ardinamir from the southeast; the green, outer, perch can just be seen. The inner one is now red and on the rock on the south side of the entrance

Martin Lawrence

Seil Sound

Entered between Degnish Point and Torsa, Seil Sound runs north between Seil and the mainland, and narrows abruptly to become Clachan Sound.

Tides

Constant –0025 Oban (–0555 Dover).

Height in metres

MHWS	MHWN	MTL	MLWN	MLWS
2·7	2·0	1·6	1·1	0·4

Directions

Rocks at the north end of Torsa, both awash and submerged, lie between one and two cables NNE of En na h-Eaglaise and must be watched, especially if heading for Cuan Sound (p.93). Drying rocks extend a cable SSW of Ardmaddy Point on the east side of the sound. None present a problem if a mid-channel course is kept.

The channel east of Eilean Tornal is clean except for a submerged rock nearly a cable ESE of the south end of the island. Two cables beyond the north end of the island drying and above-water rocks lie on both sides of the passage.

Balvicar Bay

This perfectly sheltered anchorage lies halfway up the east side of Seil Island. Enter midway between the point to the south and the island of Eilean Tornal to the north. Keep mid-channel and do not go north of the mooring area as the bay shoals out for 3 cables.

Anchorage

Mooring is preferable to anchoring and visitors moorings may be available on application to the boatyard. If anchoring use a trip line and take care to ensure good holding on the slate bottom.

Services and supplies

Balvicar Boatyard ☎ 01852 300557 on the south side of the bay has toilets and showers. Slip and winter storage up to 20m (in open), 10 and 40 ton hoists, 15-ton crane. Full boatyard facilities (including undercover repair shed) Hull, electrical and engine repairs available.

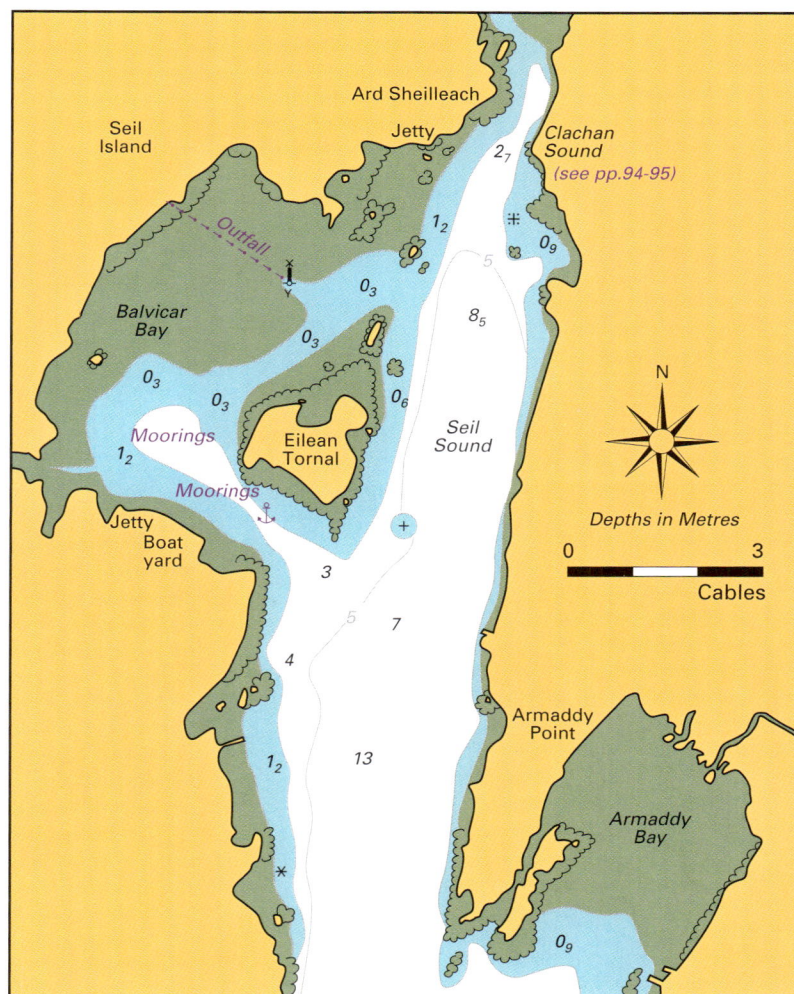

Balvicar village has shop, calor gas, Post Office, public telephone and 9-hole golf course. Clachan village (2½ miles north of Balvicar) has petrol, diesel, pub and restaurant. Buses to Oban. It is possible to reach Clachan pub by dinghy from Balvicar (see pp.94-95).

BALVICAR BAY

Balvicar Boatyard from the northeast; Eilean Tornal in the foreground

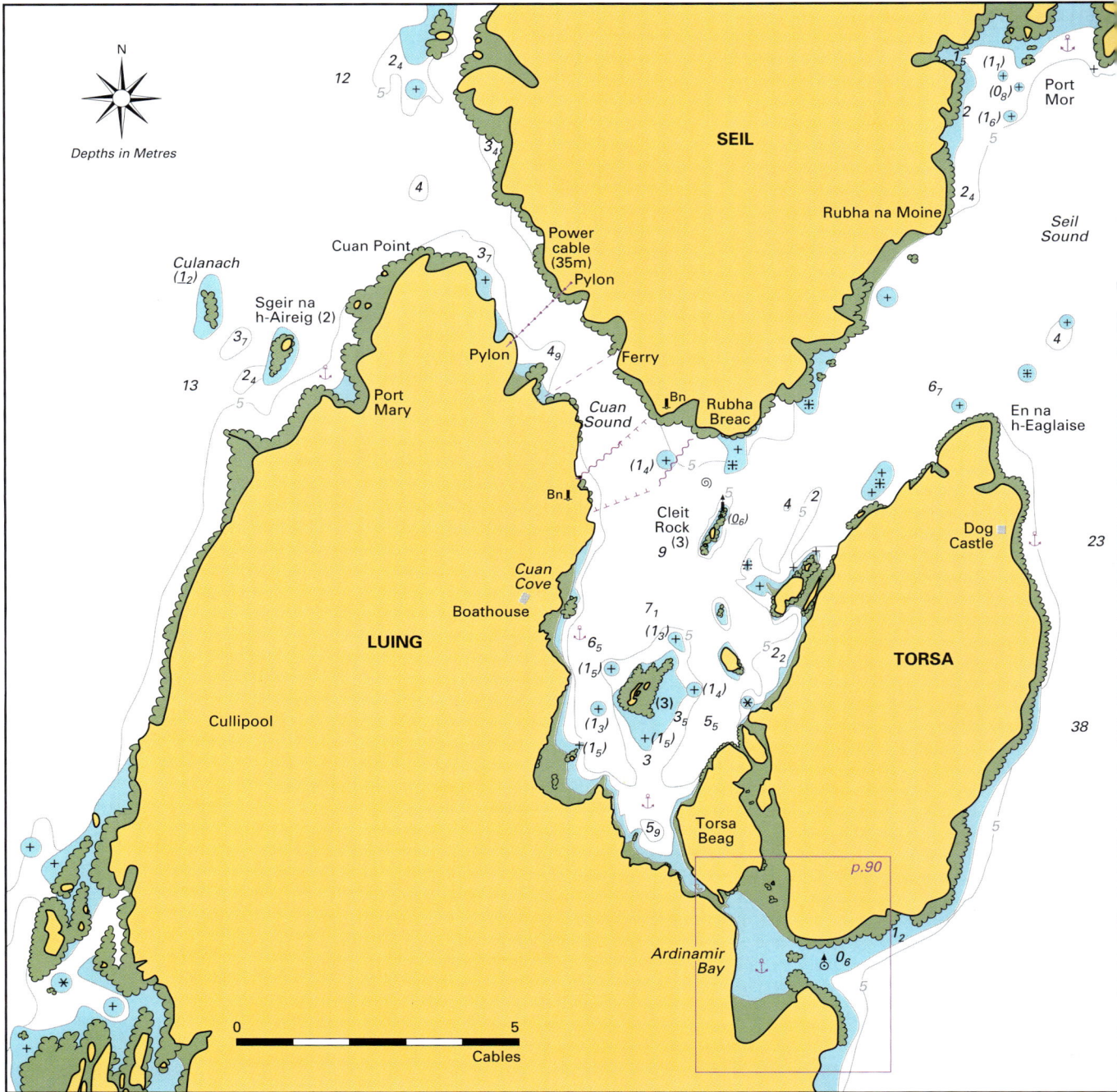

CUAN SOUND

N
Depths in Metres

12
24
5
Culanach (1₂)
Sgeir na h-Aireig (2)
3₇
2₄
5
13
34
4
Cuan Point
3₇
Power cable (35m)
Pylon
Pylon
Port Mary
4₉
Ferry
Cuan Sound
Bn
Rubha Breac
(1₄)
Bn
Cleit Rock
9 (3)
(0₆)
4 2
5
SEIL
Rubha na Moine
2₄
Seil Sound
4
6₇
En na h-Eaglaise
Dog Castle
23
Cuan Cove
Boathouse
LUING
6₅
(1₃)
5
7₁
(1₅)
(3)
(1₃)
3₅
5₅
(1₅)
3
5 2₂
(1₄)
TORSA
38
5₉
Torsa Beag
p.90
Ardinamir Bay
1₂
0₆
5
0 Cables 5

Port Mor
1₅ (1₁)
(0₈)
2 (1₆)
5

Cuan Sound

Cuan Sound is the V-shaped channel, 1 mile long and ¾ cable wide at its narrowest point, which connects the Firth of Lorn with Seil Sound and Loch Melfort. It separates Torsa island from the islands of Seil to the north and Luing to the south. The navigable channel has a least depth of 7m. Two submarine cables, marked by beacons, are laid across the Sound 1 cable west of Rubha Breac, the south extremity of Seil. Halfway between Rubha Breac and Cuan Point, the north extremity of Luing, a vehicular ferry crosses, and less than 1½ cables northwest of the ferry is an overhead power cable with a clearance of 35m.

Admiralty Chart
2326
Admiralty Leisure Folio
5611. 14, 16
Imray Chart
C65, 2800.3
Ordnance Survey
55
Cruising Scotland
p.82

Tides

For constant and heights see Seil Sound (p.91)

The flood tide runs westwards, beginning about +0430 Oban (–0100 Dover) at springs, +0515 Oban (–0015 Dover) at neaps.

The ebb runs eastwards, beginning about –0145 Oban (+0515 Dover) at springs, –0100 Oban (+0600 Dover) at neaps.

The stream reaches its greatest strength soon after turning; in the western part of the sound the spring rate in both directions is seven knots; neap rate up to 5 knots. There are strong eddies on both, especially in the vicinity of An Cleiteadh (Cleit Rock).

A passage against the tide, especially a spring tide, should only be attempted with an adequately powerful engine, and going through with the tide can also pose problems. No matter the state of tide the brief passage is always full of interest.

H King

Directions

From the south and east If approaching from Seil Sound or Loch Melfort, there is a rock which dries ¾ cable northeast of En na h-Eaglaise, the north extremity of Torsa. There is also an unmarked rock 2 cables northeast of this point. Both can be avoided by keeping either 30m off Torsa, or by going well out.

When taking the route close to the north end of Torsa maintain a northwesterly course from the point to clear a rock with less than 2m lying 1 cable west of the point. The west side of Torsa is foul and mid-channel should be kept, aiming for a yellow perch with yellow triangular topmark at the north end of Cleit Rock. This is difficult to identify from a distance, but is in transit with the farthest left of a small cluster of houses on Luing. Note that the perch is at least 8m from the northeast extremity of the rock.

An unmarked rock, which occasionally dries (see photo above), lies almost in mid-channel between Cleit Rock and Rubha Breac. The Seil side, to which it is slightly closer, is foul with another unmarked rock, and should therefore be avoided. Going towards the Firth of Lorn on the flood, a strong eddy can make it difficult to steer the recommended course between the rock in mid-channel and Cleit Rock, as there is a tendency to be swung suddenly towards the latter. Do not turn into the remainder of the sound until it is fully open, and keep to mid-channel thereafter. At the northern entrance to the sound the overfalls can be considerable and even dangerous to small vessels in strong to gale westerlies with wind against tide.

Going south of the Cleit Rock on the flood is not a safe proposition, although it can be safely circumnavigated at slack water by keeping 20m off. At HW the Cleit can give the impression of being 2 islets and on a spring flood a low standing wave, in itself not troublesome, forms between the Cleit and Rhuba Breac.

From the north and west Approaching from the Firth of Lorn, the northern entrance to the sound is identified by the pylons supporting the overhead power cable (clearance 35m). Ensure that you keep at least 2 cables off the Seil shore to avoid the submerged rock lying north of the entrance. With a strong south going ebb tide there is a strong set of current towards the Cleit Rock and course should be altered in plenty of time to cut across the tide in order to ensure that you pass clear of the northeast end of the rock which extends at least 8m north-eastwards from the perch. After passing the Cleit keep in mid-channel until you reach the north end of Torsa where the inside passage close to the point can be taken as described above for proceeding westwards.

Anchorage

There are several well-protected anchorages to the south of Cleit Rock, well clear of the tidal stream of Cuan Sound. The most straightforward approach is along the Luing shore keeping more than half a cable off to clear a drying rock off the boathouse. South of this, close the shore to ¼ cable to clear submerged rocks lying west of the 3-metre islet and then aim to pass a cable northeast of a small islet in the middle of a bay on the Luing shore. The best anchorage is west of Torsa Beag where shown on the plan.

Dog Castle, a ruined fort south of the northeast point of Torsa is a temporary anchorage which can be used if waiting for slack water in Cuan Sound.

Port Mary, at the northwest corner of Luing, is a also good temporary anchorage between the shore and the off-lying islet if waiting for slack water in the Cuan Sound. Consult the chart carefully to avoid the Culanach Rock (drying 1·2m) and the reef running south from the islet.

Cuan Sound, from the north end of Luing, at extra low spring tide, with both of the rocks north of the Cleit Rock showing

A *on Clachan Sound plan, east shore*

B *on Clachan Sound plan*

C *on Clachan Sound plan*

D *on Clachan Sound plan, Fasgadh*

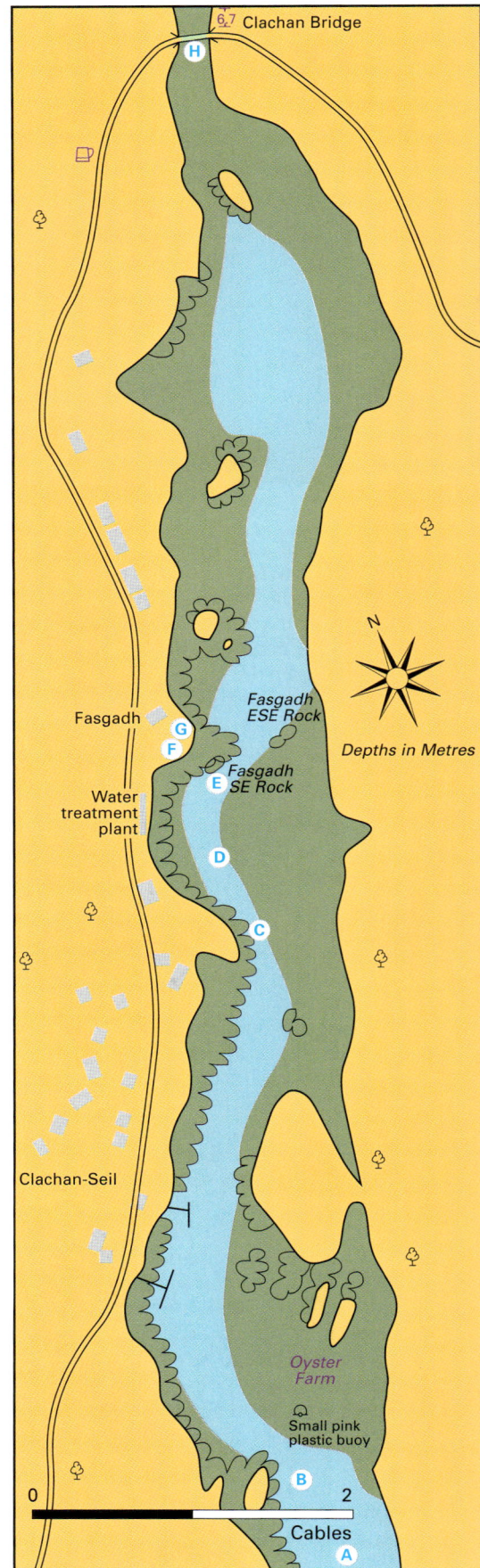

CLACHAN SOUND
NOTE: THIS PLAN IS NOT ALIGNED TO THE MERIDIAN

All photographs by David Foster

Clachan Sound

A motor boat – or a shoal-draught boat able to lower her mast easily – might find Clachan Sound a painless alternative to the Firth of Lorn on a blowy day, given enough rise of tide to get over the bar at the north end. This is reported to dry 2·4 metres (although charted as drying 1·5 metres), so that the passage is available only to shoal draught-boats towards high water. Headroom at the bridge is charted as 6·7 metres and 10 metres under the electricity cable north of it. The 2018 issue of *Antares* charts includes Clachan Sound which could make matters easier.

Tides

Tidal streams run strongly between Clachan Bridge and the north end of the sound.

Height in metres at Oban

MHWS	MHWN	MTL	MLWN	MLWS
4·0	2·9	2·4	1·8	0·7

The figures for Seil Sound are:
Constant –0025 Oban (–0555 Dover).

Height in metres

MHWS	MHWN	MTL	MLWN	MLWS
2·7	2·0	1·6	1·1	0·4

A further complication is that the tidal range north of the sound is much greater than that south of the Sound, so that at the time when one would probably choose to make the passage, the stream is flowing south, although still rising, and flowing north, at Oban.

Directions

The passage is described from south to north:
The Sound is entered east of Ard Sheillach on Seil Island, on which stand several houses. Most of the passage is occupied by permanent moorings and there are no visitors' moorings, or designated anchoring area.

To clear a shoal spit on the west side of the passage, pass ESE of the first group of four moorings, keeping close ESE of the most northerly mooring of this group, heading for a RW pole to the left of a white house on the east shore (photo A). Note that another RW pole on a rocky outcrop further right is easier to identify initially, but is not the one to steer for. A pink buoy to stbd. marks the limit of oyster beds there and should not be approached closely.

Another RW pole marks the HW line of a rock NE of Ard Sheillach on the west side of the passage, and when the pontoon landing stages north of it come into view, steer for them (photo B). Depth is about 0·5m LAT, mud and stones. Four moorings lie in this reach; pass west of them. When past these alter course towards the west shore, heading for a conspicuous wall of stone-filled gabions (a new water-treatment plant, photo C).

North of this plant stands a white house (Fasgadh, photo D); when an inconspicuous white drum on a pole is in line with the SE corner of the house steer on this line to clear drying stones on the east side of the channel. Southeast of Fasgadh stands a round-topped rock which rarely covers, and ESE of the house a rock on the east side of the channel which only uncovers at a low spring tide.

After passing the water treatment plant steer ENE for the largest tree on the right-hand slope of a small flat-topped hill (photo E), until you can see the next group of four moorings clear of 'Fasgadh SE rock'. From here steer north to pass close either side of the moorings. Following this lies a (final) scattered group of moorings, the main line of which lies to the west of mid-channel. Two submerged spits extend from the west side, about 50 and 100 metres south of the bridge. From the south east side of the moorings pass through the gap between the third and fourth mooring from the bridge, heading for the west side of the arch.

Provided the tidal conditions are favourable, proceed under the bridge and keep in mid-channel. The shallowest point lies about ½ mile north of the bridge, apparently drying 2·4 metres at chart datum, followed by a pool, and a further drying bar, where a pair of low W posts on the shore on Seil (astern) lead northeast through the deepest water. For directions north of the bar see *Puilladobhrain* p.102.

E on Clachan Sound plan

F on Clachan Sound plan

G on Clachan Sound plan

H on Clachan Sound plan

6. Firth of Lorn

Admiralty Chart
2386, 2387, 2169
Admiralty Leisure Folio
5611.9A
Imray Chart
C65, 2800.3
Ordnance Survey
55, 49
Cruising Scotland
p.87

This wide stretch of water is exposed to the Atlantic and demands respect in conditions of heavy swell and when strong wind against tide exist. If the ebb tide is running against an onshore wind conditions may be very unpleasant, particularly leaving Kerrera Sound and off Easdale and Insh Island, where the contrast with the protected passages of the Sound of Luing and southward is most marked.

The main fairway of the firth is clean and it is only to the east and southeast of the Garvellachs that there are any significant unmarked rocks.

For the purpose of this Pilot the Firth of Lorn is taken to begin at Frank Lockwood's Island,

close inshore south east of cliffs on Mull, east of Loch Buie. Carsaig and Loch Buie are included in Ch. 11, *Ross of Mull*.

Charts

2386 and 2387 respectively cover the south and north parts of the Firth of Lorn at 1:25,000. The approach to the firth is also covered, together with waters further south and west on 2769 at 1:75,000, and the remainder on 2171. Admiralty Leisure Folio chart 9 gives good coverage. Imray charts C65 and 2800.1 cover the area at scales of 1:150,000 and 1:160,000 respectively. Ordnance Survey maps are 49 and 55.

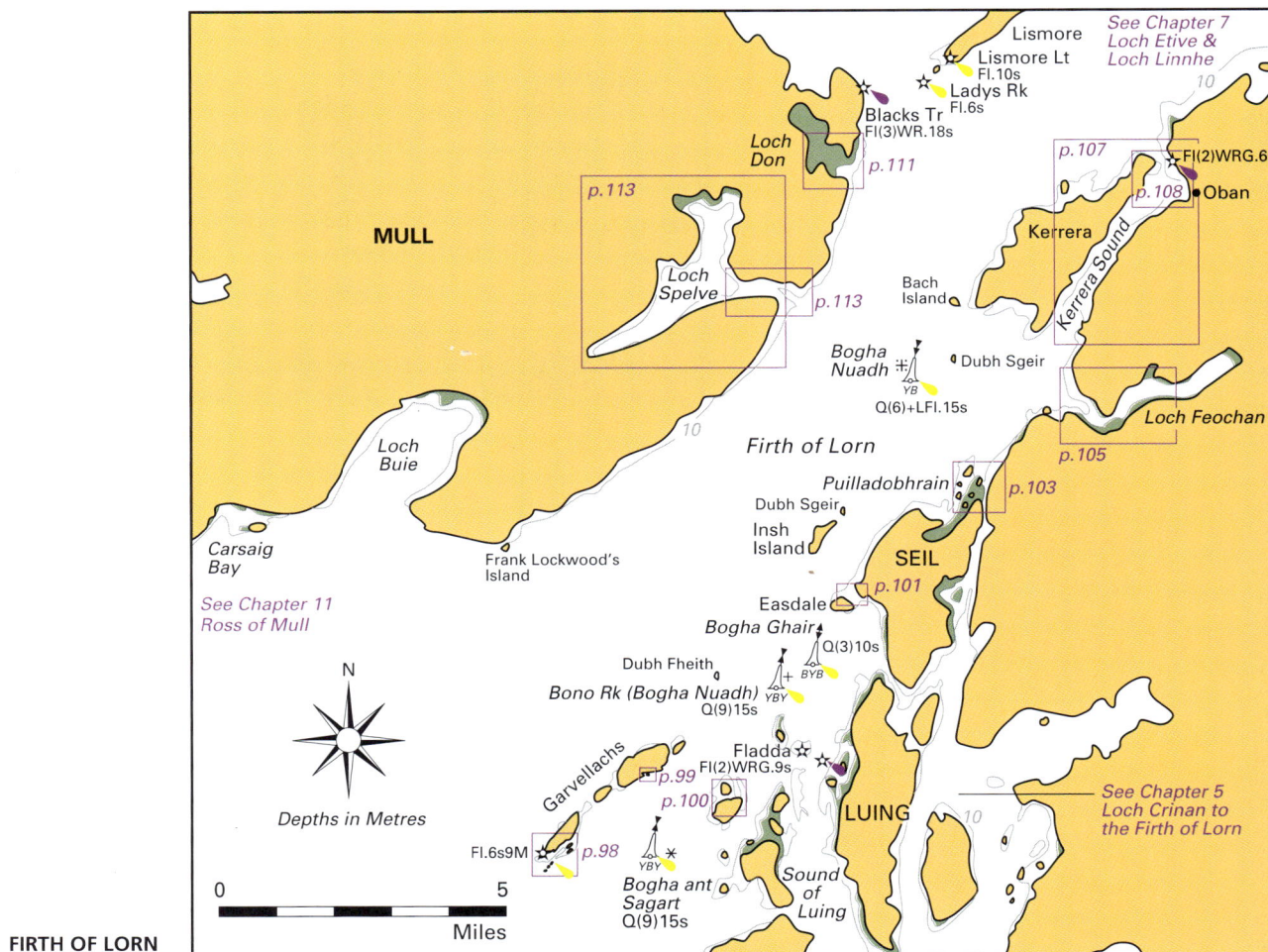

FIRTH OF LORN

Tides

In the fairway of the Firth the stream turns progressively clockwise, setting northeastwards about +0430 Oban (−0100 Dover); southwestwards about −0155 Oban (+0500 Dover). Tidal streams generally run at one to 1½ knots but southeast of the Garvellachs the spring rate is two to three knots with an eddy setting southwestwards after half-flood. Between Fladda and Easdale the spring rate is 2½ knots with up to 3 knots off Loch Don. Races form between Lismore and Mull and to the south, especially when the wind and tide are opposed.

Dangers and marks

The two main dangers are separate submerged rocks six miles apart, both named Bogha Nuadh and both marked by buoys. The more dangerous one, halfway between Fladda and Easdale, is charted at 0·9m and has a west cardinal light buoy on its southwest side; swell usually breaks on it but this cannnot be relied upon. This buoy is named on the chart as Bono Rock. Another rock with 4·3m over it, Bogha Ghair, lies 4 cables NNE of the Bono Rock buoy and is marked by an east cardinal light buoy; in moderate conditions it is not a hazard.

The second Bogha Nuadh, an awash rock 4 cables southwest of Dubh Sgeir, a 7m high islet about 1¼ miles southwest of Kerrera, is marked by a south cardinal light buoy, positioned 1 cable SSE of the rock.

Southeast of the Garvellachs there are several dangerous rocks of which the most hazardous is Bogha ant Sagart, which dries 0·3m, approximately halfway between Lunga and the Garvellachs. It is marked by a west cardinal light buoy.

Conspicuous marks are: Scarba, at 446m the highest land to the south of the Firth of Lorn; the Garvellachs; Insh Island (Sheep Island) west of Seil and Lismore lighthouse at the north end of the Firth.

Dubh Fheith, an isolated rock 12 metres high, 1½ miles northeast of the Garvellachs, is a useful reference point.

Directions

The passage northwest of the Garvellachs and Dubh Fheith presents no problem other than from steep seas when the wind is against the tide.

On a passage from or to the west side of Jura the Great Race, which extends several miles to the west of Corryvreckan, should not be crossed on the flood, particularly at springs or in strong west winds. Giving the race a good berth will usually mean passing to the west of Bogha ant Sagart. If tacking to the east of the rock give the buoy marking it a good berth and be aware of unmarked rocks to the west of Lunga and Scarba.

Edward Mason

Making for Oban or the Sound of Mull from the Sound of Luing, it is simpler, and probably quicker, to pass east of both the Bono Rock and Bogha Ghair buoys. If passing between them, give the Bono Rock buoy a berth of at least 1½ cables as it is positioned well to the southwest of the rock and its associated shoal. Bogha Ghair should not trouble most yachts but if any sea is running give it a good berth. From the north identify Scarba and then Fladda lighthouse to find the right passage.

North of Insh Island drying rocks lying more than a cable northeast of Dubh Sgeir (a 5m high rock more than ½ mile northeast of the island), are a hazard if tacking or if heading from the Sound of Insh to the Sound of Mull.

Bogha Nuadh, 1¾ miles southwest of Kerrera, lies 1 cable NNW of the south cardinal buoy which marks the rock, and the buoy should be given a berth of at least ¼ mile if passed on its northern side.

Looking back to Fladda, Scarba and the Black Isles from the Firth of Lorn

Lights

Bogha ant Sagart W cardinal light buoy Q(9)15s
Garvellachs Fl.6s24m9M (not visible from NE between 215° and 240°)
Fladda lighthouse Fl(2)WRG.9s13m11-9M
Bono Rock (Bogha Nuadh) W cardinal buoy Q(9)15s
Bogha Ghair E cardinal buoy Q(3)10s
Dubh Sgeir, ESE of Fladda, Fl.WRG.6s9m6-4M
Bogha Nuadh S cardinal buoy, two miles SW of Kerrera Q(6)+LFl.15s
Lismore lighthouse Fl.10s31m7M
Lady's Rock, ½ mile SW of Lismore, Fl.6s12m5M
Black's Memorial on Mull, one mile west of Lady's Rock, Fl(3)WR.18s14m5-3M

EILEACH AN NAOIMH

From the east or southeast make for the southwest side of a gap in the skerries, keeping closer to that side to avoid a reef, part of which is awash, on the northeast side of the gap.

From the southwest it is possible to pass between the skerries and the island, but keep closer to the skerries to avoid drying rocks on the island side.

Anchor off the old landing place southwest of the ruins, or beyond the drying rock at the northeast end of the inlet. When the rock is covered it can usually be seen showing white underwater, but note that submerged rocks extend from both ends of it.

The northeast end of the channel between the skerries and the island is awash at chart datum, with dense weed, but there are no individual rocks at a higher level, so that if there is no swell a boat of moderate draught might pass through this channel above half-tide.

Garvellachs (Isles of the Sea)

The Garvellachs are well worth visiting but the anchorages are too exposed to be suitable for staying overnight, except in settled weather and even then a swell can set in.

Admiralty Chart
2386
Admiralty Leisure Folio
5611.9A
Imray Chart
C65, 2800.3
Ordnance Survey
55
Cruising Scotland
pp.87, 88

Tides

Constant −0010 Oban (−0540 Dover).

Height in metres at Carsaig, Mull

MHWS	MHWN	MTL	MLWN	MLWS
4·1	3·1	2·4	1·8	0·6

On the southeast side of the Garvellachs, an eddy on flood runs southwestwards from about +0130 Oban.

Eileach an Naoimh

On Eileach an Naoimh (pronounced neave) there are extensive remains of 9th-century monastic buildings and a grave reputed to be that of St Columba's mother.

Right Beehive cell on Eileach an Naoimh

Below The anchorage at Eileach an Naoimh in the Garvellachs

Edward Mason

Martin Lawrence

Martin Lawrence

Garbh Eileach

This, the largest of the group, has a very small bay in the middle of the southeast side of the island which provides an occasional anchorage.

Keep the cottage open west of the west end of Sgeir a' Phuirt; a submerged rock south of the islet lies on the line shown on the plan - it is not a clearing mark. There are mooring points on the west end of Sgeir a' Phuirt and on the shore to the north of it, and at the concrete slip on the west side of the bay.

The anchorage at Eileach an Naoimh from the east. The channel between the right-hand islet and Eileach an Naiomh is awash at CD so is navigable for vessels of moderate draught above half tide

The anchorage at Garbh Eileach is very tight

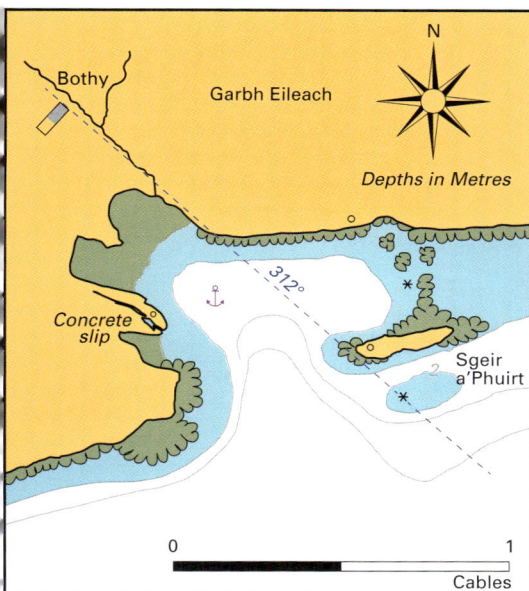

GARBH EILACH

Arthur Houston

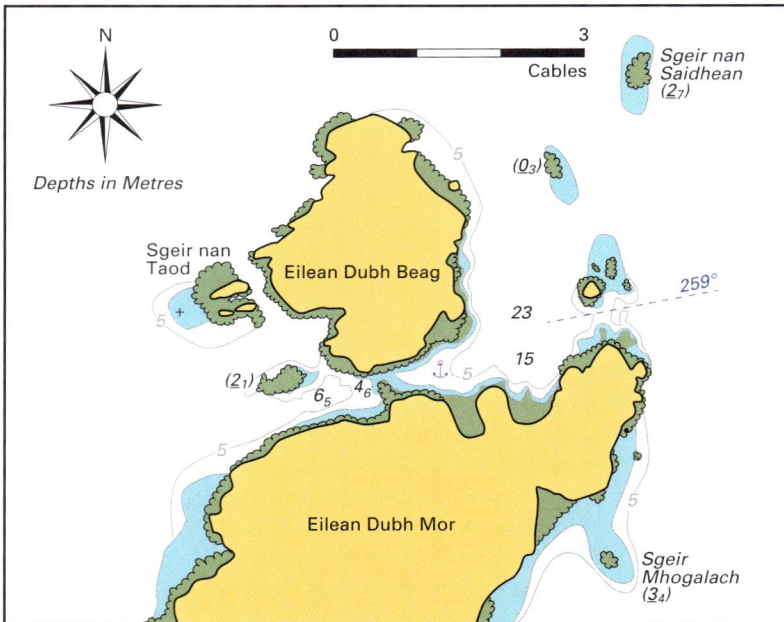

THE BLACK ISLES

Admiralty Chart
2326
Admiralty Leisure Folio
5611.14
Imray Chart
C65, 2800.3
Ordnance Survey
55
Cruising Scotland
p.88

The Black Isles from the south east showing the submerged hazards in the approach channel

The Black Isles

An attractive anchorage between the islands of Eilean Dubh Mor and Eilean Dubh Beag, 1½ miles SE of the Garvellachs. Useful for anchoring whilst waiting for a fair tide in the Sound of Luing or overnight in settled weather.

Directions

From the north keep well towards the east side of Eilean Dubh Beag to avoid a drying rock a cable east of the island.

From the east pass close south of the small islet off the north point of Eilean Dubh Mor, taking care to avoid the submerged rocks which lie either side of the eastern entrance to the channel. Minimum depth in the passage is 2·5m. Course through 259°.

Anchorage

Anchor in 4 metres in the centre of the pool between the two islands as shown on the plan (where the bottom is sand) or in 10 metres or more further out.

Both of the bays on the north side of Eilean Dubh Mor are foul with submerged and drying rocks, but it is possible to anchor off the promontory between them.

Fishermen use the very shallow passage through the narrows between the islands so show a riding light. This channel rarely dries and protects the anchorage from swell in most conditions of wind and tide.

Fladda and Belnahua

Fladda provides a temporary anchorage NNE of the island during the flood tide.

Belnahua, three cables WNW of Fladda, has the remains of extensive slate quarries, which penetrated far below sea level. It makes an interesting visit on a quiet day, but anchoring there needs care as the tide runs at five knots at springs and reefs extend more than 3 cables to the north. On the ebb, anchor in the tidal lee at the south end of the island. On the flood anchor as close inshore as possible on the east side. Keep an eye on your boat all the time; the bottom is mostly slate waste.

Martin Lawrence

Easdale Sound

Easdale was one of two main centres of the Scottish slate industry, and its character is post-industrial, with rows of miners' cottages converted to holiday homes. For the last 60 years it has been said that Easdale Sound was silting up, but a survey by a resident yachtsman shows that for the most part it is as deep as ever, except in the southwest corner.

The plan shows the approach, dangers and marks but note the large scale; the clear passage in the south entrance is less than 20m wide.

Tides

Constant −0010 Oban (−0540 Dover).

Height in metres at Carsaig, Mull

MHWS	MHWN	MTL	MLWN	MLWS
4·1	3·1	2·4	1·8	0·6

Directions

From the southeast keep the south end of Insh Island just open south of the head of the ruined pier 320°. This entrance is very narrow, the clear passage at low tide being no more than 20 metres wide and no more than 1·7m depth at LWS. After passing the pier alter course to the north, and before the slate wharf comes abeam, alter course to north west to pass about 30 metres south of the beacon on the reef on the north shore. Continue on this heading until clear of the entrance.

From the northwest identify the entrance to the sound by the cliff on its north side, about a mile southeast of the south end of Insh Island. Take care not to cut the corner, but when you have identified the beacons (always pass well north of the mid-channel beacon) approach with the south point of Insh Island astern, to pass about 30 metres south of the northern beacon (photo p.102). Steer first for the slate wharf bearing 130° and, after passing the beacon, towards the end of the ruined pier, bearing 155°.

Anchorage

Anchor off the slate wharf, about 50 metres off the end (see photo p.8), or further northwest, leaving a clear space for the passenger ferry to the island, as well as for boats passing through the sound. Poor holding in rock or weed.

Shoal-draught boats may find a berth in Easdale Harbour, especially if able to take the ground (see p.102). The bottom is stony in places.

Services and supplies

Restaurant, folk museum, pub, phone box. Bus to Oban.

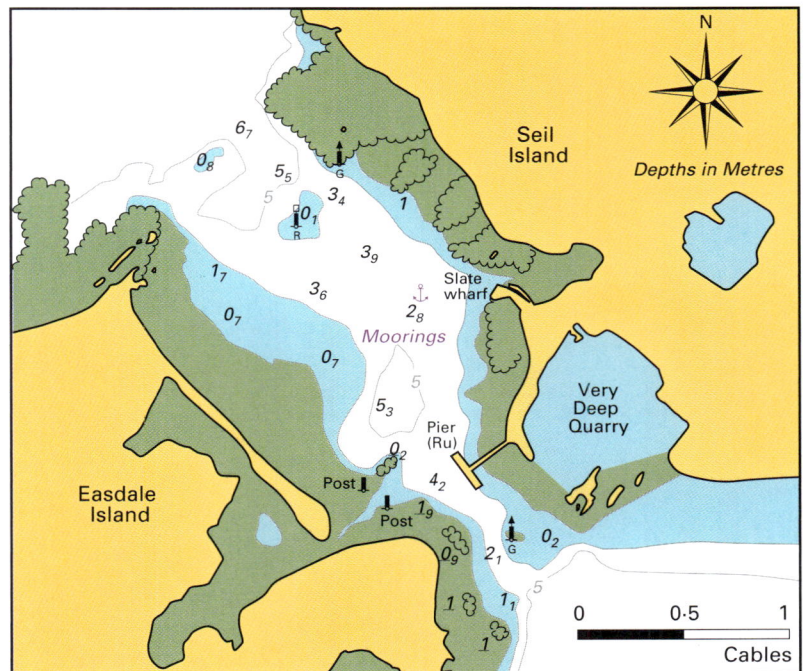

EASDALE SOUND

Admiralty Chart 2386
Admiralty Leisure Folio 5611.27A
Imray Chart C65, 2800.3
Ordnance Survey 55
Cruising Scotland pp.90, 91

Approach to Easdale Sound from the east. Keep close to the line of the face of the pier at this point to avoid rocks on the south side of the channel

Neil McCubbin

Martin Lawrence

Upper *The anchorage at Puilladobhrain with the Firth of Lorn and Isle of Mull beyond*

Lower *Easdale Sound from the west. Note that the reef extends as much as 10m south of the beacon (see p.101)*

Ardencaple Bay

This large, open bay to the southwest of Puilladobhrain offers two occasional anchorages. Anchor either immediately to the east of Rubha Garbh Airde in 5m, or east of Ardfad Point in 5-10m, mud and weed.

Approaching Ardencaple Bay from the west give the Seil Island shore a good berth and, if approaching from the north, note the 1·8m patch, 2½ cables southwest of Eilean Duin. Fish cages may be found in either of these anchorages but there is usually room for small vessels to anchor.

Puilladobhrain

A well sheltered, attractive and popular anchorage (pronounced 'Puldohran') behind tidal islands on the east side of Ardencaple Bay. It may not be easy to identify, but the rock formations of Eilean Duin (see plan) resemble a ruined castle.

Tides

Constant as Oban (−0530 Dover).
Height in metres

MHWS	MHWN	MTL	MLWN	MLWS
4·0	2·9	2·4	1·8	0·7

Directions

From the south and west identify Eilean Duin and keep a couple of cables north of it to avoid a submerged rock northeast of it. A white cairn near the north point of Seil Island kept open north of a drum (white/orange) on the north end

N

Depths in Metres

Sgeir Liath

Clachan
Bridge
hidden

Eilean
Duin

18

Dun Horses
(2_8)

Old
Slate
Quarry

Ardencaple
Bay

(2_4)

3_7

(3_1)

5

White/orange
drum

1_8

Sgeir
Bhuidhe

7$_7$

(1_2)

Eilean nam
Beathach

6

(0_5)

5

(3_7)

2_1

(1)

Cairn

2_4

Eilean
nam
Freumha

White cross

4

Wooded

2$_2$

(0_9)

(2)

(2)

3$_9$

Seil

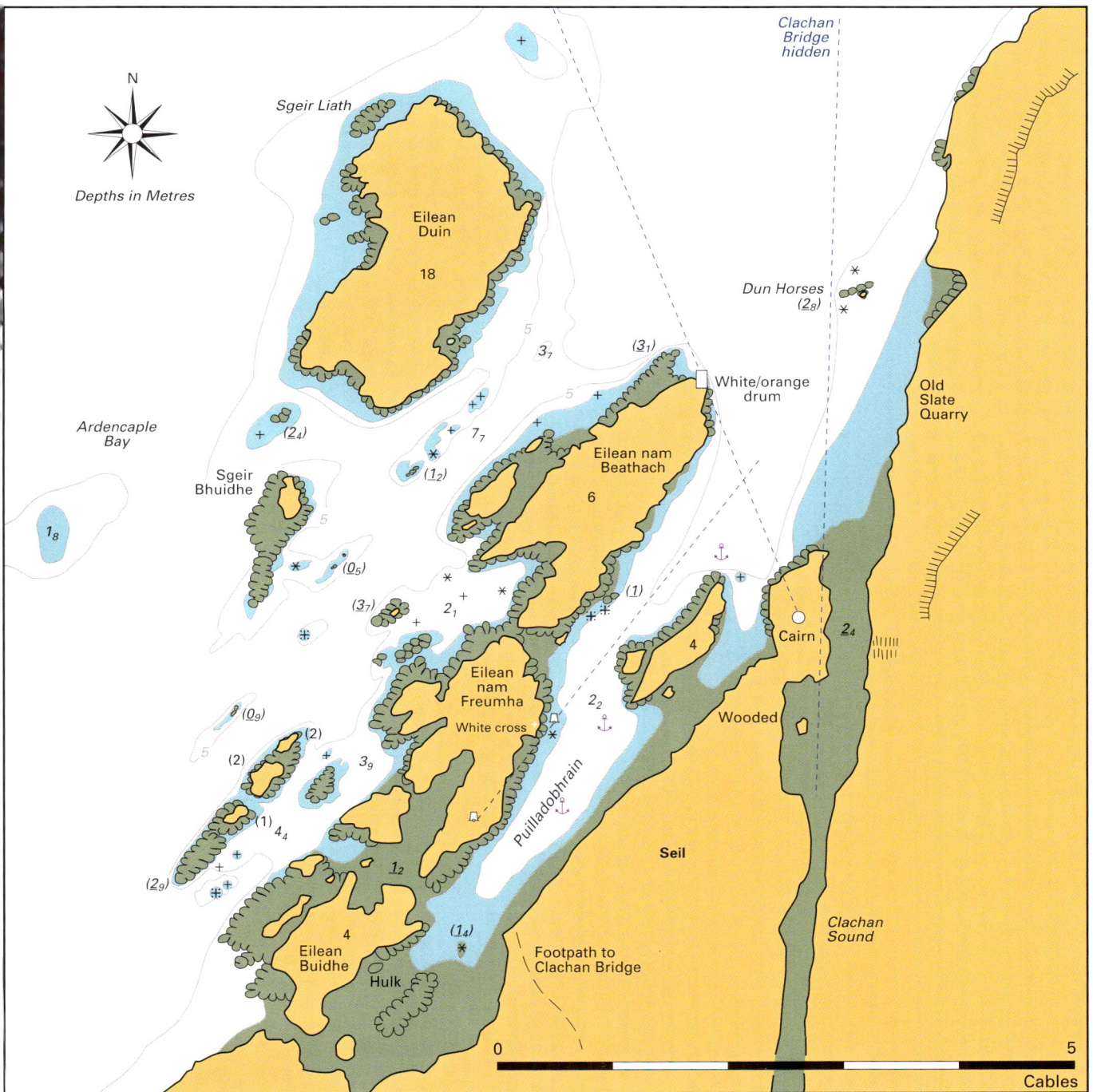

Puilladobhrain

(1) 4_4

1_2

Clachan
Sound

(2_9)

(1_4)

4

Eilean
Buidhe

Hulk

Footpath to
Clachan Bridge

0   5

Cables

PUILLADOBHRAIN

of Eilean nam Beathach leads clear of this rock. Enter by rounding the north point of Eilean nam Beathach but no more than ½ cable off, to avoid Dun Horses (dries 2·8m), a group of rocks off the mainland shore. A rock which dries at LW on the west side of the channel is avoided by keeping in mid-channel, with two cairns in line, as shown on the plan. The front cairn is almost submerged at HW. There is a drying rock close inshore on this line, the position of which is marked by a white cross on the islet.

From the north Eilean Duin is less easy to identify against Seil, but once identified, steer for it until the bridge through Clachan Sound can be seen. Continue on the same heading until the sound is shut in, when it is safe to alter course to starboard avoiding the Dun Horses.

Anchorage
Anywhere in the pool in suitable depth, 4-6m. Good holding with 20m or more of chain in black mud. Large yachts (and others if the pool is crowded) can anchor in the outer anchorage in 6-15 m.

Services and supplies
Inn at Clachan Bridge: land at the shingle beach towards the head of the pool before taking a sign-posted path over the hill (½ mile). Post Office and telephone box at Balvicar.

Admiralty Chart
2387
Admiralty Leisure Folio
5611.27A
Imray Chart
C65, 2800.3
Ordnance Survey
49
Cruising Scotland
p.91

Puilladobhrain (see p.102) from the northwest, with the drying passage of Clachan Sound and Clachan Bridge (Bridge over the Atlantic) beyond

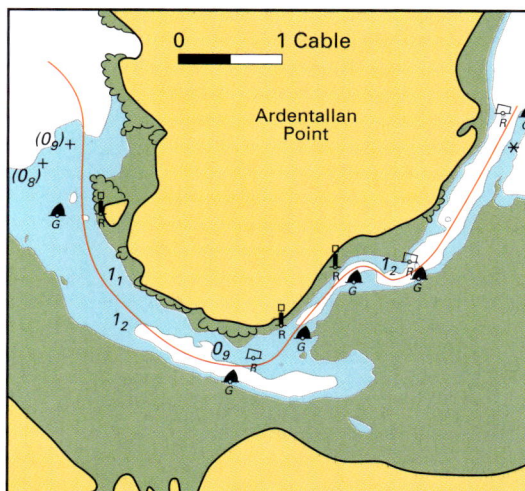

0   1 Cable

Ardentallan Point

(0_9)+
(0_8)+

1_1
1_2
1_2
0_9

LOCH FEOCHAN NARROWS

Admiralty Chart
2387
Admiralty Leisure Folio
5611.17
Imray Chart
C65, 2800.3
Ordnance Survey
49
Cruising Scotland
p.92

Loch Feochan

A picturesque loch 1½ miles southeast of the south end of Kerrera offering good shelter and facilities but with a tortuous entrance channel between sandbanks. This has been buoyed by Ardoran Marine but the directions must be followed with great care.

Tides

Owing to the shoals at the entrance, the flood does not begin to enter the loch until the level has risen 1m outside. This results in the flood running for just four hours and the ebb continuing until two hours after LW. This effect is less pronounced at neaps.

Flood begins −0355 Oban (+0300 Dover)
Ebb begins HW Oban (−0530 Dover) Sp rate 5 kn, Np 3 kn.

HW in the loch is the same as HW Oban. For heights see Kerrera Sound, p.106

There is a least depth of 0·6m in the buoyed channel at LW.

The buoyed channel at the entrance to Loch Feochan at LW. The flood tide sets a yacht strongly to the east at the first bend - on to drying banks

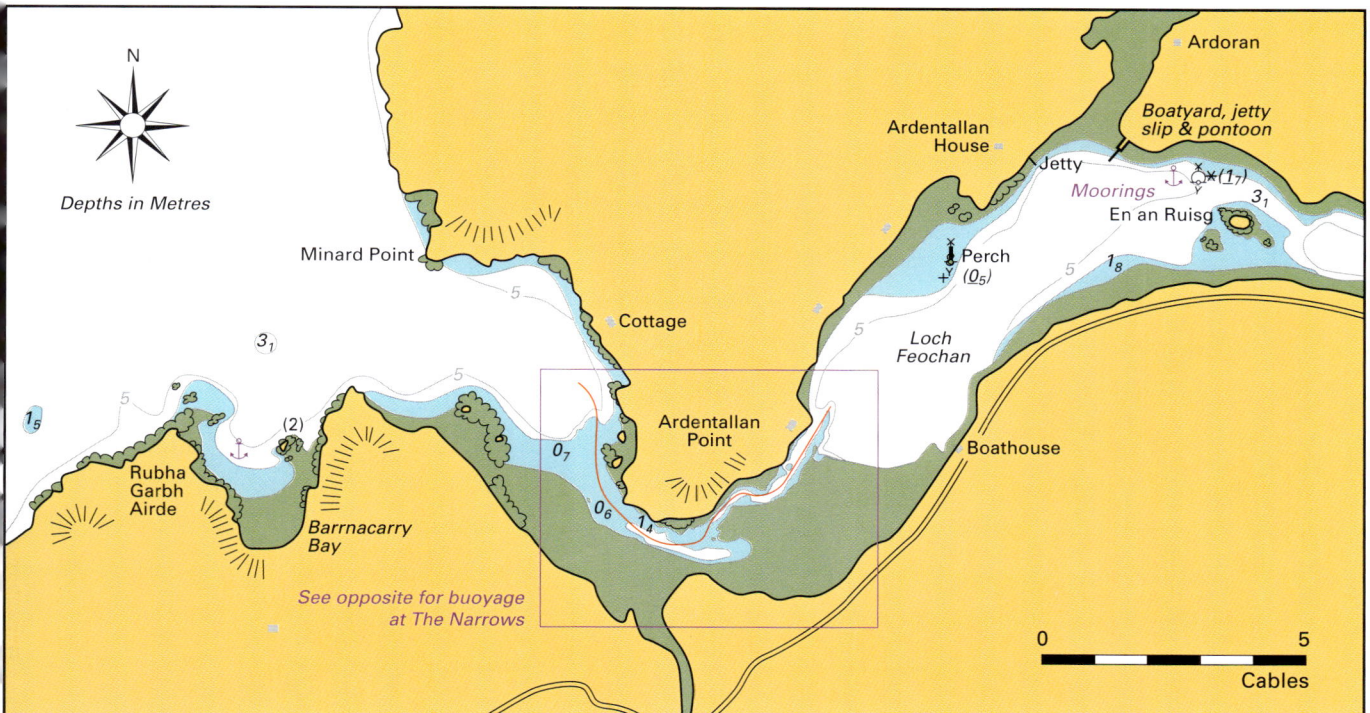

**LOCH FEOCHAN AND
BARRNACARRY BAY**

Directions

Entry for the first time should be at HW or on the first few hours of the ebb, although local boat owners familiar with the entrance take it at most states of tide.

The channel is intricate and is marked with six pairs of buoys (or buoys and perches) of which the first lie west of the point. The best depth is found by keeping mid-channel between the buoys. The strength of the flood stream at springs can drag the buoys under but this is very unlikely within one hour of HW. Upon entering the channel at the outer buoy and islet perch, hold 10m off the islet and Ardentallan Point before passing between the first set of channel buoys and following round the shore to the north, and thence between the buoys marking the drying rocks 1 cable northeast of the point.

After leaving the entrance channel note the drying rock (0·5m) marked by a yellow perch which lies in shoal water 2 cables offshore, ½ mile north of the narrow channel. If proceeding further east towards the head of the loch note that Eilean an Ruisg, one mile beyond Ardentallan Point, has rocks all round it. The passage to the north of it is cleaner, but beware of the rock drying 1·7m NNW of the island, closer to the mainland shore. It is now marked by a buoy.

Anchorage

Anchor in Ardentallan Bay off the drying inlet on north side, adjacent to the moorings and the boatyard slip. Alternatively anchor towards the head of the loch.

Services and supplies

Ardoran Marine (① 01631 566123, Ch 16 and 37) has pontoons (depth 2m), a slip and 12 ton hoist, also moorings, water, diesel, chandlery, gas, laundry, showers and toilets. Winter storage, engine and light engineering repairs.

Barrnacarry Bay

An occasional anchorage on the south side of the entrance to Loch Feochan, for settled weather or moderate southerly winds.

Directions

From the south and west keep ¼ mile offshore to avoid a 1·2m shoal ½ mile west of Barrnacarry, as well as drying rocks off the west point of the entrance. Approach the bay with the farm buildings in line with the west side of the largest (2m high) above-water rock in the bay bearing 182° to pass east of the drying rocks to the west. Anchor towards the southwest side of the bay. Good holding in fine dark sand. Subject to southwesterly swell at HW.

Admiralty Chart
1790, 2387
Admiralty Leisure Folio
5611.17
Imray Chart
C65, 2800.3
Ordnance Survey
49
Cruising Scotland
p.92

Kerrera Sound

Kerrera Sound provides a sheltered and well-marked approach to Oban from the south. Several reasonable anchorages can be found in the sound, but all of them are likely to be disturbed by passing traffic.

Navigation within the sound is governed by a Code of Practice of which a summary is given on the plan opposite and the full version can be found in the appendix. It is frequently used by large vessels and all small craft, including yachts under sail, have a duty not to impede them.

Tides

Tidal streams run at one to two knots turning about 1½ hours before HW and LW Oban

Height in metres at Oban

MHWS	MHWN	MTL	MLWN	MLWS
4.0	2.9	2.4	1.8	0.7

Directions

Entering from the south, Cutter Rock, a drying reef extending 1½ cables SSW of the Sgeirean Dubha light beacon, must be noted. Starboard and port hand lit buoys mark Sgeir an Fheurain, a drying shoal off the mainland shore, and a shoal at the mouth of Little Horseshoe Bay.

More than ½ mile further northeast the Ferry Rocks lie in the middle of the sound. The main channel runs to the northwest of them where it is marked by port and starboard hand buoys. If using this channel, follow the Code of Practice opposite and keep well to the starboard side of the channel.

To avoid large vessels in this narrow channel, small craft can pass east of the Ferry Rocks, now marked by an E cardinal buoy, and then west of the starboard hand buoy marking the shoal off Rubha Tolmach.

Two cables north of Rubha Tolmach, Heather Island lies on the west side of the Sound and is best left to port because of an unmarked shoal lying southwest of its southern point. The eastern shore of the island should be given a good berth to avoid drying rocks off its most easterly point and a reported patch with less than 2m lying about ¼ cable further east.

Lights

Sgeirean Dubha Lt Bn; Fl.(2)12s7m5M; Wh. Twr
Sgeir an Fheurain buoy; Fl.G.3s
Little Horseshoe Shoal buoy; Fl.(4)R12s
Kerrera buoy; QR
Ferry Rocks West buoy; QG
Ferry Rocks East buoy; Q(3)10s
Rubha Tolmach Shoal buoy; Fl.G 5s
Heather Island Bn; Fl.R.2·5s11m2M

Anchorage

Little Horseshoe Bay Note the position of the shoal in relation to the buoy and enter either side of the shoal but beware of the drying reef which extends nearly a cable northeast of the south point. Avoid the electricity cable when anchoring. Holding poor in heavy weed

Gallanach Most of the space is taken up by moorings although the boatyard usually keeps some for visitors. Go alongside to enquire, keeping clear of the buoys around the drying rocks in the centre of the bay. The quay dries alongside but has about 1·2m at LW neaps.

Oban Marine Centre operate the moorings and can provide diesel, petrol, water, hull and engine repairs, showers, slipping and winter storage. ☎ 01631 566088.

Horseshoe Bay is partly occupied by moorings. Inshore of them is drying foreshore; to the north lies a 1·8m submerged rock and further north the bay is mostly very deep. Space for anchoring has been left in the southwest part of the bay. Be aware of tidal eddies and shoal ground inshore.

Heather Island The small shallow bay on Kerrera, north of Heather Island, has 5 visitors' moorings laid off it. These are operated by Ardantrive farm (£10 per night) where there are showers and toilets. Meat and eggs sold at farm. Nearby seafood restaurant ☎ 07840 650669.

South and west sides of Kerrera

The anchorages given below can be approached using chart 2387 or the plan opposite and none of them suffer the disturbance from passing traffic that can be experienced in Kerrera Sound.

Gylen Castle Bay Avoid anchoring in depths of over 5m as holding is poor in the bays east and west of the promontory below the Castle. If conditions are not good for anchoring off the castle it can be approached on foot from Little Horseshoe Bay.

Barr-nam-Boc This bay was used originally by the ferry to Loch Don, Mull. Anchor in 8m, mud, shingle and weed although take care to avoid a recently laid cable which is clearly marked onshore.

Oitir Mhor Bay is situated towards the north end of Kerrera. The approach to this bay is straightforward from the north, avoiding Sgeir Dhonn (1) and keeping 1 cable east of Eilean nam Uan. The approach from the southwest, between Eilean nan Gamhna and Kerrera, is narrow and winding and not recommended without local knowledge or the *Antares* chart but the channel between Eilean nan Uan has 2·8m in the centre and can be used if entering or leaving from the northwest. Anchor in 4–8m shingle. Note that the southwest part of the bay dries out 1 cable.

Charlotte Bay 5 cables to the northeast has less shelter than Oitir Mhor Bay although both are used in settled summer weather by yachts seeking to avoid the traffic in Oban Bay.

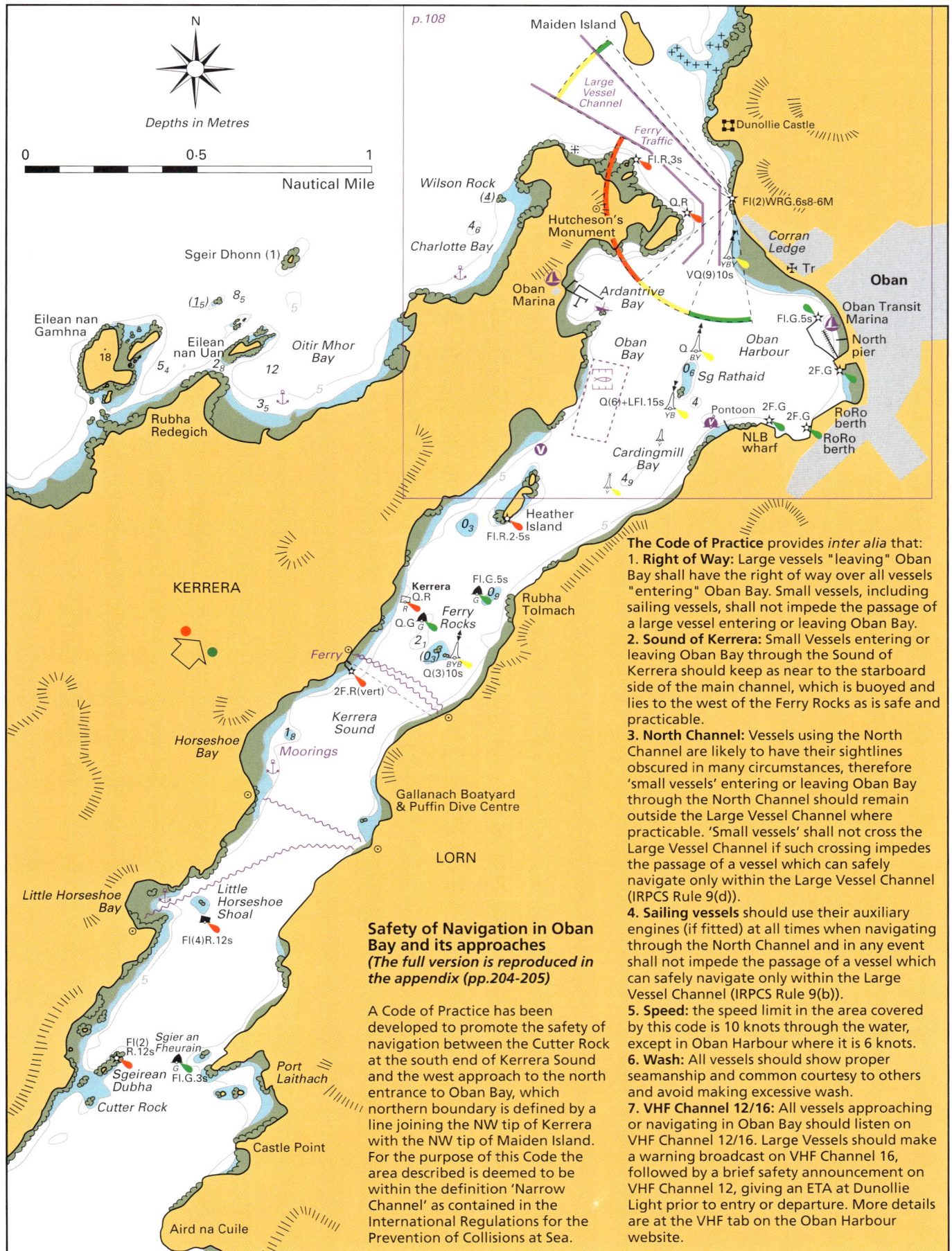

N

Depths in Metres

0   0·5   1

Nautical Mile

p.108

Maiden Island

Large Vessel Channel

Ferry Traffic

Dunollie Castle

Fl.R.3s

Wilson Rock *(4)*

Q.R

Fl(2)WRG.6s8-6M

4₆

Hutcheson's Monument

Corran Ledge

Tr

Charlotte Bay

VQ(9)10s

YBY

Oban

Oban Marina

Ardantrive Bay

Fl.G.5s

Oban Transit Marina

Sgeir Dhonn (1)

8₅

Oban Bay

Q BY

Oban Harbour

North pier

(1₅)

5

0₆

2F.G

Eilean nan Gamhna

Sg Rathaid

Eilean nan Uan

Oitir Mhor Bay

Q(6)+LFl.15s

4

Pontoon

2F.G

2F.G

RoRo berth

18

5₄

2₈

12

YB

NLB wharf

RoRo berth

Rubha Redegich

3₅

5

V

Cardingmill Bay

4₉

5

Heather Island

Fl.R.2·5s

5

KERRERA

0₃

Kerrera

Q.R

Fl.G.5s

0₉

Rubha Tolmach

R

G

G

Q.G

Ferry Rocks

2₁

Ferry

(0₃)

BYB

2F.R(vert)

Q(3)10s

Kerrera Sound

1₈

Moorings

Horseshoe Bay

Gallanach Boatyard & Puffin Dive Centre

LORN

Little Horseshoe Bay

Little Horseshoe Shoal

5

Fl(4)R.12s

Fl(2)R.12s

Sgier an Fheurain

Port Laithach

Sgeirean Dubha

Fl.G.3s

G

Cutter Rock

Castle Point

Aird na Cuile

Safety of Navigation in Oban Bay and its approaches
(The full version is reproduced in the appendix (pp.204-205)

A Code of Practice has been developed to promote the safety of navigation between the Cutter Rock at the south end of Kerrera Sound and the west approach to the north entrance to Oban Bay, which northern boundary is defined by a line joining the NW tip of Kerrera with the NW tip of Maiden Island. For the purpose of this Code the area described is deemed to be within the definition 'Narrow Channel' as contained in the International Regulations for the Prevention of Collisions at Sea.

The Code of Practice provides *inter alia* that:
1. **Right of Way:** Large vessels "leaving" Oban Bay shall have the right of way over all vessels "entering" Oban Bay. Small vessels, including sailing vessels, shall not impede the passage of a large vessel entering or leaving Oban Bay.
2. **Sound of Kerrera:** Small Vessels entering or leaving Oban Bay through the Sound of Kerrera should keep as near to the starboard side of the main channel, which is buoyed and lies to the west of the Ferry Rocks as is safe and practicable.
3. **North Channel:** Vessels using the North Channel are likely to have their sightlines obscured in many circumstances, therefore 'small vessels' entering or leaving Oban Bay through the North Channel should remain outside the Large Vessel Channel where practicable. 'Small vessels' shall not cross the Large Vessel Channel if such crossing impedes the passage of a vessel which can safely navigate only within the Large Vessel Channel (IRPCS Rule 9(d)).
4. **Sailing vessels** should use their auxiliary engines (if fitted) at all times when navigating through the North Channel and in any event shall not impede the passage of a vessel which can safely navigate only within the Large Vessel Channel (IRPCS Rule 9(b)).
5. **Speed:** the speed limit in the area covered by this code is 10 knots through the water, except in Oban Harbour where it is 6 knots.
6. **Wash:** All vessels should show proper seamanship and common courtesy to others and avoid making excessive wash.
7. **VHF Channel 12/16:** All vessels approaching or navigating in Oban Bay should listen on VHF Channel 12/16. Large Vessels should make a warning broadcast on VHF Channel 16, followed by a brief safety announcement on VHF Channel 12, giving an ETA at Dunollie Light prior to entry or departure. More details are at the VHF tab on the Oban Harbour website.

KERRERA SOUND AND APPROACHES TO OBAN BAY

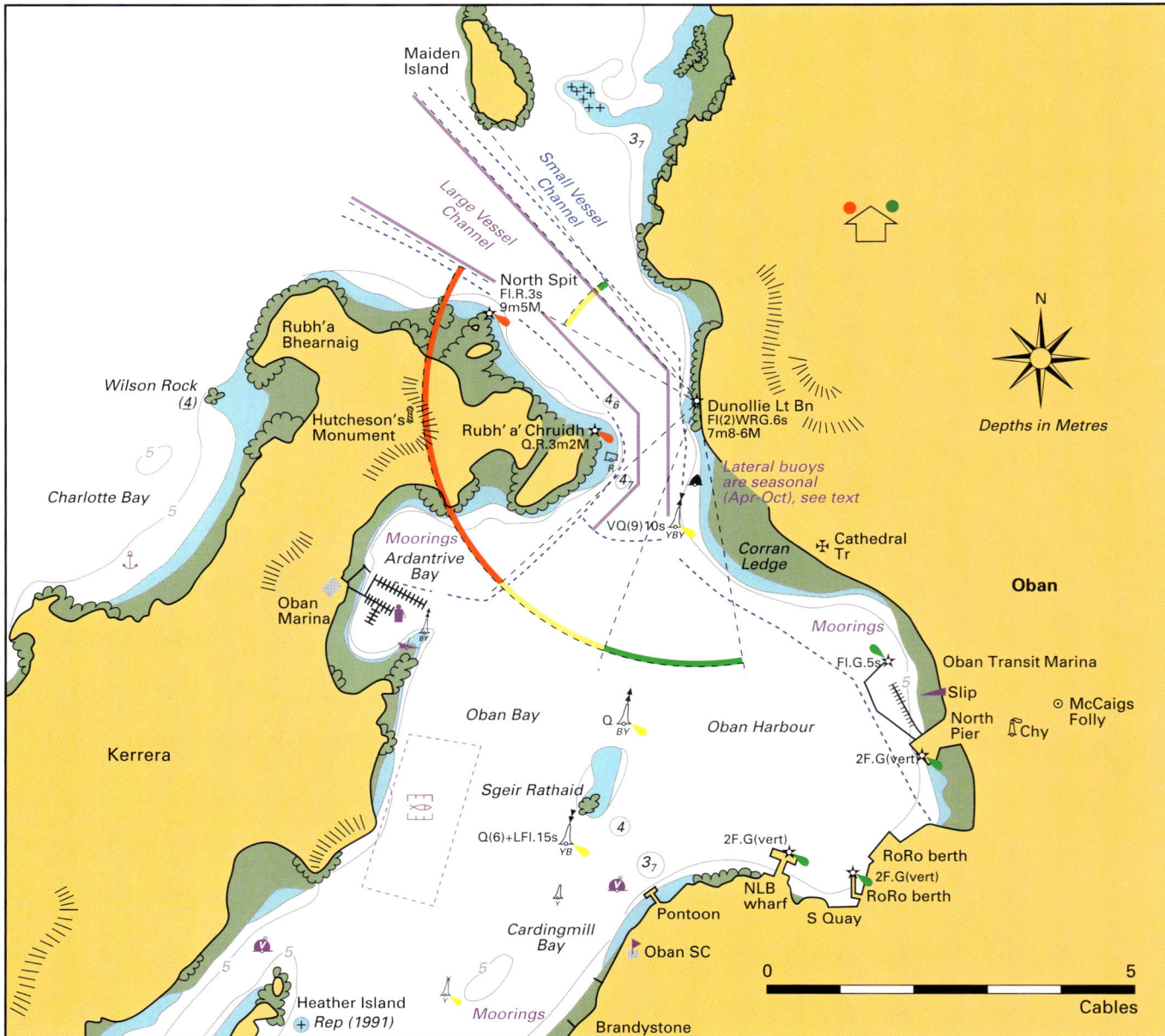

OBAN BAY

Admiralty Chart
1790, 2387
Admiralty Leisure Folio
5611.17, 28A
Imray Chart
C65, 2800.3
Ordnance Survey
49
Cruising Scotland
pp.92, 93

Oban

Oban is the principal port on the West Coast and is one of the busiest ferry ports in Britain, traffic having grown by over 50% in recent years. Leisure vessels are also on the increase following the establishment of a 50 berth transit marina at the North Pier in 2017, and with Oban becoming a popular destination for cruise liners their numerous tenders are yet another source of small craft traffic during the summer season.

As a result of all the above, a new Code of Practice for the Safety of Navigation in Oban Bay has been introduced. A summary of this is given on p.107 and the full version can be seen in the appendix. **It is important that all leisure vessels entering Oban Bay familiarise themselves with this code and follow its recommendations closely.**

Tides

Oban is a standard port (−0530 Dover).

Height in metres at Oban

MHWS	MHWN	MTL	MLWN	MLWS
4.0	2.9	2.4	1.8	0.7

For tidal streams in Kerrera Sound see p.106.
In the north entrance to Oban Bay tidal streams run at 2½ knots springs, turning about 1½ hours before HW and LW Oban. The flood stream runs northwards.

Identification

In poor visibility the town may not be easily seen from the west, being largely obscured by Kerrera. Conspicuous features are a radio mast close south of the town, and Hutcheson's Monument, a stone obelisk at the north end of Kerrera.

Directions

From the south follow the directions given on p.106 for the Sound of Kerrera as far as

Heather Island. Sgeir Rathaid is marked by a S cardinal buoy at its southern end and a N cardinal buoy at its northern end, and may be passed on either side.

From the north it is important to follow the recommendations of the Code of Practice: keep out of the deep water channel if practicable; use the engine (if fitted); listen on VHF Ch 12/16; observe the speed limit and on no account impede any vessel that can navigate only within the Large Vessel channel.

Before reaching Kerrera or Maiden Isle decide which Small Vessel channel, east or west of the Large Vessel channel, to use and adjust your course accordingly. If intending to use the eastern channel the passage east of Maiden Island may be taken but keep well towards the island (about 30-40m off) to avoid submerged rocks extending from the mainland to 100m from the island.

Where the Large Vessel channel turns south and narrows at Dunollie, keeping out of it is largely a matter of staying within the 10m contour. For a trial period, two seasonal buoys are to be laid in the positions shown on the plan. These should make it easier to judge how close inshore it is safe to go, especially on the east side where Corran Ledge and its W cardinal buoy stand further off shore than one might expect.

Lights

At night lights may not be easy to make out against those of the town; also, for the same reason, keep a particularly good lookout for other vessels.

Sgeir Rathaid South card. buoy; Q(6) +L.Fl.15s
Sgeir Rathaid North card. buoy; Q

Corran Ledge West card. buoy; Q(9)10s
Dunollie light beacon; Fl(2)WRG.6s7m8-6M
The sectored light shows white over the fairways to SSW and NW, red over Kerrera and green to the mainland side, obscured from the east side of the bay. Stone twr.
Rubh' a' Cruidh; Q.R.3m2M. Metal framework
Kerrera North Spit light beacon; Fl.R.3s9m5M. Wh. concrete column with red bands
Transit marina; Fl.G.5s
North Pier and **South Quay** both show 2.F.G(vert)
Northern Lights Wharf; 2.F.G(vert)

Anchoring, mooring and berthing

Soundings in Oban Bay and Oban Harbour are deep, the bottom shelves abruptly and where depths are suitable for anchoring there are many moorings. Accordingly anchoring is not recommended nor advisable and use should be made of the many moorings and pontoons that are available to visitors.

Mooring 15 visitors' moorings are located in Cardingmill Bay, north of the Oban Sailing Club. They are operated by the Oban Bay Berthing Co. who can be contacted on ☎ 07720 302727 to arrange payment. Moorings are also available for hire from Oban Marina (see overleaf). See also p.106 for visitors' moorings north of Heather Island operated by Ardantrive farm.

Berthing Pontoon berths are available at Oban Marina in Ardantrive Bay and the Oban Transit Marina at the north pier (see overleaf).

A pontoon for short stays only (30 minutes) and dinghy landing, is located 1 cable north of Oban Sailing Club, opposite the visitors' moorings. Water and refuse facilities. Fee payable via honesty box.

Oban Marina in Ardantrive Bay, under new management since 2017, provides the best shelter in the Oban area

Charles Warlow

Argyll & Bute Council

Oban Transit Marina, the larger vessels are berthed alongside the outer breakwater pontoon and at the North Pier itself

Oban Transit Marina

This new facility is positioned to the north of the North Pier and is administered by the Argyll and Bute Council - ☎ 01631 562892, VHF Ch 16/12 - yachts intending to berth should call *Oban Harbour* for directions.

50 visitors' pontoon berths all serviced with water and electricity; toilets and showers on North Quay. Dues vary from £12 for a daytime stop between 1100 and 1600 to £3 per metre for overnight berthing up to a maximum stay of three days.

Services and supplies

Chandlery; Caley Fisheries, South Pier and Oban Marina. Supermarkets, shops and hotels in Oban. Launderette beside Royal Hotel and at Oban Marina.

Train and bus to Glasgow. Car ferries to Mull, Lismore, Coll, Tiree and Colonsay. Car hire. Tourist information office.

Communications

Post Office, phone boxes at railway station and elsewhere.
Calmac piermaster ☎ 01631 565854
Caley Fisheries (chandlery) ☎ 01631 563354
Oban Divers ☎ 01631 566618
Oban Marina VHF Ch 80 ☎ 01631 565333
Oban Transit Marina & Harbourmaster (North Pier) ☎ 01631 562892
and VHF Ch 16/12 (during working hours)
Tourist information ☎ 01631 563122
Vale Engineering ☎ 01631 564513

Oban Marina

Ardantrive Bay, Kerrera, ☎ 01631 565333, VHF Ch 80, has 100 pontoon berths, slip, hull and engine repairs, 30 moorings, chandlery, gas, showers and toilets. 'Waypoint Bar and Grill'. Water and electricity at pontoons. Diesel berth at outer end of 'B' pontoon. 50 tonne hoist. Winter storage. A passenger ferry is provided between the boatyard and Oban.

Approaching the marina from the east or south beware a drying reef extending from the south point of the bay. There is a wreck at the outer end of the reef which covers. It is marked with a pole and in addition there is a small north cardinal buoy positioned at the northern edge of the reef.

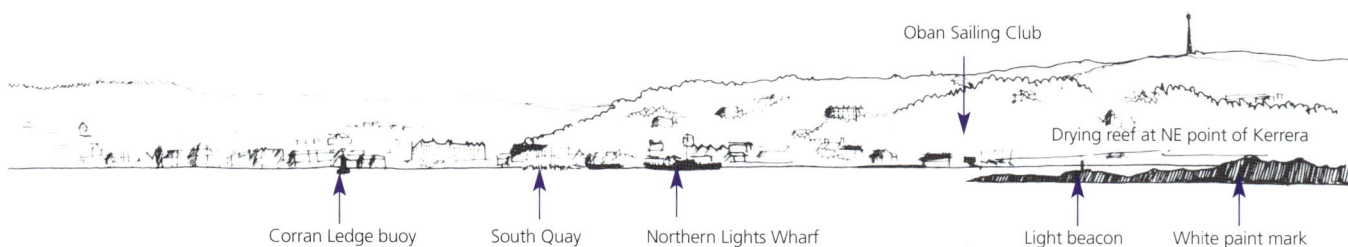

Oban Sailing Club | Drying reef at NE point of Kerrera

Corran Ledge buoy | South Quay | Northern Lights Wharf | Light beacon | White paint mark

Oban Bay north entrance, from northwest of North Spit Beacon. Railway Pier lies beyond Corran Ledge buoy

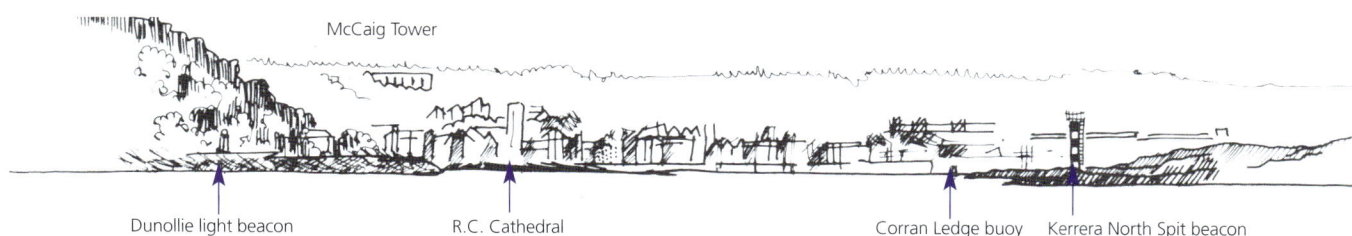

McCaig Tower

Dunollie light beacon | R.C. Cathedral | Corran Ledge buoy | Kerrera North Spit beacon

Oban Bay from north, from east of North Spit beacon

Loch Don

A curious place of shoals and drying banks, rather like a river from the east coast of England set down among mountains. The entrance is identified by a conspicuous white house at Grass Point, about two miles south of Black's Memorial light beacon.

Directions

Identify Eilean nan Caorach and the small islet Maol Donn, lying ¾ cable due south of it. On a course of 270° pass about ½ cable south of Maol Donn and continue on this course until a cable due north of Rubha nan Gall Mor.

Here steer 225° for about a cable and then the best that can be done, unless you have the *Antares* chart running in conjunction with GPS, is to feel your way in, preferably on a rising tide, watching the echo sounder when approaching the edges of the channel. Do not try to cut across the bank in the middle of the loch, which extends further east than it would appear to do, and has large boulders scattered over it.

Anchorage

There is a useful temporary anchorage off the pier at Grass Point. The holding is poor close north of the pier (which was originally the main ferry pier for Mull) but better further out. Leave room for tourist launches to approach the pier. Otherwise anchor off the fence shown on the plan, where at least a knot of tide can be experienced at springs.

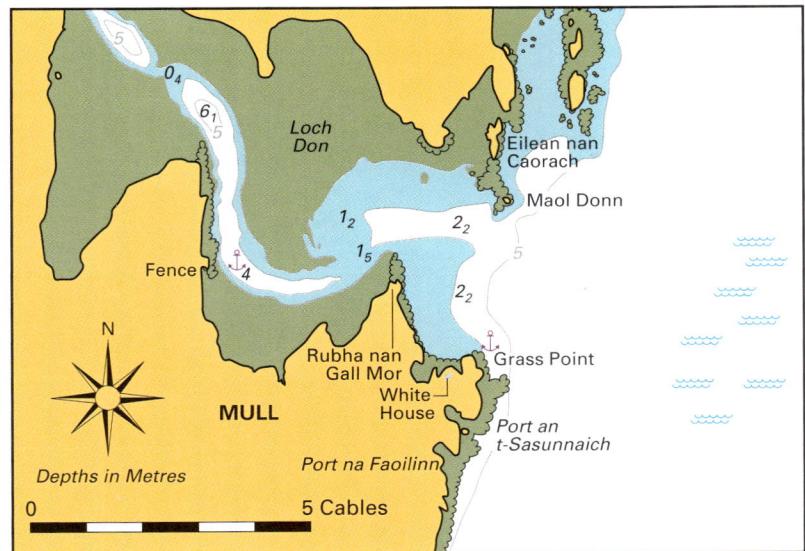

LOCH DON

Occasional anchorages

Port Donain A small bay, named on chart 2387 and shown with an anchor, 1¼ miles north of the entrance to Loch Spelve. Good shelter in offshore winds but fully exposed to east. Sand and weed.

Port Ohirnie Another small bay 6 miles west of the entrance to Loch Spelve and immediately north of Rubha nan Fear. Sheltered in winds from west to north but squally in strong winds because of the high ground onshore.

For details of the coast west of here see Ch.11, Ross of Mull.

Loch Don from the south east with Grass Point and the Ferry Cottage on the lower right

Martin Lawrence

Charles Warlow

The anchorage off Croggan, Loch Spelve

Admiralty Chart
2387
Admiralty Leisure Folio
5611.9A & B
Imray Chart
C65, 2800.3
Ordnance Survey
49
Cruising Scotland
p.89

Loch Spelve

Lying on the west side of the Firth of Lorn, Loch Spelve is completely landlocked and surrounded by an impressive range of hills, which sometimes produce correspondingly impressive squalls.

What was formerly a challenging entrance to this loch, a narrow channel with shoal water to the south and a rock on the north side, has been greatly simplified by the establishment of a lit perch on the said rock.

Tides

Const +0005 Oban (−0535 Dover).

Height in metres

MHWS	MHWN	MTL	MLWN	MLWS
4.0	2·9	2·4	1·8	0·7

Tidal streams run in the narrows at 3½ to 4 knots Sp. In-going stream begins at −0530 Oban (+0125 Dover) Out-going stream at +0015 Oban (−0515 Dover).

Directions

Approach from the southeast keeping well off both shores to avoid shoals and make to pass close west of the second point on the north side. Note that there are shoals extending northeastwards from the south shore towards this point. When west of this point, and with the vertical cliff open of the dark shoulder (see plan) bearing 092° astern, steer to keep about ¼ cable from the north shore and pass south of the green perch with ball topmark (Fl.G 5s).

Care must also be taken to avoid the rock known as The Mushroom which stands 1·5 metres above the general level of the shoal to the south and is awash at chart datum. This rock lies only just south of mid-channel and very much in the way of any boat cutting across the edge of the shoal when the tide might seem to have risen enough. Following the track indicated on the plan and passing not less than 20m off the perch clears all the dangers described.

'Papadil', one of the fleet of yachts anchored in the NW arm of Loch Spelve for the CCC Centenary muster

Anchorage

There are many possible anchorages throughout the loch, often with good holding in mud, although a steeply shelving bottom and the presence of fish and mussel farms can be a restriction in some of them.

The southwest arm of the loch provides reasonable shelter at the head. The bottom rises abruptly from 12 metres to a foreshore which dries more than ½ cable on the south and southwest sides but good holding should be found in 8-12 metres.

Camas an-t Seilisdeir lies on the west side of the loch, southwest of Rubha Riabhach. There are several fish cages but suitable space and depth should be found.

Ardura, at the west side of the north arm, is probably the best anchorage in the loch. Anchor in its southwest corner as depth permits. Extensive drying foreshore, and fierce gusts in westerly winds.

When approaching this anchorage from the narrows the passage between the mussel lines is not readily apparent until well into the loch. It is, however, quite wide and lit by flashing yellow buoys shown approximately on the plan.

In the northeast bay the bottom is mostly rock, and not good holding, and a broad drying rock lies towards the head of the bay.

On the east shore there is some shelter in the bay northeast of Eilean Amalaig, which lies about a mile north of the entrance, but entrance to it may be obstructed by mussel lines.

In easterly winds the unnamed bay ¼ mile south of Eilean Amalaig is reported to provide good holding but is shoal inshore with a drying rock lying off the south point of the bay and mussel lines impede entry from the southwest.

Croggan, just southwest of the entrance, provides good anchorage in offshore winds.

Sara Mason

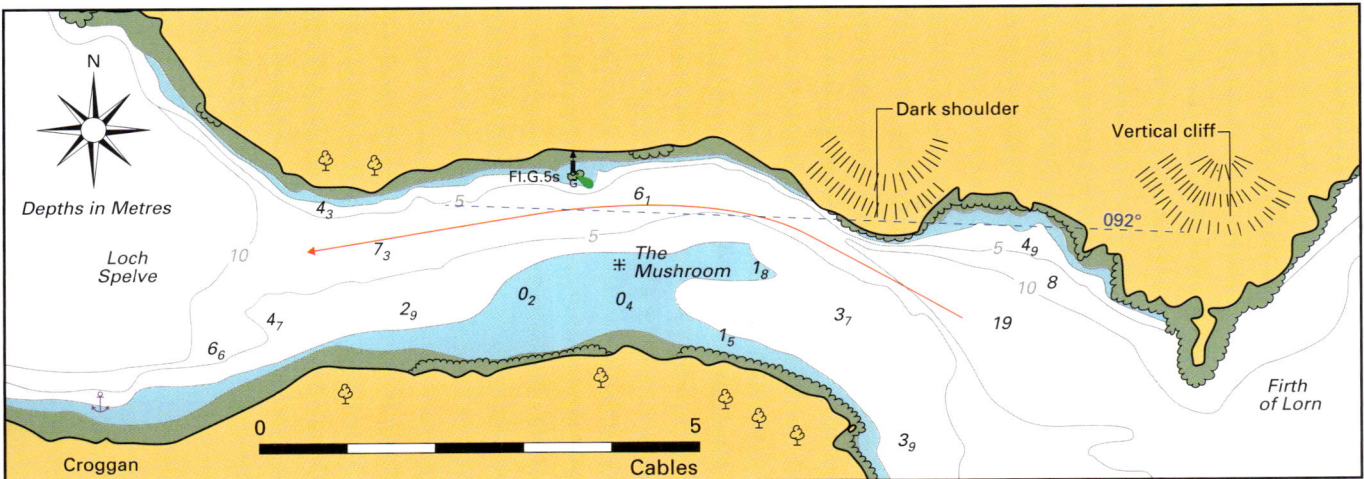

LOCH SPELVE NARROWS

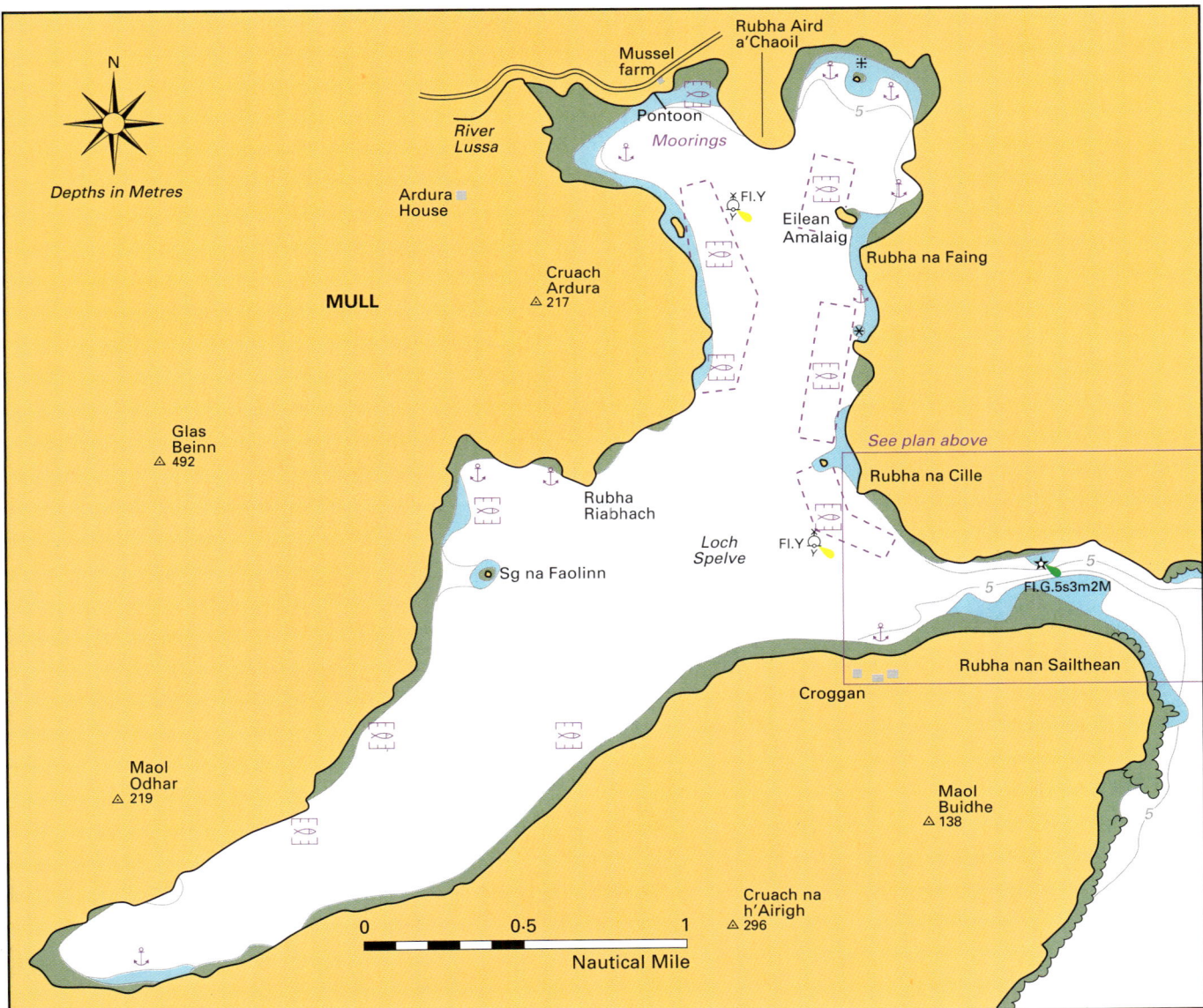

N

Depths in Metres

Loch Spelve

Fl.G.5s

Dark shoulder

Vertical cliff

092°

The Mushroom

4_3 5 6_1 5 5 4_9

7_3 10

6_6 4_7 2_9 0_2 0_4 1_8 3_7 10 8 19

1_5 3_9

Croggan Cables 0 5 *Firth of Lorn*

LOCH SPELVE

N

Depths in Metres

MULL

River Lussa

Ardura House

Mussel farm

Rubha Aird a'Chaoil

Pontoon

Moorings

Fl.Y

Eilean Amalaig

Rubha na Faing

Cruach Ardura △ 217

Glas Beinn △ 492

Rubha Riabhach

Sg na Faolinn

Loch Spelve

Fl.Y

See plan above

Rubha na Cille

Fl.G.5s3m2M

Rubha nan Sailthean

Croggan

Maol Odhar △ 219

Maol Buidhe △ 138

Cruach na h'Airigh △ 296

0 0·5 1 Nautical Mile

7. Loch Etive and Loch Linnhe

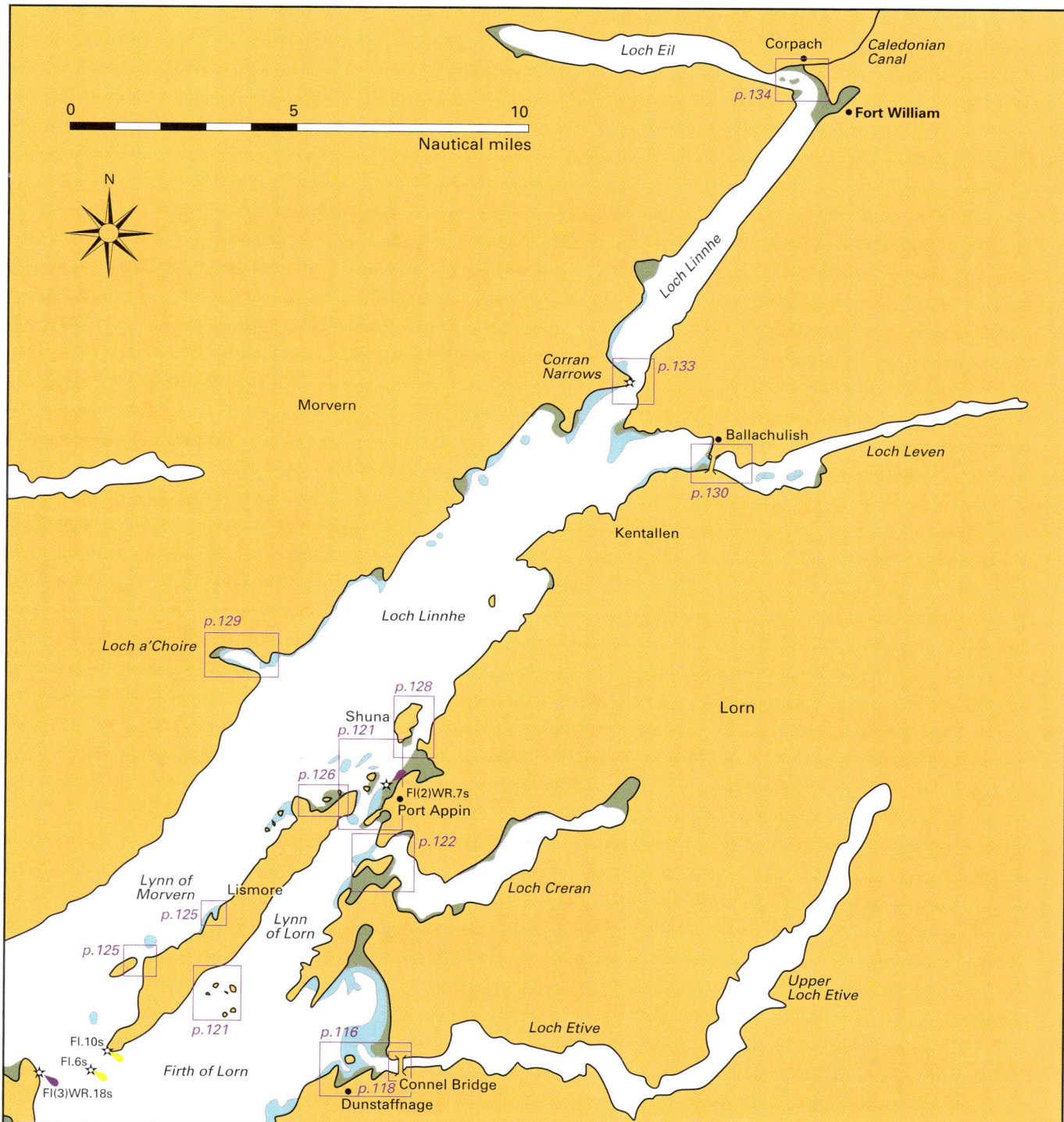

LOCH ETIVE AND LOCH LINNHE

Map labels:
- Loch Eil
- Corpach
- Caledonian Canal
- *p.134*
- Fort William
- Loch Linnhe
- Corran Narrows
- *p.133*
- Ballachulish
- Loch Leven
- *p.130*
- Morvern
- Kentallen
- Loch Linnhe
- Lorn
- Loch a'Choire
- *p.129*
- *p.128*
- Shuna
- *p.121*
- *p.126*
- Fl(2)WR.7s
- Port Appin
- *p.122*
- Lynn of Morvern
- Lismore
- Lynn of Lorn
- Loch Creran
- *p.125*
- *p.125*
- Upper Loch Etive
- *p.121*
- Loch Etive
- Fl.10s
- Fl.6s
- *p.116*
- Fl(3)WR.18s
- Firth of Lorn
- *p.118*
- Connel Bridge
- Dunstaffnage

Scale: 0 — 5 — 10 Nautical miles

N

John Anderson

Loch Linnhe is the continuation of the Firth of Lorn northeastwards from Lismore towards Fort William and the Great Glen, through which runs the Caledonian Canal. This is entered at Corpach, just beyond Fort William, at the head of the loch. In the approach to Loch Linnhe there are two channels: the Lynn of Morvern to the northwest of Lismore and the Lynn of Lorn to the southeast.

South of these, Loch Etive branches off eastward for about 15 miles into the mainland and 17 miles further up Loch Linnhe, Loch Leven heads away into the hills. Whereas the scenery in the lower reaches of these three lochs is fertile and gentle it becomes increasingly mountainous and dramatic towards their heads.

Navigation in the main part of Loch Linnhe and its approach through the Lynn of Morvern is straightforward and relatively free from dangers but the Lynn of Lorn, the area between Lismore and Shuna and the entrances to the adjoining lochs and the narrows within them, require considerable care.

The whole area is well charted to a large (1:25,000) scale but passage planning is not helped by the fact that there is no Admiralty chart giving an overall view other than chart 2635, *West Coast of Scotland*. The Imray chart C65 at 1:150,000 scale is the best alternative.

Looking northeast up Loch Linnhe with Lismore in the centre of the picture. The Lynn of Morvern lies to the left and the Lynn of Lorn to the right

Admiralty Chart
2379, 2380, 2388, 2389, 2372
Admiralty Leisure Folio
5611.18, 19, 20, 22, 23. 26B
Imray Chart
C65, 2800.4, 6, 7
Ordnance Survey
49, 41
Cruising Scotland
pp.95-100

John Anderson

The entrance to Loch Etive from the west. Connel Bridge is in the centre and Dunstaffnage Yacht Haven in the lower right hand corner

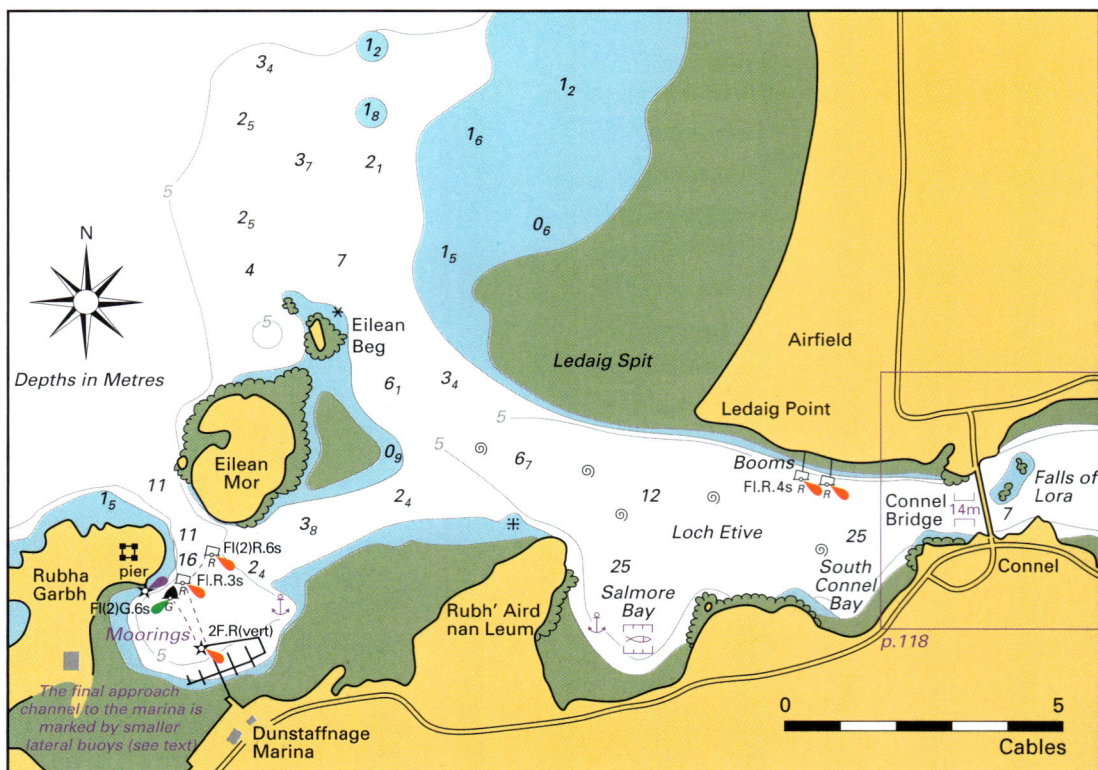

DUNSTAFFNAGE BAY AND APPROACHES TO LOCH ETIVE

Dunstaffnage Bay and approaches to Loch Etive

The central part of Dunstaffnage Bay (the inner part dries out for 2½ cables) is almost entirely occupied by moorings and marina pontoons or fish cages belonging to the The Scottish Association for Marine Science (SAMS) whose buildings lie on the west side of the bay.

The tidal stream through the bay is significant but Salmore Bay (charted as Camus Bruaich Ruaidh) 5 cables to the east and partially occupied by a fish farm, is less affected by tide.

Tides

At Dunstaffnage Bay the constant is as Oban (–0530 Dover).

Height in metres

MHWS	MHWN	MTL	MLWN	MLWS
4·1	3·0	2·4	1·9	0·8

Tidal streams in Dunstaffnage Bay normally circulate counter-clockwise but may, unpredictably, run in the reverse direction.

Directions

The principal approach to Dunstaffnage Bay and Salmore Bay is between Rubha Garbh, on which Dunstaffnage Castle stands, and Eilean Mor. If coming from the Lynn of Lorn keep at least 3 cables off Rubha Garbh-aird, the westerly point of Ardmucknish Bay, to avoid a rock, drying 0·9m, lying southwest of the point.

There is nothing to be gained by passing east of Eilean Mor and Eilean Beg as extensive drying spits lie off the east side of Eilean Mor and off Ledaig Point opposite. There is also tide to contend with, which is strong on the west-going

Admiralty Chart
2388
Admiralty Leisure Folio
5611.19
Imray Chart
C65, 2800.6
Ordnance Survey
49
Cruising Scotland
p.95

ebb. However, if you do, keep clear of a half-tide rock ½ cable northwest of Eilean Beg and pass a cable east of this islet before coming round gradually to head for the bridge.

Anchorage

Ganavan Bay A wide sandy bay between Oban and Loch Etive offering temporary anchorage. Anchor in 3-4m sand but take care to avoid the several isolated rocks and cables shown on the chart.

Dunstaffnage Bay Anchor between Eilean Mor and the moorings, clear of the fairway to Loch Etive and to the marina.

Salmore Bay (Camas Bruaich Ruaidhe), east of Dunstaffnage Bay, is entirely occupied by fish cages and permanent moorings.

South Connel Bay, east of Salmore Bay, is almost full of moorings and is more affected by the tide, but is more convenient for stores.

Dunstaffnage Marina

There are many moorings in the bay and to avoid them a buoyed channel has been established. Approach the marina from the outer (Fl(2)R.6s) port hand buoy and then pass between the inner port and starboard hand lit buoys before heading for the west end of the breakwater pontoon. Smaller, unlit red and green buoys may define the channel between the larger ones.

Call the marina on Ch 37 to request a berth but, if there is no response, tie up alongside the outer breakwater and report to the marina office. The marina offers full yacht services and

Martin Lawrence

has moorings and serviced pontoon berths for visitors. Facilities include water, diesel, chandlery, showers, toilets, restaurant, bar and accommodation. Slip with mobile 40 tonne hoist, mechanical, electrical and hull repairs. Engineer; sailmaker (Owen Sails) will collect sails for repair.

Services and supplies
At Dunbeg; general store, Post Office, bus service to Oban, rail station at Connel (2 miles).

Communications
Dunstaffnage Marina VHF Ch 37 ☎ 01631 566555
Wide Mouthed Frog restaurant ☎ 01631 567005

Dunstaffnage and the entrance to Loch Etive from the west. The yacht haven moorings are at the right beyond the castle, and Connel Bridge and Ben Cruachan at upper left

Martin Lawrence

Dunstaffnage Yacht Haven from southeast. Several more rows of pontoons have been added since this photo was taken in 2003

Connel Bridge showing the recommended course south of the Falls of Lora

Randal Coe

Admiralty Chart
2388
Admiralty Leisure Folio
5611.19
Imray Chart
C65, 2800.6
Ordnance Survey
49
Cruising Scotland
p.95

Loch Etive

Apart from the usual crop of unmarked rocks there are three specific obstacles which discourage visitors from entering Loch Etive. The first is the bridge at Connel, with a charted clearance at MHWS of 14 metres. Next, immediately east of the bridge a drying reef extending more than halfway across the channel from the north side holds back the water and causes a tidal fall, known as the Falls of Lora. Lastly, at Bonawe, five miles east of the bridge, a very high-voltage electricity cable crosses the loch, with a safe clearance at its lowest point of 13 metres.

The shores of the lower part of the loch are pastoral and well wooded. Beyond Bonawe the loch is overshadowed by high mountains with no road except at its head, and the few farms are supplied by mail boat. Fish farming is expanding rapidly. On the north side of Bonawe narrows there is a quarry from which granite is taken away by sea.

Tides

Tidal streams run at up to six knots in the narrows at Connel.

The east-going stream begins about –0345 Oban (+0310 Dover). The west-going stream begins about +0200 Oban (–0330 Dover).

Meteorological conditions may cause these figures to vary by up to 1½ hours with a tendency to be early rather than late, owing to the greater frequency of, and exposure to, westerly winds. There is almost no slack water. This information is based on research by the SAMS laboratory at Dunstaffnage.

The reefs to the east of Connel Bridge hold back the water so that at HW springs the level is 0·5 metre higher outside the loch than inside, and at LW springs it is 1·2 metres higher inside than outside. Again, there is virtually no slack water, and the stream runs very strongly through the channel south of the reef with eddies on either side. Recommended times to pass the falls vary from half an hour either side of the turn of the tide to two hours, one figure being given by the owner of a sailing yacht with a small engine, the other by the skipper of a fishing boat.

Directions

From the west the best approach is to be at the narrows a little before the tide turns eastwards so as to go through at fairly slack water. Read the above notes about tides, and allow for the tide turning up to 1½ hours early in strong southwesterly winds or if the barometer is low, or up to 1½ hours late in the opposite conditions. If you are early anchor off a blue-painted pub on the south shore (The Oyster Inn).

Steer for the space between the bottom of the first and second oblique struts of the bridge from its south tower. There is no satisfactory mark for clearing the south end of the reef, but at low tide it is uncovered and when covered it is usually defined, except at slack water, by a ripple along its south edge.

When past the bridge and about 70m from the point with a large building on it, a cable east of the bridge, turn towards a conspicuous white-gabled house amongst trees on the north shore.

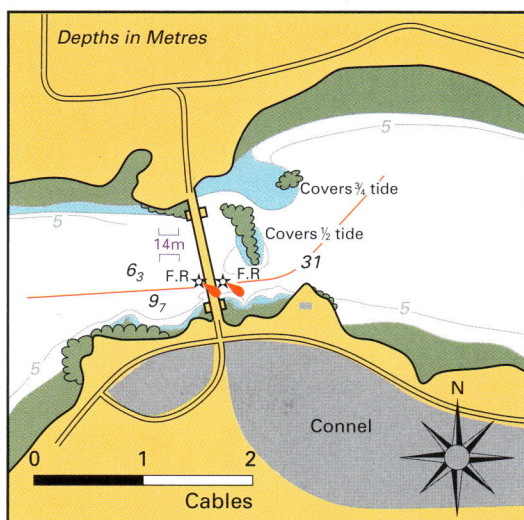

CONNEL BRIDGE NARROWS

The north side of the loch is quite clear to the Kilmaronaig Narrows and keeping towards it avoids a rock, half a mile from the bridge, just south of mid-channel. Rocks lie off the end of Dunfiunary, a point on the south shore on which stands a house with a round tower, and there are violent eddies beyond it. The tide sets strongly towards rocks on the south shore at the east end of the channel.

At Kilmaronaig Narrows, 1½ miles east of Connel Bridge, the tides turn about ten minutes later than at Connel and runs at nearly the same rate as at the falls. Strong eddies run westward along the south shore east of the narrows on the flood, and west of the narrows on the ebb, flowing east.

The channel is about half a cable wide between the northwest shore, which dries out for 50m just southwest of the narrows, and submerged rocks extending more than half way across from the islets off the southeast shore. To pass through Kilmaronaig Narrows keep 50m off the north shore until well clear of the narrows and the rocks mentioned above.

2¼ miles east of the narrows is Ardchattan shoal in mid-loch with 1·2m over it. It is best to steer to the south of the loch at this point to avoid the shoal. Otherwise, provided the shores are given a berth of at least a cable, the loch is clear as far as Bonawe Narrows and the tides are little felt.

Anchorage

Achnacreemore Bay North of the narrows. Except in onshore winds anchor at the north end of the bay's west shore, but keep clear of a rock which dries 0·6 metre, a cable south of the mouth of a burn.

Stonefield Bay (Linne na Craige) is on the south shore a mile west of the narrows. Anchor east of Eilean Traighe, towards the head of the bay.

East of Abbot's Isles on the east side of Stonefield Bay. The channel there is rather deep and the bottom rocky, and an eddy sets through it on the flood; anchor in the bight close to the islands. There may be lost moorings here.

Auchnacloich Bay, the next bay east of Stonefield, provides some shelter. Leave clear access to the pier which is used by workboats from the SAMS laboratory.

Sailean Ruadh, west of Airds Point, three miles from Kilmaronaig Narrows, is an attractive anchorage and provides good shelter in four metres; there are rocks towards the head of the inlet. A fish farm has recently been established across the mouth of this bay but there is room to pass between it and the shore at each end.

Airds Bay southwest of Bonawe Narrows has a foreshore drying out for more than half a cable beyond which the depth increases very quickly. At the concrete jetty east of the river mouth in the southeast corner of the bay underwater cables run WNW from the end of the pier and northwest from a point on shore north of the pier.

Areas on either side of the approach to the pier have been leased for permanent moorings, and the area allocated for anchorage is off the southwest shore, about ¼ mile west of the pier.

Supplies

Shop, Post Office, phone box, hotels; petrol at Taynuilt, ¾ mile from Bonawe Pier.

Connel Bridge and the Falls of Lora from the south. The ebb tide is pouring over the reef close east of the bridge

Martin Lawrence

Upper Loch Etive

The upper loch is narrow and penetrates nine miles into increasingly high mountains which with certain wind directions can produce severe squalls. Overhead power cables cross Bonawe Narrows, with a safe clearance of 13 metres at their lowest point but greater, although unspecified, clearance towards the north side.

Tides

The constant at Bonawe is +0200 Oban (–0330 Dover).

Height in metres

MHWS	MHWN	MTL	MLWN	MLWS
2·0	1·2	1·0	0·5	0·2

Tidal streams at these narrows run at 2½ knots springs on the flood, 1½ knots on the ebb.

Directions

Apart from the overhead power cable the only hazards are shoal water extending northeast from the former ferry pier at the south side of the narrows, and drying rocks extending 3 cables offshore from Ardnellan Point, the north point of Inverliver Bay on the southeast shore some 3½ miles northeast of Bonawe Narrows. The wind tends to be very fluky unless setting straight up or down the loch.

In case any shoal-draught boats should enter the mouth of River Awe on the south side of the narrows, note that power cables cross the river, ¼ mile from its mouth, with a safe clearance of four metres.

Anchorages

Most bays are very deep and there are many fish cages. The best anchorage is at the head of the loch but it is exposed to southerly fetch.

Glenoe Bay (Port an Dobhrain) On the east shore 2 miles from Bonawe. Anchoring depth reported as 4–8m. No survey of seabed.

Creag Bay Opposite Glenoe Bay. Anchor off jetty below cottage in 6–10m.

Inverliver Bay Approach from the southwest. A reef extends westward 3 cables from Ardnellan Point on the north side of the bay. Good shelter except from NW/SW winds. Anchor well offshore in at least 10m. Good holding in mud reported. Avoid fouling anchor on boulders inshore.

Camus an Seilisdeire Keep clear of the northeast point of this bay and anchor close inshore as soundings increase rapidly.

Bagh nan Dalach (Dail Bay) On the west shore between the mouths of rivers Dalach and Easach. Anchor west of the remains of old pier. Good holding in 6–8m.

Head of Loch Anchor on the west shore between the pier and an islet which dries at low water. Exposed to southerly winds. Good holding but boulders have been reported.

Lynn of Lorn

The passage from Oban to Loch Linnhe by the east side of Lismore and the Lynn of Lorn is sheltered from the west but tides run strongly and careful pilotage is needed at the north end. The passage can be negotiated with these directions and Imray chart C65, but 2379 and 2389 at 1:25,000 will be needed for exploring inshore.

Tides

The constant at Port Appin is –0005 Oban (–0535 Dover).

Height in metres

MHWS	MHWN	MTL	MLWN	MLWS
4·2	3·1	2·5	1·9	0·8

At the south end of the Lynn of Lorn the tidal stream turns NNE at +0445 Oban (–0045 Dover); SSW at –0140 Oban (+0515 Dover).

Southwest of the group of islets off the southeast side of Lismore an eddy on the flood sets southwestwards.

At the north end of the Lynn of Lorn, the tidal stream turns NNE at +0600 Oban (+0030 Dover); SSW at –0015 Oban (–0545 Dover).

Streams vary from one knot at the south end to 2½ knots at the north end at springs.

North end of the Lynn of Lorn, with the perch marking rocks extending SSW of Inn Island in the foreground and the spit extending east from Lismore beyond

Martin Lawrence

Directions

From the south keep outside of a cable off Rubha Fion-aird on the east side of the entrance and pass east of Eilean Dubh, and at least ¼ mile off the mainland shore here; pass either side of Branra Rock beacon then pass within a cable to the west of Appin Rocks starboard-hand buoy, to avoid the Lobster Stone. Pass midway between Sgeir Buidhe and Inn Island, noting the shoals extending 1½ cables SSW of it marked by a perch, and extensive shoals off the Appin shore. Between Shuna and Sheep Island (Eilean nan Caorach) keep towards Shuna to avoid shoals extending 2 cables north of Sheep Island and 2 cables northeast of Eilean Glas. However, note that Shuna has rocks extending up to a cable from its southwest shore.

Passage west of Inn Island is possible but care is required to avoid the 2m shoal in the channel and the two spits extending from Lismore, which are marked by perches. For passage through Shuna Sound see p.128.

Anchorage

None of the anchorages within the Lynn of Lorn provide good shelter but with the right wind direction they provide interesting occasional anchorage in pleasant surroundings, often off a sand or shingle beach.

The Creags There are several occasional anchorages around this group of islands. The adjacent plan shows four that can be used according to wind direction and conditions. They are mainly in 4–10m sand or shingle with weed patches (see photo p.122).

Ardmucknish (Tralee) Bay Anchor in north corner off Ard Bhatan in 6-10m sand with rock patches. Owen Sails are within short walking distance. Calor Gas at caravan site.

Camus Nathais The bay between Ru Fionaird and Ru Garbhard. Anchor in 3–9m sand and shingle.

Eilean Dubh Anchor off a shingle beach on the west side in 2–3m. Can be approached from the north or south but the depth in the latter passage is only about 1·2m.

Airds Bay East of Appin Rocks provides temporary anchorage. Exposed to southerlies. Dries out for 2 cables.

Port Appin Anchor at least 2 cables south of the pier avoiding underwater cables and moorings. 10 visitors' moorings are provided for patrons of the Pier House Hotel ☎01631 30302. **Facilities:** Shop, Post Office, water 200m north of the pier.

Eilean nan Caorach (Sheep Island) Approach with care from the southeast as the leading marks are no longer in existence. Anchor well off.

Lights

Branra Rock Bn. Fl(2)10s3m5M
Dearg Sgeir Bn. Fl.WRG.2s
Appin Rocks Buoy Fl.G 6s.
Sgeir Buidhe Light Bn. Fl(2)R.7s9M

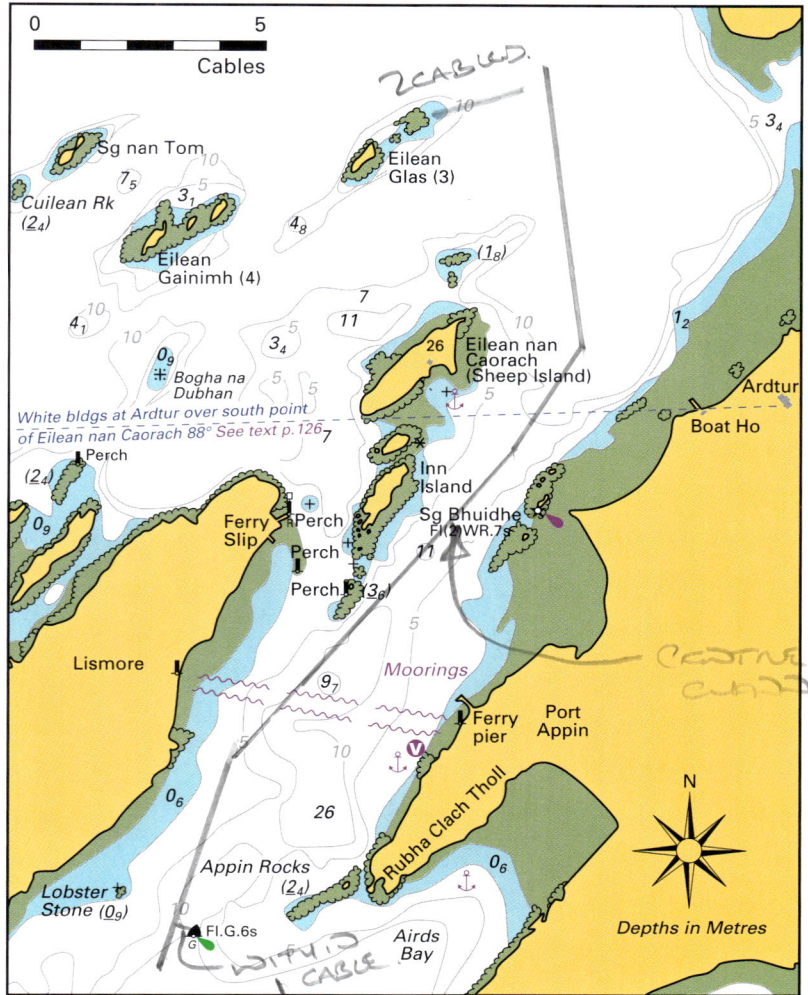

APPIN NARROWS

Admiralty Chart
2379, 2389
Admiralty Leisure Folio
5611.18, 19
Imray Chart
C65, 2800.6
Ordnance Survey
49
Cruising Scotland
p.95

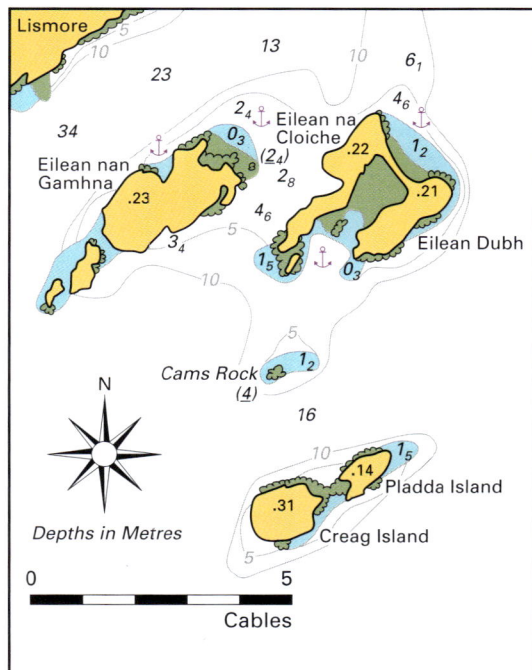

THE CREAGS

Admiralty Chart
2379
Admiralty Leisure Folio
5611.18, 26B
Imray Chart
C65, 2800.6
Ordnance Survey
49
Cruising Scotland
p.96

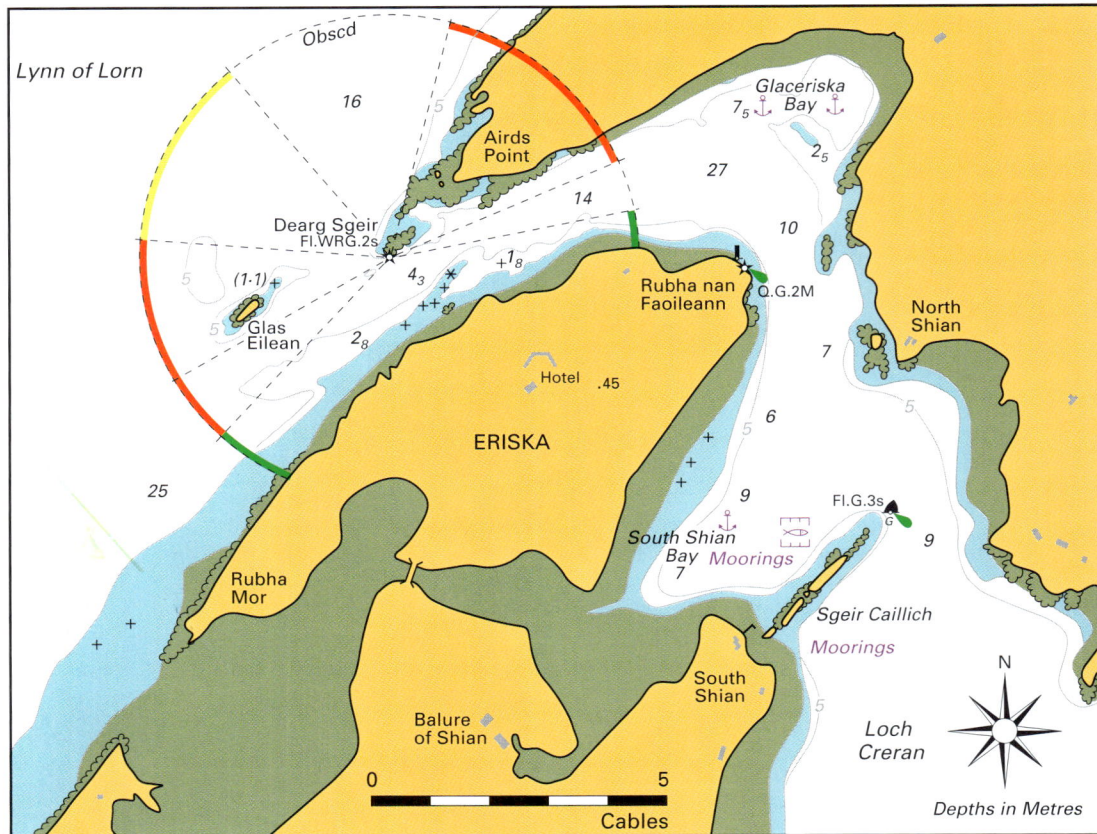

ENTRANCE TO
LOCH CRERAN

Loch Creran

Loch Creran has a narrow entrance which requires care, although it is well marked and lit. Within the loch there are many fish farms and a good number of yacht moorings. It is divided into two parts by the narrows at Creagan but the entrance to the upper loch is restricted by depth (1·5m) and a road bridge which has a clearance of 9·5m.

Tides

Tidal streams can run at up to 4 knots springs in the narrows turning at approximately HW and LW Oban. The constant at Barcaldine is +0015 Oban (−0515 Dover).

Height in metres

MHWS	MHWN	MTL	MLWN	MLWS
4·1	3·0	2·4	1·8	0·8

Directions

Enter either side of Glas Eilean and southeast of Dearg Sgeir. Keep towards Dearg Sgeir to avoid rocks extending a cable from the Eriska shore. Branra Rock beacon in line with the inside of Glas Eilean astern clears these rocks.

A cable past the beacon keep mid-channel for a while but after passing north of Eriska hold towards Eriska beacon on the starboard hand to avoid rocks on the northeast side of passage. Then pass north of the G con. buoy marking the end of the spit extending northeast from Sgeir Caillich.

Note that quite large commercial vessels visit Loch Creran and need to be given right of way in the narrow entrance channel.

At anchor off the shingle spit joining Eilean na Cloiche and Eilean Dubh in the Creags (p.121)

Edward Mason

Once inside the main loch there are no hidden dangers in the fairway but give the shores a generous berth as in places they dry for up to 2 cables off. Keeping outside the 10m contour will clear all dangers.

Approaching Caolas Creagan, Black Rocks (drying 3·7 metres), extend over a cable off a promontory 4 cables WSW of the narrows. The bridge headroom is 9·5 metres and the least depth is 1·5m so access is possible only for small shoal draught boats. The tidal streams run at up to five knots.

To navigate the Creagan narrows pass under the south span of the bridge, to avoid rocks under the northern span, and then keep to the north side until the end of the bluff on that shore where the loch opens out. At that point alter southeastwards to avoid an extensive gravel spit running south from a white house above the north shore, but keep a cable off the south shore to avoid a shoal with LD 0·2m.

Designated anchorages

Only the following anchorages may be used:

Glaceriska Bay opposite north end of Eriska. Anchor in suitable depth clear of moorings. Good holding. Store and hotel at Port Appin 1½ miles.

South Shian Bay East of Eriska, off the former ferry slip or closer to Eriska but clear of moorings. Landing at slip.

Creagan Occasional anchorage in the bay southwest of the Creagan Inn. Holding poor, use plenty of scope. Creagan Inn provides two visitor's moorings.

Head of loch Anchor in 9m, mud, at the east end about a cable from the shore and where shown on chart 2379.

Lights

Dearg Sgeir Lt. Bn. Fl.WRG.2s2m3-1M
Eriska Lt. Bn. QG.2M
Sgeir Caillich buoy Fl.G.3s

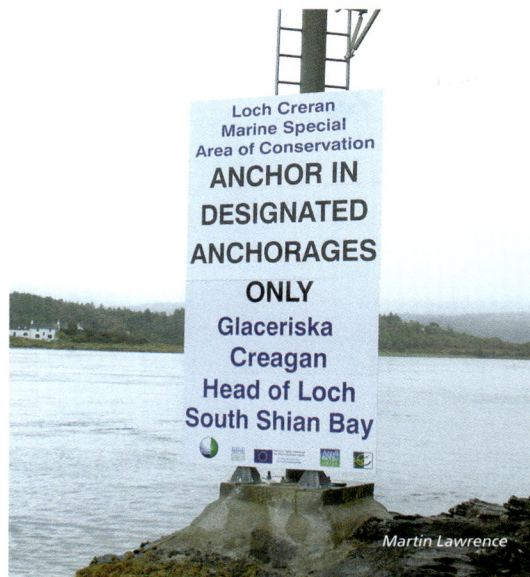

Martin Lawrence

At night approach in the white sector of Dearg Sgeir light. Appin Rocks buoy (Fl.G.6s) on the port beam will give some indication of how near to the beacon you are; the echo sounder will not be much help. Pass close southeast of the beacon until in the white sector again, and when Eriska beacon appears steer to pass close northeast of it with the Fl.G light buoy ahead. There are no lights further up the loch.

Services and supplies

Creran Marine, lying immediately west of the large shed marked on the chart as the Marine Resource Centre, is now the only yacht yard within Loch Creran: 50 moorings, short stay pontoon with water, toilets and showers. Chandlery, mechanical repairs, hull repairs and general maintenance. Other specialist repairs by arrangement.

Pub at Creagan. 5 star hotel on Eriska. Shop, Post Office and gas at Barcaldine caravan site – ½ mile.

Communications

Creran Marine ☎ 01631 720253

> **Conservation area**
> *Loch Creran is a marine Special Area of Conservation (mSAC) and a Nature Conservation Marine Protected Area because it contains very rare and fragile reefs known as serpulid reefs, horse mussel beds and flame shell beds. These habitats are extremely sensitive to physical damage and accordingly only the designated anchorages should be used, except in an emergency.*

Warning notice on the Eriska beacon at the entrance to Loch Creran

South Shian anchorage from the west

Martin Lawrence

Martin Lawrence

*Achadun Bay and castle
from the north, Bernera
Bay is in the upper part
of the photograph*

Admiralty Chart
2389
Admiralty Leisure Folio
5611.15A, 18
Imray Chart
C65, 2800.4 & 6
Ordnance Survey
49
Cruising Scotland
p.97

Lynn of Morvern

This is the main entrance to Loch Linnhe, between Lismore and Morvern, and it is generally clean and deep. It offers only occasional anchorages until the north end of Lismore is reached and, coming from the south, the strong tidal streams between Lismore and Mull have to be taken into account, but otherwise there are neither the pilotage problems nor the interest of the Lynn of Lorn.

Tides

Constant as Oban (−0530 Dover).

Height in metres

MHWS	MHWN	MTL	MLWN	MLWS
4·3	3·2	2·5	1·8	0·7

The north-going stream begins −0545 Oban (+0110 Dover).
The south-going stream begins +0025 Oban (−0505 Dover).

In the Lynn of Morvern the main body of the tidal stream runs at one knot, but on the flood a narrow stream runs northwards from Lismore lighthouse across to the Morvern shore and then northeast towards Shuna island, at 2½ knots.

On the ebb an eddy sets into Bernera Bay. Also on the ebb, at springs only, a strong stream off the Morvern shore northwest of Bernera, runs at four knots to the southeast, with overfalls.

Directions

Approaching from the south, Liath Sgeir, which dries three metres, lies a little more than a mile north of Lismore lighthouse, halfway between the lighthouse and the southwest end of Bernera Island, and slightly to the west of a line joining these two points. This is a hazard if tacking, or making direct for the Lynn of Morvern from south of Lismore.

The super-quarry at Glensanda on Morvern, west of the north end of Lismore, is a landmark on an otherwise featureless, though hazard-free shore. A boat harbour south of the loading jetty is not available to yachts except in emergency. Very large bulk carriers operate from Glensanda to the open sea, normally by way of the Sound of Mull. An announcement of their departure is usually made on VHF Ch 16.

Anchorage

Few of the anchorages in the Lynn of Morvern give all-round shelter and all have to be used with an eye on the present and forecast wind direction.
Bernera Bay lies southeast of Bernera Island, which is towards the southwest end of Lismore, and gives good shelter from northwest to southeast. Anchor in 6–8m, mud. In the approach hold to the Lismore shore to avoid the awash rock a cable due east of the small islets off Bernera Island.
Achadun Bay to the east of Rubh Ard Eirnish on Lismore. Being just across the peninsula from Bernera Bay it is a useful alternative, giving shelter from southeast to west. Anchor on the west side of the bay in 6–8m, mud. Alternatively anchor off a shingle beach in the small bay off the northeast of Bernera Island. Achadun castle ruins are a short distance from each of these bays.

Port na Moralachd (1987); the fish cage is still there though now of a different type.
The best anchorage in SW winds is just off the picture to the right

An Sailean lying about the middle of the northwest side of Lismore is a shallow inlet, suitable as an overnight anchorage only for shoal-draught boats or for those of moderate draught at neaps. There are remains of extensive limestone quarries and limekilns from which lime was shipped out in the first half of the 19th century.

Grogan Dubh, a rock with a perch just above HW springs, is the north end of a drying reef extending from the southwest point of the entrance. The deepest part of the pool is abreast of the high-water mark of this point.

Port na Moralachd located immediately south of the northwest point of Lismore provides reasonable shelter close inshore at the south side of the bay. There is no clear passage between the off-lying islands, and the only approach is from the southwest.

If coming from the north, note that submerged rocks extend over half a cable southwest of the most southerly islet. A large raft of fish cages lies off the north point of the bay (see photo).

Camus Eignaig is no more than a slight indentation in the shoreline, 2½ miles southwest of Glensanda, but it is virtually the only place on the north shore which offer good anchoring depths. In offshore winds it is a good place for a short stay and a run ashore. It can be identified as being the only place between Rubha an Ridire and Glendsanda which has a cottage near the shore.

Lights
Lismore LH. Fl.10s31m17M
Lady's Rock Lt. Fl.6s12m5M
Glensanda jetty Fl.R.3s5m4M

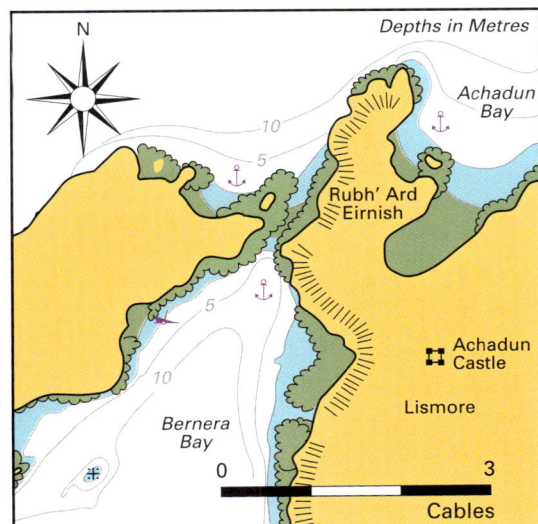

BERNERA BAY AND ACHADUN BAY

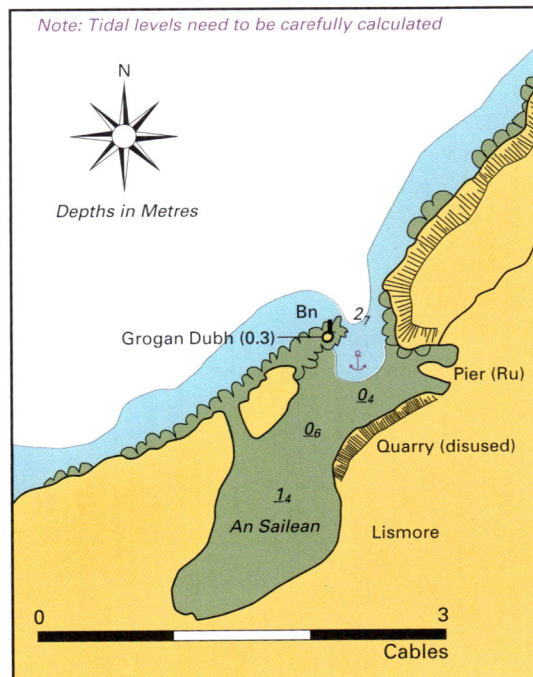

AN SAILEAN, LISMORE

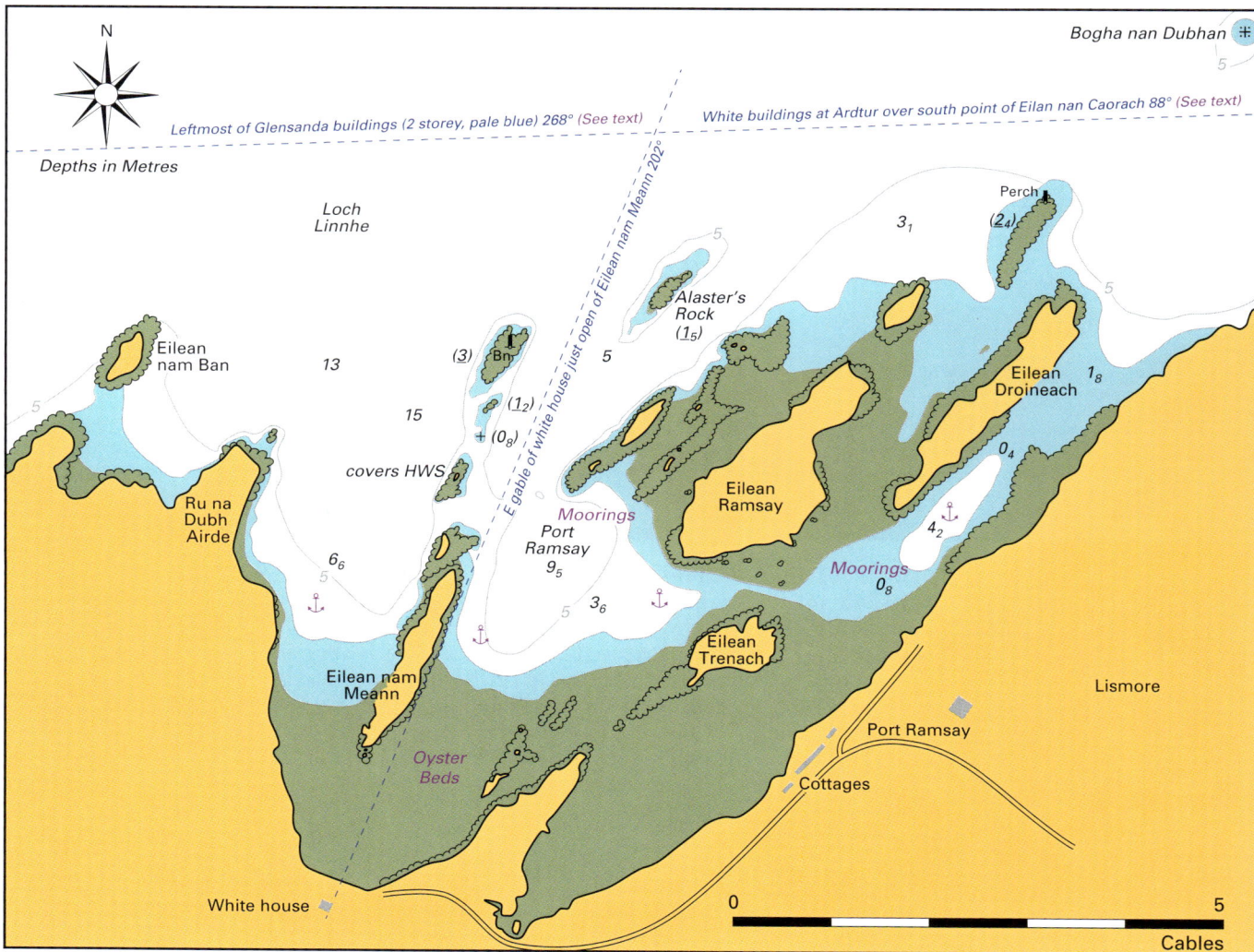

N

Bogha nan Dubhan ⌗
5

Depths in Metres

Leftmost of Glensanda buildings (2 storey, pale blue) 268° (See text)

White buildings at Ardtur over south point of Eilan nan Caorach 88° (See text)

Perch

Loch
Linnhe

3₁

(2₄)

5

3₁

*Alaster's
Rock*
(1₅)

Eilean
nam Ban

13

(3) Bn

5

Eilean
Droineach

1₈

15

(1₂)

0₄

+(0₈)

covers HWS

Moorings
Port
Ramsay
9₅

Eilean
Ramsay

4₂

Ru na
Dubh
Airde

Moorings
0₈

6₆

5

5 3₆

Eilean nam
Meann

Eilean
Trenach

Lismore

Port Ramsay

*Oyster
Beds*

Cottages

White house

0   5

Cables

PORT RAMSAY

Port Ramsay

Admiralty Chart
2379
Admiralty Leisure Folio
5611.18
Imray Chart
C65, 2800.6
Ordnance Survey
49
Cruising Scotland
p.97

Port Ramsay is one of the few secure anchorages at the southwest end of Loch Linnhe although, with many off-lying dangers in the approach, great care has to be taken in identifying the various marks before entering.

Tides

Constant at Port Appin –0005 Oban (–0535 Dover).

Height in metres at Port Appin

MHWS	MHWN	MTL	MLWN	MLWS
4·2	3·1	2·5	1·9	0·8

Directions

In the approach from the north a perch stands on the rock which dries 3 metres on the west side of the entrance, and another stands on the rock which dries 2·4 metres, two cables northeast of Eilean Ramsay. Neither of these perches is at the extreme edge of the rock. If either of these perches is missing, access is still possible but careful use must be made of the transits given below.

From the west Approach from a position no less than ½ cable northeast of Eilean nam Ban. Identify Eilean nam Meann which extends north from the south side of the bay and with

an islet at its north end joined to it by a drying reef; a rock ½ cable north of this islet probably only covers at HW springs. Drying rocks continue north to a perch with a white encapsulated radar reflector standing on the rock which dries 3 metres.

Pass about ¼ cable north of the islet north of Eilean nam Meann and when the east side of Eilean nam Meann is well open come slowly round into the anchorage, giving the east side of the islet a berth of at least ¼ cable.

From the east The main hazards are the rock marked with a perch (dries 2·4m) northeast of Eilean Ramsay and the awash rock, Bogha nan Dubhan, 2½ cables northeast of it. Alaster's Rock (dries 1·5m) lies further west: approximately 1½ cables northeast of the perch on the rock which dries 3 metres.

A transit that clears all three of these hazards is, looking east, the south point of Eilan nan Caorach, which has a bold end, in line with the white buildings at Ardtur (p.121) and a rusty roofed boathouse by the shore, bearing 088°. The same line in the opposite direction heads for a pale blue two-storey building which is the leftmost of the Glensanda buildings and is in line with the glen itself, on the reciprocal of 268°. Binoculars will be needed to pick this up.

Continue westwards along the above transit until picking up the leading line into the anchorage. To do this identify a white house on the Lismore shore south of Eilean nam Meann and keep the left-hand (east) gable just open of the east side of Eilean nam Meann on a bearing of 202°. This will take you ½ cable clear of the perch and clear of Alaster's Rock. If the house is just closed behind the island this will still clear the perch reef.

From the north Many rocks and islets lie up to a mile north of the anchorage, of which Sgeir nan Tom is furthest to the northwest, with drying rocks 1½ cables southwest of it. Pass more than ¼ mile southwest of Sgeir nan Tom or not more than a cable east of it and approach the perch on the drying rock on the west side of the entrance. When about 1½ cables north of it identify the leading line and follow the directions above for entry into the anchorage.

Anchorage

The best anchorage is off the east side of Eilean nam Meann, but no further south than the middle of the island as the head of the bay dries off nearly two cables. Good holding in stiff mud.

Alternatively, anchor between the west end of Eilean Ramsay and Eilean Trenach, though there are some moorings here. The bay west of Eilean nam Meann is also suitable, although less sheltered.

With sufficient rise of tide it is possible to enter the pool east of Eilean Droineach by the shallow (LD 0·4m) channel east of the island. Enter from the northeast but note that there is a

Martin Lawrence

stony spit off the Lismore shore roughly parallel to and near the centre of the apparent channel. The course to take is about a quarter of the width of the channel away from Eilean Droineach. Anchor in a pool abreast of the south part of the island; further southwest it is shoal, with some moorings.

The shallow channel east of Eilean Droineach from the northeast. A boulder spit lies east of mid-channel parallel to the Lismore shore

Port Ramsay at the north end of Lismore. The island in the left foreground is Eilean nam Ban. Eilean nam Meann is the long thin island right of centre

Martin Lawrence

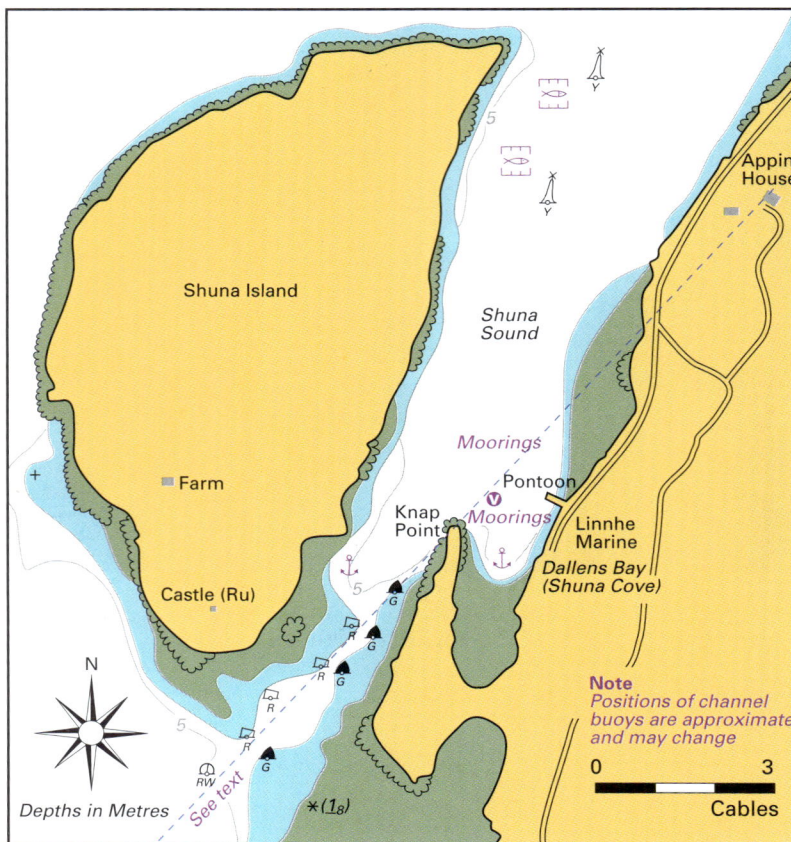

SHUNA SOUND, LOCH LINNHE

Admiralty Chart
2379
Admiralty Leisure Folio
5611.18, 20
Imray Chart
C65, 2800.6
Ordnance Survey
49
Cruising Scotland
p.98

Shuna Sound

Shuna Island lies approximately 2 miles north of Port Appin and the 3 cable wide sound between it and the mainland is easily approached from the north where the only obstructions are fish pens on the west side marked by two yellow buoys.

However, the entrance at the south end narrows to 2 cables and is obstructed by shoals. The channel through these is less than straight but regular surveys by Linnhe Marine show a least depth of 2·5 metres. It is marked with a black and white spherical buoy at its south end, followed by four pairs of lateral buoys with radar reflectors. The traditional leading line of Knap Point in line with the left side of Appin House may still be used, but with care.

Anchorage
Dallens Bay (Shuna Cove) is restricted due to the large number of moorings although some space to anchor may be found south of the moorings. Visitors' moorings are available for hire from Linnhe Marine for £15 per night.
Shuna Island Anchor off the Shuna shore, southwest of Knap Point.

Services and supplies
Linnhe Marine (℃ 01631 730401 and 077215 03981). Water and diesel is available at the Linnhe Marine pontoon. Showers and toilets are included in the mooring fee.

Loch Linnhe

The navigation of Loch Linnhe is generally straightforward but beware the clusters of rocks between Lismore and Shuna and the several drying and submerged rocks and shoals off the northwest shore of the loch, of which the most southerly is about four miles northeast of the entrance to Loch Corrie (Loch a' Choire). For Upper Loch Linnhe see p.134.

Tides
Tidal streams are weak throughout the loch except at Corran Narrows.

The north-going stream begins −0545 Oban (+0110 Dover). The south-going stream begins +0025 Oban (−0505 Dover). Constant as Oban (−0530 Dover).

Height in metres

MHWS	MHWN	MTL	MLWN	MLWS
4·3	3·2	2·5	1·8	0·7

Directions
No specific directions are needed except to keep clear of the rocks and shoals on the northwest side of the loch. These are all avoided by keeping ½ mile offshore or outside the 30-metre contour or, if these marks can be seen, keep Corran Point light beacon (p.133) open-east of Sallachan Point red beacon, bearing 048°.

Occasional anchorages
Cuil Bay on the east shore, 3½ miles north of Shuna, is a temporary anchorage totally exposed to the southwest. Shop, Post Office, at Duror 1 mile inland.

Shuna Sound. The traditional leading line leads to the south end of the buoyed channel

Eilean Balnagowan lies 1½ mile southwest of Cuil Bay. Anchor in the bay on the east side of island in 4–10m. A drying rock lies one cable northeast of the north point of the island. This is the only anchorage that gives some shelter to the southwest.

Camus Shellachan is an open bay 2 miles southwest of Corran Narrows. Give Sallachan Point a berth of 3 cables and aim for the white cottage on the northeast side of the bay. Anchor in 5m, good holding through kelp into sand.

Camus Chil Mhalieu an open bay on the west shore, 3 miles northeast of Loch a'Choire, which dries 2 cables at its head. Anchor towards the west side of the bay in 5m.

Loch a'Choire (Loch Corry)

A dramatic anchorage ringed by the Morvern hills but subject to violent squalls in strong winds. Like several other potential anchorages most of it is either too deep or too shallow, and there are many fish cages on its north side. It is worth visiting for the scenery and the Boathouse Bistro which provides 6 visitors' moorings for its patrons.

Directions

Approaching from the south keep at least 2 cables offshore to avoid a recently reported rock, (LD 1·0m), lying 1¼ cables off the mainland shore and almost 2 cables south of Ceanna Mor on the south side of the entrance. (note that the headland on the north side of the entrance is also called Ceanna Mor).

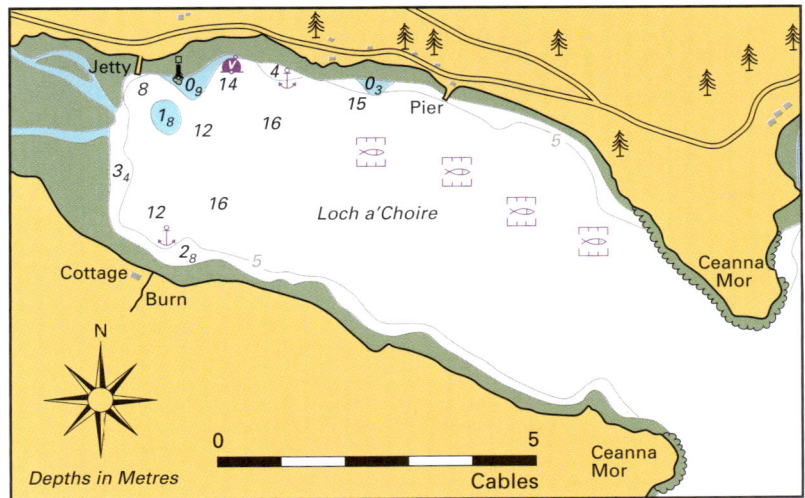

LOCH A'CHOIRE

A line of fish cages lies off the north shore of the loch and the head dries out a long way. There is a rock (drying 0·9), marked by a perch with white diamond top mark, just off the LW line. A 1·8m patch lies just south of it.

Anchorage

Anchor about a cable east of the perch at the head of the loch but the increasing number of moorings will mean anchoring in 10m or more. An alternative is to anchor off the cottage on the south side of the loch.

Services

The Boathouse Bistro (Wed–Sat 1100–2100, Sun 1100–1500) ☎ 01967 411232 to book.

The anchorage and the visitors' moorings in Loch a'Choire. The perch is just visible well to the left of the dark blue yacht

Kingairloch Estate

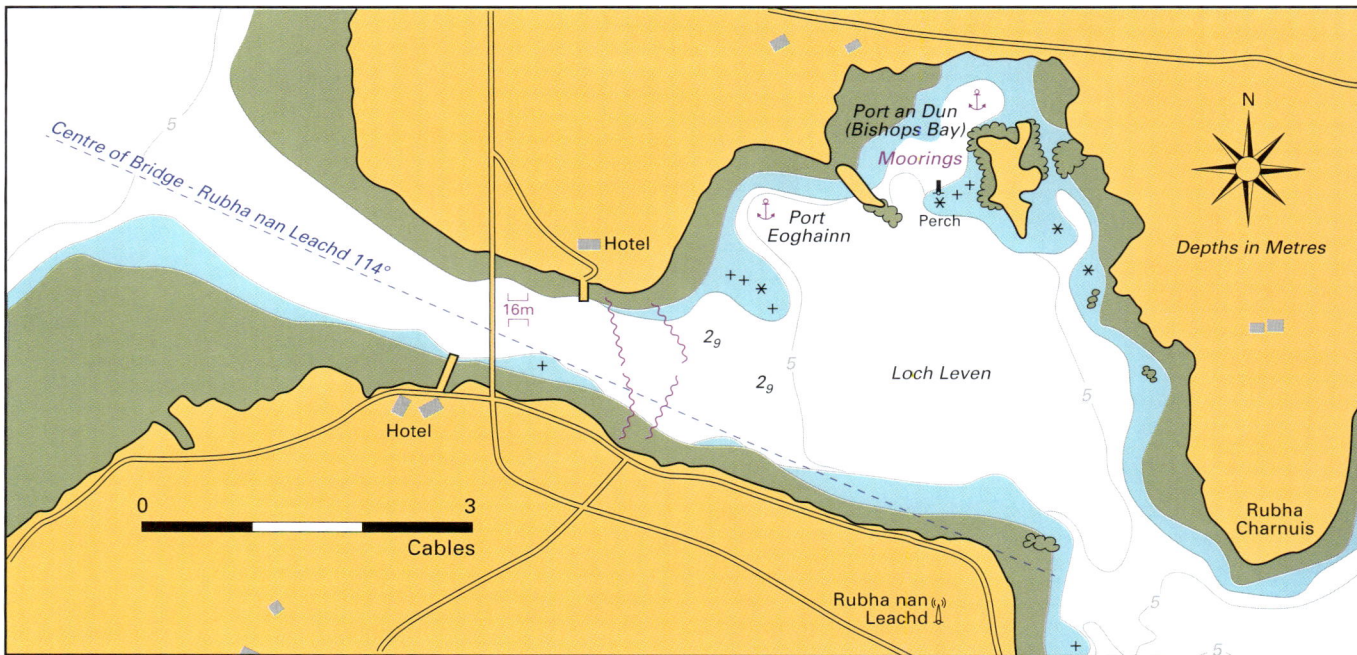

LOCH LEVEN

Loch Leven

Admiralty Chart
2380
Admiralty Leisure Folio
5611.22
Imray Chart
C65, 2800.7
Ordnance Survey
41
Cruising Scotland
p.98

Loch Leven, approached from Loch Linnhe through Ballachulish Bay, is one of the most spectacular of west coast lochs, with hills over 800 metres high crowding in on both sides. The upper five miles of the loch average less than ¼ mile wide but, apart from the scenery, would hold little attraction for a sailing yacht's crew.

The narrows, between Ballachulish Bay and Loch Leven, are crossed by a road bridge with a charted clearance of 16m. Two miles east of the bridge, Ballachulish slate quarries, on the south shore, continued in operation until about the 1950s, but since then the area between the quarries and the shore has been landscaped and now accommodates a small marina close to the Isles of Glencoe Hotel.

Tides

In the main body of the loch the tidal streams run at up to one knot, but at the narrows, and at Caolas nan Con, five miles further east, they run at more than five knots.

At the narrows:
In-going stream begins at –0515 Oban (+0115 Dover).
Out-going stream begins at +0100 Oban (–0430 Dover).

At Caolas nan Con the in-going stream begins ¾ hour later, but the out-going stream begins at the same time as at the narrows.

The tidal constant at Corran, just north of the entrance to Loch Leven is +0005 Oban (–0525 Dover).

At the head of Loch Leven the constant is +0045 Oban (–0445 Dover).

Height in metres at Corran

MHWS	MHWN	MTL	MLWN	MLWS
4·4	3·3	2·5	1·7	0·7

There are no official figures for heights within Loch Leven, but the range is likely to be substantially less than outside the narrows. Moderate overfalls occur west of the narrows on the ebb with a westerly wind.

Directions

Leaving Loch Linnhe pass south of Cuil-cheanna Spit buoy, which is slightly south of the middle of the entrance to Ballachulish Bay and note that Sgeir nan Roin lies a ½ cable off the south shore and is no longer marked with a buoy. Approach the narrows on a heading of 114° to avoid extensive shoals on each side, keeping Rubha nan Leachd, the point on the south side beyond the bridge, in line with the centre of the bridge. On reaching the bridge alter course slightly to port and keep in mid-channel to avoid a rock 60m off the south shore.

A mile east of the bridge pass south of Eilean Choinneich, a flat green island, and continue east for half a mile to avoid the rocks east of the island; the 20-metre contour should keep you clear of these rocks. Pass north of St Mungo's Islands (Eilean Munde), ¾ mile further east.

At Caolas nan Con, five miles east of the bridge, the tide runs strongly (see *Tides* above). The channel through lies on the north side of the loch and has a depth of about 2m. It is marked near both ends by decaying timber beacons which stand on the edge of shoal water to the south. Keep well to the north side when approaching and leaving the channel. Passage to the head of the loch is then clear.

Anchorages
In Ballachulish Bay

Kentallen Bay, on the south side of the entrance to Ballachulish Bay, is very deep almost to the low-water line and there are many moorings. However, ½ mile north of the bay there are six visitors' moorings laid off the old pier, provided for patrons of the Hollytree Hotel. In the approach note a rock with less than 2m over it approximately more than ½ cable northwest of the pier.

Onich, on the north side of Ballachulish Bay is totally open to the south but is suitable for offshore winds. Anchor to the east of the old pier which is reported to have submerged timber piles around it. Diesel, petrol, gas and some repairs at the garage. Shop and Post Office.

In Loch Leven

Port Eoghainn ENE of the bridge, is occupied by moorings, and the bottom, which consists of boulders, is said to be unsuitable for anchoring. A reef, part of which dries 0·3m, runs out for more than a cable on the south side of the bay.

Poll an Dunain (Bishop's Bay) east of the narrows on the north shore (see photos p.132). In the approach from the west note the extensive reef on the south side of Port Eoghainn, described above, and note that the ebb tide, which runs anticlockwise round the bay, sets across it. To avoid it maintain the course through the narrows until the inner pool of Bishop's Bay is well open.

Much of the inner pool is shallow and most of it is occupied by moorings, but it may be possible to find space to anchor. A drying rock in the middle of the entrance to the pool is marked by a thin steel perch, which almost covers at HW, with drying rocks lying east of it. Opposite the perch a drying reef extends almost ¼ cable off the west point of the entrance. The west side of Bishop's Bay dries. There is a shore footpath to the hotel at Ballachulish bridge.

Ballachulish The yacht station pontoons are in a west facing inlet west of the Isles of Glencoe Hotel. Turning space is limited. The inlet east of the hotel is deep and anchoring is inadvisable due to abandoned gear on the bottom.

Eilean Munde Occasional anchorage south of the islands, between the largest and most westerly (St Mungo's Island, on which is a graveyard and ruined chapel) and the islet on its east side. A large drying rock lies ¾ cables southeast of the next islet, with a submerged rock ½ cable further southeast. Fish cages lie between the drying rock and the most easterly island.

Eilean Choinneich Good holding is reported NNE of this island but considerable caution is required in the approaches; use chart 2380. Fish farms are to be expected.

Camus na h-Eirghe on the north shore, about four miles east of the bridge, has four visitors' moorings with pick-up buoys provided by Loch Leven Seafoods for patrons. Pontoon landing stage, cafe-restaurant and shop. ℡01855 821048.

Eilean nam Ban beyond the narrow passage at Caolas nan Con, a rather constricted pool lies behind an island close to the north shore, where a small boat can anchor.

Kinlochleven Anchorage off the wharf on the south side towards the head of the loch, though private moorings are reported to occupy all the water with suitable depths. Beyond this the loch is shoal and drying for ¼ mile. Supermarket, garage, Post Office, phone box in Kinlochleven.

Services and supplies

The pontoons at Ballachulish are operated by Lochaber Watersports, ℡ 01855 811 931 and 07729 425486, who can supply water and diesel and may be able to provide overnight berthing if their charter yachts are away. Isles of Glencoe Hotel ℡ 08448 559134 is nearby and shops and Post Office in the village ¼ mile away.

Ballachulish; the pontoon with the Isles of Glencoe Hotel to the left of it. Eilean Munde at the lower left

Martin Lawrence

Martin Lawrence

Poll an Dunain (Bishop's Bay); Ballachulish bridge just visible at the top right

Poll an Dunain (Bishop's Bay,) looking south across Loch Leven

Allan Devlin

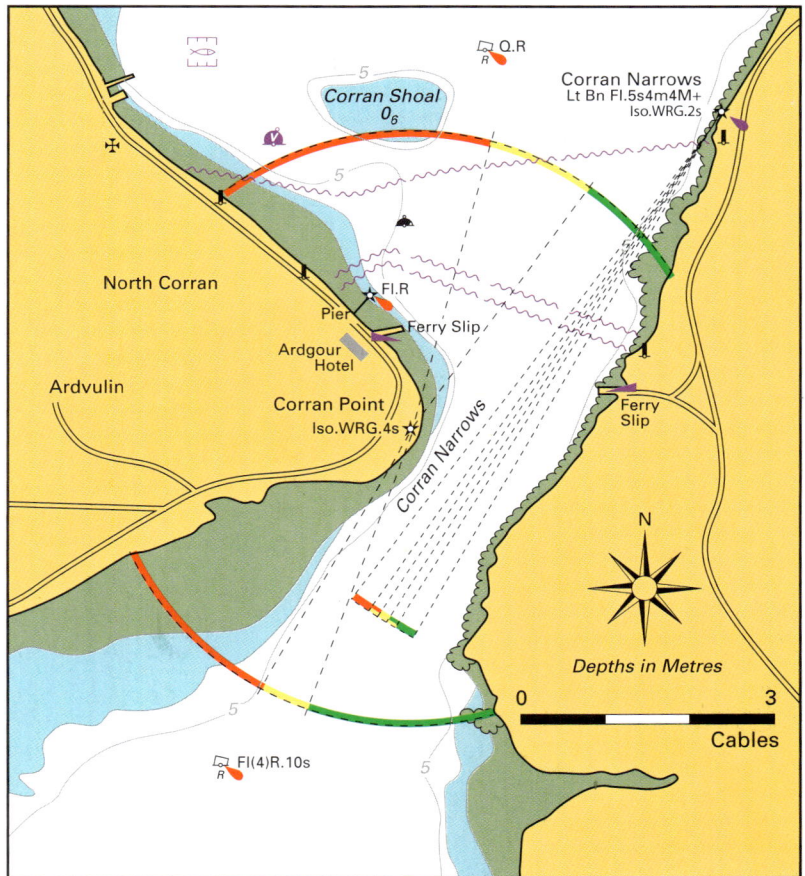

Corran Narrows

Loch Linnhe reduces to 1½ cables width at Corran Narrows, which are clear of any hazards apart from a frequently running ferry and significant tidal streams. However, the approaches from the south are confined by extensive shoals on either hand and on the starboard hand coming from the north.

Tides

The tidal stream in the narrows runs at more than five knots at springs, with eddies on both sides, mainly north of the narrows on the flood and south of them on the ebb.

The in-going stream begins –0600 Oban (+0055 Dover). The out-going stream begins +0005 Oban (–0525 Dover).

The constant is +0005 Oban (–0525 Dover).

Height in metres

MHWS	MHWN	MTL	MLWN	MLWS
4·4	3·3	2·5	1·7	0·7

Directions

Approaching from the south, the G conical buoy, 2 miles south of the narrows and marking the end of Cuil-cheanna Spit, must be left to starboard; note the extensive drying shoals south and west of Rubha Cuil-cheanna. Further north two R can buoys mark shoals to the west and should be left to port. If tacking it is possible to sail west of the buoyed channel but a careful eye must be kept on chart 2380 and the echo sounder. At night the sectored light on Corran Point and the directional sectored light on Corran Narrows Bn. mark the passage. Keep towards the southernmost port hand buoy to avoid shoals to the west of Rubha Cuil-cheanna.

The approach from the north is straightforward; Corran Shoal lies to the north of Corran Point and is marked by a single R can buoy which should be passed on its east side. If coming from Camus an Aisaig or the moorings to the northwest, Corran Shoal can be left to port but hold well towards the west shore.

Anchorage

Corran Point The bay north of Corran Point is much taken up by underwater cables, moorings and a very large fish farm. Five free visitors' moorings have been provided by the fish farm owners and should be used in preference to anchoring. Inn at Ardgour ☎01855 841225.

Lights

Cuil-cheanna Spit buoy Fl.G6s
Buoy 4c SSW of Corran Point Fl(4)R.10s
Buoy 1M SSW of Corran Point Fl(2)R.15s
Corran Point LH Iso WRG.4s12m10-7M
Corran Shoal QR
Corran Narrows Lt. Bn. ½ M NE of Corran Pt.
  Fl.5s4m4M + Iso.Dir.WRG.2s4m4M
Pier 2c NW of Corran Point Fl.R.3M

CORRAN NARROWS

Admiralty Chart
2372, 2380
Admiralty Leisure Folio
5611.22
Imray Chart
C65, 2800.7
Ordnance Survey
41
Cruising Scotland
p.100

Corran Narrows from the south

Martin Lawrence

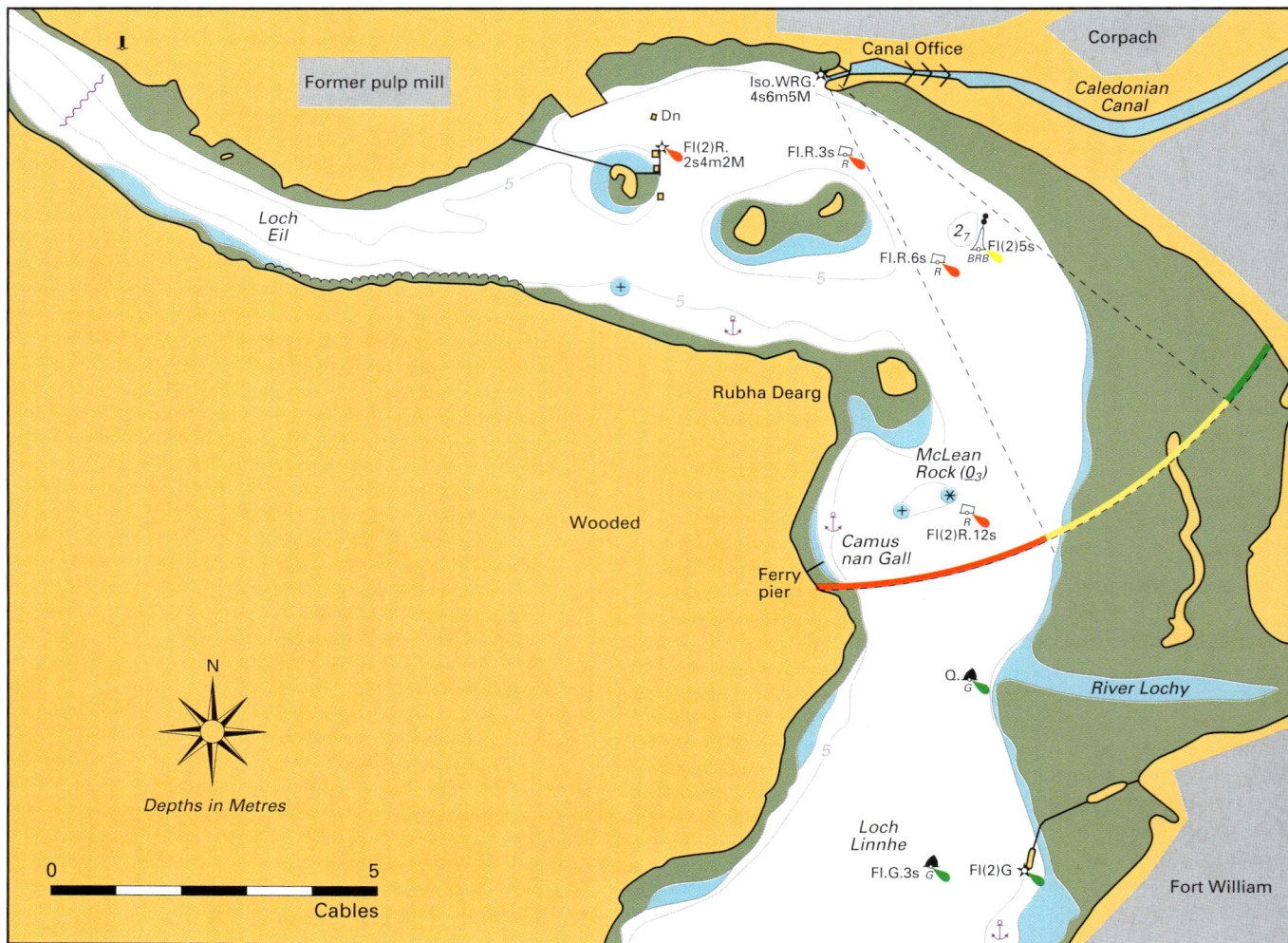

FORT WILLIAM AND CORPACH

Admiralty Chart
2372, 2380
Admiralty Leisure Folio
5611.23
Imray Chart
C65, 2800.7
Ordnance Survey
41
Cruising Scotland
p.100

Upper Loch Linnhe

The upper part of Loch Linnhe is impressive, with high mountains on each side but, like the upper part of Loch Leven, it offers little interest to the crew of a sailing yacht unless going to or from the Caledonian Canal, which leads to the east coast of Scotland, although the lochs along the canal itself are worth visiting on their own account.

Tides

The constant is +0022 Oban (–0508 Dover).

Height in metres

MHWS	MHWN	MTL	MLWN	MLWS
4·1	3·1	2·5	1·9	0·9

Directions

The loch north of Corran Narrows is generally clean except for drying banks at the mouths of burns on either side. Between Corran Narrows and Fort William various lit buoys may be encountered, but these have no navigational significance except as test sites for submarines.

Fort William stands on the east side of the loch towards the head. North of the town a long pier extends from the east shore. Beyond this the loch turns to the north towards Corpach and the canal entrance.

Approaching Corpach a G conical buoy, which is to be left to starboard, may appear to be west of the middle of the loch. McLean Rock R can buoy, 3 cables further north is to be left to port along with a further two R can buoys before arriving at the canal entrance. A black and red isolated danger buoy, 80m SSE of a 2·7m shoal patch, can be passed on either hand. Beware tidal streams which set strongly across the channel in places.

Anchorage

Camus Aisaig, 7 cables northwest of Corran Point. Anchor 1½ cables north of the slip in 5m, well clear of inshore rocks. Many fish cages.

Inverscaddle Bay 2 miles north of Corran narrows on the west side. Anchor in 8–12m.

Camus nan Gall, nearly opposite Fort William, is well sheltered and a good anchorage if needing to stop overnight before entering or after leaving the canal. If approaching from the canal beware the 2m rock a cable southwest of McLean Rock. There are several moorings though still room to anchor.

Rubh Dearg It is also possible to anchor northwest of Rubh Dearg. Trees nearby provide some shelter but the tide may be troublesome.

Fort William The Fort William Marina and Shoreline Co. (℡ 01397 772861) operate a small pontoon, south west of the town pier, for cruise ship tenders and visiting yachts. They also have two visitor's moorings.

There is temporary anchorage between the small town pier and the long pier to the north. It is shoal and drying inshore of a line between the heads of these piers.

Corpach Temporary anchorage west of canal entrance, clear of moorings and the approach to the canal. Exposed to the southwest.

Services and supplies

Shops, hotels and garages in Fort William. Showers at Lochaber Y.C. Supermarket and pub near sea lock. Corpach Boatbuilding Co. Ltd. ℡ 01397 772861 for hull, mechanical, electrical and electronic repairs. Calor Gas at garage. Bus to Glasgow, Mallaig and Inverness, train to Glasgow and Mallaig.

Caledonian Canal

The Caledonian Canal runs in a northeasterly direction from Corpach near Fort William to Clachnaharry near Inverness; a distance of about 60 miles of which about 38 are through Lochs Lochy, Oich and Ness. The remainder consists of artificial canal, which enables small craft to avoid the exposed passage round the North of Scotland.

The maximum dimensions of vessels using the canal are – length overall 150' (45·7m), beam 35' (10·6m) and draught 13'5" (4·1m). Mast clearance is 94' (29m) which is set by the Kessock Bridge over the Inverness Firth. Sea locks and main locks can be contacted on VHF Ch 74.

Opening hours

The following periods may vary and a check by telephone is advisable:

May – end September 0800–1730 (seven days a week)

October 0830–1650 (Mon–Sat)

November – early March 0900–1530 (Mon–Fri)

March – April 0830–1650 (Mon–Sat)

A lunch break between 1200–1300 is usual.

Sea locks and some inland locks may be passed outside normal opening hours on payment of an additional charge. Yachts cannot expect to pass right through the Canal in less than two days, and may well take longer.

Further information

A plan of the entire canal and comprehensive guidance for users is given in the *Skipper's Guide* issued by the canal offices at Corpach and Inverness. Up to date information as to charges and operations as well as information about delays due to repairs etc, may be had from the Canal offices at Corpach or Clachnaharry.

Martin Lawrence

Entrance to the Caledonian Canal at Corpach. Yachts are not normally allowed to stay in the basin above the sea lock and have to move up through two more locks to reach the yacht stagings

Communications

Canal office Inverness ℡ 01463 233140
Canal office Corpach ℡ 01397 772249
Corpach sea lock VHF Ch 74

Loch Eil

Approach as for Corpach, opposite, but pass south of the pair of islets off the canal entrance and head for the narrows. Beware of the rock over ½ cable offshore, 3 cables northwest of Rubh Dearg.

The flood and ebb tide set through Annat Narrows at 5 knots. The ingoing stream begins at –0435 Oban (+0220 Dover) and the outgoing at +0005 Oban (–0400 Dover). The narrows are 1 mile long and 1 cable wide but with drying shoals either side; keep mid channel.

Beyond the narrows the loch is straight to the head which is shoal, as are parts of both shores. There are extensive fish farms. Tides run at 1–2 knots in the loch.

Anchorage

Rubha Mor, immediately west of the narrows in the bay on the north shore. Approach the shore at right angles on a northeasterly course through a narrow channel between drying banks. Monitor soundings continually to avoid shoal water (0·3m and 0·6m) on each hand.

Camus Dubh Uisge, midway along the south shore of the loch, in 3–8m about a cable east of the mouth of a burn.

8. Sound of Mull and Loch Sunart

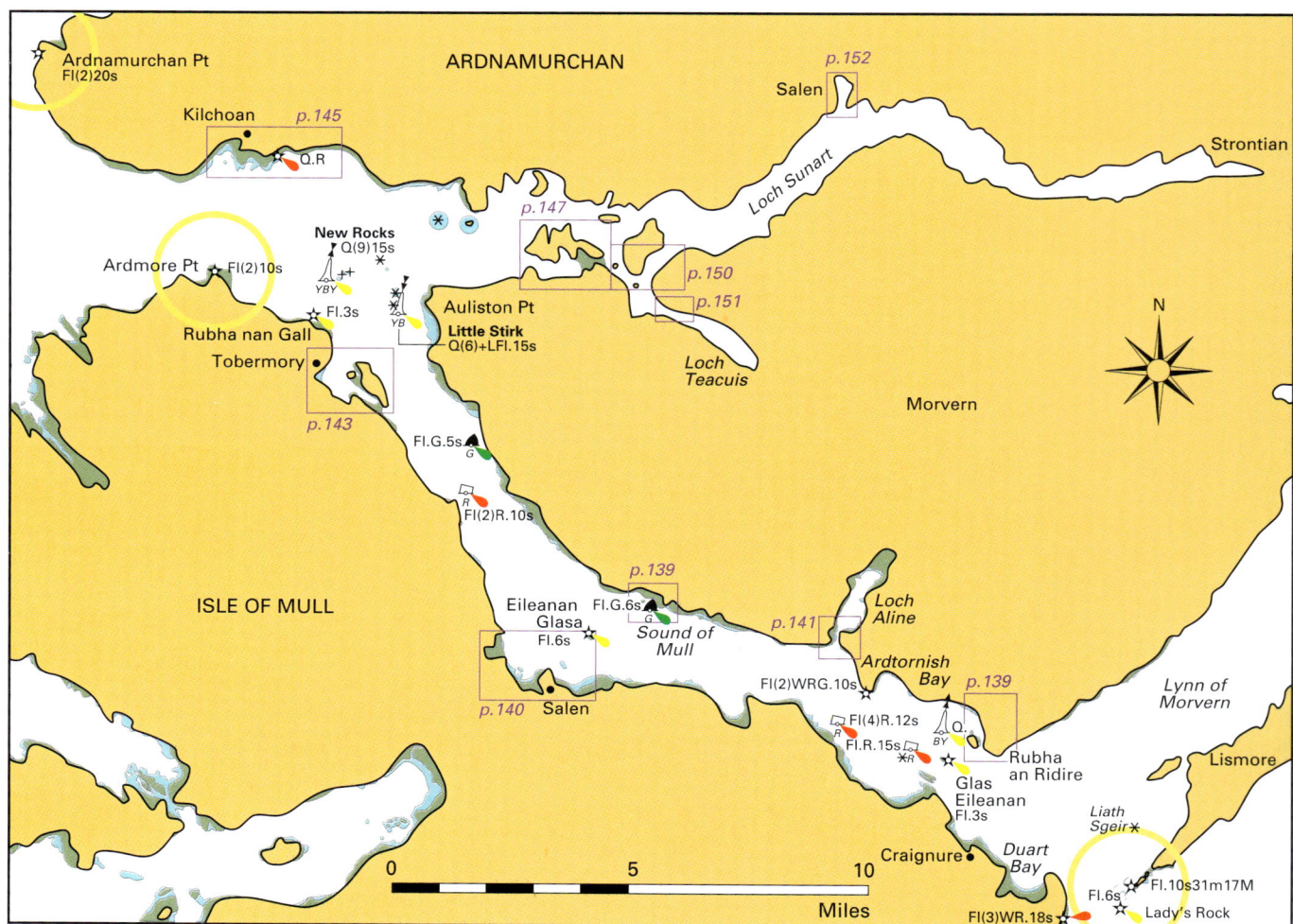

SOUND OF MULL

Lismore to the Sound of Mull

The southeast entrance to the sound is between Rubha an Ridire on Morvern and Scallastle Point on Mull, but as the passage between Lismore and Mull can be crucially affected by the tidal streams it is covered in this section.

Tides

Constant +0015 Oban (–0515 Dover).

Height in metres at Craignure

MHWS	MHWN	MTL	MLWN	MLWS
4·0	3·0	2·3	1·7	0·6

The north-going stream begins –0545 Oban (+0110 Dover).
The south-going stream begins +0025 Oban (–0505 Dover).

In the fairway between Lady's Rock and Mull tidal streams run at three knots springs, with overfalls at the windward end of the passage if the wind is against the tide. Between Lady's Rock and Lismore the ebb reaches four knots.

On the flood there are eddies and severe turbulence northwest of Lismore lighthouse, which can be very uncomfortable in heavy weather. On the ebb an eddy sets into Bernera Bay.

Directions

Approaching from the south, the tide is significant between Loch Don and Duart Point and, with a favourable current of 3kn or more

Admiralty Chart
2390, 2171
Admiralty Leisure Folio
5611.15A
Imray Chart
C65, 2800.4
Ordnance Survey
49
Cruising Scotland
p.103

at springs, hold to the Mull shore leaving Lady's Rock to starboard. Note the islets and reefs just north of Loch Don which extend fully 2 cables offshore. Give them a fair berth before closing the shore off Black's Memorial Tower where it is steep-to from there to Duart Point.

Approaching from the east the straight-forward passage is between Lismore lighthouse and Lady's Rock beacon, both of which have drying rocks extending up to ½ cable off them. With wind against a tide of up to 4 knots, a strong race can occur in this passage. If beating towards the Sound of Mull, beware Liath Sgeir (drying 3·0) which lies 2 cables west of a direct line from Lismore lighthouse to the southwest point of Bernera Island. This is the only hazard in an otherwise clear stretch of water.

From the northeast, through the Lynn of Morvern (p.124), the tide is less of a factor and apart from Liath Sgeir, see above, there are no hazards.

Anchorages

Duart Bay Both parts of the head of the bay dry off nearly four cables and it shoals rapidly beyond the low-water line. Drying and submerged rocks lie one cable NNE of the slip at Torosay on the west side of the bay but there is an occasional anchorage off the slip in five metres, clear of the rocks.

An alternative temporary anchorage in very quiet weather can be found off the stone jetty at Duart Castle, on the east side of the bay, leaving clear access to the jetty.

Craignure Bay lies 1 mile north of Duart. The best anchorage is close inshore, off the slipway, 200m northwest of the Ro-Ro linkspan and inside the moorings. Anchor in 2-4m, good holding on clean sand and convenient for the shop. Alternatively, anchor in the south corner of the bay in 4–5m and clear of moorings. Note that the small bay inside the stone pier dries out.

Martin Lawrence

The anchorage off the Torosay slipway in Duart Bay with Duart Castle on the right and and Lismore lighthouse in the distance

Exposed from north to east but good shelter in offshore winds. Shop, Post Office, hotel, inn, water, Calor Gas, ferry to Oban, buses to Tobermory, Fionnphort and Iona ferry.

Bernera Bay, southeast of Bernera in the Lynn of Morvern, is suitable for anchoring in northerly winds (see p.124).

Lights

At night the passage is well lit.
Lismore lighthouse Fl.10s31m17M
Lady's Rock Fl.6s12m5M
Black's Memorial tower Fl(3)WR.18s14m5/3M

Approach to the Sound of Mull from the southeast. The ferry is passing between Lady's Rock and Lismore lighthouse, heading for Craignure

John Anderson

Admiralty Chart
2171, 2390, 2394
Admiralty Leisure Folio
5611.15A
Imray Chart
C65, 2800.4, 5
Ordnance Survey
47, 49
Cruising Scotland
p.103

Sound of Mull

This is the usual route to the north and west, the alternative being along the exposed south side of Mull. Navigation in the sound is straightforward and the fairway is well marked and adequately lit. If tacking inshore a close watch should be kept on a large scale chart but, generally, keeping at least two cables from the shore will avoid most unmarked dangers.

The southeast half of the sound has high hills on both sides, particularly on Mull, and the wind tends to funnel along the sound, with occasional squalls through valleys. About halfway along the sound, at Salen, there is a gap in the Mull hills and a southwest wind often divides, blowing northwest and southeast from there. The converse may happen as well – in a generally northeasterly wind two yachts approaching this point from opposite directions may both be under spinnaker.

On the Morvern shore at the southeast end of the sound there are cliffs up to 250 metres high, and it is not uncommon for waterfalls on these cliffs to be blown upwards in strong southwest winds.

Tides

Tidal streams run at up to two knots at the southeast entrance to the sound, and up to one knot elsewhere.

At the southeast end of the sound:
The northwest-going stream begins about –0600 Oban (+0100 Dover);
the southeast-going stream begins about –0045 Oban (+0615 Dover).

Three miles southeast of Calve Island (Tobermory):
The northwest-going stream begins about +0500 Oban (–0030 Dover);
the southeast-going stream begins about –0045 Oban (+0615 Dover).

Note that the stream runs northwest for about 5¼ hours at the southeast end and 6¾ hours at the northwest end of the sound.

The constant throughout averages +0015 Oban (–0515 Dover).

Height in metres at Craignure

MHWS	MHWN	MTL	MLWN	MLWS
4·0	3·0	2·3	1·7	0·6

Height in metres at Tobermory

MHWS	MHWN	MTL	MLWN	MLWS
4·4	3·3	2·5	1·8	0·7

'Yeoman Bridge' is one of the five very large bulk carriers, serving the superquarry at Glensanda, which frequently use the Sound of Mull

Martin Lawrence

Directions

Coming from the south, the Glas Eileanan (Grey Isles) lie about mid-channel and can be passed on either hand; the eastern channel between the Glas Eileanan and Rubha an Ridire is the main one and is usually preferable. A north cardinal light buoy is positioned 6 cables NNW of the Glas Eileanan to assist deep draught vessels and is of no significance to yachts.

The western channel is restricted to a width of about 3 cables between Glas Eileanan and Scallastle Point by a group of rocks standing above water, of which Sgeir nan Gobhar is the most northerly. Chart 2390 also shows a rock, described as drying 0·5m, in the channel about 1½ cables east of Sgeir nan Gobhar. Recent amateur surveys have failed to find such a hazard and indicate that depths of around 20m prevail in the area where it is shown. Do not pass inside the rocks off Scallastle Point without local knowledge or the *Antares* chart.

About ½ mile WNW of the Glas Eileanan are the Yule Rocks (1·0m) marked by a R can buoy on their northeast side. Thus, if using the western passage hold well to the south of the Yule Rock buoy as the rocks are between you and the buoy marking them. 1¾ miles further up the sound, a red can light buoy near the Mull shore and a mile WSW of Ardtornish Point, marks Avon Rock over which the depth is 2·2 metres.

Eileanan Glasa (Green Isles) is a group of islets, lying 4½ miles WNW of Avon Rock of which Eilean Glasa is the largest. There is a light beacon on the north islet. The main fairway lies to the northeast, between Eileanan Glasa and Fiunary Rocks (drying 0·2m and 2·6m closer inshore) off the Morvern shore and marked by a G conical buoy.

7½ cables southwest of Eileanan Glasa and closer to the Mull shore lies a group of drying and submerged rocks, named simply as Bogha on the chart. Between these rocks and Eileanan Glasa is a shoal passage with a minimum depth of 4·3m. The Mull shore also dries out for 3 cables, both to the south of Bogha and up to 7 cables eastwards, and must be given an adequate berth. For the approach to Salen see p.140.

Between Eileanan Glasa and Tobermory harbour the sound is clear except close into either shore. Approximately halfway between these two points there is a R can buoy marking a wreck with 2·7m over it and positioned off the Mull shore. A mile further north, on the Morvern shore, a G conical buoy marks Bogha Bhuilg and shallow ground which runs a cable northwest from the rock.

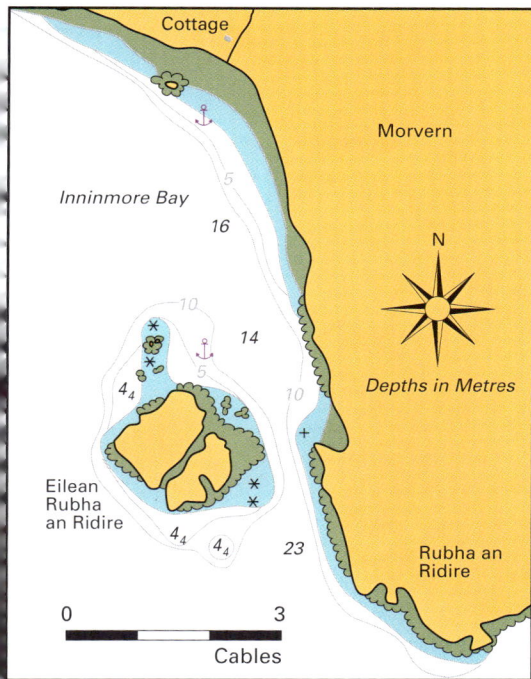

CAMAS RIDIRE

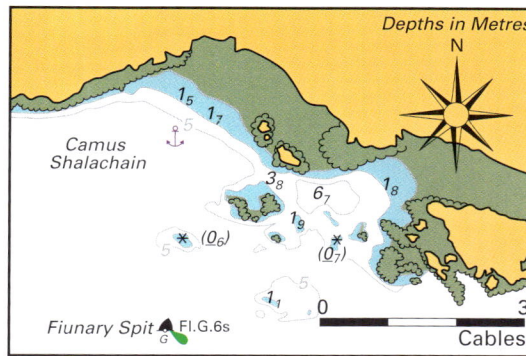

FIUNARY ROCKS

Anchorages

Camus Ridire An occasional anchorage south of Inninmore Bay, behind the islands northwest of Rubha an Ridire, at the southern entrance to the sound. Enter from either side keeping close to the Morvern shore. Anchor in 7m close to the island behind the above water and drying rocks off the north end of it which form good shelter at low water.

Inninmore Bay Anchor off the cottage in 6m sand and shingle. Sheltered from northwest through north to southeast.

Scallastle Bay lies 1 mile northwest of Craignure. Scallastle Point, which is very foul, must be given a wide berth when coming from the south (see *Directions* above). Anchor in 5m or more to be clear of an area of rocks and stones. A good anchorage in offshore winds.

Ardtornish Bay is immediately east of Ardtornish Point on which stands a sectored light beacon and a ruined castle. Anchor in 7-9m, stiff mud, anywhere in the bay. Exposed from south to southeast but surprisingly good shelter otherwise.

Fishnish Bay is about 4½ miles northwest of Scallastle Point opposite Loch Aline. Anchor in 6–7m at the head of the bay avoiding shoals close inshore. Exposed to north winds across the sound but good otherwise. The ferry terminal to Loch Aline is about 1½ miles by road.

Fiunary Rocks is a useful passage anchorage. Approach from the west, a cable off the Morvern shore. Anchor to the north of the buoy and the rocks in the bay named Camas Shalachain on chart 2390, in 8–10m. Sheltered from northwest to northeast.

Lights

Lismore lighthouse Fl.10s31m17M
Glas Eileanan (Grey Rocks) light beacon Fl.3s6M
Fiunary Rocks buoy Fl.G.6s
Bogha Bhuilg light buoy Fl.G.5s
Inninmore N card light buoy Q
Ardtornish Point Fl(2)WRG.10s8-6M
Avon Rocks light buoy Fl(4)R.12s
Eilean Glasa (Green Island) light beacon Fl.6s8M
Yule Rocks light buoy Fl.R.15s
Red buoy (wreck) Fl(2)R.10s
Rubha nan Gall lighthouse Fl.3s9M

Ardtornish Bay on the Morvern shore. Ardtornish Castle and light beacon on the right

Edward Mason

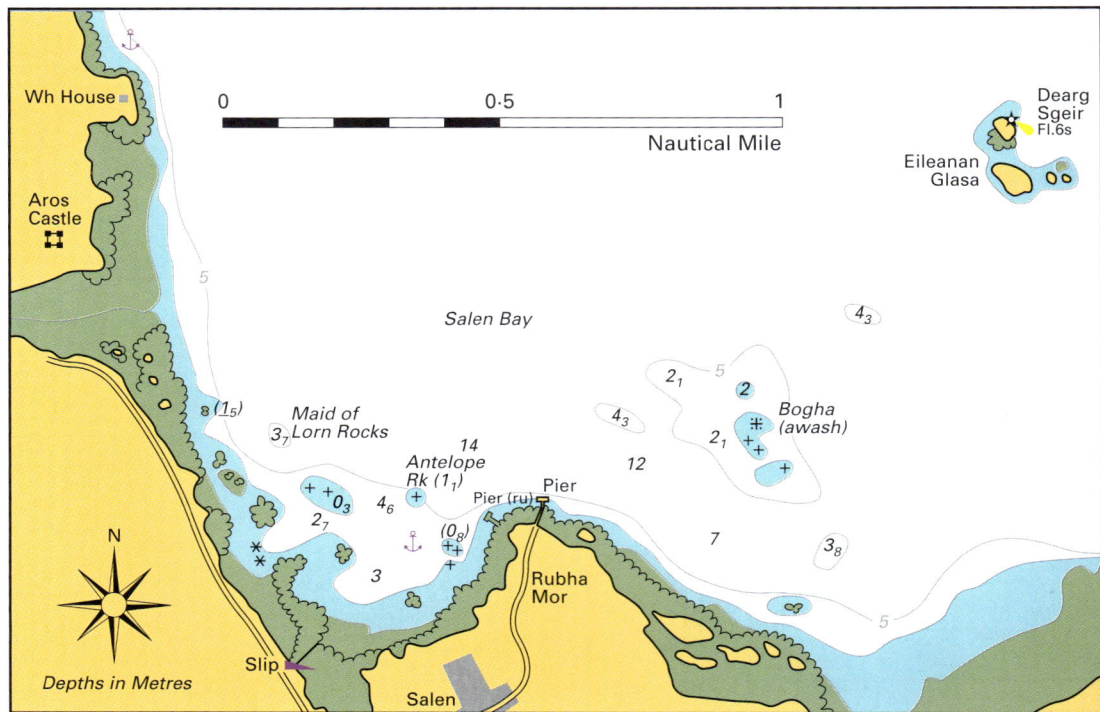

SALEN BAY, MULL

Depths in Metres

Admiralty Chart
2390
Admiralty Leisure Folio
5611.15A
Imray Chart
C65, 2800.5
Ordnance Survey
49
Cruising Scotland
p.103

Salen, Mull, from the southwest. More rocks, which are covered, lie beyond those showing

Salen

Southwest of Eileanan Glasa (Green Isles), this is a good anchorage giving protection from southeast to west, but it needs to be approached carefully because of several groups of rocks in the approach.

Directions

The approach from the east is complicated by a group of unmarked drying and submerged rocks (Bogha on chart 2390) and the fact that the Mull shore southeast of them dries out for a distance of almost 3 cables.

Accordingly, the inshore passage into Salen Bay is not advised. Instead, pass not more than 2 cables south of Eileanan Glasa on a course of 270° and alter to port when the pier on Rubha Mor bears 195°. Entering the bay aim to keep 1½ cables off the west side of Rubha Mor, to avoid submerged and drying rocks lying off it, thus leaving the Antelope Rock (LD 1·1) a cable to starboard. Anchor clear of moorings but note drying rocks extending 2½ cables from the west shore and a cable from the south. Much kelp reported in 2017.

Approaching from the north keep well off the Mull shore before closing Rubha Mor then following the above course into the anchorage.

Alternatively there is a good anchorage in the small cove north of the white house at the north point of Salen Bay. Anchor well inshore off a short stone pier.

Services and supplies

Shops, Post Office, hotels, phone box. Bus to Tobermory and Craignure. Bicycle hire. Diesel and petrol from filling station.

Loch Aline

This is the best anchorage between Oban and Tobermory (see aerial photo p.142), and better in many ways than either. Loch Aline has a variety of sheltered places within and is fairly easy to enter, even at night, and can provide most essential supplies. The facilities have recently been augmented by the establishment of pontoon berthing for visiting yachts.

Tides

Constant +0012 Oban (–0518 Dover).

Height in metres

MHWS	MHWN	MTL	MLWN	MLWS
4·5	3·2	(2·7)	(1·9)	(0·8)

Brackets indicate estimated heights as no data available.

Directions

From the west there are no offshore dangers, however if approaching from the south there is a bad reef, Bogha Lurcain, off Bolorkle Point extending one cable offshore. The leading line clearing this reef (357°) is no longer marked and the original front mark of the leading line is now an orange concrete base for a directional light. If this cannot be identified it is advisable to hold well to the west before approaching the narrows.

The entrance is narrow with a minimum depth of 2·1m and the tide runs at 2½ kn Sp (const. Oban +0012) but it is well buoyed and straightforward if the three buoys are left on the appropriate hand. The ferry to Fishnish on Mull berths at the slip on the west side. Do not enter or leave the loch at the same time as the ferry and also keep a lookout for coasters from the silica sand mine just inside the entrance.

Half a mile within the loch a yellow iron beacon with a spherical topmark marks a reef on the east side and half a mile further a similar beacon marks a more extensive reef on the west shore. Both should be given a good berth as rocks extend up to ½ cable beyond the beacons. The head of the loch dries for about half a mile.

Anchorage and berthing

Pontoons These are located on the west shore, ¼ mile beyond the inner red can buoy, and provide berths for 32 yachts. There are also 10 visitors' moorings. Water and electricity at pontoons. Showers and toilets and laundry onshore. Fuel available nearby in cans. This facility is operated by the Morvern CDC and charges are £2.60/metre per night.

Southeast corner Once through the narrows there is an anchorage in the bay to starboard. This is sheltered and out of the tide but there are many moorings and it can be difficult to find a reasonable depth. Avoid the shelf on the south side of anchorage.

Kinlochaline The head of the loch dries out approximately ½ mile but south of the LW line soundings are suitable for anchoring for almost the full width of the loch. There are moorings off the boathouse and pier on the east shore with room to anchor outside them.

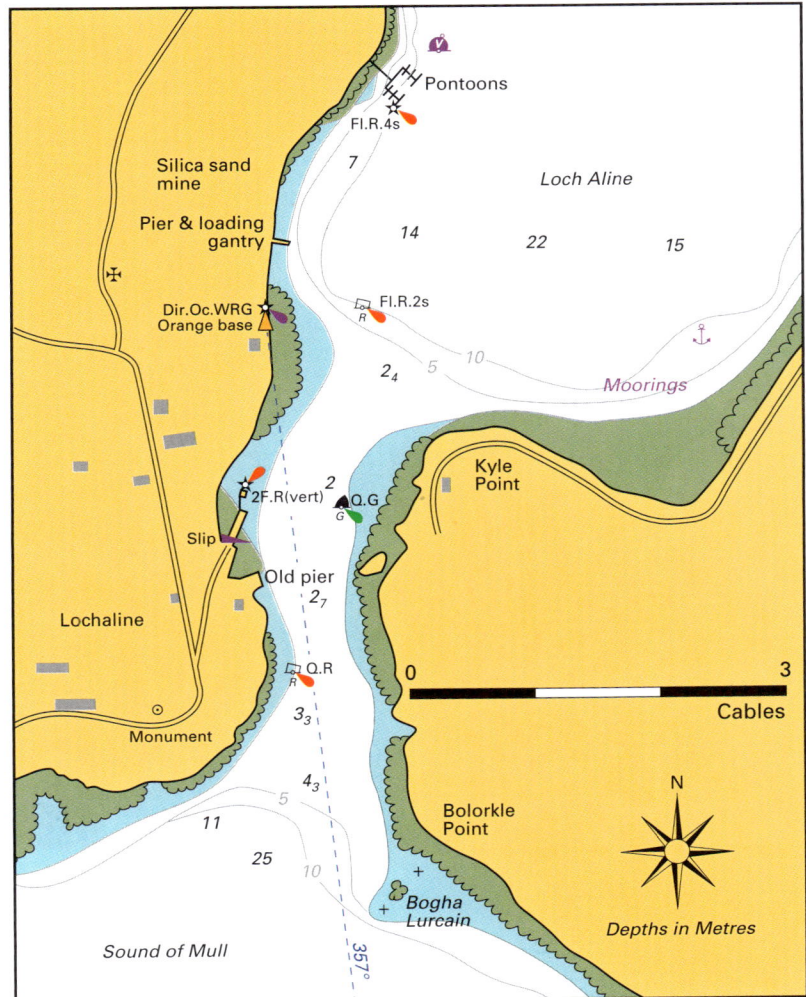

LOCH ALINE NARROWS

On the west side there is good anchorage to be found southwest or northeast of the beacon marking Sgeirean nan Ron (dries 2·7m) but note the stony shelf extending a cable from the west shore, 2 cables southwest of the beacon.

Much of the area is mud and gives good holding but rocky patches are to be found northeast of the Sgeirean nan Ron beacon.

Services and supplies

Lochaline village: Shop, 24 hour diesel and petrol pumps (card payment only), Post Office, hotel, Whitehouse Restaurant ☎ 01967 421777, dive centre, Calor Gas at shop.

Lights

Directional light Dir.Oc. WRG.6s; R 358°-002°; W 356°-358°; G 353°-356°
Outer R can buoy QR
Starboard G conical buoy QG
Inner R can buoy Fl.R.2s
Ferry slip dolphin 2FR (Vert)
Yacht pontoons Fl.R.4s

Admiralty Chart
2390
Admiralty Leisure Folio
5611.15C & D
Imray Chart
C65, 2800.5
Ordnance Survey
49
Cruising Scotland
p.103

John Anderson

Loch Aline from the southwest (p.141)

Tobermory Harbour from the east before Taigh Solais, the harbour facilities building, was built

Martin Lawrence

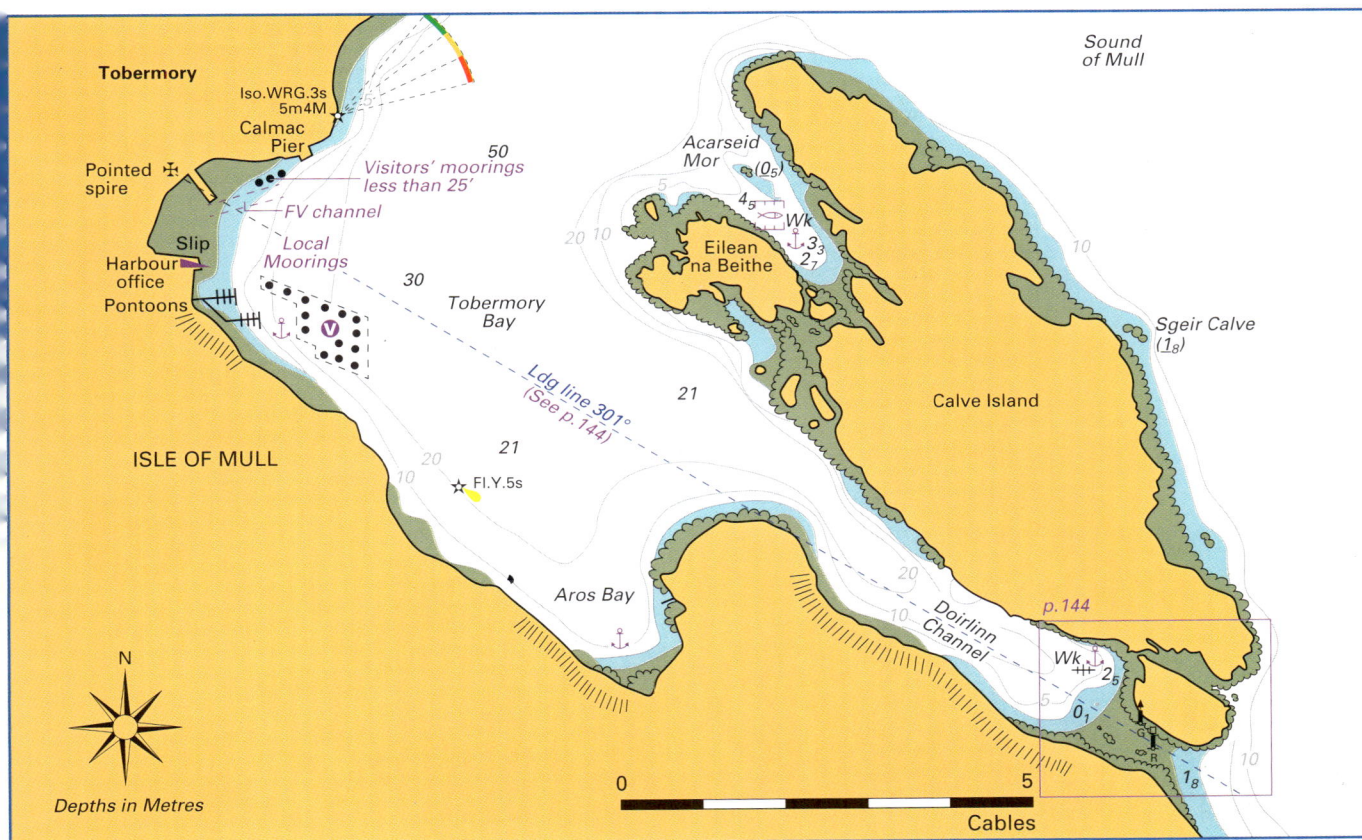

TOBERMORY BAY

Tobermory

Few yachts pass by Tobermory without stopping there as, in addition to the facilities it has to offer, it is one of the most attractive towns on the west coast of Scotland. It lies on the northwest side of a picturesque protected natural harbour and is ideally situated for taking on stores, fuel and water before heading further west. The only drawback is swell in strong winds from the NW through to NE.

Visitors' moorings and pontoons have been provided in the bay by the Tobermory Harbour Association (THA) and there is an excellent onshore facilities building.

Tides

Constant +0020 Oban (−0510 Dover).

Height in metres

MHWS	MHWN	MTL	MLWN	MLWS
4·4	3·3	2·5	1·8	0·7

Directions

The main entrance, between Calve Island and Mull, is free from dangers and the approach is straightforward but, if coming from the south, be aware of Sgeir Calve (shows at LW) off the east side of Calve Island with a shoal extending in a northwest and southeast direction for about a cable. Watch for ferry and other shipping at the entrance.

Alternatively, there is a small drying channel at the south end of Calve Island known as the Doirlinn Narrows which can be used near HW (see p.144 for plan and details).

Anchorage, berthing and mooring

Tobermory Bay An anchoring area is designated inshore of the visitors' moorings where the depth is generally in excess of 5–10 metres.

Aros Bay, at the south end of the bay, is mostly very deep but reasonable depths can be found off the ruined pier on the west side. Part of the bay may be occupied by fish farming.

The Doirlinn The anchorage is near the southeast end of Calve Island (see p.144).

Acarseid Mor, the bay between the northwest point of Calve Island and Eilean na Beithe, is useful in southeasterly weather although it contains a small fish cage and a nearby wreck. Approach from the northwest and leave the submerged reef at the entrance to port.

Pontoons with water and electricity are located where shown on the plan providing alongside berths for approximately 50 boats, although not all have 2m depth.

Moorings 28 blue visitors' moorings have been provided where indicated on the plan. The 24 hour charge for moorings is £16 for boats up to 15 tons. Fees should be paid at the THA Office or to a representative of the Harbour Committee who may be collecting from boats between 1700 and 1900.

Pontoon dues vary according to length and include electricity. Landing and going alongside for short periods to pick up or drop crew, and to collect stores, is free for visitors although a donation is requested if taking on water.

Admiralty Chart 2474, 2394
Admiralty Leisure Folio 5611.15B
Imray Chart C65, 2800.5
Ordnance Survey 47
Cruising Scotland p.104

Services and supplies

Shops, bank, hotels. Chandlery and chart agent (Seafare). Water and electricity at pontoons. Diesel at fuel berth, provided by Mackay's Garage ☎ 01688 302103. Calor Gas from Mackay's, at car park adjacent to pontoons, and from Highland Services ☎ 01688 302296. Showers, launderette at Taigh Solais, the Harbour Association building. Divers available (ask at Seafare). Bus to Craignure, ferry to Kilchoan (Ardnamurchan).

Communications

Post Office, phone box.
Piermaster ☎ 07917 832497
Seafare ☎ 01688 302277 (also VHF Ch 37)
Harbour Association ☎ 01688 302876

The Doirlinn Narrows

This is the drying channel at the south end of Calve Island and is an alternative entrance to Tobermory Bay, which can be used near HW.

Directions

At the narrows the channel is marked by tubular steel perches on either hand. Normally, there is a depth of approximately 2m in the channel for 2 hours either side of HW. The channel is well to the Calve Island side and the southeastern perch appears to be mid-channel. The traditional leading line is the church spire at Tobermory in line with the HW mark on the southwest side of the channel, about 5 cables northwest of the narrows, bearing 301°. Do not attempt this channel on a falling tide.

Taigh Solais, the new harbour facilities building, completed in 2008 and situated near the pontoons and car park

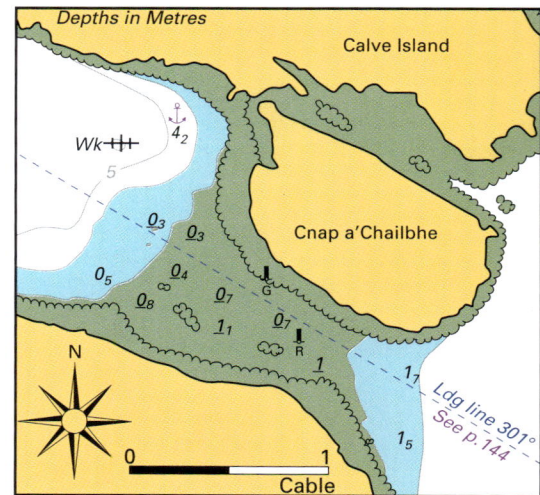

DOIRLINN NARROWS

The wreck, shown on previous editions of chart 2390 as lying almost on the leading line, has shifted northwards and no longer is a hazard if using the channel.

Anchorage

Anchor in the small bay just north of the narrows. (See photo opposite). A recent survey by *Antares Charts* shows that the wreck lies almost in the centre of the bay, as shown on the above plan. Although it now has 2·2m over it, great care should be taken with soundings to avoid fouling it and a tripping line is recommended.

Tobermory Harbour Association

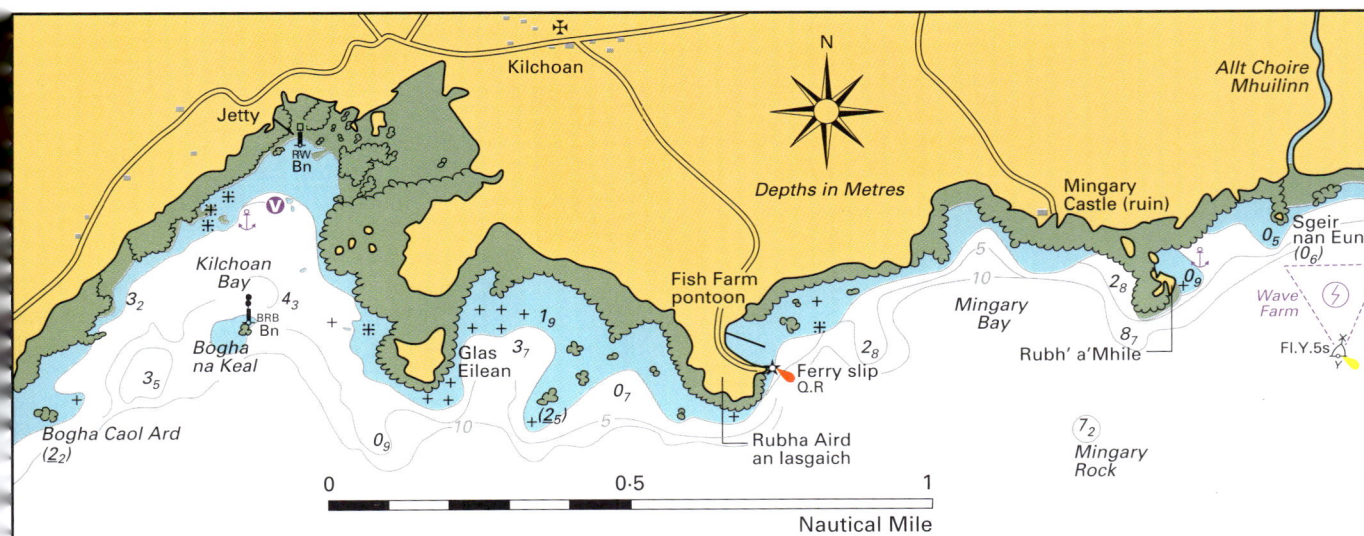

Kilchoan
Jetty
RW Bn
Kilchoan Bay
Bogha na Keal
Bogha Caol Ard (2₂)
BRB Bn
Glas Eilean
Fish Farm pontoon
Ferry slip Q.R
Rubha Aird an Iasgaich
Mingary Castle (ruin)
Mingary Bay
Rubh' a'Mhile
Sgeir nan Eun (0₆)
Wave Farm
Fl.Y.5s
Mingary Rock
Depths in Metres
N
Allt Choire Mhuilinn
Nautical Mile

KILCHOAN BAY AND MINGARY BAY

Tobermory to Ardnamurchan Point

The western entrance to the Sound of Mull is clear but north of Tobermory in mid-channel there is a large area of rocks (see p.146), with a clear passage nearly a mile wide between Mull and a west cardinal light buoy which marks the southwest side of the New Rocks. The buoy is about five miles from the western entrance and the passage should present no difficulty in moderate weather. If tacking, look out for the most southeasterly rock, Little Stirk, which dries 3·7 metres and is marked by a south cardinal buoy.

There is a wave energy array east of Sgeir nan Eun, lying within the dashed line on the plan above. It is marked on its south side by a conical yellow buoy with a cross topmark (Fl.Y.5s). 1½ cables northwest of this buoy there is an unlit, yellow, wave measurement buoy.

For the passages north and east of the rocks mentioned above see p.146, Loch Sunart. For passage round Ardnamurchan see CCC Sailing Directions, *Ardnamurchan to Cape Wrath*.

Tides

Off Rubha nan Gall:

Northwest-going stream begins +0400 Oban (–0130 Dover); Southeast-going stream begins –0045 Oban (–0615 Dover). The spring rate is about one knot.

Anchorages

All the anchorages below are fully exposed to the south and therefore essentially of an temporary or occasional nature.

Kilchoan An attractive scattered community of houses and crofts on the south facing slopes of the Ardnamurchan peninsula, Kilchoan lies on the east side of Sron Bheag on the south side of Ardnamurchan Point.

A drying rock in the middle of the bay, with a shoal area ½ cable west of it is marked by an isolated danger beacon. Drying rocks lie up to a cable off the west shore, and up to 1½ cables off the east shore. Pass a cable west and

northwest of the isolated danger beacon and anchor southwest of the vistor's moorings.

Hotel ☎01972 510222, restaurant and shop. Water, petrol, diesel, showers, toilets, rubbish disposal. Pay at box at head of slip for visitors' moorings.

Mingary Castle stands half a mile east of the ferry pier. Anchor on the northeast side of Rubh' a' Mhile, just east of Mingary Castle (ruins), but beware a covering rock reported 1 cable northeast of the point. In the approach take care to avoid the wave energy array.

Lights

Rubha nan Gall lighthouse Fl.3s17m10M
Ardmore Point Fl(2)10s18m13M (2¼M WNW of Rubha nan Gall)
New Rocks W cardinal buoy Q(9)15s (NNE of Rubha nan Gall)
Mingary Pier (Ferry slip) Q.R8m3M
Wave energy array buoy Fl.Y.5s
Little Stirk S cardinal buoy Q(6)+LFl.15s

KILCHOAN BAY AND MINGARY BAY

Admiralty Chart
2171, 2392,
Admiralty Leisure Folio
5611.15a, 13
Imray Chart
C65, 2800.1
Ordnance Survey
47
Cruising Scotland
p.117

The anchorage in the bay north of the Doirlinn Narrows

Pierre Blidon

Admiralty Chart
2394
Admiralty Leisure Folio
5611.24
Imray Chart
C65, 2800.5
Ordnance Survey
47
Cruising Scotland
pp.106-107

Outer Loch Sunart

Loch Sunart is approximately 17 miles long and runs eastwards into the mountains from north of Auliston Point. Although often by-passed by yachts using the Sound of Mull it is one of the most picturesque of west coast lochs with several attractive anchorages and some spectacular bits of rock-dodging for those who have a taste for that sort of thing.

Even in the main fairway of the loch a lot of anxiety will be spared by having chart 2394. However, the popular anchorage at Drumbuie on the south side of the loch can be reached without any difficulty.

Tides

Streams run generally at less than one knot but can vary greatly with the width and depth of the channel.

In-going stream begins about –0500 Oban (+0200 Dover); Out-going stream begins about +0130 Oban (–0400 Dover).

At Salen (Loch Sunart) the constant is as Oban.

Height in metres

MHWS	MHWN	MTL	MLWN	MLWS
4·6	3·4	2·6	1·7	0·6

Dangers

North of Tobermory and in the approaches to Loch Sunart there are three groups of rocks; the New Rocks, Red Rocks and Stirks all of which are dangerous and require care.

The New Rocks (LD 0·3m) form the westmost group and lie between 9–13 cables NNE of Rubha nan Gall lighthouse. The southwestern extremity of this group is marked by a west cardinal buoy.

The Red Rocks, lying a mile northwest of Auliston Point and unmarked, consist of three rocks, one of which dries 2·8m. Note also a patch with LD 0·5m, 1½ cables to the southeast of them.

The Stirks The Big Stirk is 0·3 m high and lies 7 cables WSW of Auliston Point and the Little Stirk, which dries 3m, lies 1½ cables south of it. The Stirks are marked by a south cardinal buoy (Q(6)+LFl.15s) lying 3 cables due south of the Big Stirk.

Further east and affecting only the approach to Loch Sunart from the west, Sligneach Mor lies ¼ mile southwest of Rubha Aird Shlignich, the north point of the entrance to Loch Sunart; it is only 0·6 metre high, drying up to a cable on all sides. Sligneach Beag, ½ mile west of Sligneach Mor, dries 3·3 metres, with other drying rocks up to a cable off its north side.

Directions

From the south use the ½ mile wide channel between the Stirks S cardinal buoy and the shore south of Auliston Point. If approaching from Tobermory pass south of this buoy before heading for Auliston Point. If beating, note that drying rocks extend in places more than ½ cable off the shore south of Auliston Point.

From the west, the traditional clearing line is the summit of Risga in line with the north point of Oronsay, 083° which will lead north of New Rocks and Red Rocks and south of Sligneach Mor and Sligneach Beag.

However, Risga may be difficult to identify and in this case it is probably best to pass about ¼ mile south of Maclean's Nose, at the base of Ben Hiant, the highest hill on the north shore of the entrance to Loch Sunart. From here, if heading for Drumbuie, steer 135° towards a waterfall on the Morvern shore, about ¾ mile east of Auliston Point, and when Sligneach Mor has been identified, head for the entrance.

Alternatively, if heading further into Loch Sunart, continue due east from Maclean's Nose towards Rubha Aird Shlignich, which is steep-to, until Sligneach Mor can be identified and then pass through the cable wide channel to the north of it.

Lights

Rubha nan Gall lighthouse Fl.3s17m10M
Ardmore Point Fl(2)10s18m13M (2¼M WNW of Rubha nan Gall)
New Rocks W cardinal buoy Q(9)15s (NNE of Rubha nan Gall)
Mingary Pier (Kilchoan) Q.R8m3M
Little Stirk S cardinal buoy Q(6)+LFl.15s

Loch Drumbuie (Droma na Buidhe)

A popular and perfectly sheltered anchorage, even in west winds, south of Oronsay at the mouth of Loch Sunart. The entrance is ½ cable wide and steep-to on both sides but, immediately north of the entrance, rocks (drying 1·2m) extend up to a cable off the west point of Oronsay. These present no problem if coming directly into the entrance from the west but take care if coming from the north.

Keep to the north side of the entrance channel as, about a cable east of the narrowest part, a submerged rock with 1·0m over it, lies ½ cable off the south shore. The north side of this rock is cleared by keeping the west end of the south side of the entrance in sight. Note also the patch with a LD of 2·1m just north of the aforementioned rock.

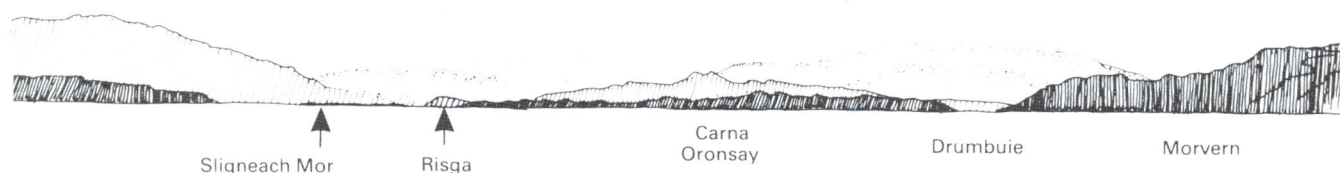

Loch Sunart approach from the west - summit of Risga in line with the north point of Oronsay - 083°

Sligneach Mor   Risga   Carna Oronsay   Drumbuie   Morvern

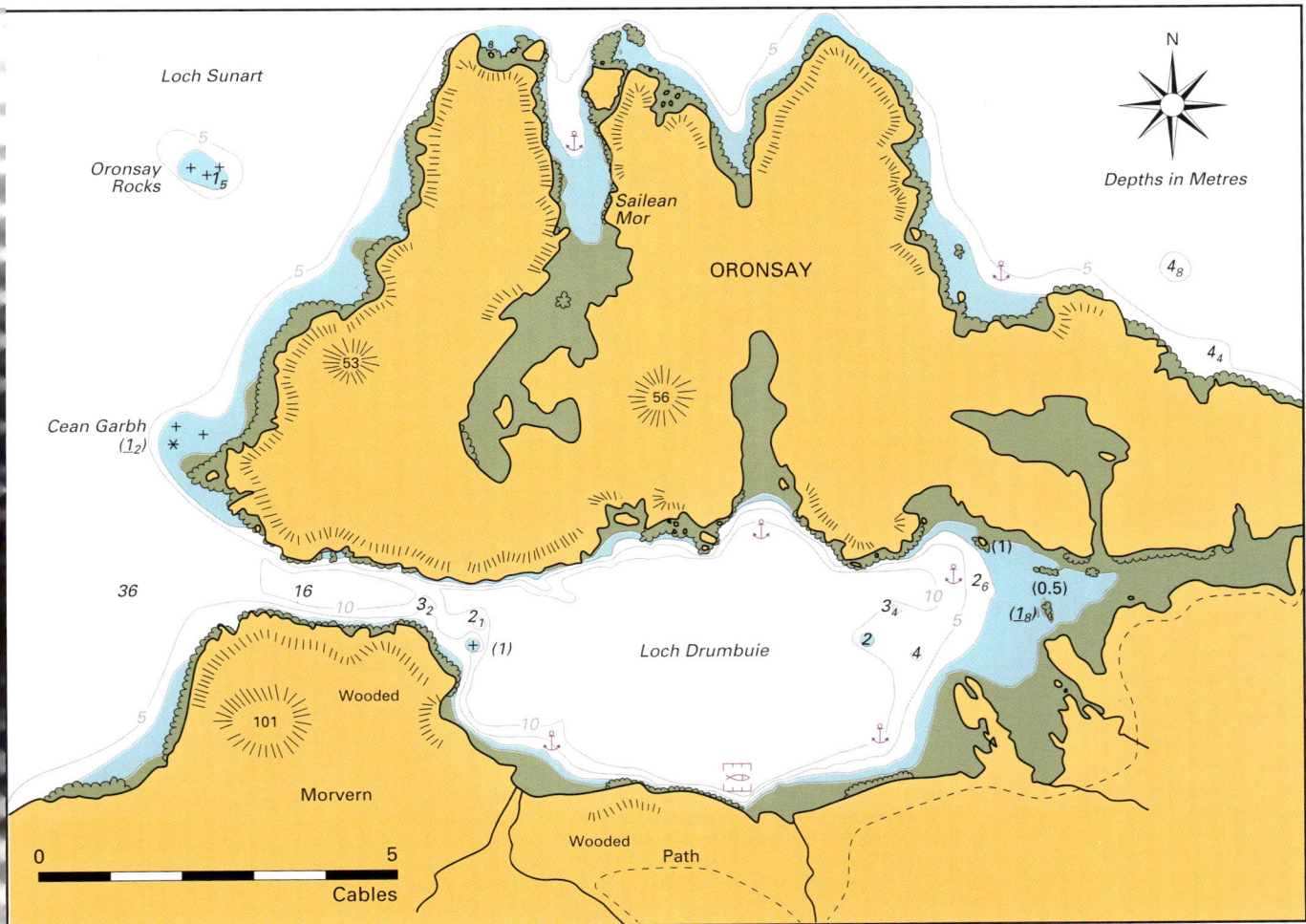

Loch Sunart

Oronsay
Rocks

N

Depths in Metres

Sailean
Mor

ORONSAY

4₈

4₄

53

56

Cean Garbh
(1₂)

(1)

36   16   3₂   2₁   3₄   10   2₆   (0.5)

2   4   5   (1₈)

(1)

Loch Drumbuie

Wooded

101

5

Morvern

Wooded   Path

0   5

Cables

Anchorage

Anchorage can be had anywhere in the loch. The main anchorages are:

SW corner of loch in 5–6m off a big isolated boulder on beach. Do not cut the corner when approaching or leaving this anchorage due to the rock mentioned above. Shoal water extends off-shore and it then shelves abruptly to 10m.

Southeast corner The bay dries but good holding in mud can be found well offshore.

North east corner Anchor anywhere in the north east part of the loch but note the 2m rock towards the centre

South of Oronsay Anchor in the mouth of the gut, in the centre, which is no longer taken up with fish cages.

Oronsay

The anchorages on the north side of Oronsay offer less frequented alternatives to Loch Drumbuie. Access is straightforward although if approaching Oronsay from the southwest, especially if coming round from Loch Drumbuie, care must be taken to avoid the Oronsay Rocks and Cean Garbh (drying 1·2m)

Anchorage

Sailean Mor is a narrow inlet on the north side of Oronsay offering good shelter from all winds. The approach from the north is clear but note the drying rocks extending north of the east side of the entrance. Anchor just inside the entrance or as far in as depth allows. The inlet dries for more than 3 cables from the head Good holding in stiff mud.

Northeast Oronsay An open bay giving good shelter from southeast to west with more space for larger yachts than Sailean Mor. Anchor in 2–8m but beware of drying rocks off the SW shore.

Glenmore Bay on the north side of Loch Sunart provides shelter on the east side of Eilean Mor, which is effectively a peninsula except at HW springs. Rocks up to ¾ cable off the east side of Eilean Mor are normally above water, but a submerged rock (LD 1·4m) lies 1½ cables northeast of them. There are fish cages as well as permanent moorings for local boats. Pass ½ cable east and northeast of the visible rocks keeping a good lookout for any which may be covered at HW, and anchor NNE of them, outside the moorings. Alternatively anchor southeast of the pontoon on the northeast side of the bay where good holding is reported.

James Scott

Looking over the CCC Centenary sunflower raft in Loch Drumbuie with Loch Sunart beyond and Carna on the extreme right

The CCC Centenary Cruise sunflower raft in Loch Drumbuie

Edward Mason

Martin Lawrence

Central Loch Sunart

A mile east of Oronsay on the south side of Loch Sunart, Carna sits in the mouth of Loch Teacuis, while on the north side between Oronsay and Carna is the small island of Risga. The main channel south of Risga is obstructed by several rocks in the apparently clear water between these islands.

The passage north of Risga is clear but there are submerged rocks on the north side of the channel, as well as rocks both submerged and drying outside each end on the south side.

A further mile from the east side of Carna the islet of Dun Ghallain off the north shore marks the beginning of a straightforward reach leading northeast to Salen.

Tides

Streams run generally at less than one knot, but north of Carna, and in the entrances to Loch Teacuis, they run at 2½ knots. At Laudale Narrows, four miles from the head of the loch, the streams run at three to 3½ knots.

In-going stream begins about –0500 Oban (+0200 Dover).
Out-going stream begins about +0130 Oban (–0400 Dover).

At Salen (Loch Sunart) the constant is as Oban.

Height in metres

MHWS	MHWN	MTL	MLWN	MLWS
4·6	3·4	2·6	1·7	0·6

Directions

In the main channel care should be taken to avoid Ross Rock (dries 0·3m) lying one cable south of Risga. There is a clearing line of 283° given on chart 2394 for avoiding Ross Rock but it is simpler to keep to the southern half of the channel between Risga and Oronsay.

Further east, Broad Rock (LD 0·5) lies almost in mid channel between Risga and Carna. It is best avoided by keeping well away from mid-channel, preferably towards Carna which is clean opposite Broad Rock, so as to avoid also the rocks east of Risga.

The narrow channel between Risga and the mainland can also be used. Hold to the north side of Risga, which is steep-to, to avoid a 1·8m rock just north of the centre of the channel.

Approaching this channel from the west beware of a rock with only 2·0m over it, 2 cables WNW of the west end of Risga; keeping the north side of Risga in line with the north end of Carna clears all hazards, including the drying rocks east of Risga.

A mile east of Carna, south of Dun Ghallain on the north shore, are several rocks drying and awash. The most dangerous is Dun Ghallain Rock, awash, ¾ cable southeast of Dun Ghallain. The north extremity of Carna in line with the 41m peak of Risga bearing 273° clears. From here on, passage is clean until Salen is reached.

Anchorage

The main anchorages in the central section of the loch are in Loch Teacuis and its approaches or at Salen. Occasional anchorages may also be found from Chart 2394 or *Antares Charts*, who have surveyed many further possibilities.

Carna

The passages either side of Carna, leading to Loch Teacuis, are among the trickiest bits of rock-dodging anywhere on the west coast. However, both of them have been recently surveyed by *Antares Charts* and the position of several of the rocks is now less speculative than previous plans have indicated.

Tides

In both channels the tidal streams run at 2½ knots springs.

In-going stream begins about –0500 Oban (+0200 Dover).
Out-going stream begins about +0130 Oban (–0400 Dover).

Height in metres

MHWS	MHWN	MTL	MLWN	MLWS
4·6	3·4	2·6	1·7	0·6

The Loch Fyne skiff 'Nighean Donn' in Loch Sunart

Admiralty Chart
2394
Admiralty Leisure Folio
5611.24, 25
Imray Chart
C65, 2800.5
Ordnance Survey
40, 47, 49
Cruising Scotland
pp.106, 107

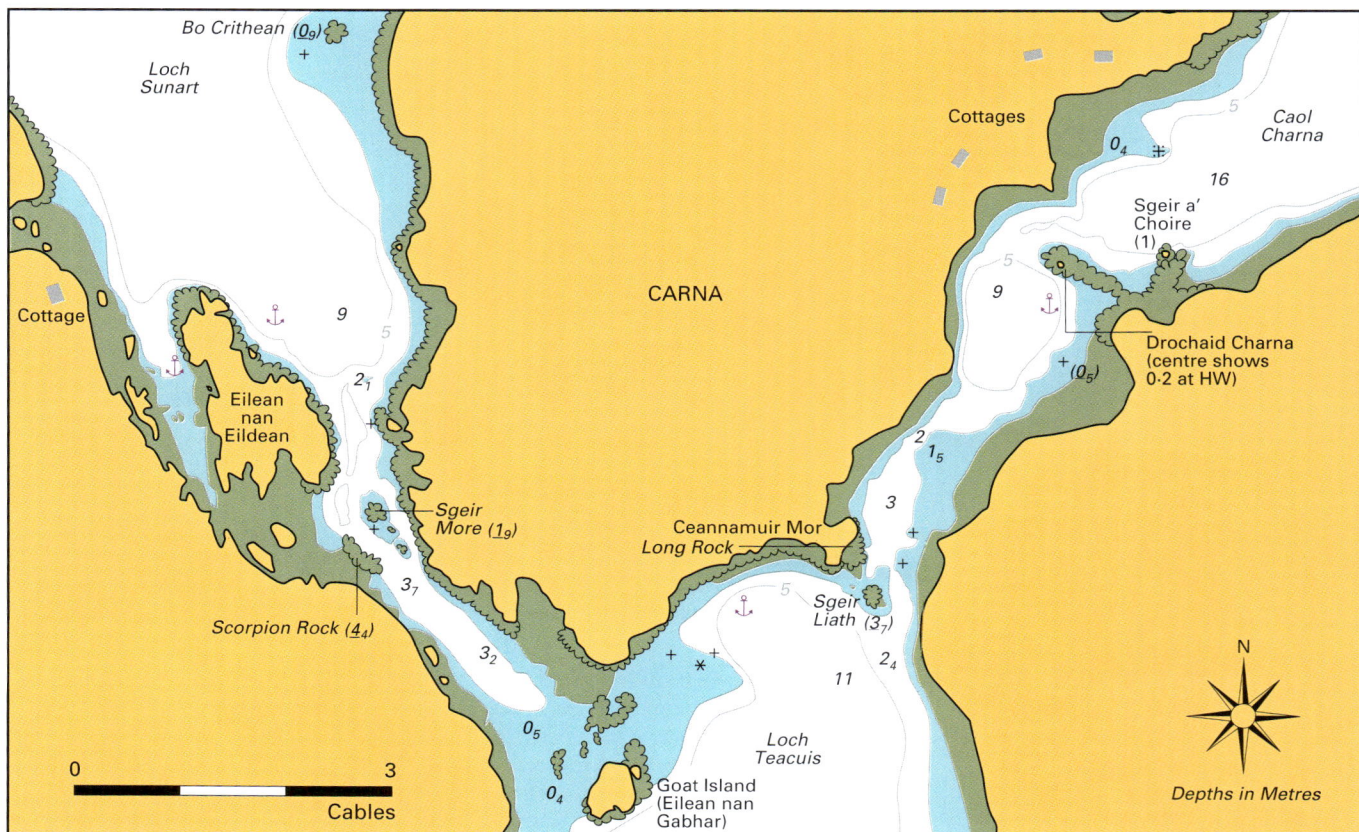

EAST AND WEST
CAOL CHARNA

Admiralty Chart
2394
Admiralty Leisure Folio
5611.24
Imray Chart
C65, 2800.5
Ordnance Survey
49
Cruising Scotland
p.106

*Looking south into the
entrance to West Caol
Charna. The Scorpion
Rock is showing in the
centre of the picture
with the tip of Eilean
nan Eildean on the right*

Bob Bradfield

Caol Charna (west passage)

This passage is named on charts as Caol
Achadh Lic, which translates as something like
'the channel of the field of stones'. Of the two
possible options, the route east of the
mid-channel rock Sgeir More (dries 1·9m), is
reasonably straight, though in places no more
than 20m wide. It is probably easier before
Sgeir More covers; the ideal time would be just
before LW neaps but bear in mind the 0·5m bar
further in.

Directions

Keep at least a cable off the west side of Carna,
to avoid Bo Crithean, and steer for the east side
of Eilean nan Eildean. If taking the eastern
passage, cross to the Carna shore when off the
south end of Eilean nan Eildean. Then keep
about 20 metres off Carna as rock ledges
extend up to 10 metres. Follow this shore for

about a cable then keep closer to the mainland
to avoid rocks which cover, northwest of Goat
Island (Eilean nan Gabhar). At this point the
channel is at its shallowest with a LD of 0·5m
which may affect the timing of the passage.

If Sgeir More is covered it may be better to
pass west of it, as Scorpion Rock (dries 4·4m)
covers only at HWS and the northwest end of
it should usually be visible. Initially follow the
course as described above but from the south
end of Eilean nan Eildean steer towards
Scorpion Rock before coming round to port to
leave it 20m to starboard. If entering with a
flood tide note that it sets strongly towards
Scorpion Rock and it may be necessary to steer
well towards the Carna shore to avoid being
carried on to it. Note also that the 'tail' of the
Scorpion projects well out into the channel and
is covered for much of the tide.

Anchorage

Doirlinn, west of Eilean nan Eildean, has a
sandy bottom but limited swinging room. A
mooring ring is fixed on the second tidal islet
southeast of the white cottage on the mainland.
The north entrance to the west kyle is a good
anchorage; within the kyle the tide runs more
strongly although the shelter is better.

Caol Charna (east passage)

The channel east of Carna is the easier to follow
as there are more rocks above water to assist
with pilotage. It also has a good anchorage
within it.

Martin Lawrence

Directions

Approach mid-channel from the northeast and identify Sgeir a'Choire, a small islet standing about a metre high off the mainland shore. Beyond it, Drochaid Charna ('bridge of Carna') extends over halfway across the passage from the southeast side, and its middle point stands just above MHWS.

Aim to pass about ¼ cable off Sgeir a'Choire and when it is abeam, turn to pass midway between Drochaid Charna and the promontory on Carna to the north of it. Then come round to port and keep midway between Carna and the west end of Drochaid Charna (drying 4·7m).

Enter the pool southwest of Drochaid Charna and then continue, keeping about ¼ cable off Carna, towards the next narrows where a reef, Long Rock, lies along the shore of the southeast point of Carna and Sgeir Liath, which dries 3·7m, lies near mid-channel. Northeast of Sgeir Liath submerged rocks extend approximately 60 metres off the mainland shore and narrow the channel, which has 2m in it.

Identify Sgeir Liath and pass east of it, keeping nearer to the rock than to the mainland, and enter into Loch Teacuis. As with the other passages in Loch Teacuis, be aware of the tide at all times so as to avoid being set towards rocks, especially when making course alterations.

Anchorage

The pool southwest of Drochaid Charna is said to provide good shelter even in strong northeast winds, although it is subject to the strong tide.

Loch Teacuis

The basin south of Carna is entered by either of the passages described above. Sgeir a' Chuilein, ½ cable off the east side of the basin, dries 1·8 metres with a submerged rock ¼ cable southwest of it, and the south side of the basin dries off ¼ mile.

A mile southeast of Goat Island the shallow Rahoy Narrows (Caolas Rahuaidh) lead to the head of Loch Teacuis. This passage should be taken just northeast of mid-channel except at the narrowest part where a rock, drying 1·7m, lies south of mid-channel and another, drying 2·6m, lies ¼ cable north of it. Pass between them in mid-channel, making due allowance for any tidal set that might take you off course. At each end of the narrows there are bars with average depths of slightly more than a metre, so avoid passing through at LWS.

The inner basin is more than a mile long with a narrower part about the middle of its length. Between this narrow part and the head of the loch, about a cable off the southwest side, there is a rock awash, close south of the 4 metre sounding on chart 2394.

The head of this basin dries off two cables, and the sides about ½ cable. Depths are otherwise moderate throughout the southeast part of the basin, and the bottom is mud.

Anchorage

Head of loch For conservation reasons, the only permissable anchorage is towards the head of the loch, about a cable southeast of a small promontory on the west side, in 3 metres. Note the awash rock a further cable to the southeast.

Outer basin This shelves abruptly almost everywhere and in places is very deep. Two possible anchorages are at the north end, just south of Carna and in the bay on the south side, just west of the entrance to Rahoy Narrows, but note that it dries out for almost a cable.

Caol Charna from the east with Drochaid Charna and Sgeir a'Choire in the foreground. Sgeir Liath can just be seen on the extreme left

> **Conservation area**
> The inner basin of Loch Teacuis is a Nature Conservation Marine Protected Area because it contains very rare and fragile serpulid aggregations which are similar to the serpulid reefs in Loch Creran (p.150) but are not yet fully developed reefs. However, they are still extremely sensitive to physical damage and yachts should anchor only at the head of the loch as described in the adjacent text to avoid the serpulid aggregations which are distributed in shallow water around edge of the inner basin.

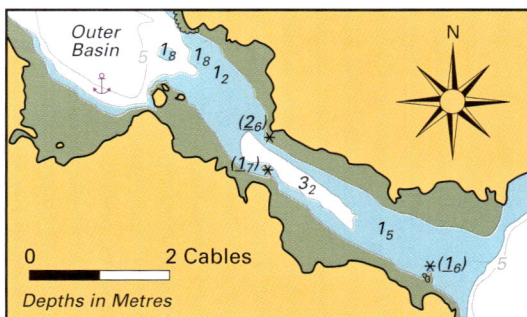

RAHOY NARROWS, LOCH TEACUIS

Admiralty Chart
2394
Admiralty Leisure Folio
5611.25
Imray Chart
C65, 2800.5
Ordnance Survey
40
Cruising Scotland
p.107

Salen

A sheltered inlet on the north side of Loch Sunart 4½ miles beyond Carna. It is the only place in Loch Sunart where water, diesel and provisions can be obtained conveniently.

About halfway up the bay is a drying reef showing 3 heads at LW across the middle third of the bay. The east end is marked by an E cardinal buoy. Keep to the east of the reef, giving the shore a reasonable berth, until the stone jetty is abeam. Do not attempt to pass west of the cardinal buoy.

Most of the bay is taken up by private moorings but anchorage can be had off the stone jetty though it is reported foul with chain and the anchor should be buoyed. 8 pontoon berths and 4 visitors' moorings are available and can be reserved up to 24 hours in advance by phone (see below).

Tides

The constant is as Oban.

Height in metres

MHWS	MHWN	MTL	MLWN	MLWS
4·6	3·4	2·6	1·7	0·6

Services and supplies

Visitors' pontoon and moorings (red buoys with orange pickups marked 'Jetty & Visitor') are all operated by Salen Jetty. Diesel by hose on pontoon. Electricity and water at pontoons. Toilets and showers. Refuse disposal and recycling. Salen Jetty also has a tearoom and a shop selling provisions and crafts.

Salen from the south; the reef shows as a pale patch with the cardinal mark to its right

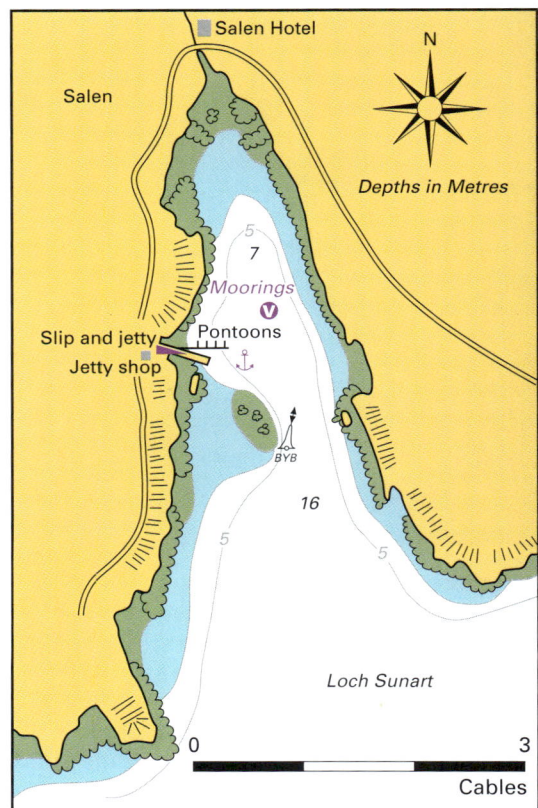

SALEN, LOCH SUNART

Communications

Salen Jetty ☎ 01967 431510 or 07909 944494
Salen Hotel - open all day ☎ 01967 431661

Iain Thornber

Bob Jones

Upper Loch Sunart

The loch continues for a further eight miles beyond Salen and it is in this part that the large-scale chart 2394 is essential.

For the first two miles beyond Salen, as the loch bends round to the southeast, submerged and drying rocks lie up to two cables off the south shore.

In the next mile, a rock with less than 2m lies 1½ cables SSW of Eilean a'Chuilinn and 2½ cables further SSW there is an awash rock. Clearance tracks to pass between these two are given on chart 2394. A 2m rock shown on chart 2394 as *Rep (1979)* has now been removed from the chart.

Rubha an Daimh, on the north shore four cables southeast of Eilean Garbh, has drying rocks extending up to two cables southwest of it. Opposite this point, at the mouth of the Laudale river, a bank of stones dries off two cables, and on both sides of the loch between Rubha an Daimh and Laudale Narrows, a mile further southeast, the foreshore dries up to ¼ mile in the bays on each side of the loch.

Immediately before Laudale Narrows, at Glas Eilean a shoal bank with a least depth of 1·2 metres extends two cables WNW of the island. From Laudale Narrows to the head of the loch the south shore is generally clean, but on the north side there are drying banks at the mouths of rivers, particularly at Strontian.

Eilean a' Mhuirich, ¾ mile west of Strontian, has a rock drying 1·8 metres ¼ cable off its south side. The head of the loch dries for half a mile.

Anchorages

Camas na h'Airbhe, on the southwest shore 1¼ miles west of Laudale Narrows, has suitable depths for anchoring close to the west side, but quickly becomes very deep away from the shore.
Garbh Eilean is a good anchorage and has reasonable depths off its southeast side.
Liddesdale, on the south shore 1½ miles east of Laudale Narrows, has reasonable depths east of the mouth of the valley, but there is probably little space clear of fish cages.
Ardnastang Bay On the north shore 2 cables east of Eilean a'Mhuirich. Keep ½ cable south of the island when approaching from the west. Convenient for Kilcamb Lodge Hotel. Call before arrival to check whether a mooring is available ☎ 01967 402257.
Strontian There are reports of sandbanks shoaling both at Strontian, for up to 2 cables, and at the head of the loch for up to 5 cables. Keep a close watch on the chart and the echo sounder in this area.

The mouth of the river at the head of the loch dries out a long way. Anchor beyond a concrete slip with a green shed east of a granite obelisk which stands on a low cliff east of the village. In easterly winds there are violent squalls from the head of the loch.

Services and supplies

At Strontian: a shop, hotel, restaurant, Post Office, phone box, Calor Gas and refuse disposal.

Loch Sunart looking west from Strontian village. Kilcamb Lodge Hotel on extreme right

9. West coast of Mull

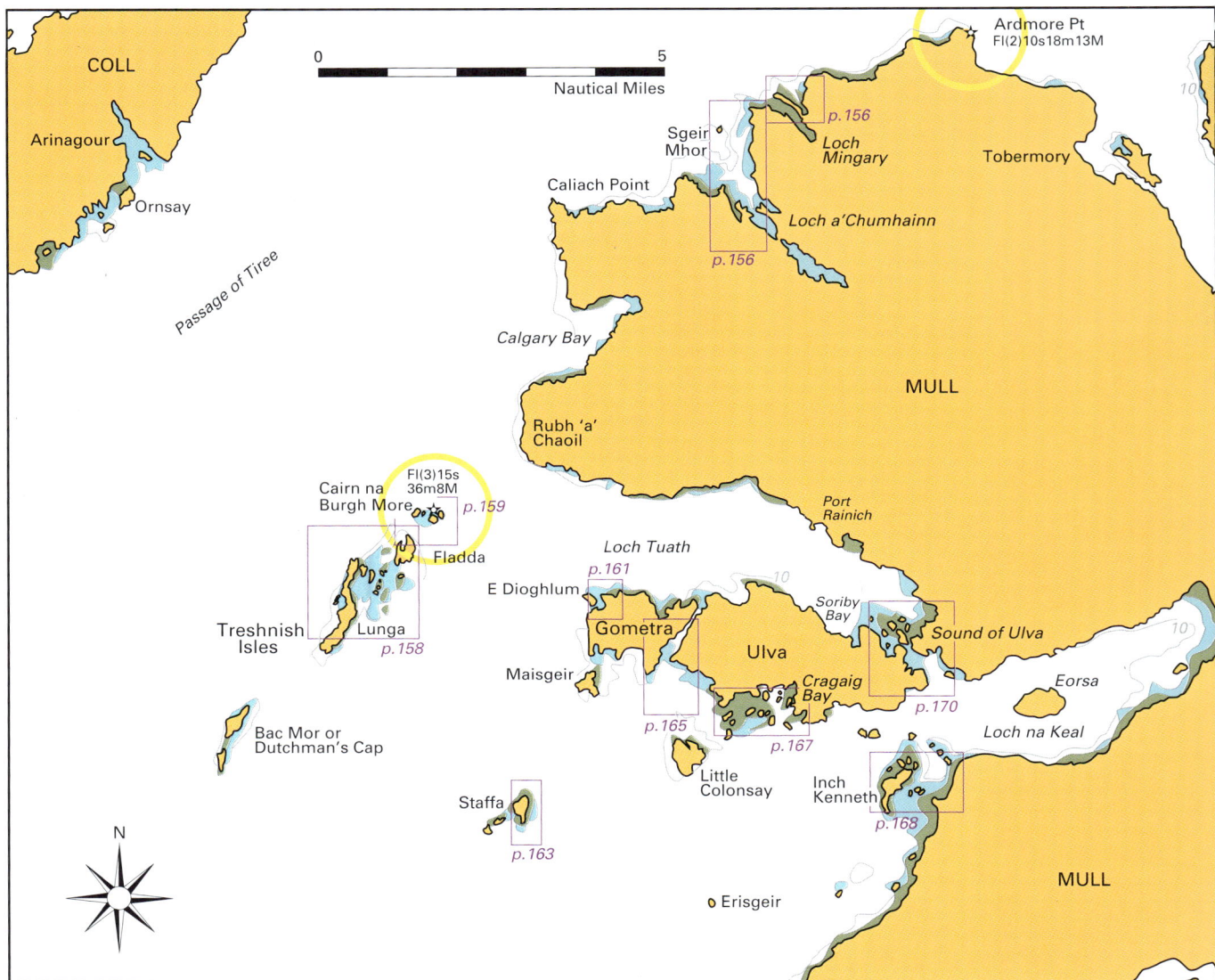

COLL

Arinagour

Ornsay

Passage of Tiree

Sgeir Mhor

Caliach Point

Loch Mingary

p.156

Loch a'Chumhainn

p.156

Tobermory

Ardmore Pt
Fl(2)10s18m13M

10

Calgary Bay

MULL

Rubh 'a' Chaoil

Port Rainich

0   5
Nautical Miles

Cairn na Burgh More

Fl(3)15s 36m8M
p.159

Fladda

Loch Tuath
p.161

E Dioghlum

10

Soriby Bay

Sound of Ulva

p.170

Eorsa

Treshnish Isles

Lunga
p.158

Gometra

Ulva

Cragaig Bay

Loch na Keal

10

Maisgeir

Bac Mor or Dutchman's Cap

p.165

p.167

Little Colonsay

Inch Kenneth

p.168

N

Staffa

p.163

Erisgeir

MULL

WEST COAST OF MULL

Admiralty Chart
2171, 2392
Admiralty Leisure Folio
5611.13
Imray Chart
C65
Ordnance Survey
47
Cruising Scotland
p.111

The navigation of the west coast of Mull requires care. The whole coast is completely exposed to the southwest and though there are many clean bays which might be used as temporary anchorages most of the sheltered harbours are rather difficult of access owing to submerged rocks.

The easiest approach is from the Sound of Mull, but in clear and moderate weather, with careful pilotage, it can be approached directly from the Sound of Islay or from the Firth of Lorn by the south side of Mull, but this means negotiating the passage between Mull and the Torran Rocks, although this is now made much easier by the establishment of buoyage by the NLB. This is described, together with the approach to the Sound of Iona, in Chapter 11, *Ross of Mull*.

Edward Mason

Northwest Mull

The passage around the north of Mull to the west is invariably made in one leg although, if against wind or tide, rounding successive headlands can become tedious. Loch a' Chumhainn (Loch Cuan), on the northwest coast, is well placed to provide a respite from the prevailing southwesterlies.

Tides

Off Caliach Point and Rubh' a' Chaoil, the next point to the south, tidal streams run at up to 2½ knots.

North-going stream begins –0510 Oban (+0145 Dover).
South-going stream begins +0115 Oban (–0415 Dover).

There are strong tidal streams around the Treshnish Isles, but not generally elsewhere. Those in the Sound of Iona are described in Chapter 11.

Tidal constants are, on average:
Bunessan: –0015 Oban (–0545 Dover)
Arinagour: Coll, +0020 Oban (–0510 Dover).

Height in metres at Bunessan

MHWS	MHWN	MTL	MLWN	MLWS
4·3	3·0	2·4	1·8	0·6

Dangers and marks

In the passage from the Sound of Mull to Iona there are, with the exceptions described below, no dangers beyond a quarter of a mile from the shore; nor are there any artificial marks. The dangers beyond ¼ mile from the shore are as follows:

Sgeir Mhor, a reef drying at half tide, three miles ENE of Caliach Point, lies ¾ mile from the shore in the mouth of Loch a' Chumhainn.

East of the Treshnish Isles, many drying rocks lie up to ½ mile beyond the line of the ESE side of the islands.

WSW of Staffa, drying rocks lie up to ½ mile from the island.

Rubh' a' Chaoil, the point 2½ miles south of Caliach Point has a drying reef extending nearly two cables from it

Keeping outside the 20 metre contour will clear all dangers, though sometimes by only a small margin. A few shallower banks further out may cause concern but the echo sounder in combination with the chart will be of help on this passage.

The most prominent point on the northwest of Mull is Caliach Point and very heavy seas can be met off it, particularly with wind against tide. It is worth taking care to be there at the most favourable time, particularly at springs or in fresh or strong winds; otherwise stand a couple of miles offshore.

Further east, around Gometra, Ulva, Inch Kenneth and off the Mull shore there are many reefs, in places extending up to a mile offshore. Some are described in the approaches to the anchorages described in this chapter but others, off the beaten track, are not and a close watch must be kept on the chart.

Lights

Eilean na Liathanaich (Bunessan) Fl.WR6s12m 8-6M
Dubh Artach (SW of Iona) Fl(2)30s44m20M
Skerryvore (SW of Tiree) Fl.10s48m23M
Cairns of Coll (N of Coll) Fl.12s23m10M
Cairn na Burgh More (Treshnish Isles) Fl(3)15s36m8M
Ardnamurchan Point Fl(2)20s55m22M

The dramatic plunging shoreline of Mull's west coast does not necessarily mean deep soundings inshore; the coast south of Inch Kenneth, above, has dangerous reefs extending up to a mile offshore

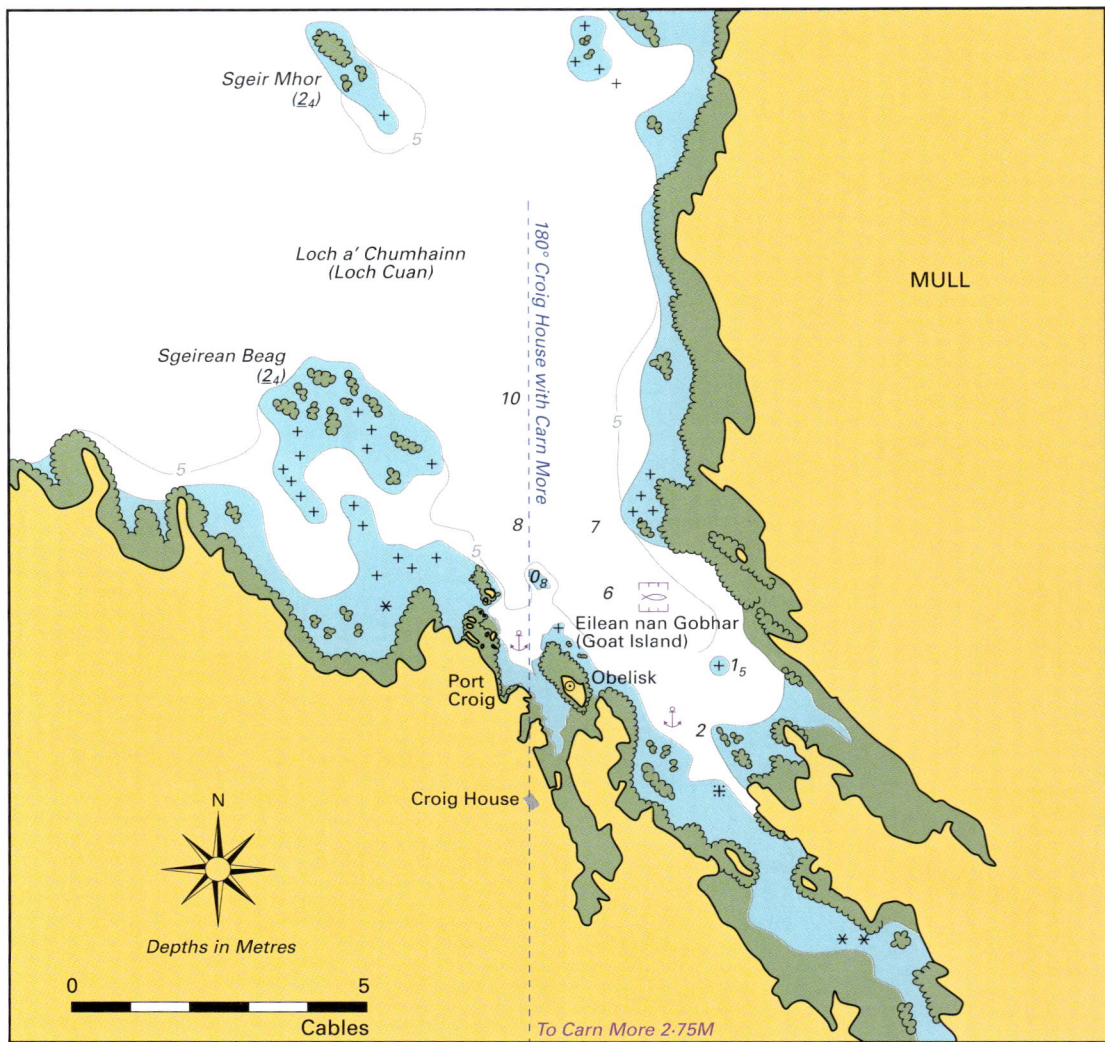

Map: Loch a' Chumhainn (Loch Cuan)

Depths in Metres

0 _____ 5
Cables

To Carn More 2·75M

**LOCH A' CHUMHAINN
(LOCH CUAN)**

Admiralty Chart
2392, 2171
Admiralty Leisure Folio
5611.13
Imray Chart
C65
Ordnance Survey
47
Cruising Scotland
p.113

Anchorages

Loch Mingary is an occasional anchorage for a quiet day. The entrance is little more than ½ cable wide between the islets south of Cuan Mor and drying reefs on the southwest side of the entrance. Be prepared to clear out if the wind or swell start to come onshore.

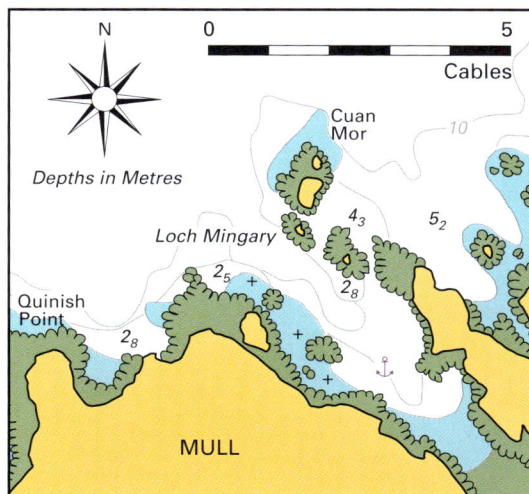

Map: Loch Mingary

Depths in Metres

0 _____ 5
Cables

LOCH MINGARY

Loch a' Chumhainn (Loch Cuan) This anchorage has more space than Loch Mingary, but it could be almost as much of a trap in an onshore wind, although a shoal-draught boat would find more shelter further in.

It is best to approach before half-flood, when Sgeir Mhor covers, although the swell will usually reveal it after that time. Sgeirean Beaga covers at the same time, so an approach can be made from northwest, or from north, passing two cables east of Sgeir Mhor.

Croig House, which is difficult to identify among the trees, in line with the ill-defined summit of Carn Mor, the highest hill to the south, bearing 180°, leads east of Sgeir Mhor. Otherwise the only mark is a stone obelisk on Eilean nan Gobhar (Goat Island), on the south side of the loch.

If near LW springs, take care to avoid the 0.8 metre patch 2½ cables north of the obelisk. Anchor either east of the promontory southeast of the obelisk, or in Port Croig, the creek northwest of Eilean nan Gobhar, but this has very little swinging room.

Shop, hotel and Post Office at Dervaig, two miles by dinghy or three miles by road.

Martin Lawrence

Calgary Bay, two miles south of Caliach Point, is another temporary anchorage if there is no swell, but perhaps less attractive than the two opposite, being accessible by road and fairly popular with tourists ashore.

Drying reefs extend ¼ mile southwest from the north point of the entrance, and submerged and drying rocks lie up to 1½ cables from the southeast side of the bay. Restaurant.

Port Croig, Loch a'Chumhainn, northwest Mull. Eilean nan Gobhar is just above the centre of the photo

Calgary Bay, Mull, with a lone yacht anchored off an unusually empty beach

Catherine Sutherland

Marks in line 195°

* (0₅)

North Rocks
(Awash LW)

FLADDA

14

4₅

Tighchoie (8)

+0₄

Foul

2₂

1₈

Sgeir
Eirionnaich

1₆

2₅

Foul

Foul

4₉

7₄

1₆

Sgeir a'
Chaisteil

3₉

5

Foul

1₆

1

3

(0₈)

5

6

Dun Cruit

10

2₂

235° left extreme of Lunga (SW) and
right extreme of Bac Mor (Dutchman's Cap)

Cruachan
101

3₃

11₁

LUNGA

N

Depths in Metres

0   5

Cables

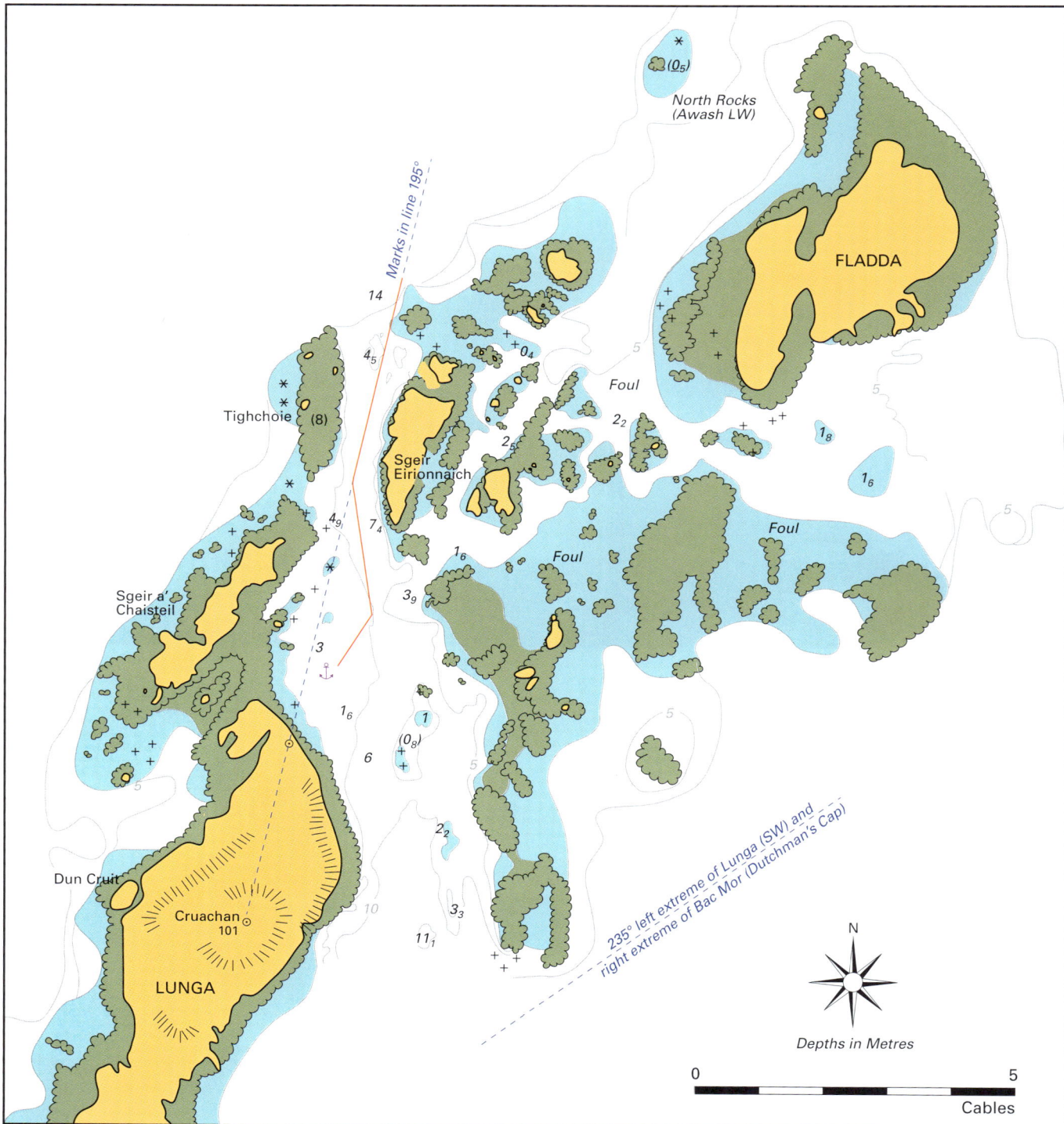

TRESHNISH ISLES

Treshnish Isles north entrance. Sgeir Eirionnaich is on the left and Tighchoie on the right, with the summit of Bac Mor showing beyond

Cairn

Bac Mor

Sgeir Eirionnaich

Cairn

Tighchoie

Martin Lawrence

Treshnish Isles

These interesting and peculiarly shaped islands are a breeding ground for grey seals and for many sea birds. The rocks and islets provide some shelter but they are rarely free from swell.

The approach, particularly from the north, needs careful pilotage, and the tide runs strongly between the islands.

The main islands are, from north to south, Cairn na Burgh More, which has ruins of a chapel and a castle on it, Fladda, which is flat; Lunga, the largest and highest of the group; and Bac Mor, otherwise known as The Dutchman's Cap.

Directions

From the north identify Tighchoie, the northwesternmost rock with a prominent rectangular block eight metres high, and the leading marks on Lunga which are stone cairns, one close to the shore and one on the summit (see photo opposite).

These cairns in line bearing about 195° lead through the outer north channel, but they – especially the lower cairn which is often no more than a few stones – may be difficult to identify.

Pass between Tighchoie and Sgeir Eirionnaich, the flat-topped island east of it, keeping the cairns in line. Once past Tighchoie, alter course to port and follow the approach lines indicated on the plan to avoid the rocks off Sgeir a' Chasteil that lie on the leading line.

From the south it is necessary to give the southernmost large drying patch, which lies due east of the summit of Lunga, a wide berth. Until recently rocks have been shown lying off the Lunga shore but the 2013 edition of chart 2652 indicates that the Lunga shore is reasonably clean. Therefore approach the southern entrance by steering towards the eastmost point of Lunga and then follow its shore round, keeping between ½ to ¾ cable off until well past a very shallow patch and an isolated rock (LD1·7m) further north.

From the east head for the midpoint of Lunga before following the southern approach and, from the northeast, keeping the south point of Lunga well open of the north point of Bac Mor, bearing 235° (photo below), leads clear of all the drying rocks east of the islands.

Anchorage

Anchor in sand east of the boulder spit at the north end of Lunga, clear of the moored pontoon that it is used by the boats for landing tourists. Some swell is likely.

Bac Mor open east of Lunga 235° clears the large area of rocks east of Lunga

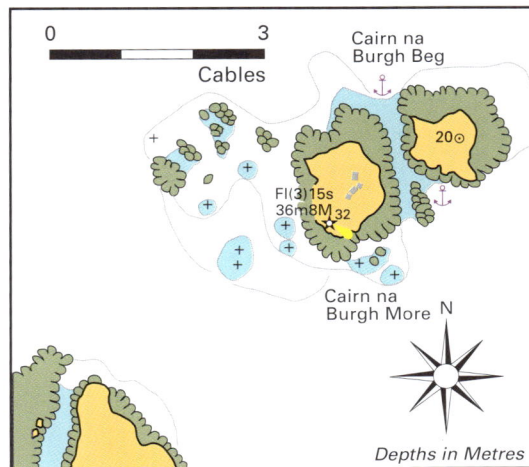

Cairn na Burgh Islands In very settled conditions theses make an interesting visit, but the tides run very strongly here. Anchor at either end of the sound between the two islands. With neither shelter nor good holding these can only be visited in the quietest weather.

Admiralty Chart
2652, 2171
Admiralty Leisure Folio
5611.11
Imray Chart
C65
Ordnance Survey
48
Cruising Scotland
p.111

CAIRN NA BURGH ISLANDS

Treshnish Isles; the Lunga anchorage

John Anderson

Cairn na Burgh Beg from Cairn na Burgh More, Treshnish Isles (p.159)

North Harbour (Acarseid Mhor), Gometra

John Anderson

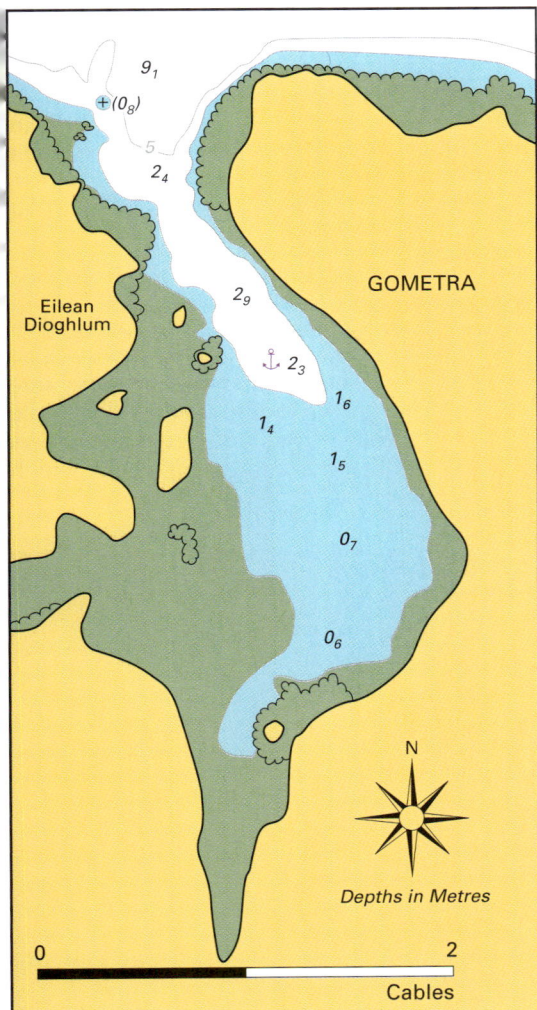
NORTH HARBOUR, GOMETRA

Loch Tuath

Loch Tuath lies between Ulva and Gometra to the south and the coast of Mull to the north. It is 6 miles in length and is clean except for a 3·6m rock, Bogha More, (LD 2·7m) which lies 2½ cables off Rubh an Suibhein on the Mull shore. There are many rocks around the approach to the Sound of Ulva, and the head of the loch should be avoided entirely unless using the large-scale chart, 2652.

Loch na Keal can be reached from the head of Loch Tuath through the Sound of Ulva but the passage is narrow and restricted by many rocks. It is best attempted above half tide and on a rising tide. It is described fully on p.170.

Tides

Sound of Ulva constant: –0010 Oban (–0540 Dover).

Height in metres

MHWS	MHWN	MTL	MLWN	MLWS
4·4	3·2	2·5	1·8	0·6

Anchorages

North Harbour (Acarseid Mhor) A popular anchorage in an almost landlocked pool at the north end of Gometra. Swinging room is somewhat restricted as most of the inner part of the inlet is too shallow for yachts of even moderate draught. Keep to the port side of the entrance to avoid rocks lying off Eilean Dioghlum, but not too close as a drying shelf of rocks and boulders lies on the east side.

Anchor towards the east shore, no further in than the north end of the islet. The bottom is sand and weed but the depth unlikely to be more than 3m. Good shelter and not subject to swell.

Gometra from the south with Loch Tuath beyond. North Harbour is slightly left of centre. The inlet below it, on the south side of Gometra, has been surveyed by Antares but is even shallower than the north anchorage

Admiralty Chart
2652, 2171
Admiralty Leisure Folio
5611.21
Imray Chart
C65
Ordnance Survey
48
Cruising Scotland
p.111

Martin Lawrence

Port Rainich, Loch Tuath, from the northeast

Port Rainich is not named even on the large-scale chart and is difficult to find. It lies behind Eilean Rainich on the north side of Loch Tuath, about four miles from the entrance, and is best found by identifying Torloisk House, a large house among trees on the hillside, from which Port Rainich is ESE. It is an occasional anchorage, open to the south and could be subject to swell. Swinging room is limited.

An Carraigean, the rock at the outer end of the reef on the south side of the entrance, does not normally cover. Enter from southwest rather closer to An Carraigean than to Eilean Rainich to avoid drying rocks at the south end of the island, and then turn north towards the head of the inlet, keeping closer to Eilean Rainich. Anchor when the south high-water line of Eilean Rainich is in line with the north point of Eilean Dioghlum at the south side of the entrance to Loch Tuath.

Ballygown Bay lies a mile east of Port Rainich and suffers from the same drawbacks though it offers more swinging room. A submerged rock, Bogha nan Ceard drying 1·1m, lies almost 1½ cables southeast of the western point of the bay, Torr an Aird.

To avoid this, approach from well offshore on a northerly course steering for the centre of the bay. Anchor in about 3m when Torr an Aird is abeam. Close to Ballygown Restaurant ☎ 01688 500113.

Soriby Bay lying at the southeast extremity of Loch Tuath has a good reputation for shelter and holding although it is open to the northwest. Drying and submerged rocks lie more than a cable WNW of Eilean Liath which is about the middle of the south shore of the bay. Anchor at the south end of the west side of the bay, or in the mouth of the inlet in the southeast corner of the bay, but not far in as there are submerged and drying rocks which close the entrance.

Martin Lawrence

At anchor off Fingal's Cave, Staffa

Staffa

With its basalt columns and several sea caves, of which Fingal's Cave is the best known, Staffa is one of the most spectacular natural features on the west coast.

Approach the island from the southeast with Erisgeir astern. The anchorage is off the landing place which is about 1½ cables from the south end. Avoid straying to the north of the approach line as sunken rocks extend up to 2 cables offshore. The island is owned by the National Trust for Scotland who have provided a concrete landing stage for use by excursion launches, though landing is often impossible owing to swell.

Anchorage

The plan shows the approximate location of rocks on the east side of the island. Those immediately northeast of the landing place have been recently surveyed by *Antares Charts*.

The usual anchorage is off the landing place at the north end of Am Buachaille, but there are no marks for avoiding any of the rocks; the bottom is rocky and falls away sharply and the anchor should be buoyed.

A gap in the rocks two cables NNE of the landing place, with moderate depths, might be less affected by seas from the west but, again, there are no marks for avoiding the rocks. It should be approached with care from the north, preferably using the *Antares* chart.

The wind and sea can get up quickly and an eye should be kept on the boat at all times; ideally, boats should not be left unattended except in the most settled conditions. When going ashore do not leave dinghies at the landing place used by the launches.

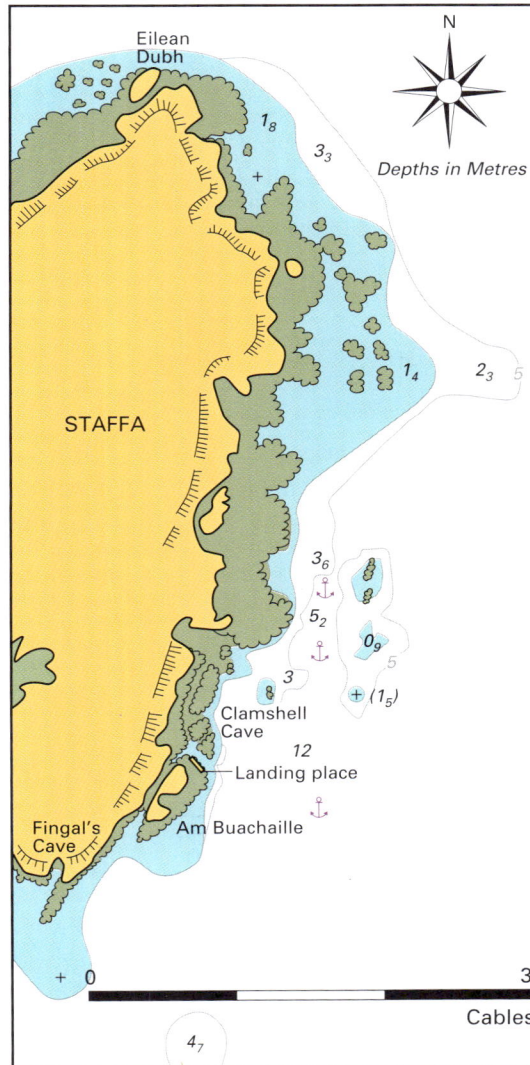

STAFFA

Admiralty Chart
2652, 2171
Admiralty Leisure Folio
5611.11, 21C
Imray Chart
C65
Ordnance Survey
48
Cruising Scotland
p.111

Staffa from SSW. The Buachaille stands at the right, with drying rocks showing beyond it

Martin Lawrence

Admiralty Chart
2652, 2171
Admiralty Leisure Folio
5611.21
Imray Chart
C65
Ordnance Survey
48
Cruising Scotland
p.111

Loch na Keal

This is the principal inlet on the west coast of Mull and its exploration is rewarding. There are so many rocks that it would be unwise to enter without chart 2652 but it is also well covered by the Admiralty Leisure charts. There are no villages around the loch and the main interest is in the pilotage and the anchorages themselves.

Tides

Ulva Ferry constant: –0010 Oban (–0540 Dover).

Height in metres

MHWS	MHWN	MTL	MLWN	MLWS
4·4	3·2	2·5	1·8	0·6

Tidal streams are not significant.

Dangers and marks

There are a great many unmarked rocks, especially off the south sides of Ulva and Gometra; these are described in greater detail in relation to each anchorage. Only those affecting passage in and out of the loch generally are described below.

Maisgeir, a reef mostly above water, extends six cables south of the west end of Gometra; however it is black and low-lying and difficult to see at dusk or in hazy weather.

Little Colonsay has a passage four cables wide northeast of it which is clear except for drying rocks which lie more than a cable north of its north west end, as well as a 2·1 metre patch two cables off its north side, and a rock 1 metre high 1½ cables north of its east end. Rocks with less than 2m over them also extend over 2 cables southwest of the island.

Erisgeir, about the middle of the entrance to the loch, 2¼ miles south of Little Colonsay, is a conspicuous islet 22 metres high with drying rocks more than ½ cable off its north and west sides, and a detached rock drying 4·4 metres more than a cable south of it.

Inch Kenneth, on the southeast side of the loch, has submerged and drying rocks extending up to two miles SSW of it, some of them a mile off the Mull shore. All these are avoided by keeping the east point of Ulva (which may not be easy to identify) open of the northwest side of Inch Kenneth bearing 027°.

Rocks above water and drying extend four cables north of Inch Kenneth. The light beacon at the entrance to Loch na Lathaich on the Ross of Mull bearing 208°, open of the northwest side of Inch Kenneth leads close west of these.

Geasgill Islands between Ulva and Inch Kenneth have rocks drying up to ½ cable all round, except south of Geasgill Mor, the larger island, and a drying reef extends one cable east of the southeast point of Geasgill Mor.

MacQuarrie's Rock which dries 0·8 metre, ½ mile south of the east point of Ulva, is the most dangerous rock in the loch. Various transits using the Geasgill Islands and other islands lead clear of the rock.

The traditional clearing mark is the south extremity of Garbh Eilean, northeast of Little Colonsay, touching the north extremity of Geasgill Beag bearing 266°(1); an easier line to identify is the south side of Geasgill Mor in line with the south side of Little Colonsay bearing 259°.

To pass north of MacQuarrie's Rock, keep the south side of Little Colonsay open north of Geasgill Beag bearing 255°(2). Once east of the point half a mile northeast of Geasgill Mor, alter course so that Little Colonsay is almost hidden behind it 252°.

MacQuarrie's Rock is safely passed when the west side of the Sound of Ulva begins to show north of the east extremity of Ulva, bearing 348°.

Eorsa, in the inner part of Loch na Keal, has drying rocks up to a cable off its east end, and Scarisdale Rocks extend east from a point 1¼ miles east of Eorsa.

Directions

The straightforward approach is south of Little Colonsay and north of Erisgeir; pass a cable south of Geasgill Mor and choose a suitable clearing mark to avoid MacQuarrie's Rock.

If continuing to the head of the loch pass either side of Eorsa but then keep to the north side of the loch which is clean outside a cable from the shore. Alternative passages should be tried only with chart 2652.

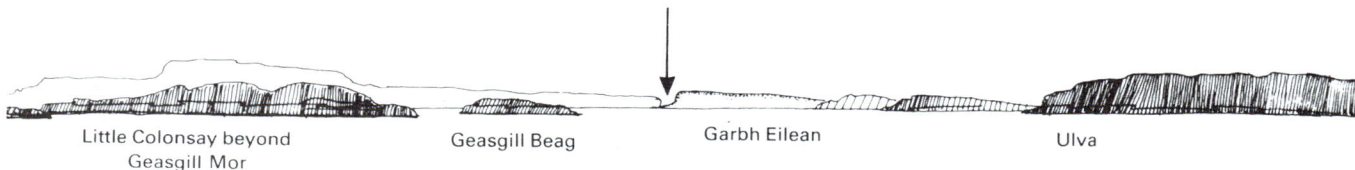

Little Colonsay beyond Geasgill Mor — Geasgill Beag — Garbh Eilean — Ulva

1. To pass south of MacQuarrie's Rock: Garbh Eilean and Geasgill Beag 266°

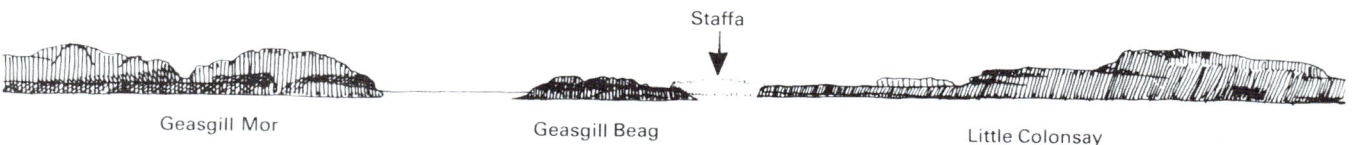

Geasgill Mor — Geasgill Beag — Staffa — Little Colonsay

2. To pass north of MacQuarrie's Rock: Little Colonsay and Geasgill Beag 255°

Gometra Harbour

This sheltered inlet lies between the islands of Gometra and Ulva, north of Little Colonsay. It is well protected except from strong southerlies. It continues NNE as a drying channel separating the two islands, across which lies a bridge.

Directions

Drying rocks lie up to a cable off the east side of Rubha Bhrisdeadh-ramh (Broken Oar Point), the promontory on the west side of the entrance. Sgeir na Skeineadh, a detached rock three cables east of the promontory, dries 3·2 metres, and the Bogha Ludden patch of rocks (LD 0·7m) lie 2 cables further southeast. Care should be taken not to mistake the next bay to the west for Gometra Harbour.

Approach with the Sound of Iona astern between Staffa and Little Colonsay and pass one to two cables east of Broken Oar Point. Keep mid-channel in the narrow entrance and anchor in the basin beyond, near the east shore which is the cleanest; drying rocks lie up to a cable from the west side and ¼ mile from the head of the inlet.

There is much weed on the bottom and holding can be poor. Substantial seas come in with strong southerly winds.

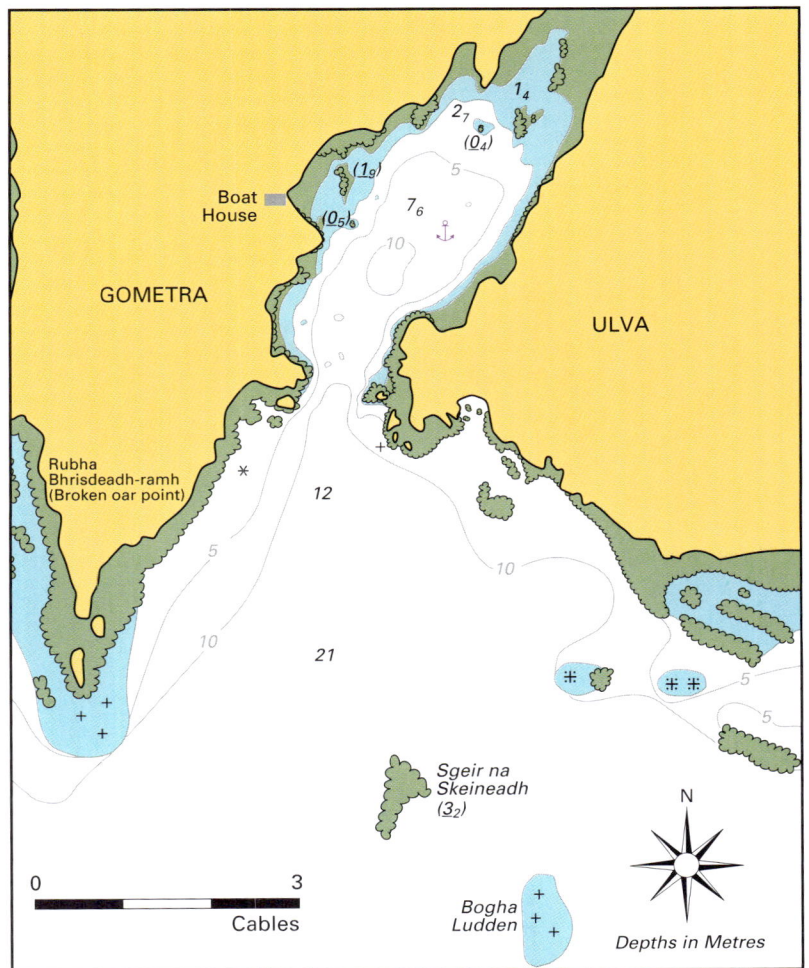

GOMETRA HARBOUR

Gometra Harbour from the southeast. Note that Bogha Ludden and Sgeir na Skeineadh are out of the photo

Gometra Harbour (p.165) looking towards the entrance

Cragaig Bay; the inlet to the west of the promontory opposite Eilean Reilean

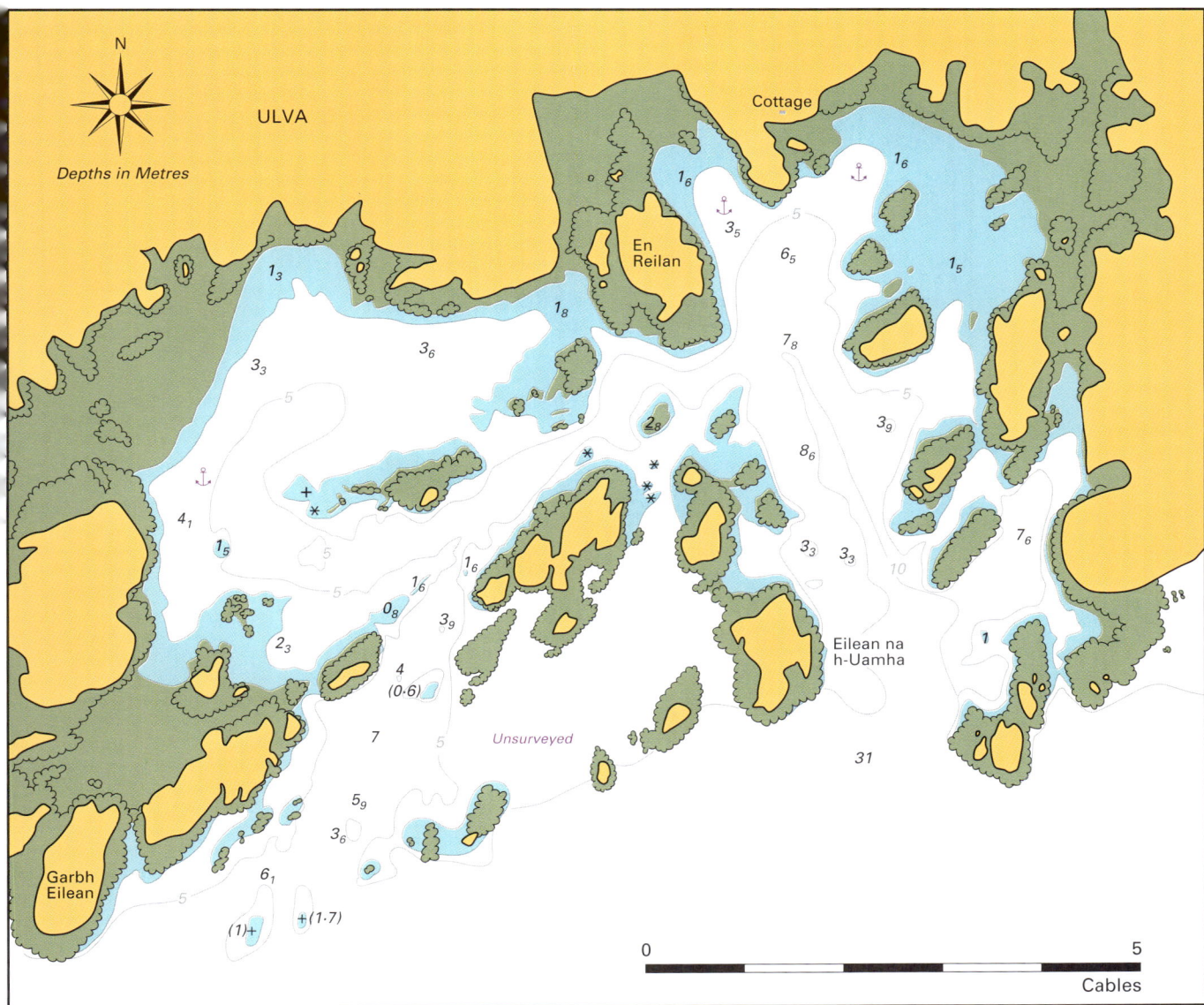

CRAGAIG BAY

Cragaig Bay

This small sheltered anchorage lies on the south coast of Ulva, northeast of Little Colonsay. Cragaig Bay is filled with islets, one or two of which have sandy beaches attached to them. There is only one straightforward inlet, the entrance to which lies east of Eilean na h-Uamha which is grass-topped, 1¼ miles ENE of Little Colonsay.

Tides

Ulva Ferry constant: –0010 Oban (–0540 Dover).

Height in metres

MHWS	MHWN	MTL	MLWN	MLWS
4·4	3·2	2·5	1·8	0·6

Directions

From some way off the entrance is difficult to make out but, heading east, as it comes abeam it opens up, leading to an inconspicuous stone cottage under the more easterly of the twin peaks of Ulva.

Approach in 6–8m, leaving Eilean na h-Uamha to port, heading for the cottage on the shore, When Eilean Reilan is abeam to port alter course slightly to port and anchor in the gut in 4m. The bottom is sandy mud giving good holding. Alternatively anchor southeast of the cottage.

In either of these anchorages a sea comes in in strong southerlies and better shelter can be found at the west end of the large basin in the northwest of the bay. There is no simple way of reaching this unless using the *Antares* chart, which has identified a channel leading to it with depths of 4–5 metres along it entire length.

Without the aid of GPS and the *Antares* chart it might be possible to make this passage in calm weather and near LW, preferably on a rising tide and with a lookout on the bow, though these are unlikely to be the prevailing conditions if the better shelter is needed.

Ashore, there is a good track to Ulva Ferry passing by an abandoned village with the ruins of a water mill nearby.

Admiralty Chart
2652, 2171
Admiralty Leisure Folio
5611.21
Imray Chart
C65
Ordnance Survey
48
Cruising Scotland
p.111

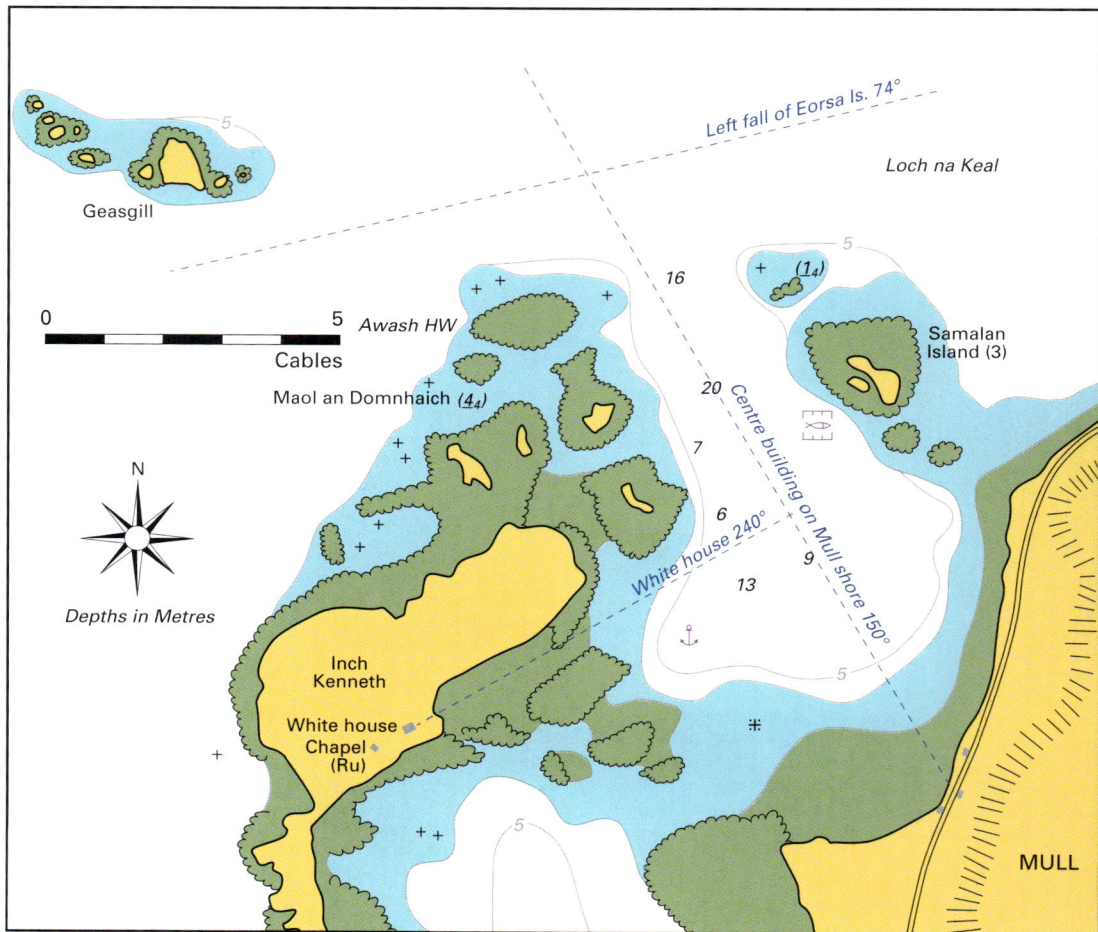

Geasgill

Left fall of Eorsa Is. 74°

Loch na Keal

16

(1₄)

Samalan
Island (3)

0   5   *Awash HW*

Cables

20

Maol an Domnhaich *(4₄)*

7

Centre building on Mull shore 150°

N

6

White house 240°

9

Depths in Metres

13

Inch
Kenneth

White house
Chapel
(Ru)

5

MULL

INCH KENNETH

Inch Kenneth

The anchorage is east of the island and is approached from the north. It combines shelter from the west with the impressive backdrop of the cliffs on Mull (photo p.155) The ruined medieval chapel on the island is well worth a visit.

Directions

Rocks extend four cables north of Inch Kenneth; Sunday Rock (Maol an Domhnaich), the broad rock three cables from the island, rarely covers (dries 4·4 metres) but other drying and submerged rocks lie up to a cable further northwest. On the east side of the entrance, rocks drying and awash lie two cables northwest of Samalan Island and there are fish cages up to almost 2 cables southwest of the island.

Approach from NNW keeping the centre building (*Clachandhu* on chart 2652) of three on the southeast shore bearing 150° midway between visible rocks and leave the fish cages to port.

When Inch Kenneth House is open south of the cliffs on the south side of the northeast part of the island, bearing 240° (see below), turn towards the island and anchor in about five metres; the bottom shoals abruptly further in.

Holding has been reported as poor but there is much clean sand and it should not be too difficult to get an anchor well set. The anchorage is subject to violent squalls from the cliffs of Mull in southeast winds.

Admiralty Chart
2652, 2171
Admiralty Leisure Folio
5611.21
Imray Chart
C65
Ordnance Survey
48
Cruising Scotland
p.111

Inch Kenneth House just showing 240°

Martin Lawrence

Ulva Sound from the southeast

Ulva Sound from the northwest

Martin Lawrence

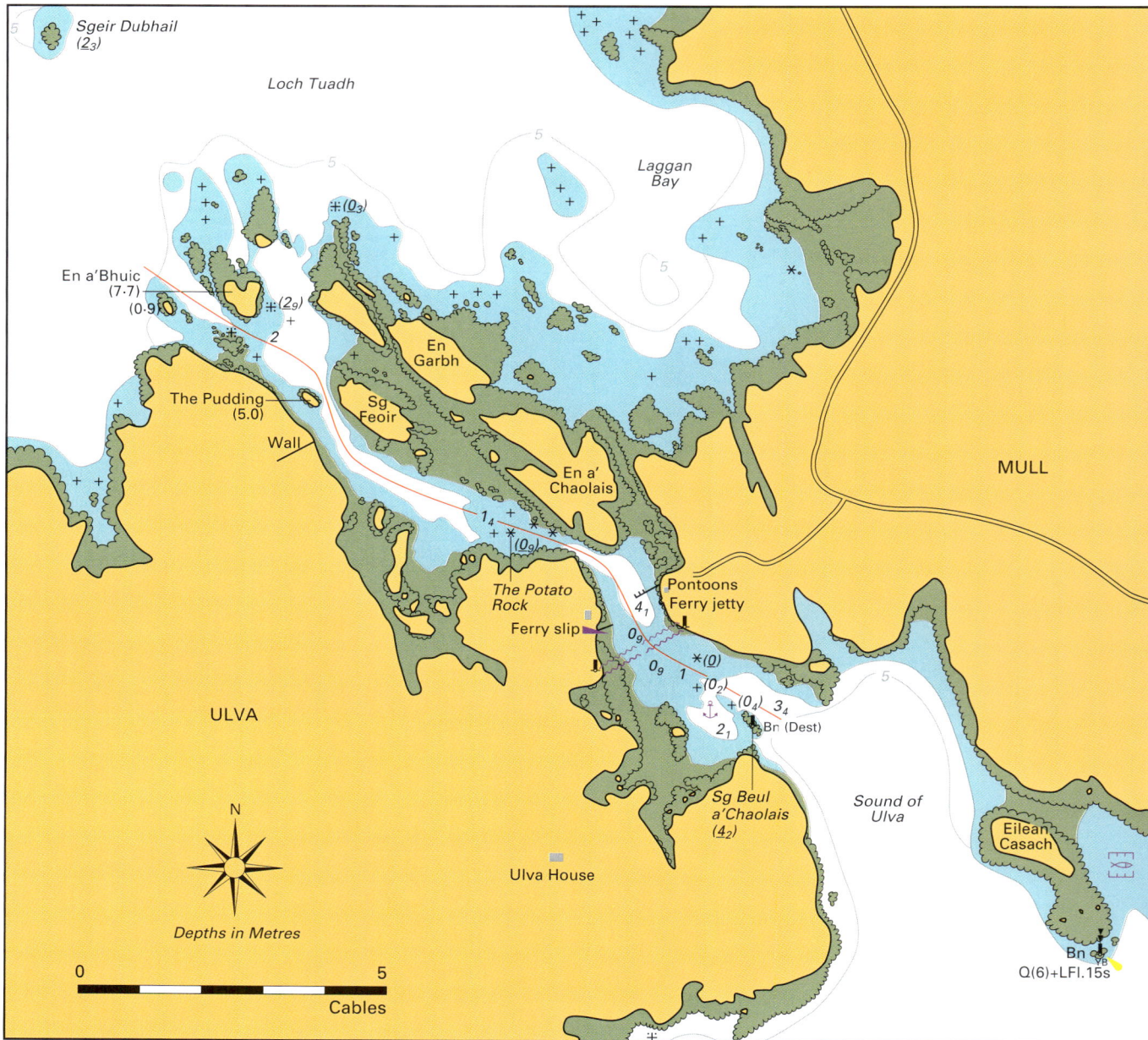

ULVA SOUND

Ulva Sound

Admiralty Chart
2652
Admiralty Leisure Folio
5611.21
Imray Chart
C65
Ordnance Survey
48
Cruising Scotland
p.111

This narrow sound separates the islands of Ulva and Mull. It is studded with rocks, shoals and sandbars, some of which have not been sufficiently identified for inclusion on the plan above. Accordingly a passage through the sound should only be attempted above half tide, preferably when it is rising, and even then with caution. Special care is needed at the eastern end of the sound, north of the ferry, where the north-going flood tide can reach 2kn at springs.

Tide

Constant –0010 Oban (–0540 Dover).

Height in metres

MHWS	MHWN	MTL	MLWN	MLWS
4·4	3·2	2·5	1·8	0·6

The flood runs northwestwards but tidal streams are not significant except at the eastern end, near the ferry.

Directions

Approaching the sound from the south note and avoid MacQuarrie's rock (see p.164). In the mouth of the sound, where it narrows to two cables north of the east point of Ulva, Sgeir Beul a' Chaolais (which means 'the rock at the mouth of the sound') dries 4·2 metres with a low concrete beacon on it. Northeast of it drying rocks extend a cable south of the north point of the entrance. Leave Sgeir Beul a'Chaolais fairly close to port and head for the ferry slip on Ulva but note that soundings reduce to less than a metre before reaching the pontoons.

Proceeding northwards through the narrows north of the ferry and south of Eilean a'Chaolais keep a sharp lookout for rocks. The deepest water at the narrows is on the south side. At, and beyond, the narrowest part of the channel avoid straying towards the drying rocks south and west of Eilean a'Chaolais. The Potato Rock', a broad submerged rock the north side of which is usually marked by an orange buoy, lies on the south side of the channel. Pass 6–8m north of the orange buoy.

If the orange buoy marking the Potato Rock is not there, or if mooring pickup buoys make identification difficult, a useful transit astern is an electricity transformer on a pole, above the ferry house toilet block, on the Mull shore in transit with a conspicuous peak on the skyline.

For the next leg of the channel the aim is to sight a stone wall on the Ulva shore south of The Pudding, a 5m high islet, and to use this wall as an approximate course to adopt for passing south of Sgeir Feoir. Do not keep close to Sgeir Feoir. During the summer, moorings are laid for excursion boats and a safe line is to pass close to these moorings.

When the channel east of The Pudding is well open alter course and leave The Pudding to port. Thereafter alter course to pass close south of Eilean a Bhuic, noting and leaving the sunken rocks and the westmost above water rock (0·9m) to port before reaching the open waters of Loch Tuath.

Proceeding southwards from Loch Tuath leave Sgeir Dubhail to port and after identifying Eilean a' Bhuic and The Pudding further east, enter the sound by keeping Eilean a'Bhuic close to port and thereafter leave the Pudding Rock to starboard.

Using the leading line of the wall on the shore of Ulva and the moorings mentioned above, pass through the central section of the sound. When approaching the narrows at the east end of the sound keep 6–8m north of the orange buoy marking the Potato Rock and then hold towards the Ulva shore until clear of the narrows. (See note above if the orange buoy is not there.)

Berthing and anchorage

There is a pontoon on the Mull shore with finger pontoons for up to 8 visiting yachts in depths varying from 5·5–3m on the outer and middle berths respectively. Water, electricity, diesel, WiFi and toilets. Pontoon manager ☎07557378953 Restaurant and visitor centre on Ulva.

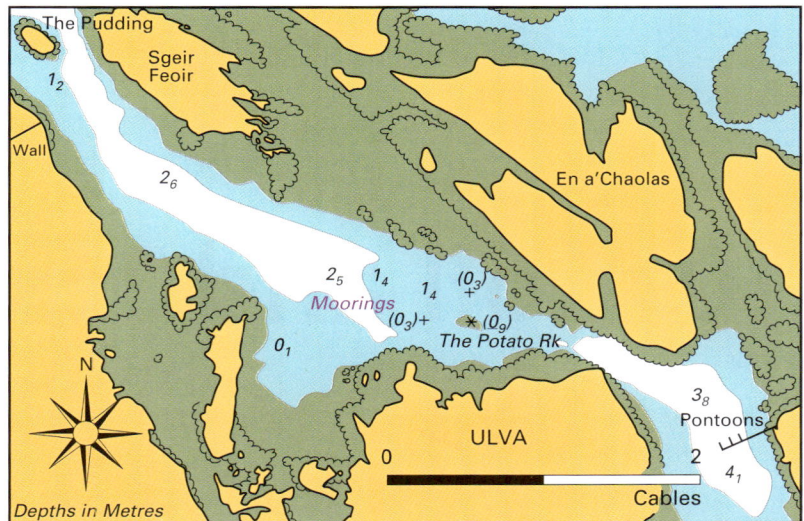

ULVA SOUND NARROWS

Do not anchor amongst the moorings or pick up any of them unless invited by a local boat owner to do so.

WNW of Sgeir Beul a' Chaolais Anchor in the slightly deeper water between Sgeir Beul a' Chaolais and the islet a cable west of it. When approaching the anchorage from the north east beware of the isolated rocks and shallows northwest of Sgeir Beul a' Chaolais.

Anchorages in upper Loch na Keal

Eorsa ENE of the island on the 5 metre line. Keep at least a cable off the southeast and east sides of the island to avoid drying rocks.

Dhiseig SSE of Eorsa. Temporary anchorage is possible southeast of Eorsa to land a party to climb Ben More. A stony bank lies off the mouth of the two burns, outside which the bottom falls away steeply.

Scarisdale provides better anchorage but access is beset by sunken and drying rocks on both hands. A' Chrannag, the 116 metre hill at the south east end of Ulva over the north edge of Eorsa bearing 270° astern leads to a pool with moderate depth south of Scarisdale Rocks. Use chart 2652 and note carefully the position of rocky shoal patches on either side of the entrance.

The visitors' pontoon at Ulva Sound with the Boathouse Restaurant across the sound on Ulva

Mull and Iona Community Trust

10. Coll and Tiree

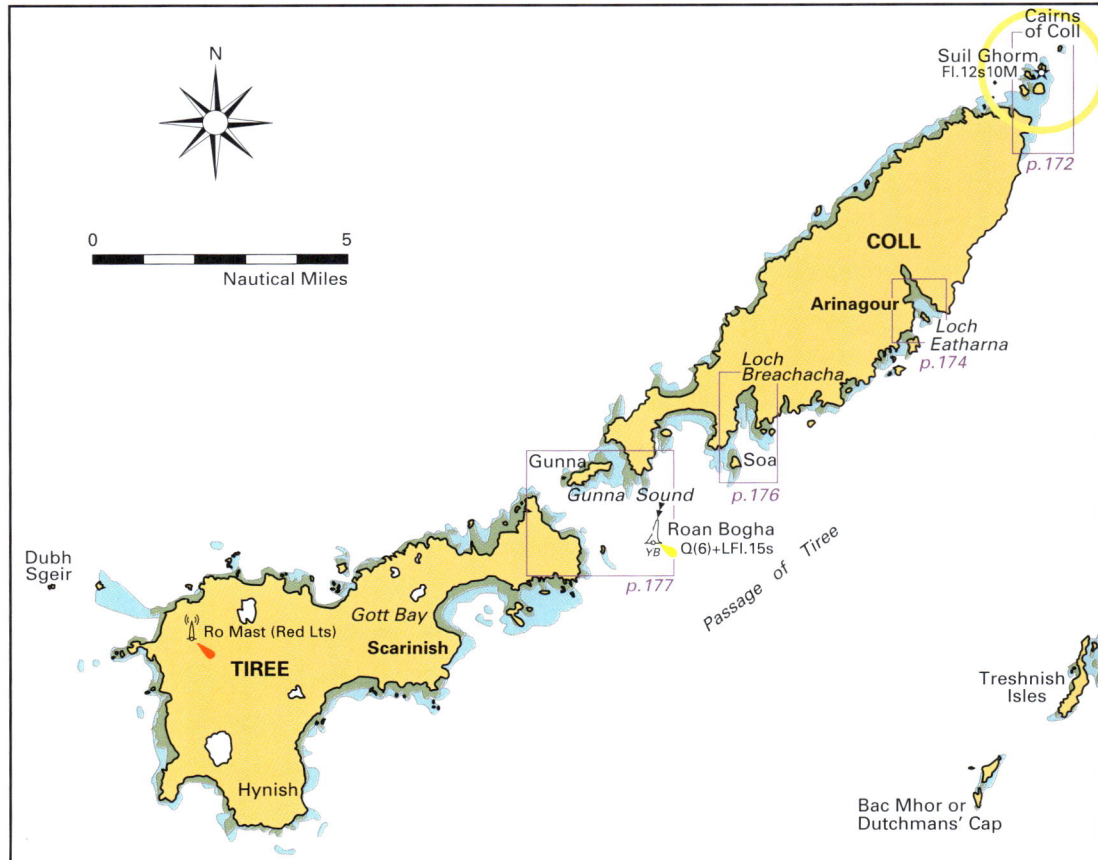

COLL AND TIREE

Admiralty Chart
2171, 1778
Admiralty Leisure Folio
5611.13
Imray Chart
C65
Ordnance Survey
46
Cruising Scotland
pp.114–5

These islands, separated by Gunna Sound, lie five to seven miles off the west coast of Mull. They are mostly low-lying and exposed and neither of them has an anchorage which is secure, let alone comfortable, in winds from all directions.

Tiree is flat and fertile but the anchorage in Gott Bay offers little protection from the weather. Coll is slightly higher, and very rocky, particularly at its northern end where the Cairns of Coll extend some one and a half miles northward from the northern tip of the island. The northern section of the east coast of Coll is relatively free of off-lying dangers, but south of Arinagour there are many off-lying rocks and some overfalls. The western sides are very exposed and offer no shelter except in offshore winds during settled weather.

Both islands may be visited from the Sound of Mull or from Iona, or from anchorages in between, the distance from Tobermory to Arinagour, or from Iona to Gott Bay being about 20 miles.

Tides

In the Passage of Tiree, the channel between Coll and Tiree and Mull, tidal streams run at up to 1½ knots at springs – enough to cause an unpleasant sea with wind against tide. Off Caliach Point and around the Treshnish Isles tidal streams increase to 2½ knots.

Off the middle of the southeast side of Coll;

Northeast-going stream begins –0430 Oban (+0230 Dover)
Southwest-going stream begins +0200 Oban (–0330 Dover).

Towards the south end of Tiree;

Northeast-going stream begins +0600 Oban (+0030 Dover)
Southwest-going stream begins at HW Oban (–0530 Dover).

A direct passage can be made from the Sound of Islay. Dubh Artach may be passed on either side but if passing north of it keep well south of the Torran Rocks, as there are submerged rocks south of those which are visible.

For ten miles west of Iona the bottom is very uneven, causing overfalls which are dangerous with any wind or swell.

For Gunna Sound see p.177.

Coll

The north end of Coll is a place that can only be explored in settled weather but if an opportunity occurs it is well worth taking. The use of the *Antares* chart for the Eilean Mor anchorage is strongly recommended.

Anchorages

Eilean Mor Off the north end of Coll, a pool among the skerries on the south west side of Eilean Mor provides some shelter to anchor and watch birds and seals on a quiet day.

Note the Cairns of Coll, an unmarked reef ½ mile north east of Suil Ghorm light beacon, and rocks, submerged and drying lying east and south of Eilean Mor. Identify An Glas Eilean and approach from the east; pass north of it and head NNW towards a sandbar joining the two skerries west of Eilean Mor, keeping a cleft in the profile of An Glas Eilean astern. Look out for drying rocks noted on the plan on either hand. The tide sets through between the skerries at up to two knots.

Sorisdale Bay, an excellent occasional anchorage, ½ mile south of the north end of Coll. An underwater power cable is landed on the west side of the bay, and a detached drying rock lies off the northeast point. Anchor in 3m on sand towards the east side of the bay off a large concrete block on the promontory. Beware of the power cable and a reef on the southwest side of the bay.

Map labels:
Cairns of Coll (4)
0 — 5 Cables
Suil Ghorm Fl.12s
•34 Eilean Mor
An Glas Eilean
COLL
Sorisdale Bay
N
Depths in Metres

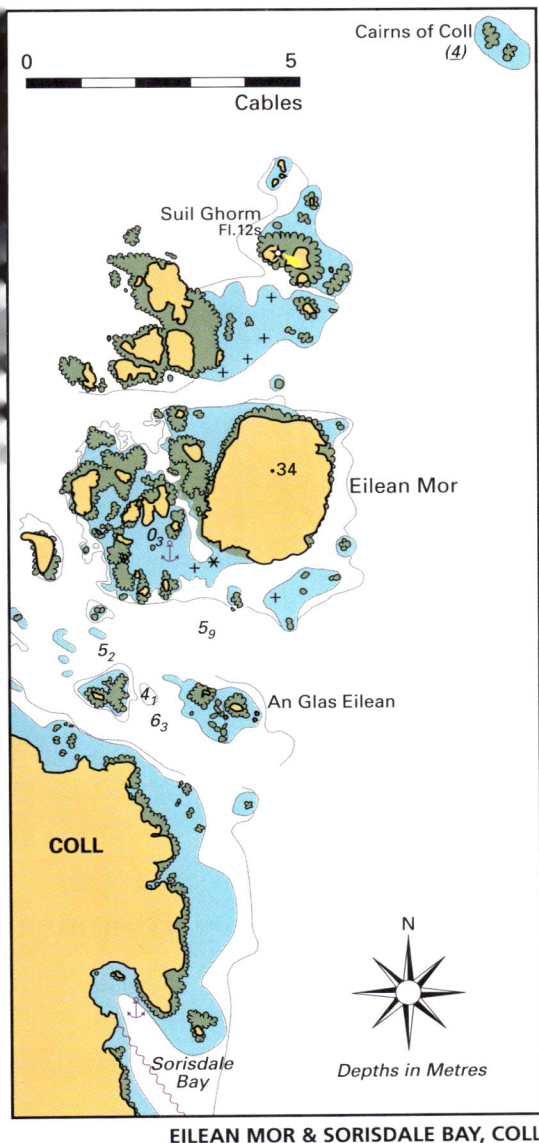

EILEAN MOR & SORISDALE BAY, COLL

The anchorage in Sorisdale Bay, Coll

Charles Warlow

Passage

Between the Sound of Mull and Arinagour there are no particular hazards apart from drying rocks within the line of headlands on the northwest coast of Mull. There is no way of identifying Arinagour until it is fairly close to, when houses will begin to appear. Bearing in mind that the approach to the coast of Coll will be made obliquely, make for a point about a quarter of its apparent length from the south end of the island.

Approaching Tiree from southeast the most conspicuous features on the island are Beinn Hough on the west side of the island (119m) with a radar installation near its summit, and Ben Hynish (138m) at the south point of the island. A small latticed communications tower stands at Scarinish, ½ mile southwest of the south point of Gott Bay and about five miles northeast of Ben Hynish.

Crossing from the north end of the Sound of Iona there are no particular hazards.

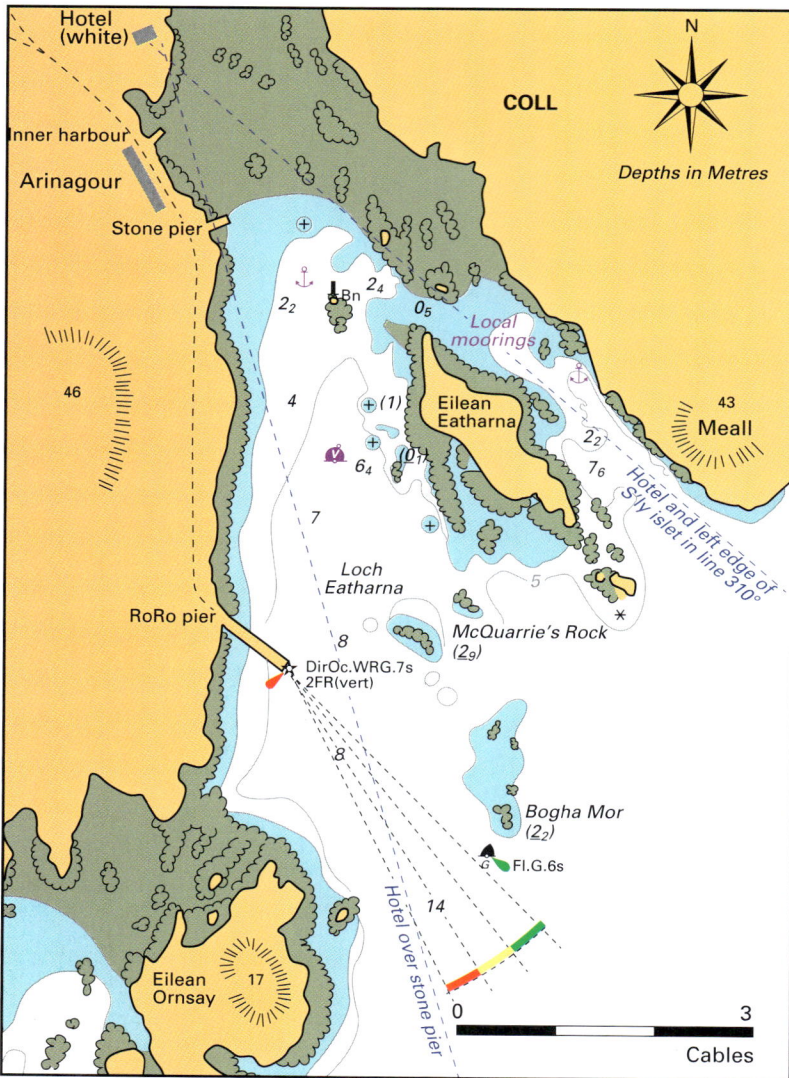

LOCH EATHARNA

Directions

If approaching from southwest keep more than a cable off Ornsay at the southwest point of the entrance, to avoid a submerged rock there. From any direction identify Bogha Mor green conical buoy and leave it well to starboard.

Steer to pass close east of the head of the concrete RoRo pier to avoid McQuarrie's Rock, unmarked, drying 2·9 metres, a cable east of the pier. Keeping the right side of the hotel in line above the root of the stone pier at Arinagour village will clear it.

Anchorage

The main anchorage is west of Eilean Eatharna and there are three trots of visitors' moorings north of the concrete pier which occupy almost the full width of the loch.

The most northwesterly of drying rocks off Eilean Eatharna has a stone beacon on it. Anchor in clean sand between the beacon and the stone pier. There is limited space to the northeast of the beacon.

Alternatively use the eastern anchorage. Enter from a position midway between the Meall and the outer islet and steer a northerly course to acquire the leading line with the hotel in line with the left edge of the southerly islet bearing 310° as indicated on the plan. This line will place the hotel below and just left of the conspicuous church and leads into the anchorage clear of all dangers. Swinging room is limited but it is better than the main anchorage when a southerly swell is running.

A half-tide passage north of Eilean Eatharna can be used – with great caution – in quiet weather. See also photo on opposite page.

Lights

At night Bogha Mor buoy is lit Fl.G.6s and the head of the concrete pier has lights 2F.R(vert), so that the approach as far as the visitors' moorings is fairly simple.

Services and supplies

Two shops, hotel ☎01879 230334. Showers and launderette at Community Hall. Calor Gas. Diesel and petrol (not always available). Post Office, phone box at stone pier. Water tap at the back of toilets on the stone pier. Bicycle hire from Coll Hotel.

Loch Eatharna (Arinagour)

A popular anchorage in the middle of the southeast side of Coll with a clean sandy bottom, but exposed to any sea running, even a southwesterly swell along the coast, which is aggravated by the shallowness of the loch.

Tides

Constant is +0017 Oban (−0513 Dover).

Height in metres

MHWS	MHWN
4·4	3·2

Admiralty Chart
2474
Admiralty Leisure Folio
13
Imray Chart
C65
Ordnance Survey
46
Cruising Scotland
p.114

The inner harbour and old stone jetty at Arinagour

Martin Lawrence

Looking across Loch Eatharna to Arinagour.
Since the photograph was taken the moorings in both the eastern and western anchorages have multiplied greatly

The head of Loch Eatharna from the north with the passage north of Eilean Eatharna at upper left

Martin Lawrence

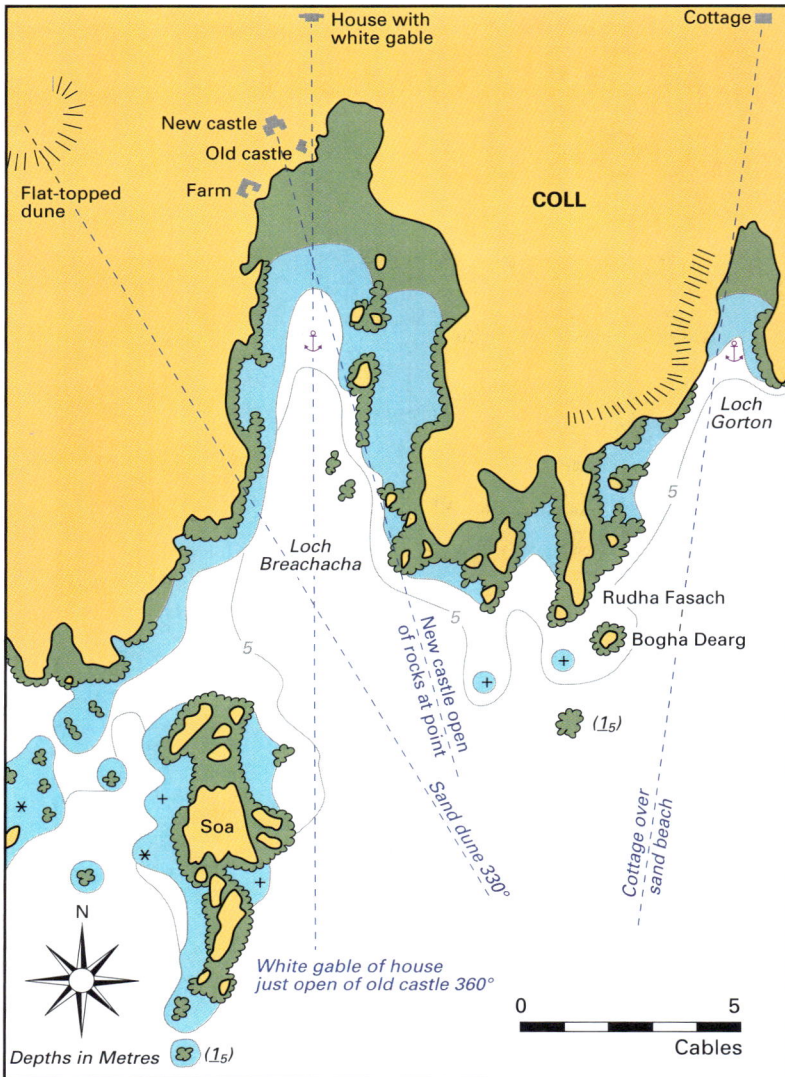
LOCH BREACHACHA

Loch Breachacha

An occasional anchorage towards the southwest end of Coll, identifiable initially by Soa Island, 15m high, and nearer at hand by the old and new castles, of which the new one is a grey castellated 19th-century building with symmetrical wings and small corner turrets. The inlet is sandy and open to any southerly swell. There are many rocks on both sides of the entrance and inside the loch.

Directions

The 20-metre contour clears all dangers. Steer with the highest point of the sand dunes to the west of the loch bearing 330°. When the 'new' castle appears clear west of above-water rocks at the east point of the entrance, all rocks to the south of that point are cleared.

A line to clear rocks within the loch is to keep the white gable of a prominent house which stands on the skyline behind the old castle just open of the right-hand side of that castle 360°; this line leads rather close to drying rocks in the middle of the loch. The house in the photograph below is showing well open of the old castle. The loch shoals very gradually but evenly; anchor as far in as depth allows.

Crossapol Bay

This bay should not be entered without the large-scale chart 2474. Do not use the old chart 2475 without the Block Correction to NM 2749/07, which shows two recently 'discovered' awash rocks in the centre of the bay.

Directions

Approaching from the east keep at least ¾ mile south of Soa to avoid drying rocks and shallow patches extending south and southwest from it. From the west take great care to keep well south of Sgeir nan Garbhanach, the rock (dries 3·2) south of Rubha nam Faochag.

Approach Crossapol Bay on a course of 015° with Roan Bogha buoy bearing 195° astern and a small but conspicuous sand 'bunker' on the skyline above the grassy dunes bearing 015° (see photo on opposite page). Keep on this line, taking care not to be carried off it by the tide, until well past the awash rock

Loch Breachacha from seaward showing, from left to right, the farm, the new castle, the old castle, and the house with a white gable referred to in the text

Loch Gorton

Loch Gorton is a narrow sandy bay one mile east of Loch Breachacha (see plan) providing an occasional anchorage in offshore winds.

From the south keep the white cottage over a sandy beach and anchor on a line between a cleft in the rock to port and the first low summit to starboard in 3m. Bottom sand.

o port and Eilean Tomulam is 2 cables abeam
o starboard. Then alter course gradually to
ort bringing the white house at Crossapol to
ear 292° and maintain this course to pass
approximately halfway between Sgeir nan
Cuiseag and Sgeir Dubh in the northwest
corner of the bay. Enter the pool and anchor in
3–5m, sand with some weed.

Anchorage

This anchorage provides shelter from west
through north to east but can be subject to swell
in winds from other directions, though the pool
has been reported to be comfortable in breezy
conditions from the SSW. In settled offshore
weather it is perfectly feasible to anchor off the
extensive sandy beach at the head of the bay.

Feall Bay

This bay, lying 3½ miles northeast of Gunna
Sound, provides occasional anchorage on the
west coast of Coll in fine settled weather. It is a
good stopping place if waiting for the tide in
Gunna Sound and provides shelter from east to
SSW. If coming from the north take care not to
confuse it with Hogh Bay which is 1½ miles
further northeast. Feall Bay has a small islet on
its southern edge; Hogh Bay has nothing.

Directions

From the north head in for the break in the sand
dunes that is just right of the centre of the bay
as viewed looking south. The bottom is sand
with rock outcrops about 1m above the sand.
At LW these rocks are at least 3m under water.
If using the approach recommended there is a
large sand 'lane' with no rocks in it leading all
the way in. Anchor in 2–6m on sand 'lane'.

Gunna Sound

The passage between Coll and Tiree is used by
boats on passage to the Outer Hebrides from
south of Mull. There are several dangerous
rocks but the two most hazardous are marked
by light buoys.

Tides

Tidal streams run at up to three knots causing heavy
overfalls at the windward end with an opposing tide.

Northwest-going stream begins +0535 Oban (+0005 Dover)
Southeast-going stream begins –0120 Oban (+0540 Dover)

Directions

From the south and east identify Roan Bogha
south cardinal buoy and pass either south or ¼
mile north of it. Identify Placaid Bogha green
conical buoy and pass south of it.

From southward, an alternative course is to
pass a cable west of Creachasdal Mor heading
360°. Do not alter course northwest until
Placaid Bogha appears about the middle of the
northwest entrance so as to clear Bogha
Hoshmish, a rock drying 2·3 metres two cables
off the northeast point of Tiree.

From the north and west make for the centre

Edward Mason

of the channel to avoid rocks on either hand,
but especially drying rocks up to two cables all
round the north point of Tiree. Identify and
pass south of Placaid Bogha buoy and follow
the reverse of the directions above.

Lights

Roan Bogha light buoy Q(6)+LFl.15s5M
Placaid Bogha light buoy Fl.G.4s

Anchorage

Port Ruadh (previously Clach Chuirr) on the
southwest side of the sound gives some shelter
from south and west. Underwater power cables
marked by a beacon on the southwest side of
the bay runs ENE towards Coll, but there is
space to anchor on either side of them in 3m,
sand. Another cable beacon inshore from the
south side of the bay may mark a disused cable
which crosses the sound from the southeast
point of the bay.

Gunna There is a good occasional anchorage
off the island of Gunna which can be entered
quite easily from the south using chart 2474.
Anchor northwest of the small islet in 5m,
clean sand.

The sand 'bunker' bearing 015° leads clear of awash and drying rocks in the approach to Crossapol Bay

Admiralty Chart
2474, 2171
Admiralty Leisure Folio
5611.26A
Imray Chart
C65
Ordnance Survey
46
Cruising Scotland
p.115

GUNNA SOUND

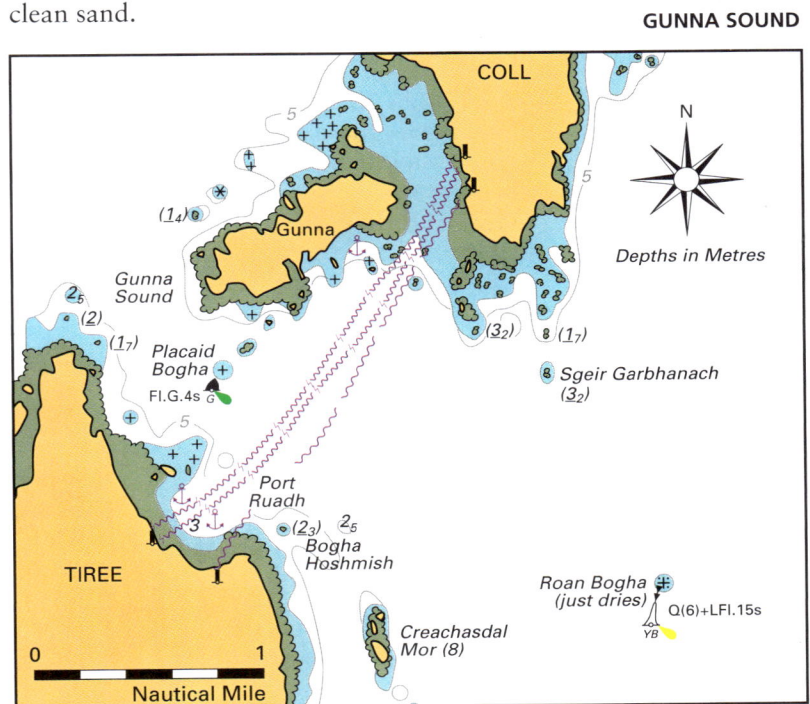

Martin Lawrence

Gott Bay, Tiree

Admiralty Chart
2474, 1778
Admiralty Leisure Folio
5611.26A
Imray Chart
C65
Ordnance Survey
46
Cruising Scotland
p.115

Tiree

If the anchorages on Coll are all best enjoyed in settled weather, those on Tiree require even more favourable conditions if they are to be visited in safety and comfort.

Gott Bay

A broad sandy bay towards the northeast end of the southeast side of Tiree exposed over a wide area and only suitable for anchoring overnight in settled westerly or calm weather. It is initially identified by the latticed communications tower ¼ mile south of Scarinish. Submerged and drying rocks lie ¼ mile southwest of Soa at the northeast side of the entrance.

10 visitors moorings have been laid in two trots northwest of the pier. The cost is £12 per night, payable at MacLennan Motors office on the pier head. Alternatively, anchor clear of the pier and moorings in 3-4m, sand. A stone slip on the west side of the pier is convenient for landing from a dinghy.

Tides

The constant is +0007 Oban (−0523 Dover)

Height in metres

MHWS	MHWN	MTL	MLWN	MLWS
4·1	3·0	2·3	1·7	0·6

Lights

Scarinish LtHo Fl.3s11m16M
Gott Bay pier Ldg Lts 286·5°F.R

Services and supplies

Diesel, petrol, Calor Gas; garage near pier, Maclennan Motors ☎01879 220555. No water at pier. Restaurant at Sandaig, The Glassary ☎01879 220 684. Ferry connection to Oban. Airport for flights to Glasgow.

Scarinish

This is the main village on Tiree but the creek and its drying harbour can only occasionally be used by yachts if there is no sea coming in. Towards HW or at neaps there might be a temporary berth at the old pier, or anchoring in the middle of the creek may be possible but avoid obstructing access to the drying harbour.

Cul Bo, nearly a cable SSE of the east point of the entrance, dries 1·8 metres. The east end of a white house with a red roof at the head of the creek bearing 330°, over the west end of the jetty at the harbour, leads clear WSW of this rock.

Supplies

Shops, Post Office, phone box, hotel.

Milton Harbour

Lights F.G (front) and Oc.G.5s (rear) on a bearing 349° lead west of detached drying rocks to a quay at the east side of a rocky creek east of Soa in Gott Bay. This tiny harbour, which is shown on chart 2474, is quite insufficient even for the fishermen who use it, and should not be approached by a yacht except in an emergency.

Hynish

On the northeast side of the south point of Tiree, east of Ben Hynish, is a masonry pier and dock built by Alan Stevenson in 1825 as a shore station for Skerryvore lighthouse, and the buildings are now used as a lighthouse museum.

Hynish is occasionally visited by yachts on rare occasions in very settled weather; some shelter from southward is given by the point Am Barradhu and drying rocks lie up to ¼ mile south of this point.

The pier dries alongside and the dock fills with sand, but a reservoir built to retain water to flush out the sand awaits restoration.

The drying harbour at Hynish

Martin Lawrence

Martin Lawrence

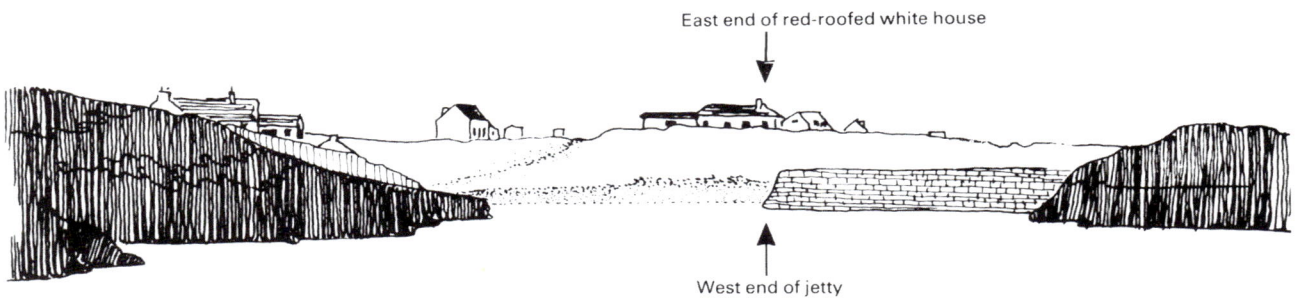

East end of red-roofed white house

West end of jetty

Skerryvore lighthouse

Standing on a group of drying rocks ten miles SSW of Tiree, Skerryvore lighthouse is only likely to be of interest to yachts on a direct passage from Islay to the Outer Hebrides.

Drying rocks lie three miles southwest and one mile northeast of the lighthouse, and the bottom between the lighthouse and Tiree is very uneven with rocks both submerged and awash.

Strong tides run round Skerryvore with overfalls, and yachts should pass at least five miles southwest of the lighthouse in a depth of not less than 15 metres.

Scarinish, Tiree, and the leading line for entry into the harbour

Peter Mackay

Skerryvore from a Northern Lighthouse Board helicopter

11. Ross of Mull

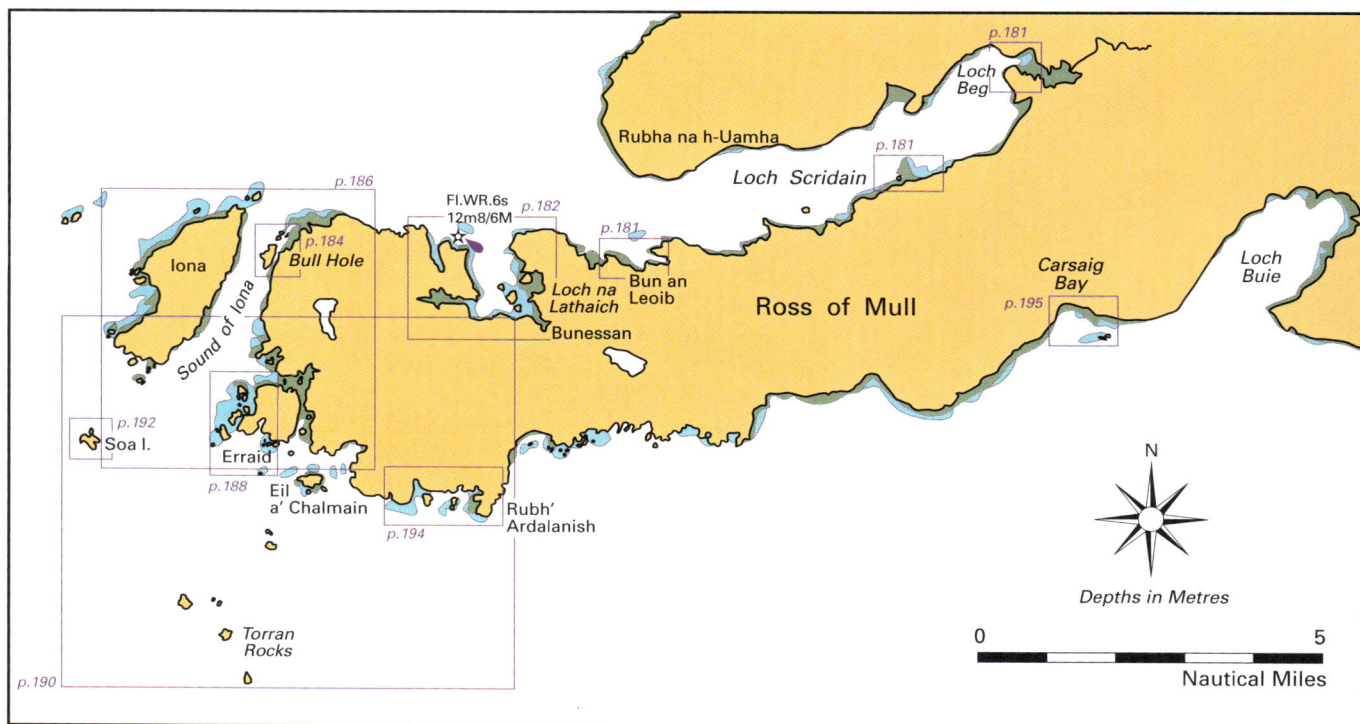

ROSS OF MULL

Extending over fifteen miles westward from the head of Loch Scridain to the north and Loch Buie to the south, the Ross of Mull, with the island of Iona at its western extremity, has some of the best anchorages to be found on a circumnavigation of Mull.

This chapter will describe, firstly, Loch Scridain and the north coast of the Ross, which gives some welcome shelter from the prevailing wind for yachts cruising the otherwise exposed

'Antares' anchored in Tinker's Hole whilst surveying this popular anchorage on the Ross of Mull in 2009

Edward Mason

west coast of Mull. The Sound of Iona and several excellent anchorages to be found near there will follow and finally the passage eastward along the south coast of the Ross to Loch Buie, where the area that was described in Ch. 6, *Firth of Lorn* is re-joined.

Loch Scridain

Loch Scridain, running five miles ENE on the north side of the Ross of Mull, has no really good anchorages. The north side is fairly clean but on the south side several groups of drying rocks extend half a mile from the shore; of these the most significant are described below.

Dangers

Bogha Mor, three cables off the entrance to a bay on the south side of the entrance to the loch, dries 0·6 metre, with a submerged rock two cables ENE of it. The Eileanan na Liathanaich fully open of Ardtun, the nearest point to the west, bearing 270°, leads close north of Bogha Mor.

An Carraigean Three miles further east, three cables offshore, ¾ mile ENE of the promontory Ard Fada, dries 0·6 metre.

Bogh' an Rubha ¾ mile ENE of An Carraigean, two cables offshore, dries 2·1 metres. Ardchrishnish House open of Ard Fada bearing 249°, leads close north of both An Carraigean and Bogh' an Rubha.

Sgeir Alltachd, a reef drying three metres, extends four cables from the shore, with other drying rocks east of it, four miles from the entrance, opposite Kilfinichen Bay. It is now marked at its extremity by a N cardinal buoy and an E cardinal buoy lies 7 cables east of it.

Anchorages

As the head of the loch is approached, the steepness of the surrounding cliffs and mountains (the anchorage in Loch Beg is the closest that a yacht may get to the summit of Ben More) makes the loch prone to fierce squalls, making holding in the anchorages difficult in bad weather.

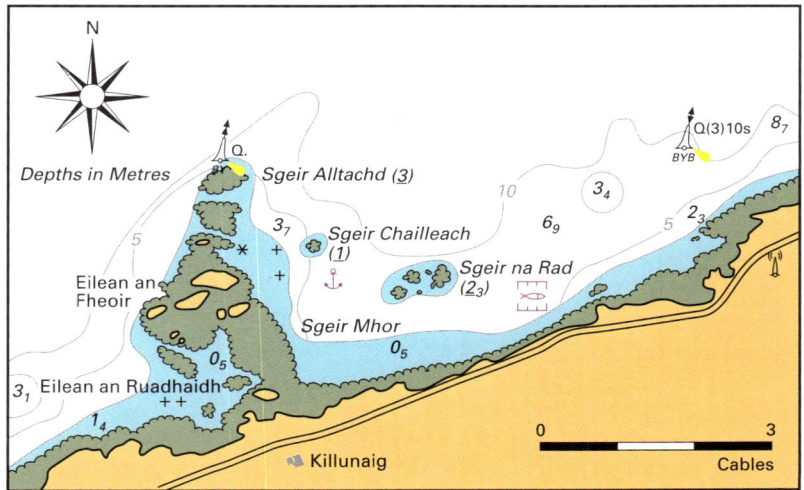

BUN AN LEOIB

Bun an Leoib, on the south side of the entrance to Loch Scridain, provides shelter from the west behind the above-water rocks Sgeir Leathen and Sgeir Mor, but little shelter from northwest and north.

Pass to one cable north of Sgeir Mor to pass inside Bogha Mor, and anchor either on the south side of the bay or NNE of a tidal islet ¾ cable off the southwest side of the bay.

A drying reef extends a cable east of the islet, with other drying rocks between the reef and the south shore.

Eilean an Fheoir, five miles from the mouth of Loch Scridain, provides some shelter on its east side. The outermost rock, Sgeir Alltachd, (dries 3m) is marked by a N cardinal buoy; it is nearly two cables northwest of Eilean an Fheoir which stands on the reef.

Sgeir Chailleach, more than a cable ENE of Eilean an Fheoir, dries one metre.

EILEAN AN FHEOIR

Kilfinichen Bay, on the north side of the loch is a good anchorage in offshore winds. Keep a cable off the west point of the entrance to the bay to avoid Sgeir Mhor, which dries 2·1 metres. Anchor on either side of the loch in 8m.

Loch Beg, at the north side of the head of the loch, has impresssive surroundings but little shelter from wind. Most of the loch dries out or is soft mud but better holding can be found in the narrows and as far in as the anchor symbol is shown. It is subject to any sea running up Loch Scridain and violent squalls in easterly winds. Hotel at Pennyghael, 1½M.

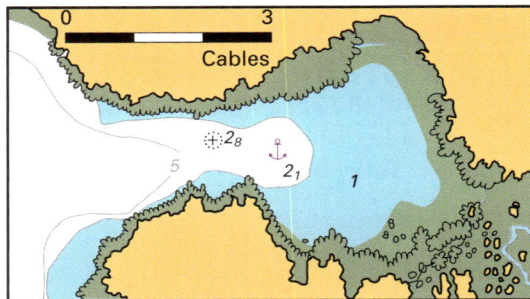

LOCH BEG

Admiralty Chart
2169, 2771
Admiralty Leisure Folio
5611.8, 10
Imray Chart
C65
Ordnance Survey
48
Cruising Scotland
pp.108–110

Looking northeast up Loch Scridain, Ben More on the left

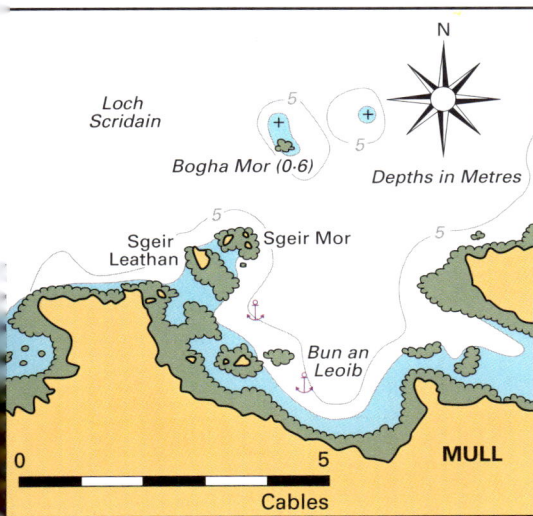

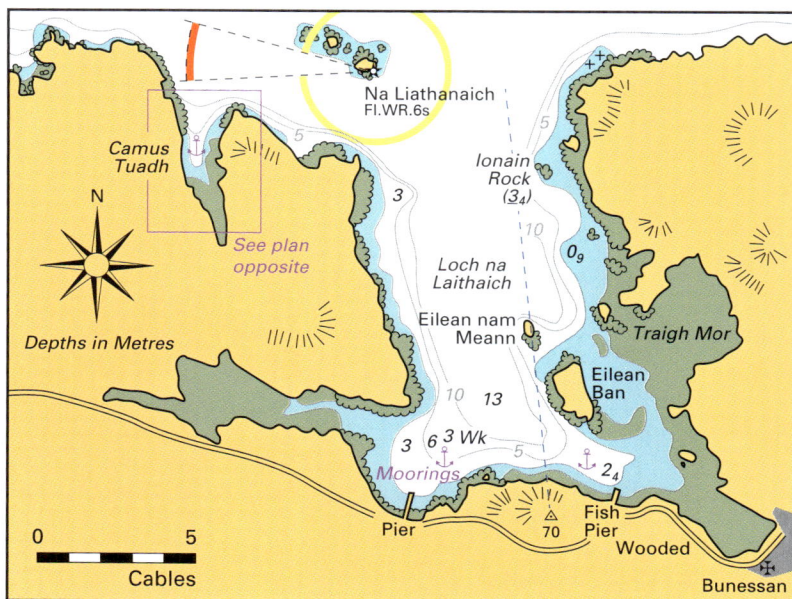

LOCH NA LAITHAICH

Admiralty Chart
2617, 2771
Admiralty Leisure Folio
5611.8, 10
Imray Chart
C65
Ordnance Survey
48
Cruising Scotland
pp. 109–111

*Bunessan, Loch na
Laithaich, from the
northeast*

Loch na Laithaich (Bunessan)

This well-sheltered loch lies on the north of the Ross of Mull, 3 miles east of Iona Sound. It is about 1½ miles long with a straightforward entrance marked by the only light beacon on the entire coast, apart from that on Cairn na Burgh More, north of the Treshnish Isles.

Tides
Constant –0015 Oban (–0545 Dover).

Height in metres

MHWS	MHWN	MTL	MLWN	MLWS
4·3	3·0	2·4	1·8	0·6

Dangers and marks

Eileanan na Liathanaich is a group of islands and rocks off the west side of the entrance to the loch. The largest and most easterly island has a light beacon on its south side. Rocks above water and drying extend a cable WNW of the western island, and a detached drying rock lies ½ cable northeast of the eastern island.

Ionain Rock, drying 3·4 metres, extends 1½ cables from the east side of the loch. Towards the southeast corner of the loch are two islets, Eilean nam Meann and Eilean Ban, which is the larger and further southeast. Eilean nam Meann in line with a prominent hill on the south side of the loch, Cnoc an t-Suidhe 173°, leads west of Ionain Rock.

Approach either side of Eileanan na Liathanaich, but look out for lobster pot floats around the islands. When inside the loch keep towards the west side which is clean.

Anchorages

Southwest corner in three to four metres, mud, clear of the moorings and fish cages. This part of the loch is now well used for mooring and anchoring. Use a tripping line.

Southeast corner south of Eilean Ban. Anchor clear of the approach to the pier and no further east than a line between the pier and the east side of Eilean Ban as it is shoal and drying beyond this. The bottom is mud with some weed. Show an anchor light at night.

Services and supplies

Post Office, shops and hotel at Bunessan in the southeast corner of the loch. Water at pier. Diesel at filling station 2½ miles along road to Fionnphort. Bus service to Oban and Iona ferries.

Martin Lawrence

Anchorages between Loch na Laithaich and Sound of Iona

The coast between Loch na Laithaich and the Sound of Iona presents an apparently unbroken line of rock with no obvious anchorages, apart from Camus Tuath. However, there are two further possibilities offering varying degrees of shelter; these have recently been surveyed by *Antares Charts* and the results are reproduced here.

All of these anchorages give more shelter from the prevailing southwesterly winds and tidal streams than most of the anchorages in the sound of Iona but only Camus Tuath could be described as being more than a temporary anchorage.

Camus Tuath, lying approximately ¾ mile west of Loch na Lathaich, is a narrow bay that dries at its head. If approaching from the north leave Eilean na Liathanaich well to port to avoid drying rocks extending west of it. Keep to the west side of the bay and anchor in the centre, once past the drying rock on the east side, in 4-5m sand and shell. It is an occasional anchorage, exposed from northwest to northeast, but otherwise it provides good protection from the south with good holding.

The disused granite quarry at the head of the bay on the east side supplied, by way of the ruined stone pier, the stone for the building of the Skerryvore and Ardnmurchan lighthouses.

Traigh na Margaidh is not named as such on the chart (only on the OS map) but it lies immediately west of Rubh' Eilean an t-Santachaidh and ½ mile west of Camus Tuath and can be recognised by the white sand beaches.

Enter keeping towards the east side of the bay and anchor off the sandy beach in the southeast corner. A temporary anchorage and fully exposed to the north, but delightful in settled weather when the two beaches can be enjoyed, especially at low water. The anchorage can be subject to swell.

Bagh Inbhir h-Aibhne, again named only on the OS map, lies about ½ mile east of the entrance to the Sound of Iona. The entrance is between rocky islets off Rubha nan Cearc and a drying reef extending a cable north from the western point of the bay. The end of this reef is surmounted by a small islet which never covers.

Enter midway between the above islets and anchor towards the western side of the bay as far in as depth and swinging room allow. Below half tide the shelter improves but the anchorage is only temporary at best and should not be used in winds from anywhere between west through north to northeast.

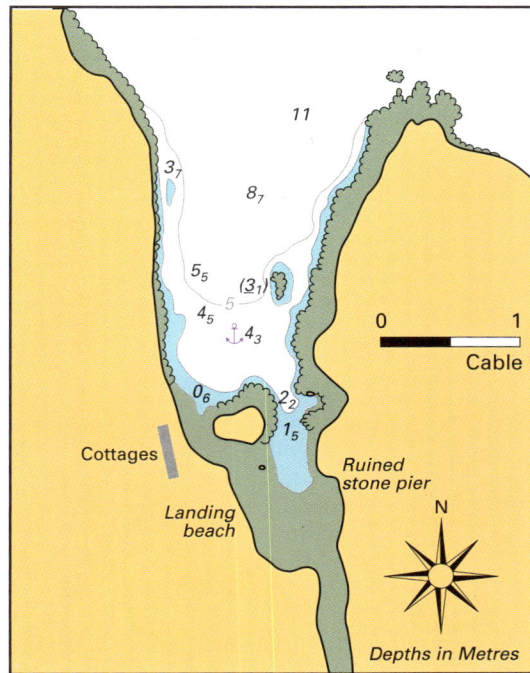

CAMUS TUATH

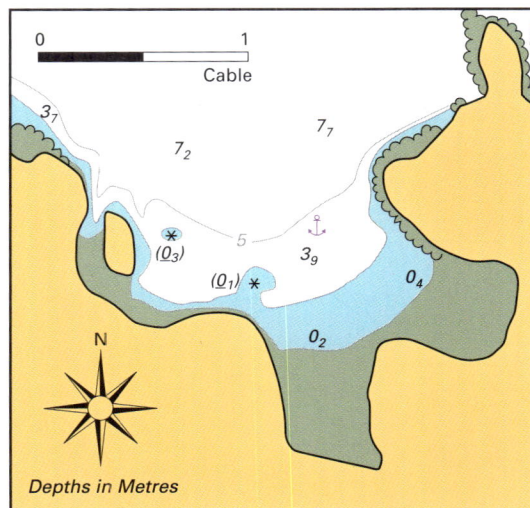

TRAIGH NA MARGAIDH

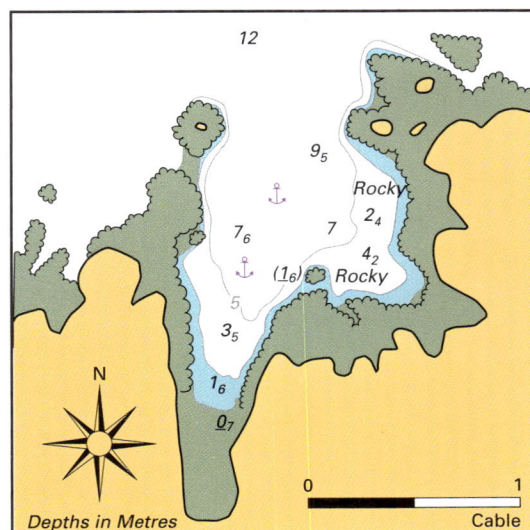

BAGH INBHIR H-AIBHNE

Bull Hole

This is a sheltered anchorage between Eilean nam Ban and Mull, near the north end of the Sound of Iona (see p.187), but it can be subject to tidal swell. Much of the basin at the north end is only deep enough for shoal-draught yachts except at neaps, and there are many moorings.

Directions

The anchorage must be entered from the south. Coming from the north end of Iona Sound note that Breug may cover at HWS and also note the drying rocks extending north and south from Eilean Liath and off the southwest point of Eilean nam Ban. However, this point should not be given too wide a berth as there is shoal water ¾ cable southwest of it (see p.187).

Within the inlet keep closer to the Mull shore leaving the Little Bull (dries 0·5m), marked by a perch, to port, then keep mid channel to avoid the Limpet rock (dries 0·5m) off the Mull shore.

Anchorage

Most of the area north of The Bull, with water deep enough for anchoring, is occupied by moorings. If anchoring further south avoid fouling the water pipe, and leave a fairway for the ferry which berths at the quay on Eilean Nam Ban, north of The Bull. The bottom is sand but it is virtually impossible to avoid being tide rode.

There is fair weather anchorage between Eilean nam Ban and Eilean Liath in 4m which may be suitable in some winds.

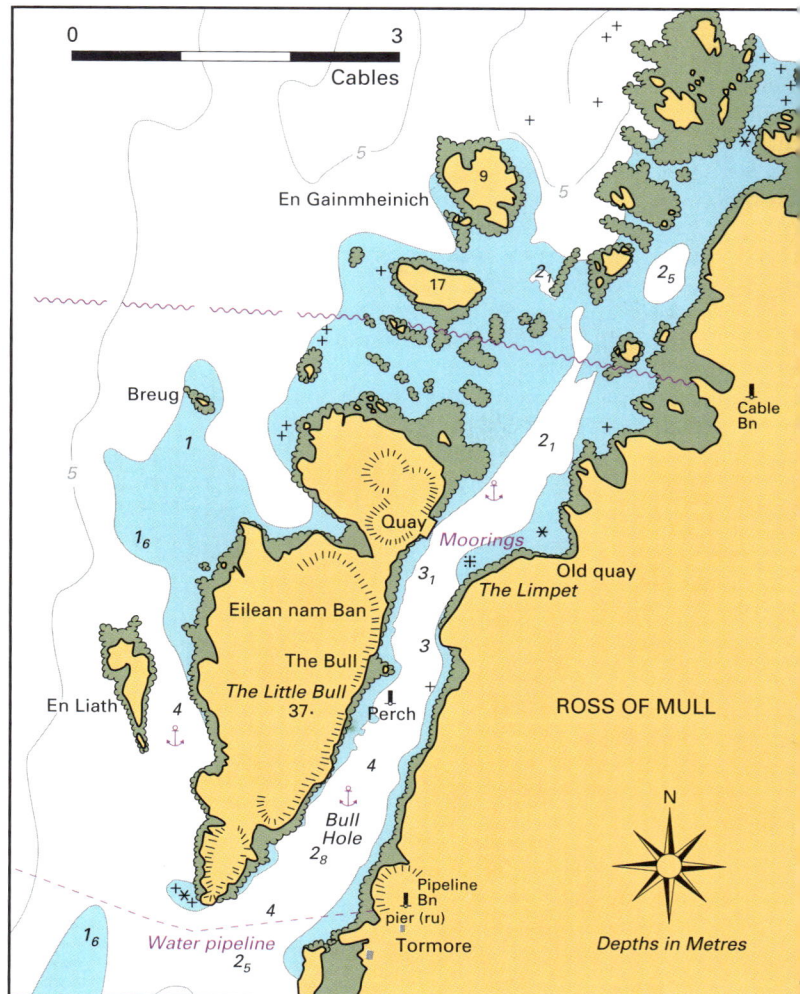

BULL HOLE, SOUND OF IONA

The anchorage off the ruined pier at the south entrance to Bull Hole

Anchorage off the village at Iona. Martyrs' Bay on the left and the ferry slip to the right (p.187)

At anchor off Iona. Space should be allowed for the ferry and care must be taken to anchor clear of the electricity cables (p.187)

N

Depths in Metres

Eilean Annraidh

0_1

5   5

Port na Fraing

Bagh Inbhir h-Aibhne
p.183

Dun I
·99

Boat shed

Eilean nam Ban

Bull Hole

p.184

Cathedral ⴲ

IONA

1_6 1_3

1_6

1_9

0_1

Slip

Martyrs' Bay

Fionnphort

Pier

ROSS OF MULL

4   Q(6)+
LFl.15s
YB

G 1   Bo na Sliganach Fl(2)G.6s

Sound of
Iona

Fl.G.5s G 2_9
Bogha
Choilta

p.188

4_1

Eilean na-h-Aon
Chaorach
(12)

(3_9)

324°

Cathedral tower 012°

Erraid

1_9

3_5

2_5

Tinker's
Hole

David Balfour's
Bay

En nam Muc

2_5

2_5

0   1
Miles

Dubh
Sgeir

4_7

Rankin's
Rock

Bogha hun
a Chuhoil (1_3)

Q(6)+
LFl.15s
YB

Sgeir na
Caillich

3_8

Eilean a
Chalmain

SOUND OF IONA

Sound of Iona

The Sound of Iona is about four miles long, and is straightforward for yachts drawing 2m or less. The Mull shore is very foul throughout but the rocks on the Iona side are well inshore. The tide runs strongly through the sound and in some conditions sets up a nasty sea.

The approach from the north poses few problems but from the south care is needed to avoid the Torran Rocks and then make the passage through the islets and rocks to the southwest of Erraid. This is described on p.190.

Tides

At Iona the constant is –0005 Oban (–0535 Dover).

Height in metres

MHWS	MHWN	MTL	MLWN	MLWS
4·0	3·0	2·2	1·5	0·5

Tidal streams in the sound run at up to 2½ knots. There is some uncertainty about the times at which the tides turn, but the following is a guide:
North-going stream begins +0515 Oban (–0015 Dover);
South-going stream begins –0015 Oban (–0545 Dover).

Dangers and marks

The most conspicuous reference marks are the cathedral on Iona north of the village, and the hill Dun I, 99 metres, ½ mile NNW of the cathedral. In the south part of the sound many rocks lie up to three cables off the Mull shore, and two cables off Iona.

A green conical buoy near the east shore marks a 2·9m rock, Bogha Choilta, and lies two cables west of the nearest drying rocks.

The principal hazard is the shoal bank which stretches across the middle of the sound from Iona village to Eilean nam Ban, ½ mile north of Fionnphort, on which the depth is only 0·1 metre in places.

South of the bank are a south cardinal buoy, and a green conical buoy on the west side of a submerged rock, Bo na Sliginach, ¼ mile off the Mull shore. North of the bank, rocks dry up to a cable off either shore.

Breug, an isolated rock 1½ cables west of the north end of Eilean nam Ban, covers at HW.

Directions

Approaching from the north, the cathedral tower is a prominent landmark. Enter the sound mid-channel and then, depending on draught and the state of the tide there is a choice of courses.

Yachts over 2-metres draught, if it is near LW springs, should pass no more than ½ cable southwest of the south end of Eilean nam Ban, then parallel to the west shore of Mull for half a mile keeping Bull Hole just open astern, before altering course to pass between the green conical buoy and the south cardinal. The shallowest part of the bank lies close west of this course. *Antares Charts* surveyed this route in 2017 and found a least depth of 2·9m though they warn that depths are liable to change over time.

Yachts of moderate draught, and deep-draught yachts within four hours of HW springs, can pass about a cable off the Iona shore between a point abreast of the cathedral and the south end of the village. A short steep sea is raised here when the tide turns against the wind. Towards the south end of the sound keep west of a line joining the two green conical buoys.

From the south pass west of Bogha Choilta green conical buoy. At a point about ¼ mile south of the south cardinal buoy the course to take past the mid-sound bank will depend on draught and the state of the tide; if over 2-metres draught and near LW springs turn to pass between the south cardinal buoy and Bo an Sliginach green conical buoy; then head obliquely towards the Mull shore to keep Bull Hole just open, until Eilean Annraidh at the north end of Iona is touching Eilean Liath, west of Eilean nam Ban. Then pass no more than ½ cable southwest of Eilean nam Ban and continue towards the middle of the sound.

Otherwise pass west of the south cardinal buoy and follow a course a cable off Iona until past the cathedral.

Anchorages

There are no sheltered anchorages on Iona and yachts intending to stay overnight usually anchor in Tinker's Hole (p.189) or Bull Hole (p.184). Temporary anchorage when visiting Iona can be found as follows:

Martyrs' Bay (photos p.185) south of the ferry slip provides temporary anchorage in 3m sand outside the local boat moorings and avoiding the cables. The anchor should be buoyed. Ensure that the anchor is well set as the tide is strong and there is considerable risk in leaving a yacht unattended especially if change in tidal stream takes place.

Port na Fraing lying north of the Cathedral may be preferable to Martyrs' Bay as the anchorage is clear of moorings and there is less tidal current. However, care must be taken to anchor clear north of the power cable and well offshore, ½ cable, to obtain suitable depth. Good holding reported when care is taken to avoid weed patches.

Fionnphort Temporary anchorage WNW of the ferry slip on the Mull shore, avoiding both the cables and the approach to the slip.

Erraid Pier There is a good occasional anchorage in the bay north of Erraid. Approach from the northwest, noting the drying reef extending almost a cable from the south shore, and anchor in 2-3m, sand, about a cable northwest of the pier.

Services and supplies

Shops and phone box at both Iona and Fionnphort. Hotels and Post Office on Iona. Water tap on the end wall of public toilet at the jetty on Iona. Other supplies at Bunessan.

Admiralty Chart
2617
Admiralty Leisure Folio
5611.10
Imray Chart
C65
Ordnance Survey
48
Cruising Scotland
pp.108–110

0 _____ 5
Cables

Sound of Erraid

Bogha ant'
Searraich
(3̲5̲)

Sound
of Iona

Eilean
Ghomain

Pier

1

● Old observatory

4₇

(0₂)

0₃

Cnoc Mor
73

4₂

0₇

1₈

0₄

1₆

(0₂)

4₆

12

2₁

ERRAID

(2₉)

2₅

5₃

2₅

(4₂)

(Seldom covers)

1₃

Eilean
Dubh
·34

3₆

Tinker's
Hole

7₃

Steamer
Passage

7₂

·54

5

Traigh Gheal or
David Balfour's Bay

Eilean
nam Muc
·40

(2₃)

2₄

5

5

(3₉)

N

Dubh Sgeir

Rankin's
Rocks

(1)

(2)

Depths in Metres

(0₈)

Neil McCubbin

Tinker's Hole

This small anchorage, sheltered but occasionally subject to swell, is one of the most popular on the west coast and can become quite crowded at times. Tinker's Hole lies between Eilean Dubh and the west side of Erraid at the south end of the Sound of Iona. In places it is less than ½ cable wide and on the east side the shore consists of sheer walls of pink granite.

Tides

At Iona the constant is –0005 Oban (–0535 Dover).

Height in metres

MHWS	MHWN	MTL	MLWN	MLWS
4·0	3·0	2·2	1·5	0·5

In Tinker's Hole:

North-going stream begins about +0445 Oban (–0045 Dover).
South-going stream begins about –0130 Oban (+0530 Dover).

Directions

From the south and east, approach the anchorage leaving Rankin's Rocks to starboard. The sketch plan shows all dangers but note especially the rock (dries 2·3m) south of En Dubh. The shores on either hand at the entrance can be approached closely and any dangers clearly seen on the white sandy bottom.

From the Sound of Iona the usual route is through the Steamer Passage between Eilean nam Muc and Eilean Dubh, a narrow channel used by the Iona cruise steamer and fishing boats. There is no clear leading line for this and careful consideration of chart 2617 is required along with the above plan. Approaching from the Sound of Iona stand off until Eilean nam Muc is identified and a clear passage to the east of it, through to Rankin's Rocks, can be seen before entering it. Avoid this channel if a heavy swell is running.

It is possible to approach Tinker's Hole from the north, preferably with local knowledge and above half-tide, though a recent survey by *Antares Charts* has identified at least one channel that can be used at any state of the tide. However, no visual pilotage directions are available for this other than those that can be deduced from the adjacent plan, which is based on their survey. Experienced rock-dodgers may, in fine weather, on a rising tide and with a lookout on the bow, care to explore this route. Those equipped with *Antares* charts on their plotter will have no problem.

Anchorage

Anchor in the pool between Eilean Dubh and Erraid, wherever convenient. At times the tidal stream runs strongly here and the east side of the pool is more out of the tide. Mooring rings at the head of the bight on the Erraid side are available to restrict swinging.

Note a submerged reef extending 20 metres south from the northwest point of this bight, which point defines the edge of the tidal stream. Lobster keep-boxes are sometimes moored in the fairway.

The anchorage is often crowded at the height of the season and, in suitable weather, additional space can be found north of the main anchorage.

The anchorage in Tinker's Hole, looking north

Admiralty Chart
2617
Admiralty Leisure Folio
5611.10
Imray Chart
C65
Ordnance Survey
48
Cruising Scotland
p.108

Iona

Sound of Iona

G
Fl.G.5s

Rubha na Aird

Ross of Mull

Erraid

Bagh a Ghnoic
Maoileanaich

Eilean
nam Muc

Dubh Sgeir

Soa Island
p.192

Bogha hun
a Chuhoil
Q(6)LFl.15s
YB

p.188

Sgeir na
Caillich

Port nan Ron

Beinn a
Chaol-achaidh
·102

p.194

Eilean a'
Chalmain

Bogha nan
Ramfhear
(1₄) BY Q

Rubh'
Ardalanish

(3₆)
Dearg Sgeir

Ruadh Sgeir
Bn
(ruin)

Na Torrain

Torr an t-Saothaid

Torran Rocks

Torran Sgoilte

N

Depths in Metres

0   3
Nautical Miles

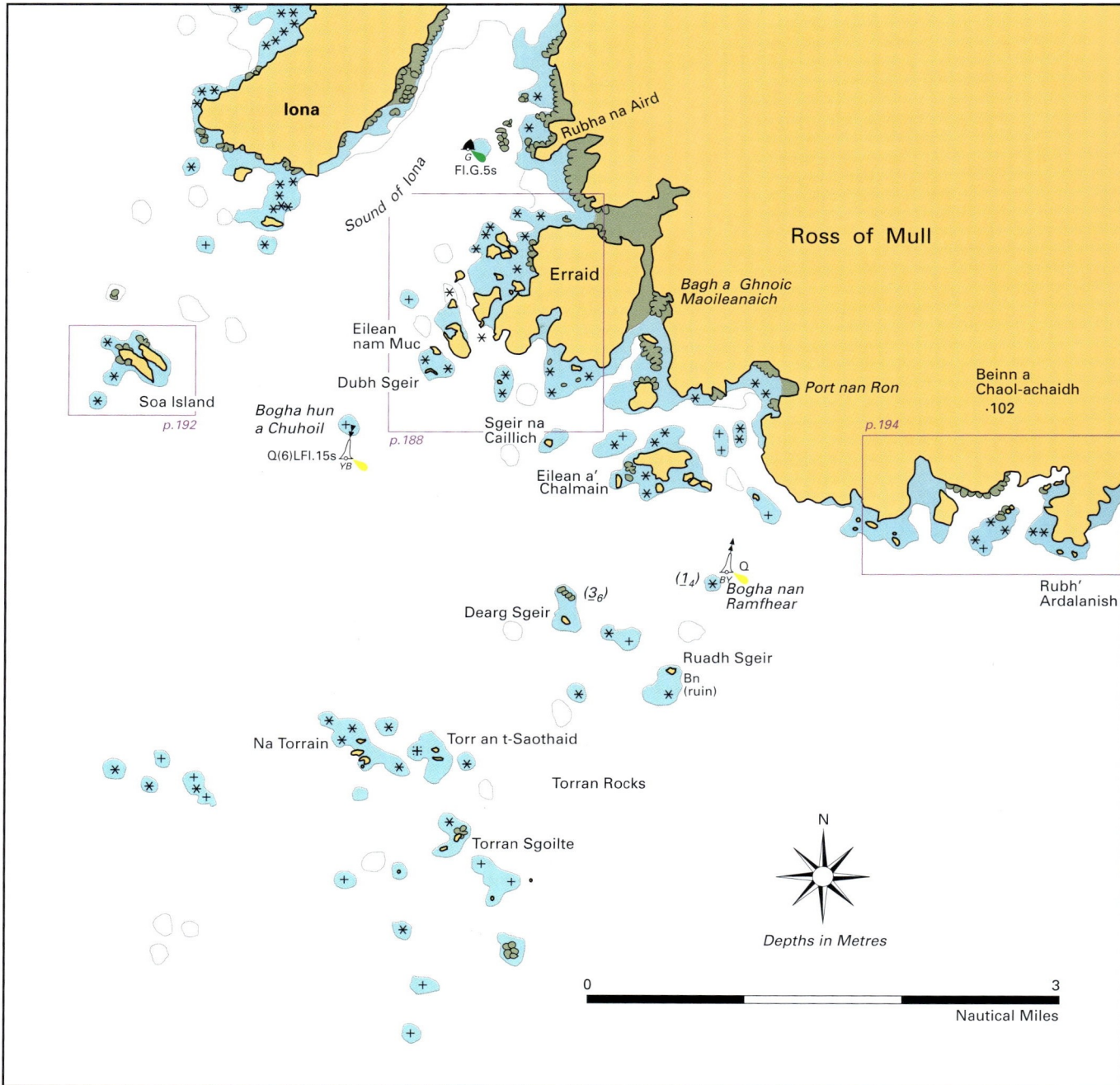

Sound of Iona to Ardalanish

Navigation along this section of coastline is complicated by the Torran Rocks, which cover an area of four miles by four miles and lie southwest of the Ross of Mull. Further complications arise because of the rash of island, skerries and sunken rocks that lie close to the southwest extremity of the Ross of Mull.

However, there is a clear inshore passage between the latter and the Torran Rocks that recently has been greatly simplified by the establishment of two buoys by the NLB. Even so, in poor visibility care has to be taken that plotted courses are maintained as in places there is little room for error because of hazards on either hand.

Tides

At Iona the constant is –0005 Oban (–0535 Dover).

Height in metres

MHWS	MHWN	MTL	MLWN	MLWS
4·0	3·0	2·2	1·5	0·5

East of the Torran Rocks the streams do not exceed 1kn Sp.
Northwest-going stream begins +0415 Oban (–0115 Dover).
Southeast-going stream begins –0210 Oban (–0350 Dover).

Dangers and marks

Eilean a' Chalmain three miles west of Ardalanish, has a drying rock nearly a cable southwest of its south point. The unnamed islet two cables southwest of Eilean a' Chalmain is a useful reference point.

Sgeir na Caillich is an islet six cables west of Eilean a' Chalmain.

Martin Lawrence

Na Torrain is a group of three above-water rocks in the middle of the Torran Rocks and provide the key to pilotage within the area. From the south these are 23, 15 and 19 metres high, and Torr an t-Saothaid, ½ mile east of Na Torrain, is about 18 metres high. These are sometimes mistaken at a distance from the east for Soa Island, several miles further north west.

Ruadh Sgeir, the most easterly of the Torran Rocks, on which there is the stump of a stone beacon, must be clearly identified in approaching from the east.

Bogha na Ramfhear, which dries 1·4 metres, lies seven cables NNE of Ruadh Sgeir and can be frequently seen breaking. It is marked by a N cardinal buoy.

Dubh Sgeir, two cables southwest of Eilean nam Muc, is the most southwesterly islet off Erraid.

Bogha hun a Chuhoil (LD 1·6) lies 6½ cables southwest of Dubh Sgeir and is marked by a S cardinal buoy lying a cable due south of it.

Soa Island, 34 metres, stands 1½ miles SSW of Iona.

Dubh Artach lighthouse, 10 miles SW of the Torran Rocks, has a broad red band round it.

Directions

The passage eastward is generally easier than westward, as the various marks are more easily identified before the dangers become critical.

Eastbound passage From a position about 3 cables west of the G buoy marking Bogha Choilta at the south end of the Sound of Iona steer about 195° for the S cardinal buoy marking Bogha hun a Chuhoil. When the north end of Eilean nam Muc bears due east alter to port and aim for a point 2 cables south of Dubh Sgeir. From here steer a course of 118° to leave

Sgeir na Caillich and the small islet southwest of Eilean a' Chalmain about a cable to port.

Pass about a cable north of the N cardinal buoy marking Bogha na Ramfhear and then adopt a course for either the Firth of Lorn or Colonsay.

Alternatively, some distance will be saved if the Steamer Passage is used (p.189). Note the warnings concerning its identification and the drying 2·3m rock in the middle. On emerging from the passage give Rankin's Rocks a good berth to port, as a drying rock lies almost a cable south of them, and join the course described above.

Westbound passage Coming from the east identify Rubh' Ardalanish and pass about 3 cables off it and then take the inshore passage keeping approximately ½ mile off the Mull shore and passing north of Bogha nam Ramfhear and its N cardinal buoy, and leaving Eilean a Chalmain, Sgeir na Caillich and Rankin Rocks to starboard

If coming from east of Colonsay and the south steer 330° for Beinn a' Chaol-achaidh, the highest hill of the west part of the Ross of Mull, before picking up the inshore passage.

When approaching the west end of the inshore route note the position of Bogha hun a Chuhoil and its buoy and aim for a point 2 cables south of Dubh Sgeir. Here, alter on to a course of 324° towards the Sound of Iona and continue until the tower of the cathedral on Iona bears 012°. This will avoid the shoal patch of 1·9m northwest of Eilean na Muc. For directions within the Sound of Iona see p.187.

As with the eastbound passage, some distance will be saved if the Steamer Passage is used, see above and p.189.

Erraid and Tinker's Hole from the south; Rankine's Rocks on the lower right and Eilean nam Muc on the extreme left with the Steamer Passage to the right of it. Note that the 2·3m rock in the passage is showing

Martin Lawrence

Bagh a' Ghnoic Mhaoileanaich from the south

The anchorage on Soa. The drying rock to the northwest of Dubh Sgeir can be seen breaking, as can Greave, much further off

Occasional anchorages

Traigh Gheal on the south side of Erraid, known as David Balfour's Bay after the hero of *Kidnapped*, is a delightful daytime anchorage, but a trap if the wind strengthens from between south and southwest (see plan p.188 and photo p.13). The approach is straightforward.

Bagh a' Ghnoic Mhaoileanaich, between Erraid and Mull, provides an occasional anchorage in settled weather, with the use of chart 2617.

Port nan Ron has also been used occasionally in settled weather but the bay has many rocks at its head. Use chart 2617, or the *Antares* chart, and approach with great care.

Soa

Soa Island lies 1½ miles southwest of Iona and, in fair weather, temporary anchorage in 3–6m with very restricted swinging room is possible as far in as the inlet will allow. The bottom is sandy patches with heavy weed, larger sandy patches may be found further in. Use chart 2617 and approach from the northeast. Hold close to the northwest point of Dubh Sgeir (see sketch plan below) as a rock drying 0·2m lies only ½ cable off it. Greave rock (dries 2·6m) will usually show and there are sunken and drying rocks extending almost ½ mile to the southwest of Soa. Watch for tidal drift when approaching and leaving.

Martin Lawrence

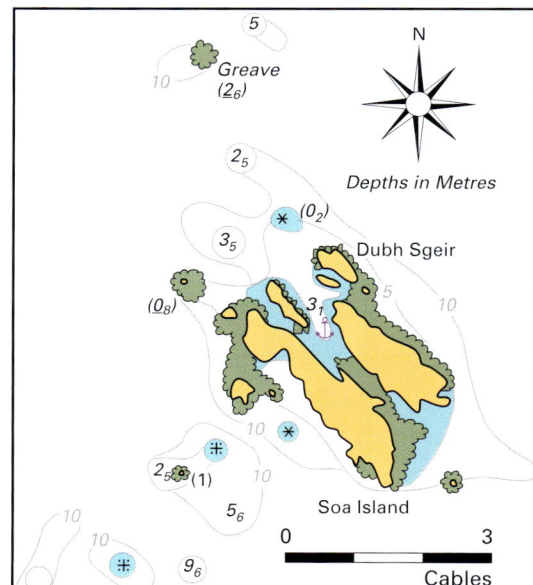

SOA ISLAND

The anchorage at Ardalanish looking southwest (p.194)

Traigh Gheal anchorage, Ardalanish, looking northwest (p.194)

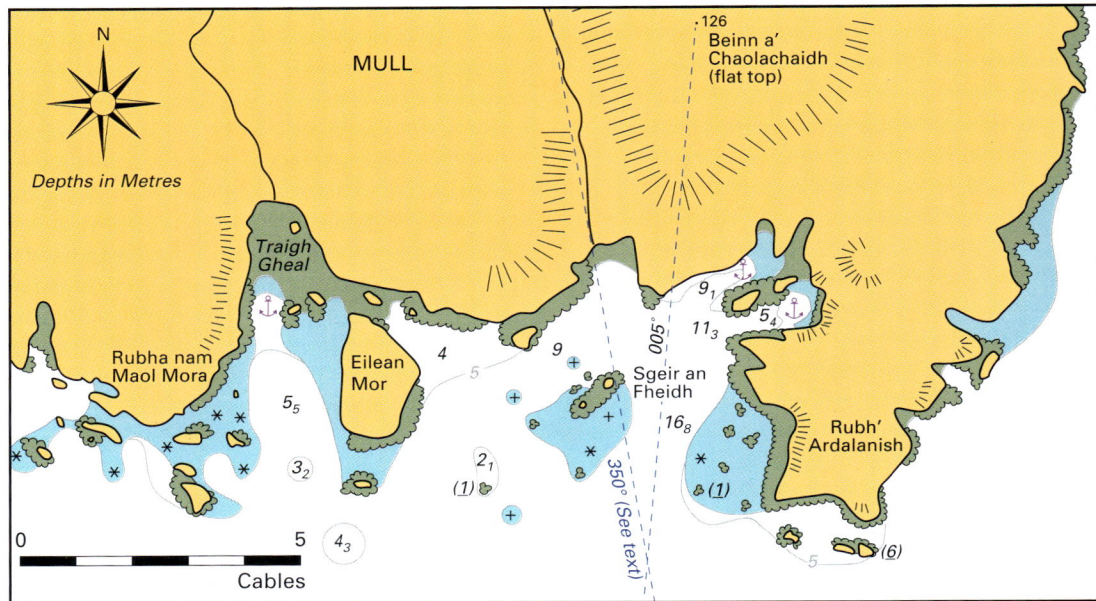

ARDALANISH

Admiralty Chart
2617, 2169, 2386
Admiralty Leisure Folio
5611.8
Imray Chart
C65, 2800.1
Ordnance Survey
48
Cruising Scotland
p.108

Ardalanish

Heading westwards to Iona the first and only anchorage on the south coast of Mull, apart from Carsaig Bay (opposite), is the attractive inlet on the west side of Rubh' Ardalanish, the most southerly point of the Ross of Mull. (photo p.193) The entrance cannot be seen from offshore but Rubh' Ardalanish is prominent.

Directions

Do not cross the 20-metre contour until Sgeir an Fheidh has been identified, which at most states of the tide appears to be two separate rocks, the largest of which is pudding-shaped. Approach with the northeast rock in line with a deep valley 350°, and then pass midway between the rock and the west side of Rubh' Ardalanish on a course of 005°.

Anchorage

Anchor anywhere in the inlet in sand with some weed, but note that it shoals to the north. Swinging room is limited. The northerly inlet can also be used but it has less depth and swinging room. Both these anchorages should be avoided in unsettled conditions.

Traigh Gheal, not to be confused with Traigh Gheal on Erraid, (see p.192) lies on the west side of Ardalanish Bay and is an attractive anchorage off a sandy beach in settled weather but is likely to be subject to swell (photo p.193).

Ardalanish to Firth of Lorn

From Rubh' Ardalanish to Fladda or Corryvreckan is 20 miles and, provided the Mull shore is not approached to within less than 2 cables, there are no hazards and the tidal streams are weak.

Heading east, passage planning is principally a matter of ensuring that arrival coincides with a favourable tide through the various tidal gates that may be encountered. It must also be borne in mind that the south coast of Mull is often a lee shore and has no anchorages offering secure shelter from the south west until Loch Spelve is reached.

For Directions for the Firth of Lorn see Ch.6 (p.96)

Tides

Tides are weak between Frank Lockwood's Island and the Garvellachs, reaching one knot at springs.

Northeast-going stream begins +0430 Oban (–0100 Dover).
Southwest-going stream begins –0155 Oban (+0335 Dover).

East of the Torran Rocks:

North-going stream begins +0415 Oban (–0115 Dover).
South-going stream begins –0210 Oban (–0350 Dover).

Lights

Dubh Artach LtHo Fl(2)30s44m20M
Rubha a'Mhail LtHo(Islay) Fl(3)WR.15s45m24/21M
Eileach Naoimh Lt. Bn. (Garvellachs) Fl.6s9M

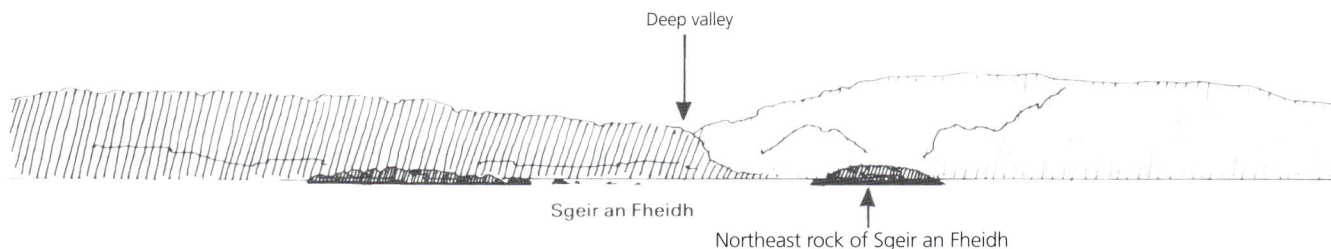

The leading marks for the outer approach to the Ardalanish anchorage - northeast rock in line with deep valley 350°

Carsaig Bay, Mull, from the south

Anchorages

Carsaig Bay A fair-weather anchorage 2 miles west of Loch Buie, subject to swell in southerly winds and squalls in northerlies. Note the rocks extending 4 cables west of Gamhnach Mhor and a cable east. Anchor off the north side of the islets or in the bight to northwest. There is 1·3m alongside the quay at half tide; two iron beacons mark rocks on the east side of the approach.

Loch Buie This has no shelter from seaward and only very occasional anchorage at the head, east of Eilean Mor. Drying rocks lie one cable east of the islet on the east side of Eilean Mor; there are several moorings used by small working boats.

For anchorages to the east of Loch Buie see Ch. 6, Firth of Lorn (pp.111-113).

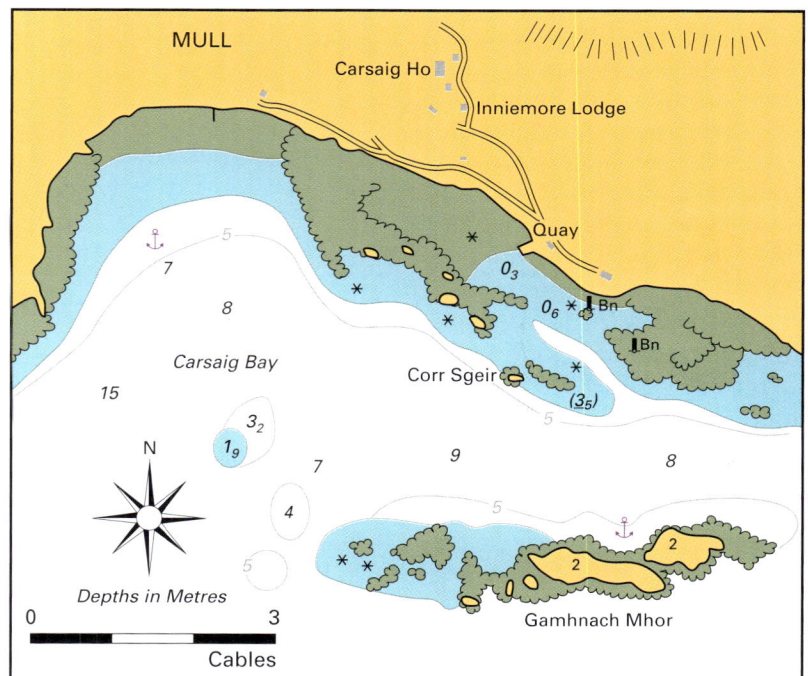

CARSAIG BAY, MULL

Appendix

Charts and other publications

Despite the increasing use of electronic charts and the alternative paper charts that are available, the full-sized Admiralty chart remains the original source material for all methods of navigation and, for those who can afford the cost and space needed for a full portfolio, it will still be the ideal, though for many it may have been relegated to a backup role.

However, for those with plotters using raster-based electronic charts, the familiar Admiralty chart name and numbering system is still very relevant. For these users, as well as the traditionalists, this Appendix includes a full list of Admiralty charts for the area covered by this book as well as a drawn chart index which also shows the extent of the Admiralty Leisure Folio No. 5611.

The latter is an economical and space-saving alternative to a portfolio of full-sized Admiralty charts and covers the area from Kintyre to Ardnamurchan - identical to that of this book - at a price approximately equal to that of two full size charts. These A2-sized charts carry all the information that the cruising yachtsman will need and in some instances, for instance from Fladda to the Sound of Mull, they are better for planning a passage at a reasonable scale than their full-sized counterparts. Even so, an overall view is often needed and for this the Imray charts C64 and C65 at a scale of 1:150,000 offer a very convenient solution. Imray also publish a chart pack of 1:50,000 scale charts for the area between Crinan and Ardnamurchan, 2800 *Isle of Mull and Adjacent Coasts*, for use with their chart C65.

Throughout this book mention has been made of *Antares Charts*: extra large scale plans produced from recent surveys and intended for use with GPS in conjunction with laptop PCs and tablets. These are more fully described in the Introduction on p.5 and key plans showing the location of all *Antares* charts for Kintyre to Ardnamurchan is included on pp.198-199 of this Appendix.

Admiralty charts

The following Admiralty charts relate to the waters covered by this volume. They are grouped according to their scale and listed in geographical order from south to north:

Group (i) charts are at a scale of 1:75,000 or smaller. Several of this group of charts omit any detail within inshore waters but are valuable for passage planning.

Group (ii) charts are at a scale of 1:25,000 and will enable many more lochs and anchorages to be explored.

Group (iii) charts are principally large scale plans, many of which are included in sketch form in these Sailing Directions.

Group (i)

2635	Scotland, West Coast	500,000
2724	North Channel to the Firth of Lorn	200,000
2126	Firth of Clyde, South	75,000
2199	North Channel, Northern part	75,000
2798	Loch Foyle to Sanda Island	75,000
2168	Approaches to the Sound of Jura	75,000
2169	Approaches to the Firth of Lorn	75,000
2171	Approaches to the Sound of Mull	75,000
1770	Islay to Skerryvore	100,000
1796	Barra Head to Ardnamurchan	100,000

Group (ii)

2475	Sound of Gigha	25,000
2476	West Loch Tarbert, Port Ellen, Crinan	Various
2481	Sound of Islay	25,000
2396	Sound of Jura (South)	25,000
2397	Sound of Jura (North) & Loch Sween	25,000
2343	Gulf of Corryvreckan and approaches	25,000
2326	Crinan to Firth of Lorn	25,000
2386	Firth of Lorn (South)	25,000
2387	Firth of Lorn (North)	25,000
2389	Loch Linnhe (South)	25,000
2388	Loch Etive and Approaches	25,000
2379	Loch Linnhe (Mid)	25,000
2380	Loch Linnhe (North)	25,000
1791	Caledonian Canal	Various
2390	Sound of Mull	25,000
2392	Sound of Mull (West Entrance)	25,000
2394	Loch Sunart	25,000
2617	Sound of Iona	25,000
2652	Loch na Keal and Loch Tuath	25,000
2771	Loch Scridain	25,000

Group (iii)

1790	Sound of Kerrera	10,000
2320	Loch Crinan	7,500
2372	Corran Narrows and Corpach	10,000
2474	Scalasaig, Tobermory, Arinagour, Gott Bay, Gunna Sound, Loch Breachacha, Loch Eatharna	Various

Admiralty Leisure Folios

Admiralty Leisure Folios consist of up to 30 A2-size sheets, directly reproduced from part of the equivalent full size Admiralty charts, printed on plain paper and sold in an acetate wallet. The coverage of individual sheets in Folio No. 5611, Kintyre to Ardnamurchan, is shown below. Chart No. 1A covers the whole area.

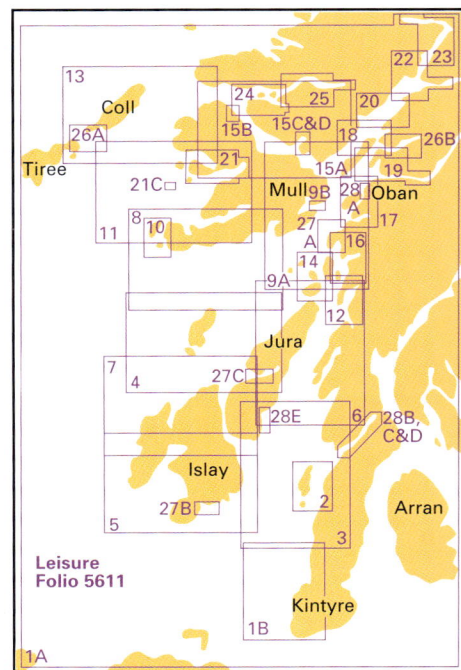

Muck

Sd of Arisaig

2380

Fort William & Corpach
2372

2171

2392

2394

2207

2380

Loch Leven
2380

Loch Sunart
2394

Loch Sunart

2380

Loch Leven Narrows

Coll

Tobermory Hr
2474

L Eatharna
2474

Sound of Mull
2390

Loch Linnhe

Corran Narrows
2372

Gunna Sound

2474

1778

Glensanda Hr
2389

L Ceran

Loch Etive
2388

Tiree

Sound of Mull
2390

Lochaline
2390

796

2474

Treshnish Isles

2652

2379

Passage of Tiree

L Tuath

Lismore

2474

Ulva

MULL

Loch Etive
2388

2724

2771

2387

2390

Staffa

2389

Firth of Lorn

●Oban

Dunstaffnage B to Connel Bridge
2388

2169

2617

L Scridian

1790

Iona

2171

Soa I

2326

L Melfort
2326

2382

Torran Rocks

Garvellachs

2386

Upper Loch Fyne

3746

Scarba

2382

2723

2397

App to Finnart
3746

1770

Colonsay

2343

Loch Crinan
2476

2381

Loch Long

Scalasaig Hr
2474

Loch Sween
2397

1906

Oronsay

JURA

Sound of Jura

Loch Gilp
2381

Loch Striven

1994

1778

Lower Loch Fyne

2168

L Tarbert
2481

2169

Caladh Hr
1906

1906

1907

NATO Fuel Jetty
1907

Burnt Is

Firth of Clyde

E Loch Tarbert
2381

1867

2383

●*Rothesay Hr*

2396

2475

1867

2481

2476

ISLAY

Gigha I

2126

ARRAN

2220

2491

2221

Port Ellen
2476

Brodick
1864

2168

Kilbrannan Sound

Lamlash
1864

Holy I

2131

Cambeltown Loch
1864

Cambeltown Hr 1864

N

Cambeltown NATO Pier 1864

Rathlin I

Mull of Kintyre

2494

Sanda I

Kintyre to Ardnamurchan

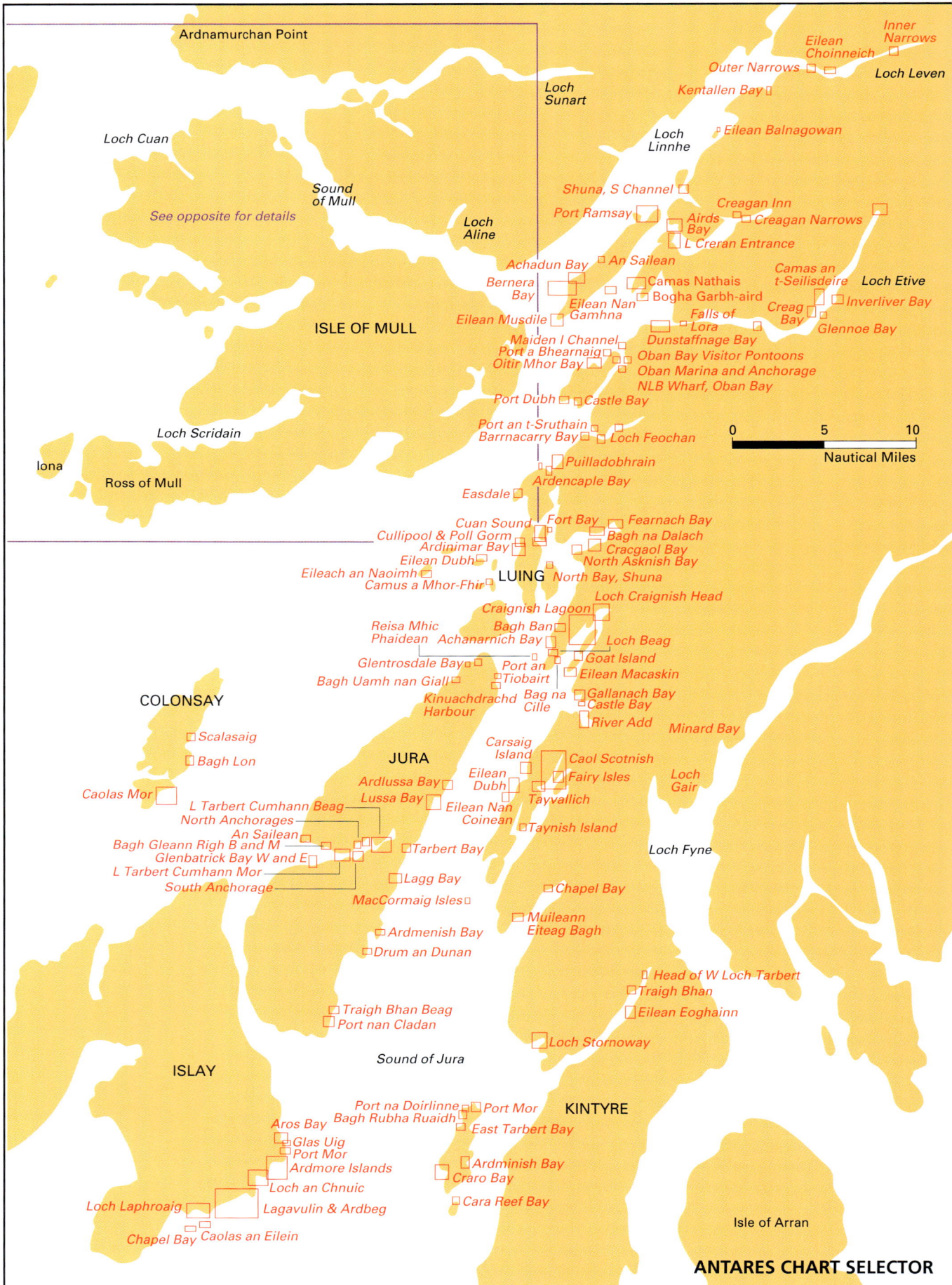

Ardnamurchan Point

Loch Cuan

Sound of Mull

See opposite for details

Loch Aline

Loch Sunart

Loch Linnhe

Inner Narrows

Eilean Choinneich

Outer Narrows

Kentallen Bay

Loch Leven

Eilean Balnagowan

Shuna, S Channel

Port Ramsay

Creagan Inn

Airds Bay

Creagan Narrows

L Creran Entrance

Achadun Bay

An Sailean

Camas Nathais

Camas an t-Seilisdeire

Loch Etive

Bernera Bay

Eilean Nan Gamhna

Bogha Garbh-aird

Creag Bay

Inverliver Bay

ISLE OF MULL

Eilean Musdile

Falls of Lora

Glennoe Bay

Maiden I Channel

Dunstaffnage Bay

Port a Bhearnaig

Oitir Mhor Bay

Oban Bay Visitor Pontoons

Oban Marina and Anchorage

NLB Wharf, Oban Bay

Port Dubh

Castle Bay

Loch Scridain

Port an t-Sruthain

Barrnacarry Bay

Loch Feochan

Iona

Puilladobhrain

Ross of Mull

Ardencaple Bay

Easdale

Fort Bay

Fearnach Bay

Cuan Sound

Bagh na Dalach

Cullipool & Poll Gorm

Cracgaol Bay

Ardinimar Bay

North Asknish Bay

Eilean Dubh

LUING

Eileach an Naoimh

North Bay, Shuna

Camus a Mhor-Fhir

Loch Craignish Head

Craignish Lagoon

Reisa Mhic Phaidean

Bagh Ban

Loch Beag

Achanarnich Bay

Goat Island

Glentrosdale Bay

Port an Tiobairt

Eilean Macaskin

Bagh Uamh nan Giall

Gallanach Bay

COLONSAY

Kinuachdrachd Harbour

Bag na Cille

Castle Bay

River Add

Minard Bay

Carsaig Island

Caol Scotnish

JURA

Eilean Dubh

Fairy Isles

Loch Gair

Scalasaig

Ardlussa Bay

Tayvallich

Bagh Lon

Lussa Bay

Eilean Nan Coinean

Taynish Island

Caolas Mor

L Tarbert Cumhann Beag

North Anchorages

An Sailean

Bagh Gleann Righ B and M

Tarbert Bay

Loch Fyne

Glenbatrick Bay W and E

L Tarbert Cumhann Mor

South Anchorage

Lagg Bay

Chapel Bay

MacCormaig Isles

Muileann Eiteag Bagh

Ardmenish Bay

Drum an Dunan

Head of W Loch Tarbert

Traigh Bhan

Eilean Eoghainn

Traigh Bhan Beag

Port nan Cladan

Loch Stornoway

Sound of Jura

ISLAY

Port na Doirlinne

Port Mor

KINTYRE

Aros Bay

Bagh Rubha Ruaidh

East Tarbert Bay

Glas Uig

Port Mor

Ardmore Islands

Ardminish Bay

Loch an Chnuic

Craro Bay

Loch Laphroaig

Lagavulin & Ardbeg

Cara Reef Bay

Chapel Bay

Caolas an Eilein

Isle of Arran

ANTARES CHART SELECTOR

0 5 10
Nautical Miles

ANTARES CHART SELECTOR

Antares Charts

Throughout this book mention has been made of *Antares Charts*, a portfolio of extra-large scale plans produced from recent surveys and intended for use with GPS in conjunction with a variety of plotting software applications on PCs and tablets. They are more fully described in the Introduction on p.5.

The portfolio now contains so many plans that a simple list of them does not adequately illustrate their location, especially when a number of them have unfamiliar names. So, with the kind permission of Bob Bradfield of *Antares Charts*, we have reproduced here his chart selector which shows at a glance all the plans for the area covered by this book.

These are up to date as far as and including the 2018 issue. New charts are constantly being added and a full list of all the current and possible future charts can be seen on the *Antares* website: *www.antarescharts.co.uk*

Imray charts

The area included in this book is covered by the following Imray C series of charts which are all drawn at around 1:150,000 scale (except where noted), with inset plans, on waterproof material, in folded format and sold in an acetate wallet at approximately A4 size. They can also be obtained flat by special request. See the previous page for the area covered by each chart.

| C64 | North Channel to Crinan | 1:160,000 |
| C65 | Crinan to Mallaig and Barra | 1:155,000 |

In addition, more detail is shown on the Imray chart pack 2800, Isle of Mull and Adjacent Coasts. This is a collection of charts at A2 size drawn mainly at 1:50,000 with a 1:160,000 overall plan. The plan below illustrates the coverage of these charts which are printed on tough wet strength paper and supplied in a plastic wallet:

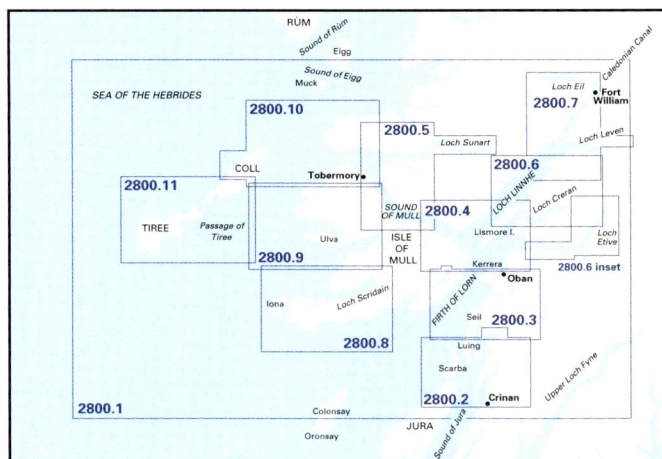

Ordnance Survey maps

1:50,000 Landranger maps cover Kintyre to Ardnamurchan as follows:

OSL40	Mallaig and Glenfinnan, Loch Shiel
OSL41	Ben Nevis, Fort William & Glencoe
OSL46	Coll & Tiree
OSL47	Tobermory & North Mull
OSL48	Iona & West Mull, Ulva
OSL49	Oban & East Mull
OSL50	Glen Orchy & Loch Etive
OSL55	Lochgilphead & Loch Awe
OSL60	Islay
OSL61	Jura & Colonsay
OSL62	North Kintyre & Tarbert
OSL68	South Kintyre & Campbeltown

Availability of charts

Admiralty chart agents for the west of Scotland are: ChartCo, Unit 5 St Luke's Place, Glasgow G5 0TS, ℡ 0141 429 6462 *www.bookharbour.com*

Imray, Laurie, Norie & Wilson Ltd are also Admiralty chart agents and can supply charts by post from: Wych House, The Broadway, St Ives, Cambridgeshire PE27 5BT ℡ 01480 462114 *www.imray.com*

Other outlets in the Kintyre to Ardnamurchan area which may stock a selection of local charts are:

Crinan Boatyard Ltd, Crinan ℡ 01546 83232
Seafare, Tobermory ℡ 01688 302277

Ardfern Yacht Centre, Ardfern ℡ 01852 500247
Alba Yacht Services, Dunstaffnage ℡ 01631 565630
Craobh Marina, Loch Melfort ℡ 01852 500222

Admiralty publications

West Coast of Scotland Pilot, 2014 1st Edition (NP 66B), with supplements to date
Tidal Atlas N Coast of Ireland and W Coast of Scotland (NP 218)
Admiralty Tide Tables Vol 1 (NP 201)
Admiralty List of Lights Vol A (NP 74)

Other publications

Almanacs

The Cruising Almanac, Cruising Association, Imray
Reeds Western Almanac, Adlard Coles Nautical
Reeds PBO Small Craft Almanac, Adlard Coles Nautical

General books

Cruising Scotland, Mike Balmforth & Edward Mason, Imray
The Scottish Islands, Hamish Haswell-Smith, Canongate
An Island Odyssey, Hamish Haswell-Smith, Canongate
The Hebrides, An Aerial View of a Cultural Landscape, Angus and Patricia Macdonald, Birlinn
Exploring Scotland's Heritage – Argyll and the Western Isles, J.N. Graham Ritchie & Mary Harman, RCHM
The Islands of Scotland, Scottish Mountaineering Club
The Archaeology of Argyll, J.N.Graham Ritchie, Edinburgh University Press
The Buildings of Scotland, Argyll & Bute, Frank Arneil Walker, Penguin
Land of Mountain and Flood, McKirdy, Gordon & Crofts, Birlinn
Scottish Anchorages, Charles Warlow, obtainable through www.scottishanchorages.co.uk

Contact telephone numbers and websites

Imray charts, sailing directions
℡ 01480 462114; www.imray.com

Clyde Cruising Club
℡ 0141 221 2774; www.clyde.org

Citylink bus travel enquiries
℡ 0990 505050; www.citylink.co.uk

Rail travel enquiries
℡ 0345 484950; www.nationlrail.co.uk

CalMac (MacBraynes ferry enquiries)
℡ 0800 066 5000; www.calmac.co.uk/timetables

Sail Scotland
www.sailscotland.co.uk

Stornoway Coastguard
℡ 01851 702013

Belfast Coastguard
℡ 02891 463933

RYA Scotland
℡ 0131 317 7388; www.ryascotland.org.uk

Association of Scottish Yacht Charterers
℡ 01852 200258

West Highland Anchorages and Moorings Association
℡ 01786 822840

Quick reference table of provisions, services and supplies

Figures following a reference letter indicate the distance in miles from the landing place
Camping Gaz may not be available at all locations indicated by 'C'

Page	Place	Water A Alongside by hose T Tap on jetty N Nearby tap	Shop S Supermarket L Local store B Basic supplies only	Diesel A Alongside, by hose M Marine diesel near G Garage, autodiesel	Petrol P Garage often some distance away	Calor Gas C	Repairs H Hull M Marine engines E Electronics	Chandlery Y Yacht F Fishing I Ironmonger	Visitors' Moorings V (including hotels) P Pontoon	Catering R Restaurant B Bar S Showers	Cash A ATM B Bank P Post Office	Rubbish disposal D
18	Campbeltown	A	S	A	P	C	HME	I	P	RBS	ABP	D
	Rathlin	A	B						P	RBS		D
22	Gigha	T	L	G	P	C			VP	RBS	AP	
30	Port Ellen	A	S	M	P	C	HME	I	P	RBS	AP	D
34	Lagavulin	N		M			HM	Y/F	V	S		D
35	Ardbeg	N							V	R		
40	Port Askaig	A	L	M	P	C				RB	P	D
43	Bowmore		S	G	P	C				RB	ABP	D
44	Portnahaven	N	L	M			HME			RB		D
52	Scalasaig	A	L	G	P	C				RB	P	
56	Craighouse	T	L	G	P				V	RBS	P	D
64	Castle Sween		L			C				R		D
65	Tayvallich	T	L			C			VP	RB	P	D
72	Crinan	A	B	A		C	HME	Y	VP	RBS		D
75	Ardfern	A	L	A		C	HME	Y	P	RBS		D
87	Craobh Marina	A	B	A		C	HME	Y	P	RBS		D
89	Kilmelford	A	L	A		C	HME	Y	VP	RBS	P1	D
89	Melfort Pier	T							V	RBS		D
91	Balvicar	N	B	G 2½	P 2½	C	HME				P	D
101	Easdale								V	RB		D
104	Loch Feochan	A		A		C	HME	Y	VP	S		D
110	Oban Marina	A		A		C	HME	Y	VP	RBS		D
110	Oban	A	S	M	P	C		Y/F	VP	RBS	ABP	D
116	Dunstaffnage	A	L1	A	P	C	HME	Y	P	RBS	AP1	D
121	Port Appin	N	L						V	RB	P	D
122	Loch Creran	A					HME	Y	VP			D
128	Dallens Bay	A		A	P 2	C 2			VP	S		D
130	Kentallen	N							V	RB		
131	Ballachulish	A	L ½	A	P	C			VP	RBS ½	A ½	D
135	Corpach	A	S	A	P	C	HME		P	RBS	AP	D
137	Craignure		L	G	P	C				RB	P	D
140	Salen (Mull)		L	G	P					RB	AP	D
141	Loch Aline	A	L ½	M ½	P ½	C ½			VP	RB ½ S	P ½	D
143	Tobermory	A	S	A	P	C		Y	VP	RBS	ABP	D
145	Kilchoan	N	L ½	M ½	P ½				V	RB ½	P	D
152	Salen (Loch Sunart)	A	L	A					VP	RBS		D
153	Strontian		L			C				RB		D
170	Ulva Sound	A		A					P	R	P1	
174	Arinagour	N	L	G	P	C			V	RBS	P	
178	Gott Bay (Tiree)	N	L	G	P	C			V	RB 2	P	D
182	Bunessan	N	L	G 2½	P 2½					RB	P	D
186	Iona	N	L							RB	P	
187	Fionnphort	T	L	G	P					RB	AP	D

Round the Mull to Crinan and Ailsa Craig to Belfast

Distances given in miles

	Sanda Island	Deas Point	Mull Of Kintyre LtHo	Cara I. south end	McArthur's Head	McCormaig Isles	Tayvallich	Dorus Mor	Crinan	Ailsa Craig	Corsewell	Belfast Roads
Sanda Island		5·7	8·5	27·5	37·0	44·5	54·5	59·3	59·0	15·9	22·3	39·0
Deas Point	5·7		2·8	21·8	31·3	38·8	48·8	54·6	54·3	21·6	27·6	38·6
Mull Of Kintyre LtHo	8·5	2·8		19·0	28·5	36·0	46·0	50·8	50·5	24·4	29·9	40·2
Cara I. south end	27·5	21·8	19·0		12·0	17·0	27·0	31·8	31·5			
McArthur's Head	37·0	31·3	28·5	12·0		13·0	23·0	27·4	27·1			
McCormaig Isles	44·5	38·8	36·0	17·0	13·0		10·0	14·8	14·5			
Tayvallich	54·5	48·8	46·0	27·0	23·0	10·0		24·8	24·5			
Dorus Mor	59·3	54·6	50·8	31·8	27·4	14·8	24·8		3·0			
Crinan	59·0	54·3	50·5	31·5	27·1	14·5	24·5	3·0				
Ailsa Craig	15·9	21·6	24·4								14·6	42·5
Corsewell	22·3	27·6	29·9							14·6		19·0
Belfast Roads	39·0	38·6	40·2							42·5	19·0	

Crinan to Loch Aline and Tobermory via Fladda LtHo and via Cuan Sound

Distances given in miles

	Crinan	Fladda LtHo	3 cables W of S end Sheep Island	Easdale Pt via Fladda Sound	Lismore LtHo / Lady Rock	Duart Point	Glas Eilanan (Grey Isles)	Ardtornish Point	Loch Aline Ferry Pier	Eilean Glasa (Green Isle)	Tobermory Pier
Crinan		10·6	14·4	13·7	23·2	24·4	27·6	29·6	30·7	34·7	42·4
Fladda LtHo	10·6		3·8	3·1	12·6	13·8	17·0	19·0	20·1	24·1	31·8
3 cables W of S end Sheep Island	14·4	3·8		1·2	8·8	10·0	13·2	15·2	16·3	20·3	28·0
Easdale Pt via Fladda Sound	13·7	3·1	1·2		10·0	11·2	14·4	16·4	17·5	21·5	29·2
Lismore LtHo / Lady Rock	23·2	12·6	8·8	10·0		1·2	4·3	6·3	7·4	11·5	19·2
Duart Point	24·4	13·8	10·0	11·2	1·2		3·2	5·2	6·3	10·3	18·0
Glas Eilanan (Grey Isles)	27·6	17·0	13·2	14·4	4·3	3·2		2·0	3·1	7·1	14·8
Ardtornish Point	29·6	19·0	15·2	16·4	6·3	5·2	2·0		1·1	5·1	12·6
Loch Aline Ferry Pier	30·7	20·1	16·3	17·5	7·4	6·3	3·1	1·1		4·5	12·2
Eilean Glasa (Green Isle)	34·7	24·1	20·3	21·5	11·5	10·3	7·1	5·1	4·5		7·8
Tobermory Pier	42·4	31·8	28·0	29·2	19·2	18·0	14·8	12·6	12·2	7·8	

Easdale Point to Fort William via Lynne of Lorn and Morven

Distances given in miles

	Easdale Point	Loch Spelve SW Corner	Puilladobhrain	S entrance Kerrera Sound	N entrance Kerrera Sound	Dunstaffnage	Port Appin Lt. via Lynn of Lorn	Lismore LtHo / Lady Rock	Port Ramsay via Lynn of Morvern	Cuil-Cheanna Spit Buoy	Ballachullish	Corran Narrows	Fort William Pier
Easdale Point		9·4	4·9	6·6	10·4	13·6	18·8	10·5	19·0	28·3	31·7	34·1	41·3
Loch Spelve SW Corner	9·4		8·7	8·6	11·2	14·0	18·0	9·0	17·5	27·2	30·6	33·0	40·2
Puilladobhrain	4·9	8·7		2·8	6·6	9·8	15·0	7·8	16·3	24·5	27·4	30·3	37·5
S entrance Kerrera Sound	6·6	8·6	2·8		3·8	7·0	12·2	8·2	16·7	21·7	25·1	27·5	34·7
N entrance Kerrera Sound	10·4	11·2	6·6	3·8		3·2	8·4	4·4	12·8	17·9	21·3	23·7	30·9
Dunstaffnage	13·6	14·0	9·8	7·0	3·2		7·6	6·0	14·5	17·1	20·5	22·9	30·1
Port Appin Lt via Lynn of Lorn	18·8	18·0	15·0	12·2	8·4	7·6		10·0	1·8	9·5	12·9	15·1	22·3
Lismore LtHo / Lady Rock	10·5	9·0	7·8	8·2	4·4	6·0	10·0		8·5	18·9	22·3	24·7	31·9
Port Ramsay via Lynn of Morvern	19·0	17·5	16·3	16·7	12·8	14·5	1·8	8·5		10·6	13·8	16·2	23·4
Cuil-Cheanna Spit Buoy	28·3	27·2	24·5	21·7	17·9	17·1	9·5	18·9	10·6		3·4	2·4	9·6
Ballachullish	31·7	30·6	27·4	25·1	21·3	20·5	12·9	22·3	13·8	3·4		5·8	13·0
Corran Narrows	34·1	33·0	30·3	27·5	23·7	22·9	15·1	24·7	16·2	2·4	5·8		7·2
Fort William Pier	41·3	40·2	37·5	34·7	30·9	30·1	22·3	31·9	23·4	9·6	13·0	7·2	

From Tobermory and from Fladda LtHo to the West Coast of Mull

Distances given in miles

	Tobermory Pier	Loch Drumbuie	Ardnamurchan LtHo	Caliach Point	Lunga, Treshnish Isles	Gometra Harbour	Ulva Sound, S Entrance	Inch Kenneth	Bull Hole	Fladda LtHo	Arinagour	Gott Bay
Tobermory Pier		5·0	9·8	11·0	18·6	22·7	25·4	25·0	29·8		17·2	27·8
Loch Drumbuie	5·0		12·2	14·4	22·0	26·1	29·8	29·4	33·2		20·2	31·8
Ardnamurchan LtHo	9·8	12·2		8·5	16·1	20·2	23·9	23·5	27·3		11·8	25·0
Caliach Point	11·0	14·4	8·5		7·6	11·7	15·4	15·0	18·8		6·8	17·3
Lunga, Treshnish Isles	18·6	22·0	16·1	7·6		6·2	10·5	10·2	10·3		8·5	14·2
Gometra Harbour	22·7	26·1	20·2	11·7	6·2		6·2	5·6	9·6		13·5	18·8
Ulva Sound, S Entrance	25·4	29·8	23·9	15·4	10·5	6·2		2·0	12·0		18·3	23·7
Inch Kenneth	25·0	29·4	23·5	15·0	10·2	5·6	2·0		11·3		18·0	23·4
Bull Hole	29·8	33·2	27·3	18·8	10·3	9·6	12·0	11·3		29·0	18·4	18·8
Fladda LtHo									29·0			
Arinagour	17·2	20·2	11·8	6·8	8·5	13·5	18·3	18·0	18·4			12·6
Gott Bay	27·8	31·8	25·0	17·3	14·2	18·8	23·7	23·4	18·8		12·6	

RECOMMENDED SMALL VESSEL ROUTES AT OBAN

www.obanharbour.scot

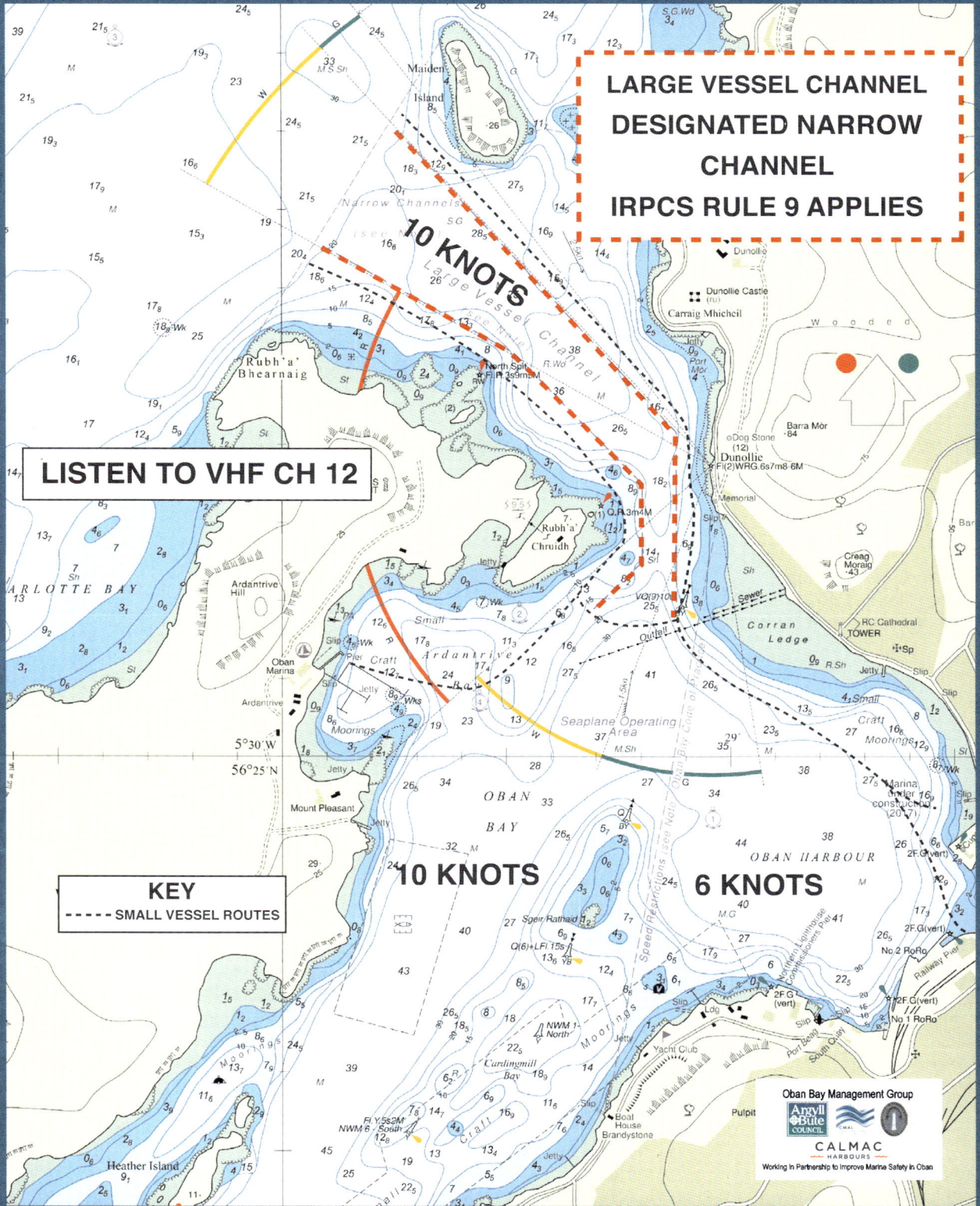

LARGE VESSEL CHANNEL
DESIGNATED NARROW CHANNEL
IRPCS RULE 9 APPLIES

10 KNOTS

LISTEN TO VHF CH 12

10 KNOTS

6 KNOTS

KEY
- - - - SMALL VESSEL ROUTES

Oban Bay Management Group
CALMAC
HARBOURS
Working in Partnership to Improve Marine Safety in Oban

NOT TO BE USED FOR NAVIGATION

CODE OF PRACTICE FOR OBAN BAY, NORTH CHANNEL & SOUND OF KERERRA

www.obanharbour.scot

This Code of Practice was developed through extensive consultation with a wide range of commercial and leisure users of Oban Bay. It has no standing in law but following the key principles of common sense, sound seamanship and common courtesy and drawing on the experience of many users of Oban Bay over many years it provides advice on how to navigate safely through the Bay. Nothing in this Code of Practice relieves the master/ skipper from their responsibility for the safety of their vessel and all those on board. Similarly, nothing in this Code of Practice constitutes a deviation from or variation to the International Regulations for Preventing Collisions at Sea 1972 as amended (IRPCS), published in Merchant Shipping Notice No. 1781/COLREG 1 or relieves the master/ skipper from their responsibility for complying with the IRPCS.

For the purposes of this Code of Practice, the following expressions shall have the associated meanings as described below: -

Large Vessel A vessel of more than 20 metres in length overall, and/or a vessel with a draft in excess of three (3) metres.

Large Vessel Channel The deep water route through the North Channel marked on the appropriate charts and sailing directions as being for use by 'large vessels', which is considered to be a "narrow channel" as defined in IRPCS Rule 9.

Oban Bay Those waters lying to the south of a line from the north-west tip of Kerrera (Rubh 'a' Bhearnaig) to the north-west tip of Maiden Island and to the north of a line drawn east-west through Sgeirean Dubha light tower (Cutter Rock Beacon, Kerrera Sound)

Oban Harbour That part of Oban Bay lying to the east of a line drawn between Dog Stone to the north and Brandy Stone to the south.

Small Vessel A vessel other than a Large Vessel.

CODE OF PRACTICE

1. Right of Way Large vessels "leaving" Oban Bay shall have the right of way over all vessels "entering" Oban Bay. Small vessels, including sailing vessels, shall not impede the passage of a large vessel entering or leaving Oban Bay.

2. Sound of Kerrera Small Vessels entering or leaving Oban Bay through the Sound of Kerrera should keep as near to the starboard side of the main channel, which is buoyed and lies to the west of the Ferry Rocks as is safe and practicable.

3. North Channel Vessels using the North Channel are likely to have their sightlines obscured in many circumstances, therefore 'small vessels' entering or leaving Oban Bay through the North Channel should remain outside the Large Vessel Channel where practicable.

'Small vessels' shall not cross the Large Vessel Channel if such crossing impedes the passage of a vessel which can safely navigate only within the Large Vessel Channel (IRPCS Rule 9(d)).

4. Sailing vessels should use their auxiliary engines (if fitted) at all times when navigating through the North Channel and in any event shall not impede the passage of a vessel which can safely navigate only within the Large Vessel Channel (IRPCS Rule 9(b)).

5. Speed the speed limit in the area covered by this code is 10 knots through the water, except in Oban Harbour where it is 6 knots.

6. Wash All vessels should show proper seamanship and common courtesy to others and avoid making excessive wash.

7. VHF Ch 12/16 All vessels approaching or navigating in Oban Bay should listen on VHF Channel 12/16. Large Vessels should make a warning broadcast on VHF Channel 16, followed by a brief safety announcement on VHF Channel 12, giving an ETA at Dunollie Light prior to entry or departure. More details are at the VHF tab on the Oban Harbour website.

8. Seaplanes A seaplane service operates to and from Oban Bay. The aircraft commander should ensure that the area is clear of surface craft before landing or taking off and shall, when on the surface, be governed by the IPRCS.

9. Berthing 'Large vessels' berthing at the NLB berth, ferry berths or North Pier require sea room to manoeuvre onto or off the berths. For example: ferries loading over the bow will swing into the northern half of Oban Bay to give room to line up for the berth; those loading over the stern will initially, swing into the southern half of Oban Bay and then head towards the northern half to give sea room to back down onto the berth at Railway Pier. All vessels are to keep clear of 'large vessels' so manoeuvring.

10. Anchorages Mariners should note the designated anchorages portrayed under the port information tab on the web site.

11. Cruise Ship Tenders cruise ship tenders ferrying large numbers of passengers between cruise ships anchored in Oban Bay and the shore are often to be seen; mariners should keep a good and wary lookout for these vessels.

BE SAFE - BE SEEN

Very small vessels such as kayaks, paddleboards and inflatables should make every effort to ensure that they are easily visible from the bridge of large vessels by use of brightly coloured clothing and lights when appropriate – the attention of people in these vessels is drawn to the 'Be Safe – Be Seen' guidance available from the website *www.obanharbour.scot*.

Gaelic for yachtsmen

In order to find the word you want it is helpful to know a little bit about Gaelic grammar. Gaelic words change in a number of ways to form the plural, feminine, possessive, the dative and vocative case of nouns, the past tense of verbs etc. Changes will be found at the beginning, at the end and also in the middle of a word, for example:

cinn see *ceann*
eich genitive and plural of *each* horse
mara genitive of *muir* sea

The change most likely to cause difficulty in looking up a word is the insertion of *h* after a consonant at the beginning· This alters the sound of the preceding letter (*bh* and *mh* and pronounced like English *v*, *ph* is pronounced *f*). Thus if you are looking for a word beginning with *bh, ch, dh, fh, gh, mh, ph, sh, th*, look it up in the list without the *h*, for example:

bhàn see *bàn*
ghlas see *glas*
mhòr see *mòr*

Some names, particularly those of islands ending in 'a' or 'ay', are of Norse origin. Anyone at all familiar with French and Latin will see correspondences there, for example Caisteil – also Eaglais and Teampuill.

Many words are compounds made up of several often quite common parts, frequently linked by na - nam - nan. The following are the most usual forms of words which commonly occur in Gaelic place names. They often set out to describe the physical features and so give some clues to identification. Some of them occur almost everywhere; most lochs have a Sgeir More and an Eilean Dubh, or vice versa.

Meanings of common Gaelic words

In the entries which follow: Gaelic words are in bold; English equivalents follow in bold within square brackets; information about case, plurals etc. are italicised and the meanings in English are in regular text.

àird, àrd height, (high) promontory
abhainn [**avon**] river
acarsaid anchorage
achadh [**ach**] field
àilean [**aline**] green field
aiseag ferry
allt [**ault**] burn, stream
aonach hill, moor
aoineadh steep rocky brae
aonach (steep) hill, moor
àrd see **àird**
àros house
asgadh shelter
àth ford
ault see **allt**
avon see **abhainn**
bà see **bò**
bac (sand)bank
bàgh bay
baile town, village, farm
bàn white, pale, fair
bàrr top, summit, height

beag [**beg**] little
bealach (mountain) pass, gorge
beàrn gap, crevice
beinn [**ben**] mountain, hill
beithe birch-tree
binnean pointed hill, peak
bò, *possessive and plural* **bà** cow
bogha, bodha [**bo(w)**] submerged rock, rock on which waves break
bodach old man
breac [**breck**] *adjective* speckled, spotted; *noun* trout
bruach bank, hillside
buachaille herdsman, shepherd
buidhe yellow
caileag girl
cailleach old woman
caisteal castle
caladh harbour
calltainn hazel
camas, camus bay, creek
caol, caolas, [**kyle**] narrow(s), strait
carraig rock
ceann, *possessive and plural* **cinn** [**ken**] head, point
cill [**kil**] church, monk's cell
clach stone
clachan village (with a church)
cladach shore, beach
cnap [**knap**] (small) hill, lump
cnoc [**cnok, knock**] hillock
còig five
coille wood, forest
coire [**corry**] kettle, cauldron, whirlpool, steep round hollow in hillside
coll hazel
craobh tree
creag rock, crag, cliff
crois cross
cruach stack, rick-shaped hill
dà two
darach [**darroch**] oak
dearg red
deas south
dòbhran otter
doirlinn isthmus, (connection to) an island which is accessible at low tide
domhain deep
donn brown
drochaid bridge
druim back, ridge
dubh black, dark
dùn fort, mound
each, *possessive and plural* **eich** horse
ear east
eas waterfall
eilach mill-race; mound
eilean island
fada long

aich meadow
aing sheep-pen, fank
eàrna alder-tree
èith bog
iacal tooth
ear, *possessive and plural* fir man
ireach moor, hill
liuch wet
raoch heather
garbh rough, harsh
geal white, bright
geòdha, geò deep cleft in cliffs, chasm
gil glen, water course
glas, grey, green
gleann glen, narrow valley
gobhar goat
gorm blue, green
gualainn shoulder; slope of hill
ar west
asg fish
nbhir [inver] river mouth, confluence
nnis [inch] island, river meadow
olaire eagle
ken see ceann
kil see cill
kyle see caol
lag hollow, pit
leac slab, flat stone
learg hillside, plain
leathan broad, wide
leth half
liath grey
linne pool, channel
loch lake, arm of the sea
lochan small loch, lake
long, *possessive* luinge ship
machair sandy grassed area behind a beach, low-lying plain
maol [mull] headland, bare rounded hill
mòinteach moorland, mossy place
mol, mal shingle (beach)
mòr [more] big, tall, great
muir, *possessive* mara sea
mullach summit
òb (sheltered) bay, harbour
odhar dun-coloured
oitir sandbank
òrd, ùird hammer
òs river mouth
plod, pool, pond
poll, puill pool
port port
rath fortress
rathad road
rhu see rudha
rìgh king
rinn promontory
ròn seal

ruadh red, reddish-brown
rudha, rubha [rhu] point of land
seachd seven
seann old, ancient
sga(i)t skate
sgarbh cormorant
sgeir skerry, rock
sgùrr rocky peak
sròn nose, (nose shaped) promontory; jutting ridge
srath strath, low-lying valley
sruth current
taigh, tigh house
tarbh bull
tioram dry
tobar well
tràigh beach, strand
trì three
tuath north
tulach hillock
uamh cave
uaine green
ùird see òrd

Scottish Exercise Areas including SUBFACTS

Warnings of areas allocated for exercises are given by Liverpool, Belfast and Stornoway Coastguards along with the weather forecasts at the times given in the Introduction

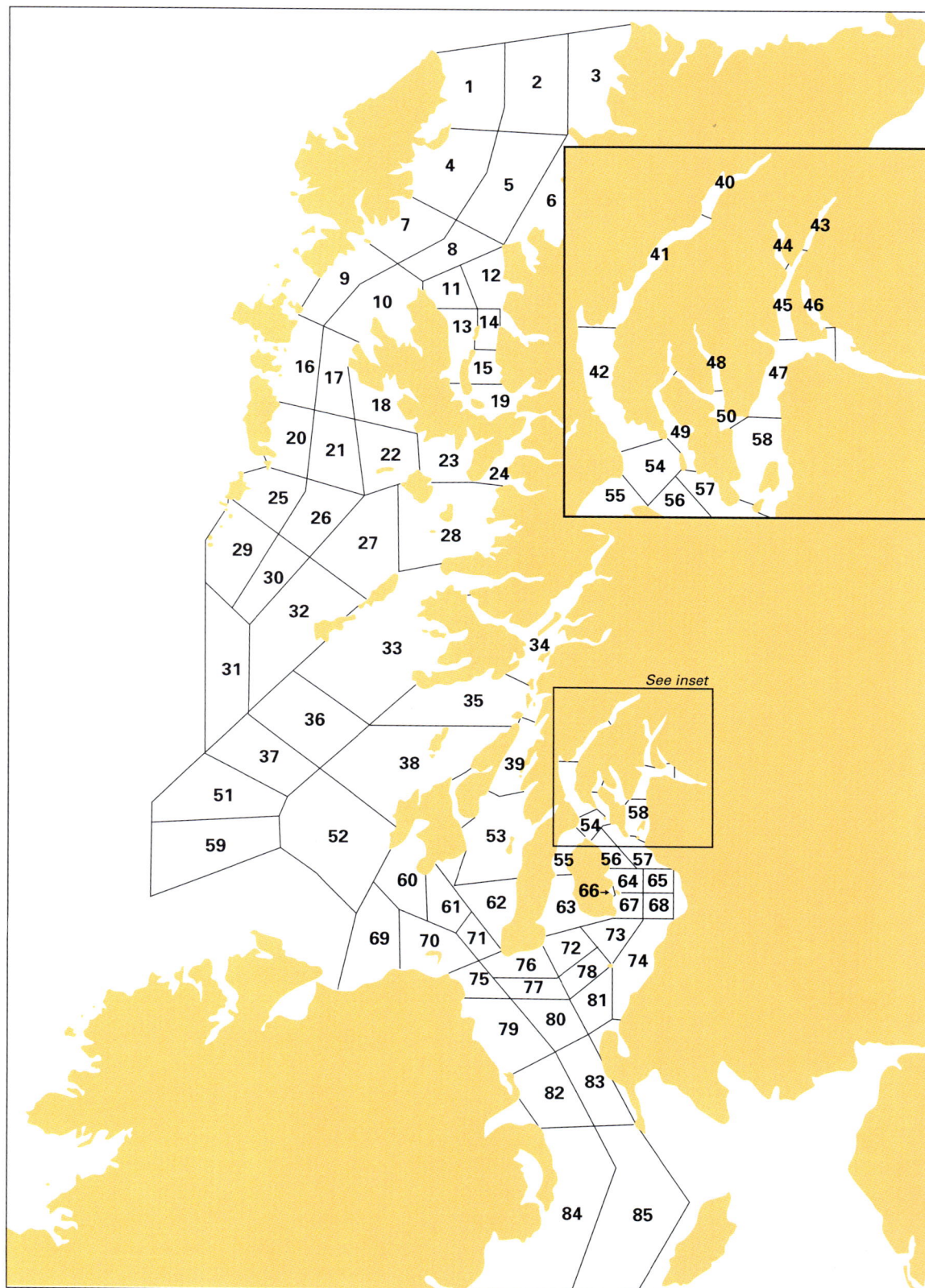

See inset

1. Tolsta
2. Pulteney
3. Eddrachillis
4. Erisort
5. Clynelish
6. Broom
7. Shiant
8. Balblair
9. Hermitray
10. Waternish
11. Flodigarry
12. Longa
13. Portree
14. Rona
15. Raasay
16. Wiay
17. Pooltiel
18. Bracadale
19. Crowlin
20. Boisdale
21. Dalwhinnie
22. Canna
23. Rum
24. Sleat
25. Hellisay
26. Edradour
27. Hawes
28. Eigg
29. Sandray
30. Glenturret
31. Tullibardine
32. Tiree
33. Staffa
34. Linnhe
35. Mull
36. Mackenzie
37. Blackstone
38. Colonsay
39. Jura
40. Fyne
41. Minard
42. Tarbert
43. Long
44. Goil
45. Cove
46. Gareloch
47. Rosneath
48. Striven
49. Ettrick
50. Rothesay
51. Place
52. Orsay
53. Gigha
54. Skipness
55. Lochranza
56. Laggan
57. Garroch
58. Cumbrae
59. Boyle
60. Islay
61. Otter
62. Earadale
63. Davaar
64. Brodick
65. Irvine
66. Arran
67. Lamlash
68. Ayr
69. Skerries
70. Rathlin
71. Kintyre
72. Stafnish
73. Pladda
74. Turnberry
75. Torr
76. Sanda
77. Mermaid
78. Ailsa
79. Maiden
80. Corsewall
81. Ballantrae
82. Magee
83. Beaufort
84. Ardglass
85. Peel

Index

The rocks don't move...

Maybe, but 'new' rocks are discovered and countless other things change. If you see anything, however minor, in these Directions that needs amending or updating please email the editor at:

sailingdirections@clyde.org